To Lindsay
with love +
Comradeship

Zackie

DEFIANT *desire*

To Lindsay,
Towards a great future —
WOZABAI!
Glen.

M

DEFIANT *desire*

Mark Gevisser and Edwin Cameron

Routledge / New York London

Published in 1995 by

Routledge
29 West 35th Street
New York, NY 10001

11 New Fetter Lane
London EC4P 4EE

First published by Ravan Press
PO Box 31134 Braamfontein 2017
South Africa

Library of Congress Cataloging-in-Publication Data

Defiant desire: gay and lesbian lives in South Africa / edited by Mark Gevisser and Edwin Cameron.
   P. cm.
Includes bibliographica; references and index.
ISBN 0-415-91060-9 – ISBN 0-415-91061-7
1. Gays–South Africa–Identity 2. Lesbians–South Africa–Identity. 3. Gays–South Africa–Social conditions. 4. Leabians–South Africa–Social conditions. 5. Gay rights–South Africa. I. Gevisser, Mark. II. Cameron, Edwin, 1953-
HQ76.3.S5D43 1994
305.9'0664'0968–dc20
                                      94-22150
                                        CIP

British Library Cataloguing-in-Publication Data also available.

Contents

Four — *Making noise: Queer cultural forms*

Five — *Making waves: Lesbian and gay activism*

Six — *Testaments*

Foreword to the International Edition

This book was published in South Africa in March 1994, shortly before the country went to the polls in its first democratic election, which installed Nelson Mandela as the head of an African National Congress-led government.

South Africa is the first country in the world to offer gay and lesbian people explicit protection in its constitution: Section 8 of the Chapter on Fundamental Rights outlaws unfair discrimination on the basis of sexual orientation. Indeed, in his first presidential pronouncement, during his victory speech on the Grand Parade in Cape Town, Nelson Mandela made a point of saying that discrimination against gays and lesbians would no longer be tolerated.

Two months later, opening South Africa's first gay film festival, the new Minister of Safety and Security for the FWV province, Jessie Duarte, offered herself as a patron of GLOW (Gay and Lesbian Organisation of the Witwatersrand) and said: "Not only are there legal injustices to be done away with, but mindsets and cultures have to be done away with too. It's one thing for you to have your rights and equality in the law, it's quite another to have them each day in the street, at work, in the bar, in public places where you socialize and where you cruise."

Here was a head of police asserting gay peoples' entitlement to legal partnerships, to full police protection, even to soliciting sex in public places. Standing in the audience was a senior divisional commander of the South African Police Services. There was, all around, a sense of arrival which was utterly new in South African gay politics. The "gay cause" had moved inside. It may even have become fashionable.

Almost in response, the annual October gay pride event, which has taken place in Johannesburg since 1990, has decided this year to transform itself from a "March" to a "Parade". To some gay South Africans, the dialectic of pride and protest has been resolved: there is nothing more to fight for, no more need for angry protest. We are surely free. Let us then celebrate.

Certainly, there is much that is worthy of celebration. Not only that we, as gays and lesbians, have the law on our side but that all South Africans have now claimed equality before the law. But now the hard work begins. Constitutional equality by no means guarantees an end to social discrimination. And, more importantly, the constitution is interim, valid only until the next elections in 1999. It is up to the current legislature to draft a final constitution, and the process will be public; one in which all South Africa's political parties and ideologies will compete.

Foreword

The gay equality clause slipped quietly into the interim constitution, with little public debate. But the apparent consensus over this issue is fragile indeed: South Africa remains, in parts, a deeply conservative and religious land. Given more obvious political divisions, a conservative coalition, a "Moral Majority" across racial lines, has yet to emerge. But its time may come: the ANC could well find resistance, both within its ranks and elsewhere, to its socially progressive policies on sexuality, reproductive rights and gender equity. Who is to say that an unpopular clause on sexual equality will not be jettisoned in order to salvage other aspects — like land rights or economic equity — considered more important to reconstruction and development?

To its credit, the ANC has to date stood firmly by its principles. Challenged on national television during the election campaign by fundamentalist Christian and Muslim religious parties, ANC Western Cape leader Allan Boesak — himself a minister of the church — defended the rights of gay people to equality. Also during the campaign, spokesperson Baleka Kgositsile, now a leader of the women's caucus in parliament, unequivocally affirmed the ANC's commitment to its gay equality platform.

But, already, there are signs of dissent within the ANC's own constituency. Some student activists at the historically black universities are resisting "non-homophobia" as a principle of the national student movement: this from a constituency that has long been in the vanguard of anti-apartheid politics. Whether the gay anti-discrimination clause makes it into the final constitution will depend on the savvy of the gay community — on both its lobbying skills and its ability to operate as a powerful and coherent political minority.

There is an opinion within the gay community that we should keep quiet in the next few years; that the more noise we make, the more conservative backlash there is likely to be. But such a strategy is shortsighted. No matter how fashionable a "cause" becomes, there has to be a powerful organisation on the ground to ensure that lofty constitutional principles are indeed applied. The unfair discrimination prohibition of Section 8 could mobilize the kind of mass-based lesbian and gay movement that does not yet exist in this country.

But while gay equality might be an indivisible ingredient of a truly democratic dispensation, it is not a national priority. An all-out assault on all fronts might thus be counter-productive. Gay South Africans need to choose, very carefully indeed, the rights which they will assert through Section 8 in the next few years: immediate legalization of gay partnerships, for example, might not be as pressing a concern as revoking anti-gay criminal laws — and it might provoke precisely the kind of reactionary hostility that could blow "sexual orientation" out of the interim constitution.

Given South Africa's brutal history of racial discrimination and deliberate economic impoverishment of its majority, gay and lesbian South Africans have to endeavor, more than ever, to fold their concerns into this country's growing culture of human rights. Single-issue gay politics have never worked here.

Whatever the political and legal consequences of Section 8, its very exist-ence has given gay society in South Africa an unprecedented vitality; a robustness that is markedly different from the marginal and subterranean lives many of us have lived.

This even in the face of a growing AIDS epidemic that is having an ever-deepening impact on our society. One of our contributors, Linda Ngcobo, died before publication, and another, Koos Prinsloo, died shortly thereafter. Prinsloo, who is rated as perhaps the most gifted short story writer the Afrikaans language has ever produced, chose not to conceal the fact that he was gay and that he had AIDS.

His funeral was public and was covered on national television. If we are to pinpoint signal moments in the "coming out" of gay South African society, Koos Prinsloo's funeral must surely be marked, with pain but also with grim pride, as one of them.

And the South African publication of *Defiant Desire* must be marked, more unequivocally, as another. Coming as it did during the electoral campaign, it too has contributed materially to this new openness; to the growing debate on the na-ture and needs of South Africa's gay and lesbian citizens. Even now, six months after its publication, we remain astonished at the richness and diversity of South African gay and lesbian experiences unearthed by our contributors. We hope you will be too.

Mark Gevisser
Edwin Cameron
August 1994

Acknowledgements

We thank the Embassy of the Federal Republic of Germany and the Centre for Applied Legal Studies at the University of the Witwatersrand for financial assistance in producing this book. We are particularly grateful to a group of individual donors, including William Barlow, Eric Eikenboom and Leslie Smith, Michael Emanuel, the late Colin Fletcher, Nic Griffin, Keith Kirsten, Mark Nowitz, Howard Sacks, and Vincent Baasch and Ted Kahn, whose generosity and support enabled us to make the book bigger and cheaper.

Thanks are also due to Marie Human and the Bailey's African Photo Archives, Hugh McLean, Dhianaraj Chetty, Julia Beffon, Donald Dunham, Stephen Roche, Martin Nel, Alan Lazar, Cathi Albertyn, Lydia Levin, Bridget Brand, Lynn Reynolds, Joe Garmeson, Ann Smith, Tielman Henkel, Roz Posel, Rachel Holmes, Rob Nixon, Ann McClintock, Alisa Solomon, Marilyn Neimark, Jane Bower, Bronwyn Adams, Glynis Hutton, Ferial Haffajee, Tony Sparks from the Gay Library in Johannesburg, the *Weekly Mail & Guardian*, and to the members of GLOW, OLGA, ABIGALE, Yachad and Sunday's Women, who supported this project by generating ideas and submitting proposals and contributions.

Very special thanks are due to Shaun de Waal. He acted with generosity and insight as our editorial consultant. We are grateful to everyone at Ravan Press, particularly Ingrid Obery, who with Glenn Moss initially proposed this project, and who nurtured it through three exacting years of conception and production. Barry Burland undertook a final arduous proof-reading of the manuscript.

And finally, thanks to Cecelia Cancellaro and all at Routledge whose enthusiasm for this book and its subject have helped bring it to an international audience.

Mark Gevisser
Edwin Cameron
12 January 1994

Etymological note:
On 'moffie'

In South African slang, the word 'moffie' covers a range of interrelated senses, including 'male homosexual', 'effeminate male' and 'transvestite'. In its most widespread usage, it refers to the first category, but its more specific meaning of 'transvestite' is also found in the Cape coloured community.

A number of possible etymologies have been put forward. The most plausible relates it to 'mophrodite', a variation of 'hermaphrodite'. The word 'mofrodiet' is also used in Dutch (Jean and William Bradford, *The Oxford Dictionary of South African English*). A reference to 'mophrodites' in Henry Fielding's 1742 novel *Joseph Andrews* seems to indicate opera-singing castrati, or to conflate the two terms (and would also have connotations of transvestism).

'Moffie' is used exclusively in slang. Given this, roots in sailor slang — with the port city of Cape Town as a possible South African origin — seem credible. The word 'mophy' is recorded in *Sea Slang* of 1929 and by slang lexicographer Eric Partridge. It is 'a term of contempt among seamen for delicate, well-groomed youngsters'.

Other possible roots for 'moffie' are from Afrikaans 'mof', meaning a muff, sleeve or socket, as well as a bastard, cross-breed or undersized animal; or 'moffie', meaning a mitten. In these instances, semantic links are extremely tenuous. It has also been suggested that 'moffie' comes from the English 'mauve', a colour associated by some with homosexuals. This notion seems somewhat far-fetched.

The word 'moffie' has had an overwhelmingly derogatory implication, based on homophobic social responses. Recently, however, it has been reappropriated by homosexuals and transvestites in referring to themselves, losing some of its negative connotations. This is partly due to an ironic, camp tradition containing elements of self-mockery, and partly a political statement in the manner of African Americans, who have appropriated the insulting term 'nigger' (for instance the black rap group Niggers with Attitude). It is analogous to the way in which homosexual activists in England and America have taken over the word 'queer' (as in the pressure group Queer Nation).

It must be borne in mind, though, that the connotation is in the mouth of the speaker. Many homosexuals in South Africa may thus use the word 'moffie' of themselves, but still resent its use by homophobes.

Shaun de Waal

ONE —
Overviews

DEFIANT DESIRE:

An Introduction

Mark Gevisser and Edwin Cameron

Seizing the moment

Defiant Desire is a celebration of the lives of gay men and lesbians in South Africa. It does not and cannot claim to be a complete picture of gay and lesbian experience in this country. Rather, it tries to highlight some of the issues, the problems, the contradictions and the connecting points that make up our lives.

The book takes as its starting-point that there is no single, essential 'gay identity' in South Africa. What has passed for 'the gay experience' has often been that of white, middle-class urban men. The political and social cost of this perception, both in how we are represented and in how we are seen, has been enormous. If *Defiant Desire* has one aim, it is to expand — or at the very least re-examine — this narrow definition of 'gay identity'.

So we present a collage of essays, memoirs, polemics and pictures that acknowledge and explore some of the many facets of South African homosexual experience. In these pages you will find black youths from the townships, white mineworkers, lesbian sangomas, rich white 'entertainers' from the suburbs, coloured moffie drag queens, cross-racial working-class couples, political prisoners and sex workers. Much of this work is path-breaking, particularly that which details for the first time the extent to which homosexuality exists and flourishes in black communities and cultures.

Certainly, there is much in this book that stems from and reflects the urban mainstream. And while we record with pride the way this particular subculture has managed to claim space in the face of sometimes severe opprobrium, we also examine its limitations. To what extent and why have women and black people largely been excluded from 'mainstream' gay culture? What parallel cultures have existed, and how have they organised themselves? And how has the increasingly vocal presence of blacks and women transformed both the style and ideology of a South African 'gay identity'?

This in turn leads to the hardest question of all. What, if anything, do we all — blacks and whites and workers and professionals and men and women — actually share? Is there, could there have been, should there yet be, a common 'South African gay identity'? Perhaps the book, like South Africa's growing lesbian and gay movement itself, attempts to weave these people together with a thread of common experience, that transcends our differentness and affirms our gayness, of being 'out of order' — in the eyes of the law, the authorities and the heterosexual establishment.

* * *

This book is being completed in 1993, at the time of South Africa's transition to democracy. For three years now, since the unbanning of the liberation movements in 1990, our identities and aspirations have been unshackled. South Africans have explored, argued and exchanged ideas as never before. In bloody township battles, in tortuous constitutional negotiations, in campaigns leading up to a first democratic election, in unprecedentedly open media, South Africa's forty million citizens are staking claim to their future.

Defiant Desire is a product of these times: an attempt to engage in the current debate over what we want this land to be. For lesbian and gay South Africans, 'liberation' is a particularly loaded word. What role does sexual politics play in this time of transition? What do the struggles of those experiencing oppression in various ways — as blacks, as women, as gays and lesbians — have in common? Does their claim for equal rights, for democracy and dignity, tie them together in some way? Or does the call for equal rights for gays and lesbians detract from more urgent matters at hand — the righting of the wrongs of apartheid?

Defiant Desire attempts to answer these questions by examining, in depth, the relationship between lesbian and gay politics and the quest for democracy in South Africa. The majority activist contributors to this book are adamant that the struggle for justice and true liberation in this country must include a commitment to lesbian and gay equality. And, after much lobbying, the African National Congress came to agree. A clause in the ANC's proposed Bill of Rights (emulated in that of the Inkatha Freedom Party and the Democratic Party) outlawed discrimination on the grounds of sexual orientation, and this is reflected in the present draft Constitution.

And yet the status of gay and lesbian issues in the broader movement for democracy remains tenuous: gay issues continue to be seen as both frivolous and

4

'un-African'. The contributions by Nkoli, Chan Sam, Kleinbooi, Chetty, Lewis and Loots, and, most notably, McLean and Ngcobo, suggest that the claim that homosexuality is a 'bourgeois Western phenomenon' which 'contaminates' the purity of African civilization is untrue. The essays of Gevisser and Holmes cast light on why and how this notion came about.

Homosexual experience in South Africa is unique, precisely because of our history of division and resistance. Our identities have been formed by our country's history of racial struggle. And our identities have been deformed by a system that classified us into those with freedom and those without. Apartheid legislated who we were, what work we could do, where we could live, who we could associate with, what we could read and see and what kind of sex we could have. Apartheid even tried even to dictate to us our self-conception and our self-regard.

Asserting a lesbian or gay identity in South Africa is thus more than a necessary act of self-expression. It a defiance of the fixed identities — of race, ethnicity, class, gender and sexuality — that the apartheid system attempted to impose upon all of us.

South African homosexual experience is also unique because of the demographic divergences our country reflects. From the 'developed world', we inherit notions of sexual freedom and gay subculture; from the 'developing world' we gain the imperatives of struggle, resistance, and social transformation. Charting the development of a lesbian and gay identity in South Africa means examining the way these ideas have interacted with each other: how they have clashed, and what their potential may ultimately be to consolidate into a potent lesbian and gay liberation movement — the first ever in Africa.

For all the above reasons, there is a moment that must be seized. *Defiant Desire* reflects and attempts to make something of this moment. Which leads to another of the book's aspirations: to assist in establishing a climate in which South African lesbian and gay studies can emerge. The more that is published by and about gay South Africans, the more interest there will be, from publishers, from academic institutions, and from the reading public. Only a few years ago, working class and peasant tradition, labour history and women's studies were largely ignored in South Africa; now these are at least taken seriously by publishers and the academic world. We have similar brave hopes for lesbian and gay studies.

About the contents

Challenging the idea of a single, essential 'gay identity' has meant compiling a book that registers an enormous range of voices, styles and attitudes. *Defiant Desire*'s form is necessarily as diverse as its content. The chapters range from critical essays to attempts at historical reconstruction, to personal accounts, to memoirs that flirt with fiction. This means that a consistent style is neither possible nor desirable: each piece has determined its own form. Some contributions are intensely personal; others are abstracted and systemic studies.

In South Africa, as elsewhere, there is a personal politics to self-description. We all call ourselves something different: gay, moffie, lesbian, dyke, queer.

What for one is a submission to language stereotyping is for another an assertive reappropriation of language. And so we have let each contributor determine the terms of his or her personal identification.

The book begins with Gevisser's history of lesbian and gay organisation in South Africa, 'A different fight for freedom'. By giving a detailed account of gay and lesbian organisation from the bars and house-parties of the 1950s through the law reform movement of 1968 to the gay upsurge in the 1980s and the current wave of more radicalised lesbian and gay activism, Gevisser creates a context for the rest of the book. He also synthesises many of its themes: the interplay of sexual identity with the politics of race, class and gender; the interaction between middle-class whites and working-class blacks in the creation of a gay subculture; the reasons for so-called lesbian 'invisibility'.

Gevisser explores how homosexuals first consciously came together in lei-sure-time activity (clubs, bars, sports teams) to satisfy basic social needs before formalising themselves into self-consciously gay groups and then political move-ments. He looks at the relationship, in South African lesbian and gay subcultures, between confrontation and accommodation; between political advocacy and social support; between activism and acting out; between 'apolitical' conservatism and radical liberationism.

The two contributions in Section Two perhaps best explain the political reasons for this book — describing the oppression to which gays and lesbians are subject in South Africa. In 'Unapprehended felons', Cameron explores the South African legal system's letter and its spirit towards homosexuality, and assesses how the various constitutional models deal with non-discrimination towards lesbian and gay rights.

In 'Keeping sodom out of the laager', Retief looks at the ways the apart-heid system has policed sexual minorities. Retief points to the link between apartheid oppression and gay oppression, and his central point is that sexual polic-ing was an intrinsic project of apartheid: it helped consolidate Afrikaner Calvinist control by upholding 'Christian National' values in the face of what was charac-terised as a 'threat to white civilization'. Anything deemed threatening — including gays — was 'expelled from the laager'.

* * *

Despite the apartheid state's repression, various gay and lesbian subcultures devel-oped in South Africa. Some of these are examined in Section Three, 'Making space: Queer societies'. Given the homophobic society in which they have had to develop, these 'queer societies' are necessarily 'outsider' subcultures. They are de-fined by masquerade, resistance, subterfuge and sublimation.

We see masquerade and resistance in the way Chetty's moffie drag queens from the 1950s and 1960s and McLean and Ngcobo's township youths of the pre-sent day wilfully and often playfully subvert their preordained gender and sex roles. We see subterfuge in the way Johannesburg's 'Health Clubs', as described by Galli and Rafael, served as clandestine sexual meeting-places for closeted gay men in the

1950s and 1960s. We see sublimation in the way Miller's gay men and women of Welkom, on the surface conservative Afrikaners, have to bury their true identities deep underground.

What is astonishing is that these 'queer societies', even while marginalised and derided, are very much part of the larger communities in which they operate. In 'A drag at Madame Costello's', Chetty reclaims a critical piece of our history. Using clippings from *Drum* and *Golden City Post* as well as personal interviews, he reconstructs the moffie drag balls of the 1950s and 1960s. His work demonstrates that homosexuality and drag are an indivisible part of the history and culture of the Western Cape's coloured communities. 'A drag at Madame Costello's' was written as commentary to the series of remarkable photographs published in this volume — all taken at a 'Moffie Drag' in Madame Costello's Woodstock living-room in 1958. Ian Berry's photographs have a notable sympathy and sensitivity, and provide a glimpse of full lives lived behind a facade of dominant stereotypes.

'Lesbian Gangster', originally published in *Drum* under a different name, gives us a vivid glimpse of lesbian cross-dressing. It also shows how some lesbians, as outlaws, might have found common ground with other outlaws — gangsters — within Cape Town's coloured communities: a provocative illustration of how marginalised groups can make a common virtue of defiance.

In 'Moffies en manvroue', Lewis and Loots also demonstrate the central role of the 'moffie' scene in the Cape's coloured communities. But, by exploring the relationships of two working-class couples, their essay also demonstrates how these four people have managed to assert and develop their sexual identity and create alternate families within hostile territory. The authors' decision to record their informants at length in the Afrikaans-based Western Cape vernacular makes for challenging reading. But so much humour and creativity is embedded in this language that the effort is rewarded.

Work originating from or examining the Western Cape coloured communities (including Achmat's memoir, 'My childhood as an adult molester', which appears as a Testament in Section Six) constitutes perhaps the largest single segment of 'queer society' examined in the book. This is appropriate. These communities, by nature fluid, hybrid and permeable, contain the oldest, most developed and least-explored gay South African subculture; nowhere else in this country have homosexuals been so integral to a culture.

But homosexuality is an integral part of other black South African cultures too. In 'Abangibhamayo bathi ngimnandi', McLean and Ngcobo unearth the extent to which homosexual codes are embedded in contemporary township culture. Their informants — 20 township men, some of whom are members of the Gay and Lesbian Organisation of the Witwatersrand (GLOW) — lead lives unexpectedly integrated into township culture. They are children of parents who know of their sons' homosexuality, and lovers of 'straight' men, or *injongas*, who collude in the masquerade that their sexual partners are 'women.' The mechanics of this charade make for sometimes startling reading. The piece details an intricate taxonomy of homosexual behaviour and sexual role-play, and looks at the way this imitates — and subverts — the heterosexual paradigm.

In a similar way, Chan Sam used the GLOW Lesbian Forum to collect narratives of black lesbian life. While 'Five women' is not as comprehensive as the study of McLean and Ngcobo, it presents five moving vignettes, one of which is of a *sangoma* (traditional healer) who looks at the relationship between her sexuality and her vocation. The apparent tradition of lesbian *sangomas* is an aspect of our history that warrants more research.

Despite some of their rural roots, all Chan Sam and McLean and Ngcobo's informants live in the big city. They thus have access to overt gay and lesbian communities. By contrast, Mike Olivier's profile of Vera Vimbela, a rural woman from the Transkei who is organising gays and lesbians in Umtata, signals the difficulties of being black, gay, and rural.

While Chan Sam and Olivier record the lives of black lesbians, Beffon's 'Wearing the Pants' looks, briefly but vividly, at butch/femme role-playing in white lesbian relationships. Like 'Abangibhamayo bathi ngimnandi', it raises provocative questions about the homosexual impulse to imitate heterosexual paradigms. Like McLean and Ngcobo, Beffon finds subversive possibilities within these relationships.

* * *

While Section Three looks at 'making space', Section Four, 'Making Noise', looks at the way cultural forms arising out of queer societies are used both to define the values and codes of these societies and to confront heterosexuals with their existence. In 'The Arista Sisters', Krouse recounts how he and a group of other gays doing their national service (a whites-only obligation) put on a drag-show. The masquerade both entertained the troops and subverted the overbearing patriarchal structure of the army. But Krouse also examines the South African Defence Force's ambivalence to homosexuality — the fact that the SADF 'needs moffies' to serve as a counterpoint to what it means to be a 'real man' — and describes the 'queer societies' that gays establish for themselves within the SADF.

In a similar vein to drag, another popular expression of 'queer society' is South Africa's highly developed form of gay slang. Gerrit Olivier's 'From Ada to Zelda' provides an introduction to this slang, which creates a gay alphabet out of women's names. He looks at its possible use as a means of concealment on the one hand and of self-identification on the other. In an appendix to 'Abangibhamayo bathi ngimnandi', McLean and Ngcobo note that *isingqumo*, the township gay slang, serves the same function.

Along with drag and language, the emergence of a 'gay press', in the form of the newspaper *Exit*, has become another important vehicle for popular expression. In 'Exit', Davidson and Nerio look at the role that this newspaper has played in the politics and formation of a gay subculture.

If drag, *moffietaal* (gay language) and the gay press are popular cultural expressions of queer society, then the recurrent theme of homosexuality within

8

South African literature is one of their 'high art' equivalents. In 'A thousand forms of love', De Waal examines the way five gay writers represent, through various means of deferral and sublimation, male homosexual desire. De Waal tracks a theme of transgression, running from ID Du Plessis through William Plomer (who flags his homosexuality only through innuendo), Damon Galgut, Stephen Gray and, finally, Koos Prinsloo.

De Waal's essay is an important contribution to an already established discourse. Two volumes of gay writing have been published in South Africa: Hennie Aucamp's *Wisselstroom*[1] and, more recently, the Congress of South African Writers' *The Invisible Ghetto*.[2] Aucamp's anthology of Afrikaans fiction has prodded a lively debate within the Afrikaans academy on the nature of gay Afrikaans writing. Besides literature, however, there are several other 'high art' forms which cry out for analysis from a gay perspective. These include the extensive role of homosexuality in mainstream South African theatre (most notably the work of 'high-art' draggers like Pieter-Dirk Uys and Nataniël); as well as homophilic fine art, both as rooted in South Africa's 'grand masters' (such as Alexis Preller) and in its latest incarnation in the work of young artists like Stephen Cohen and Mallory de Cock.

* * *

Gevisser notes in 'A different fight for freedom' that claiming 'gay space' — the making of 'queer societies' and assertion of 'queer culture' — is always a precursor to the establishment of a lesbian and gay liberation movement. In South Africa, as elsewhere, there has been something of a progression from bar culture, to social support organisations, to political activism. Section Five 'Making waves: Lesbian and gay activism' examines the current political activity arising out of South Africa's lesbian and gay subcultures, and the relationship between this and the broader liberation struggle.

The section begins with two personal accounts, both by gay men, one black, one white, who were jailed for political reasons during the last years of formal apartheid. Both Simon Nkoli and Ivan Toms worked to integrate their gay identities with their anti-apartheid activism. Theirs are classic prison stories, but with a difference: for both Nkoli and Toms, physical imprisonment worked very strongly as a metaphor for the closet, and 'freedom' thus has several resonances.

In 'Wardrobes' Nkoli tells of his coming out, first to his family and then to his co-accused in the 1986 Delmas Treason Trial. His account of the way almost every *sangoma* in Sebokeng township tried to 'cure' him provides yet another insight into the workings of homosexual identity within urban township life. The graphic description of his coming out within the walls of Pretoria Central Prison reveals a behind-the-scenes battle at the Delmas Trial not previously told.

In 'Ivan Toms is a fairy?', conscientious objector Toms — the first white jailed for conscientious refusal to do military service — recounts the smear-campaign conducted against him by the South African Defence Force. Toms also addresses the more surprising subject of the implied homophobia he encountered within the anti-apartheid End Conscription Campaign. Both Nkoli and Toms bear witness to how difficult it has been for gay people to come out within the liberation movement.

In 'Identity crossfire', Kleinbooi too writes about the difficulties of being gay in the liberation movement, and, conversely, about the difficulties of being black in the gay movement. He records his alienation from both black and gay campus groups and provides an account of how compromising it is to juggle the political identities of 'black' and 'gay' within so charged and politicised a society. Toms describes how he found common ground with the cause of black South Africans through his own experience of oppression as a gay man. But Kleinbooi takes issue with any suggestion that the two can be equated: 'To say that heterosexism is the same as racism is actually trivialising racial oppression,' he urges.

Nevertheless, the linking of racial oppression and sexual oppression has been a common perception and strategy of lesbian and gay liberation groups in South Africa. As Gevisser notes in 'A different fight for freedom', there has been a major shift from the 'apolitical' (read conservative) gay movement of the 1980s to the liberationist gay movement of the 1990s, which has taken as its starting-point the need to fold lesbian and gay issues into the agenda of the broader anti-apartheid movement. The success of this strategy is charted in 'The lavender lobby', in which Fine and Nicol describe the way the Organisation of Lesbian and Gay Activists (OLGA) lobbied the African National Congress to include a clause protecting gays and lesbians from discrimination in its proposed Bill of Rights. And the physical manifestation of this new liberationism is described in 'Pride or protest?', in which Gevisser and Reid give an account of GLOW's annual Lesbian and Gay Pride Marches that have taken place since 1990.

But in 'Pride or protest?' we also see the dilemmas caused by the gay movement's new radicalism: most white gay men are alienated from the movement, and GLOW's own constituency of younger black men and women still feels the need for social support before embracing political activism. And in Holmes' 'White rapists made coloureds (and homosexuals)', we see another major problem faced by this new liberationism — one that Toms and Nkoli painfully enunciate — the continued homophobia that exists within the 'democratic movement'.

Holmes offers a complex analysis of the defence put up for Winnie Mandela during her 1991 kidnapping and assault trial. Mandela claimed that she had ordered four youths to be 'removed' from a Methodist manse to protect them from sexual abuse by the minister, Paul Verryn. Holmes unpicks the homophobia in this defence: the fact that homosexuality was simply equated with sexual abuse and thus with betrayal of the cause and bad parenting. Holmes demonstrates how Mandela set herself up as 'good mother' as opposed to Verryn as 'bad father'. She concludes that the Mandela defence was 'queerbashing with family values'.

All the above writers look at the tenuous relationship between gay politics and the broader democratic movement. Armour and Lapinsky's 'Lesbians in love and compromising situations' in its turn examines the equally tenuous relationship between lesbian politics and the gay movement. Through a survey of feminist organisation in Cape Town, they unearth the roots of a specifically South African lesbian consciousness, touching on the issues of lesbian marginality within gay politics and lesbian separatism.

In South Africa, AIDS has long ceased to be depicted as only a 'gay disease': the grim arithmetic of heterosexual transmissions has rendered sexual stereotyping of those at risk redundant. But the gay community has been brutally and disproportionately hit by HIV. No account of gay lives in South Africa would be accurate without including it as a central theme. Pegge's 'Living with loss in the best way we know how' describes how the epidemic has spread through Cape Town's gay community and how gay men have responded to the crisis.

Placing this essay in the section on lesbian and gay activism is appropriate. North American- or European-style AIDS activism has not developed in South Africa. Nevertheless, given the compounded stigma of illness, sin and contamination that mars public perceptions of AIDS in South Africa, the work that Pegge documents constitutes an especially necessary and courageous form of activism. The fight against the spread of HIV and for fair, compassionate and appropriate services should be as much part of gay movement's agenda as more recognisably 'political' issues.

The last contribution in this section, Ricci's 'Of gay rights and the pitfalls of the "PC"', serves as a dissenting — or at least cautionary — voice to what precedes it. Ricci scoffs at 'political correctness', which he sees as gaining currency in South Africa. He notes that 'it would be sad indeed if South Africa went from reactionary "old" oppression to trendy "new" oppression without any stage of true democracy in between.' He warns the budding South African gay and lesbian movement 'to guard against the "PC" idiocies and excesses of far more established and powerful protest groups', and takes issue with several gay holy cows. These include the very use of the word 'gay'.

* * *

The concluding section of the book, 'Testaments', is a collection of personal memoirs. Prinsloo's 'Promise you'll tell no-one' and Achmat's 'My childhood as an adult molester' explore the complex comings to sexual consciousness of two children. John's 'Pretended families' examines the moment at which a gay man and a lesbian decide to have a child together. Mayne's 'In memory of Rocky' is an obituary. Their trajectory, in simple narrative terms, is one from birth, through parenting, to death.

In more thematic terms, the section gives us four very different glimpses of moments in lives that are informed by homosexual consciousness but not dictated by it. Prinsloo's work, treading on and sometimes trampling over the line between memoir and fiction, shows the mutability of sexual identity at a formative time in its protagonist's life. Achmat, by skilfully weaving an account of his coming of sexual age into a rich and textured description of his home-life in Salt River, gives powerful voice to the indivisibility of sexual, social, community and political consciousness. John explores the difficulties of being a gay parent, but also the common ground he and the mother of his child have with all parents.

11

And, finally, Mayne uses the form of the obituary to its full creative and expressive potential. The untimely AIDS-related death of a friend allows her to remember his life and her own, the 30-year relationship between them, and the difficult and complicated positions they both held in their society — she as a white lesbian, he as a coloured gay man. Mayne's tribute is a fitting close to the book, perhaps just as Gevisser's account of Linda Ngcobo's funeral is a fitting opening. The time of our community's greatest potential power, constitutionally and socially, is also a time when many of us are at risk of infection with HIV, or are succumbing to the epidemic, as Rocky and Linda Ngcobo have.

Though Mayne recounts the loss of a friend through AIDS, she also shows how friendship can generate dignity and pride and transcendent bonds. These can surpass the divisions which our blackness or whiteness, our maleness or our femaleness, our HIV infection — or our freedom from it — impose upon us. In this her account is not a memorial of the past, but a hopeful marker for the future.

Inclusiveness, assertion and pride

One of our contributors states that the impact of Johannesburg's first two annual pride marches, in 1990 and 1991, was undermined by the way the media focussed on the presence of drag queens. Should the lesbian and gay movement, in its attempt to present a serious and compelling argument for equality, allow drag queens to participate in a pride march? This is a continuing discussion among gay activists and writers, both in South Africa and abroad[3], and the issue cuts to the heart of the difficult relationship between personal identity and political strategy. It is an issue we have had to confront in editing this book. Should we present an upright, buttoned-down image of gay life and culture? Would we play into society's stereotypes by including photographs of 'moffies' in drag, by boasting about butch dykes and sexually promiscuous men, rather than by representing only 'normal' boy-and-girl-next-door homosexuals?

The simple answer to these questions is that we will not do to those among us what society has done to all of us: we will not marginalise — or deny a voice to — anyone. We will rather celebrate our diversity, and honour those forms it takes which most courageously and assertively flaunt what is common to all of us — that society disparages us for being different, no matter how buttoned-down some of us may appear on the surface.

A more complicated answer is that since we reject the very notion that there is an 'essential' gay identity in South Africa, no one of us can claim to represent a single, unchangeable 'gay' or 'lesbian' image. This book's own 'activism' is, as we stated earlier, to present the multiplicity of gay and lesbian experience. This contains within it as much complexity, difficulty and possibility as heterosexuality. Excising more difficult manifestations of homosexuality might proffer strategic rewards. But valuing strategy over truth is in itself a form of self-censorship. Furthermore, the product, a conforming and inoffensive representation of the homosexual, is as stereotyped and one-dimensional as the very images it tries to counter

Introduction

— the pansy, the drag queen, the child-molester, the disease-carrier. And, like all one-dimensional stereotypes, it can be knocked down as easily as it is erected.

A more lasting acceptance and tolerance of sexual minorities will come about only once we are acknowledged in all our complexity; only when society understands the extent to which we are embedded within it and thus imbued with its own quirks and pathologies, its own range of values and attitudes. And until lesbian and gay communities themselves accept the sometimes inconvenient deviances and dissents they encompass, we cannot hope to persuade society at large to embrace the same project.

Johannesburg, June 1993

Notes

1 Hennie Aucamp (ed), *Wisselstroom* (Human & Rousseau: 1990).
2 Matthew Krause and Kim Berman (eds), *The Invisible Ghetto: Lesbian and Gay Writing from South Africa* (COSAW: 1993).
3 See Marshall Kirk and Hunter Madsen, *After the Ball: How America will Conquer its Fear and Hatred of Gays in the 1990s* (Plum: 1990).

A different fight for freedom:

A history of South African lesbian and gay organisation from the 1950s to 1990s

Mark Gevisser

Prologue: Linda Ngcobo's funeral

There were hundreds of mourners at the funeral service for Linda Ngcobo in Soweto's Phiri Hall on Saturday 13 February 1993. Ngcobo died unexpectedly of AIDS-related renal failure at the age of 28. He was a founder-member of GLOW, the Gay and Lesbian Organisation of the Witwatersrand, and the organiser of the annual Miss GLOW drag show, the highlight of gay Soweto's calendar. He was also a loyal son who lived with his family in their township home, and a choir-member in the charismatic African Apostolic Church of which his father is an elder and lay preacher.

And so, on the day of his funeral, two communities gathered to bury Linda Ngcobo and lay claim to his spirit. Among the congregationists, the men wore suits and women dressed from head to toe in white; in the charismatic African style of prayer, they chanted and swayed and thumped, moving up to heaven with the force of their faith the body lying in the coffin before them. They sat, a sea of white waves, on chairs in the hall. Behind them stood at least two hundred men and a smattering of women; black gays and lesbians from Soweto, Ngcobo's comrades from GLOW and the clandestine gay networks that criss-cross this sprawling township.

Some of Ngcobo's gay comrades came in jacket and tie. A few arrived in full explosive drag. A few more represented that peculiar androgyny of township drag borne of scant resources and much imagination, nodding at gender-inversion

14

with no more than a frilly shirt, a pair of garish earrings, a touch of rouge, a pair of low-heeled pumps, a third-hand wig. Most, however, wore t-shirts with the GLOW logo, a pink triangle framing a raised, clenched fist. For, in the township tradition of the slain freedom-fighter, this was to be a political funeral: an expression of grief that was also a consecration to further struggle.

Earlier in the week, at a memorial service organised by GLOW, a confrontation had erupted between Ngcobo's friends and his father; offered an opportunity to speak, the old man had railed against his son's gay friends, damning their sin. The GLOW members were furious, and decided to organise their own feast after the burial rather than attend the family one. Ngcobo's father showed remorse; he and his family had always known about and accepted their son's homosexuality, and, he apologised, he had been moved to speak by the heat of the moment. GLOW was welcome at the funeral, he added, and a space had been made in the programme for the gay organisation to speak.

And so, in Phiri Hall, a strange truce held. Neither Ngcobo's friends nor his church was prepared to relinquish their claim over his body. In the GLOW part of the programme, veteran black gay activist Simon Nkoli spoke, making explicit Ngcobo's homosexuality in what was as much a memorial to a dead comrade as an impassioned plea for tolerance and a call-to-arms for rights. In the traditional style of funeral oration, Nkoli peppered his speech with hymns, and, despite the controversy (and even blasphemy) of his words, the congregation joined in with his call-and-response. After Nkoli's speech, a young GLOW member in drag led the gay mourners through a modified version of 'We are a gentle, loving people'. Here was a group of conservative church people, witnessing the spectacle of a man in women's clothing singing at the funeral of the son of one of their elders! Here was a moment of power, if not revenge, for the gay people of Soweto; here too a rare moment of tolerance.

During Nkoli's speech, the GLOW banner was unfurled behind the coffin, effectively screening the church elders, seated on the raised stage behind the banner, from the congregation. It was as if GLOW had replaced the church as the institution watching over Linda Ngcobo. After the GLOW section of the programme was over, the church service resumed; a preacher labelled GLOW as Ngcobo's 'friends of the flesh' and explained how the departed had 'repented for his sins' on his deathbed. But still the GLOW banner stood its ground, held prominently and tautly above the coffin.

And now the gay mourners devised a brilliant, if subconscious, theatrical ruse. Two people were required to hold the banner; Ngcobo's friends arranged for its bearers to be relieved, unnecessarily, every two minutes. And so, as the preacher railed on about repentance and sin, a constant procession of gay men, many in drag or demi-drag, paraded up and down the central aisle of Phiri Hall. The aisle became a ramp, the gay guys models, performing their identity before the white-clad congregation, reminding the congregation, even as the preachers preached about friends of the flesh, that they were there and proud, friends of Linda Ngcobo and part of the community, like it or not.

There were moments, as the vast funeral procession moved from the hall down to the Avalon Cemetery, Soweto's anarchic dustbowl of a burial ground, that were reminiscent of any of the dozens of political funerals that had taken place there before. A group of t-shirt-clad comrades toyi-toying before the coffin; the singing of more conventional freedom songs interspersed with 'Hey hey, ho ho, homophobia's got to go!'; the clenched and raised fists protruding out of impossibly-packed busses; the tensions, of course, between a political movement and a family laying claim to a departed soldier.

Linda Ngcobo's death, like all deaths, like all AIDS-related deaths, violent deaths, deaths in detention, deaths of heroes and untimely deaths, was a coming of age for the young men and women mourning him that day. Linda Ngcobo's funeral was as brazen and complex and contradictory, yet as inevitably affirming, as the black gay movement Ngcobo himself had helped found and entrench. Ngcobo was one of the first black men to declare his homosexuality publicly and draw others around him; he was also the first black gay leader to die an AIDS-related death. His death caused panic, confusion and fear. But his funeral did, undoubtedly, consecrate a social and political movement that had been growing in black urban communities since the mid-1980s; one with its counterpart in a white movement that had itself been germinating, slowly, in South African soil for over four decades.

***

Linda Ngcobo's funeral raises more questions than this account of lesbian and gay organisation in South Africa could ever answer. What is the history of gay identity that led to this moment of consecration in a dusty township cemetery, and where is it to be found? Given the history of apartheid South Africa, where identities were so rigidly defined, why is a 'gay identity' so elusive and undefinable? Given the specificity of class, race and ethnicity in South Africa, is it even possible to pin down a 'gay identity' using the terminology of Western culture? When I — a white man — called myself 'gay' and Linda Ngcobo — a black man — called himself 'gay', did we mean the same things? When I call myself 'gay', do I mean the same things as middle-aged white men and women who participated in a homosexual subculture in the 1950s and 1960s? Is it right to tell a history in such a way that makes of these men and women my fathers and mothers? Is there a line of consciousness that leads from middle-class white homosexuals who called themselves 'queer' in the 1950s through to hip young black kids who now call themselves 'queer', with a new subversive edge, in the 1990s?

And are there homosexual 'norms' which can be picked out of random points of South African history and strung together into a coherent narrative of gay identity? Lesbian and gay historiography is now split between 'essentialists' and 'constructionists'.[1] The former group, believing that there is an essential gay consciousness linking all gay people, would probably answer 'yes' to the above questions. The latter group, believing that sexuality is determined by specific cultural, historical and social contexts, would probably answer 'no'. While this account does attempt to tell the 'story' of gay social and political life in South

16

Africa from the 1950s to the present day, it does so from the 'constructionist' perspective: the narrative coherence of the story which follows is undermined, quite consciously, by the understanding that it is impossible to identify a single, cohesive 'gay' identity.

This account is of necessity episodic and subjective. It is by no means exhaustive and is not an empirical study. Given the sparse documentation of lesbian and gay history in this country, I have had to construct a narrative from fragments: the vivid but subjective memories of a half-dozen older men and women; a wonderful red leather-bound scrapbook bequeathed to the Johannesburg Gay Library which happens to include much information about Durban; incomplete newspaper-clipping files; the ideologically charged interpretations of activists; the work of the very few other people who too have attempted to document homosexual experience in South Africa.

Despite all the above problems and limitations, the funeral of Linda Ngcobo compelled me to continue with the project none the less. As I stood in Phiri Hall behind the black gay mourners behind the hymn-singing congregants, I felt a proud commonality with Linda's black friends around me, despite our differences; we were all gay, all South African. My strongest feeling was this: we cannot afford to 'lose' Linda Ngcobo as we have lost to obscurity so many before him. In his name, some beginnings at South African gay and lesbian history must be attempted, fragments though they may be.

As I stood at the back of Phiri Hall I realised, too, that even if this account cannot tell the 'whole story', it can, at least, restate the very issues the funeral itself raised: the interplay of sexual identity with the politics of race, class and gender; the different relationships of middle-class white people and working-class black people to a homosexual subculture; the marginality and invisibility of lesbian voices in both black and white gay subcultures; the relationship between outrageous sexual dissidence and gender inversion on the one hand and 'straight-acting' conformity on the other; the choices, faced by gay South African politics, between confrontation and accommodation; the division between political advocacy and social support; the relationship between activism and acting out, as seen so clearly, at Linda Ngcobo's funeral, in the confusion of toyi-toying drag queens and ramp-walking comrades.

Finally, this is a history of gay and lesbian organisation rather than of sexual identity in South Africa. As such, it focuses on those who have called themselves 'queers' or 'moffies' or 'gays' or 'lesbians' or 'dykes' — on those who have self-consciously identified themselves with homosexual subcultures rather than that far greater number who have engaged in homosexual sex or homophilic relationships on the margins of these subcultures. Because these subcultures have, until very recently, been white, male and middle-class, this account reflects, to a large extent, white, male and middle-class experience. Rather than claiming that women and black men belonged to a subculture when they patently didn't, I hope to show why they did not, and how their later entry into the subculture worked to transform and reconceive both style and ideology.

One
The roots of a subculture: the 1950s and 1960s

Between drag queens and child-molesters

By the mid-1950s, the public image of homosexuals swung between two stereotypes: the child-molester and the drag queen. While *Drum* and *Golden City Post* sold newspapers by focussing on the coloured 'Moffie Drag' subculture in and around Cape Town, printing sensational 'exposés' of coloured drag queens and competitions, a 1956 police swoop of the Esplanade, Durban's pre-eminent cruising place, resulted in the arrest of 30 men who were charged with indecent assault. In his judgement, the magistrate, JL Pretorius issued sentences ranging from six to 15 months, declaring that 'your type is a menace to society and likely to corrupt and bring about degradation to innocent and unsuspecting, decent-living young men and so spell ruin to their future...'[2]

Between these two stereotypes, however, homosexual subcultures existed in the major cities (Johannesburg, Cape Town and Durban) relatively unharassed — and had done so at least since the war a decade previously. Just as gay communities were established in urban centres in the United States in part because of the uprooting impact of the depression and World War II, the various urbanising influences of South Africa — first the mining rushes that created Johannesburg, then the flood of people from the rural areas in the 1920s and 1930s — meant that there were people in the cities, away from their families and home communities, able for the first time to practise 'personal autonomy': to 'come out' as part of a homosexual subculture.[3]

With the exception of Cape Town, where there had long been a 'moffie' culture based in the Cape Malay communities, these subcultures were white, male, and generally middle-class. But, in South Africa's apartheid history, the influx of white people into the towns was paralleled by the system of black migrant labour: the single-sex compounds, where men were divorced from home communities, created 'breeding grounds' for 'circumstantial homosexuality'. Certainly there were those black men who practised homosexuality for lack of a more appealing heterosexual alternative, but there were also those who 'found themselves', and who remained in town, living homosexual lives, rather than returning to either wives or the possibility of marriage in their rural areas. Given South Africa's history of 'separateness', there were very few places where mobile white homosexuals and migrant black homosexuals met. Not surprisingly, those spaces that did exist were the much-mythologised 'melting pots' of South Africa's past: Fietas and Sophiatown in Johannesburg, District Six in Cape Town.

American gay historians have noted that World War II played perhaps the single most important role in the creation of a self-identified gay subculture.[4] In South Africa too, the war, with its concentration of transient men in uniform, had a formalising effect. In the port-cities of Durban and Cape Town, gay men found public space within the quayside subculture that blossomed around docked warships. In Johannesburg, gay life sprouted in Joubert Park, where there was an army camp during the war, and the area became known for its bars; even though these bars were 'straight', they were patronised by gay Johannesburgers looking to meet off-duty soldiers. That, says 'Gareth', who was in his late teens at the time, 'is how Joubert Park became the first gay place in Johannesburg. Most of the bars closed up as soon as the war ended. But the people who had moved into flats around the park to be near the bars remained.'

The end of the war saw a far larger percentage of single people living away from their families. The Hillbrow/Joubert Park area, with its proximity to town and its cheap high-density accommodation, became an obvious and acceptable neighbourhood for young people to live alone. Not surprisingly, gay men and lesbians flocked there. Cruising areas also developed during the war because of their proximity to soldiers and sailors: Park Station adjacent to Joubert Park in Johannesburg, the Esplanade alongside the docks in Durban, the Sea Point Promenade and Gardens area in Cape Town. Along with a few of the bars, these cruising venues remained active after the war and, in all three cities, gay men continued to have public meeting places into the 1950s.

'Sporting Women': Lesbian subcultures in the 1950s and 1960s

Lesbians, despite being entirely ignored by both the law and the media, experienced far greater pressure to remain closeted and had far fewer public gathering places. In South Africa, as in the West, a homosexual male's entry into the gay subculture is often via the bar or the cruising ground.[5] In North America and Europe, lesbian bars and subcultures did exist in the 1950s — most notably in Greenwich Village in New York, but also in smaller cities like Buffalo and Vancouver.[6] Particularly during the 1960s, these communities folded into the burgeoning Women's Movement, and lesbians found, in feminism, a philosophical framework for living lives independent of men.

While there is a history of women's organisation in South Africa, it has focussed primarily on workplace rights and the anti-apartheid struggle (the famous 1956 march of 20 000 women on Pretoria's Union Buildings being a case in point). In the 1950s and 1960s, it certainly did not address itself to issues of sexuality; neither did it situate itself within feminist ideology. With no feminist movement in South Africa and little bohemian subculture to speak of, lesbians thus found it even more difficult than gay men to find space.

Nevertheless, alongside and often intersecting with more visible gay male subculture, lesbian communities existed after the war in South Africa's major cities — often in the form of small cliques of friends organised by profession (teachers, nurses, lawyers). Entry into these cliques was by word of mouth in the workplace and often required much intrepid inventiveness. 'Hannah' is a businesswoman who moved to Johannesburg after the war. Through a close gay friend she met while working, she was introduced to the gay male subculture; through a personal newspaper advertisement ('Lady interested in motor mechanics wishes to meet same'), she met her first lover and became involved in a tight-knit circle of lesbians.

'Ellie', her lover of 16 years, is a physical education teacher who 'picked up' her first lover in 1955 while working in a record store: the pick-up was an art-student who introduced Ellie to a 'bohemian artsy' world in which there were many gay men and women. Through surreptitious conversation in staffrooms and at sports meetings, Ellie met many other lesbian teachers too.

It was a fiercely clandestine world. 'Jackie', a teacher who met Ellie at a swimming gala, remembers that

> *you only came alive on the weekend. During the week you kept up all pretences. I had my hair set every week, and wore high heels, skirts and make-up. I wouldn't have dreamed of going to a movie in town in slacks.*

For many lesbians of this generation and class, wearing slacks in public became the yardstick of liberation, and both Ellie and Jackie remember vividly the thrill of first wearing slacks to town.

The cliques developed, says Hannah, as a safety mechanism: 'women who had jobs just could not afford to be disclosed.' Occasionally, there would be interaction between the cliques: Ellie, for example, became involved at one point with a group of women from Pretoria,

> *very Afrikaans, very insular, civil servants who were terrified of being found out. They were an outdoorsy crowd. Their idea of a Sunday afternoon was to get together over a weekend and go hiking and fishing at Hartebeespoort Dam.*

There were, however, some public 'safe' venues open to lesbians. In the late 1950s, for example, a woman called Chick Venter ran a club near Park Station in Johannesburg. 'It was downstairs in a basement,' recalls Ellie, 'and very rough. The walls were covered with fishnets with bottles hanging off them. That was the style in those days.' While most of Chick Venter's clientele was male, it was one of the few venues at the time where 'unaccompanied women' could go. Ellie, with her 'arty' connections, also became involved in the coffee-house scene: the East African in Jeppe St, for example, was a largely-straight venue frequented by gay people.

On the whole, though, lesbian social life at the time revolved around private parties in flats. In Johannesburg, cliques developed around certain party-givers, one of whom was Hannah, outspokenly open and well into her 30s by the mid-1950s. Hannah lived in Reynard Hall, a building almost exclusively occupied by lesbians and gay men and renamed 'Radclyffe Hall' by Hannah's set. '*The Well of Loneliness* was our Bible,' says Ellie, and, in an attempt to emulate the lesbian author, pipe-smoking was a fad for a while. Hannah remembers that

> *I had a helluva lot of parties. There was always terrific music, and tens of beautiful women crammed into my little flat. I had very young people mixing with me. Because they were living at home and couldn't let their hair down, they used my place as a gathering point. As we say in gangster-talk, it was a 'safe-house'.*

In those days, the women recall, the butch scene was far more entrenched than it is now, and gendered rituals were *de rigueur*: the butches wore slacks, kept their hair short, and were expected to get drunk; the femmes wore dresses, bobbed their hair, and were in great demand. Because there was a general antipathy in the subculture to wearing dresses, however, the rituals often became wonderfully stylised: since, eventually, everyone, butch and feminine wore slacks, regardless of gender assignation, at some parties guests were required to wear pink or blue bowties to signify their roles. Today, says Hannah, 'when I go to a party people say "do you want to lead or shall I?" It's become very liberal now. Those days you knew where you were and you stayed there.'

Apart from the flatland party scene and the occasionally welcoming bar, club or coffee-shop, the other significant gathering place for lesbians in the 1950s and 1960s, as now, was to be found in the sporting clubs. In smaller cities, this was often the only option: 'Cleo', a woman active in Durban in those years, remembers that

> the only way you could meet someone was through cricket —
> there was no other place... We knew that 'those girls' played
> cricket, so we joined too... The girls used to play at Albert
> Park, and every week we'd have a 'Plaza Night': we'd meet at
> someone's home for supper, a few drinks, and a game of darts.[7]

Cleo recalls too that women's soccer teams were also havens for lesbians, but for a 'rougher' type.

In Johannesburg, Hannah responded to an advertisement for a 'No-Man's Cricket Team', and became a member of the Kennet Club in Kensington:

> You'd go there every Saturday to practise, but it was also a
> social gathering. You'd arrive and quickly cast your eye
> around. But of course, you'd never actually mention that you
> were queer, which is the word we used those days. Everyone
> knew the score, but it was very hush-hush.

At the same time, Ellie and Jackie were members of a women's hockey team. The hockey league was more formal and serious. But, says Jackie,

> while the cricket teams were more obviously gay, there were a
> lot of gay women in the hockey teams too. There were some
> teams that were well-known for gays. Like the Transvaal Scot-
> ties — they were the captains of gay. But it was also never
> discussed. There were lots of hockey parties where no husbands
> or boyfriends ever came, and that was the perfect place to find
> someone. But even there, we all wore our little dresses, which
> was ridiculous, because sporting women are incredibly butch,
> even the femme ones.

Lesbian communities thus did exist, but were much more clandestine than their gay male counterparts. Firstly and most obviously, heterosexual institutions like marriage were far more restrictive for women than for men: there was room in society for the 'gay bachelor', for independent and transient men, but the pressure on women to marry and bear children was — and remains — greater. Secondly, the lesbian cliques that did exist tended to involve women in the service professions who needed to go to great pains to keep their identity secret. And thirdly, there were men in the gay community who had the economic independence to become 'community leaders' by taking the attendant risks of public life. Many of the male 'entertainers', for example, were wealthy: they had the means and the space to throw large parties. In contrast, lesbian parties, in Johannesburg at least, took place in cramped flats and on balconies rather than on patios and around pools. 'Heather', a Johannesburg teacher, recalls that

> *we were all poor and hard-working. You have to remember that in those days women as a matter of course earned much less than men. And also, we were by definition independent. We didn't have men to look after us. So we had to earn a living. And for middle-class women in the 1950s that was unusual. There were very few professions open to us, and we could not afford to lose our jobs — there was no hubby to go running back to. This dictated how we ran our lives.*

'Queens, tarts and sailors':
The gay bar and party scene in the 1950s and 1960s

For men active in the 'scene' there was, as there is now, a far greater variety of options: bars, outdoor cruising places and private parties. In Johannesburg, after the demise of the wartime Joubert Park scene, the gathering place in the late 1940s became the bar at the Carlton Hotel — a huge, square tomblike venue crowded with enough people that, according to one habitué, 'the queens could find their corner and carry on undetected.' Later, the scene shifted back to Joubert Park, to the Astor on Smit Street, and then, in the late 1950s, the lounge-bar at The Waldorf Hotel, on the corner of Rissik and Bree, took over. 'Joe', who moved from Durban to Johannesburg in 1959, recalls:

> *It was a place with atmosphere, with the strict dress code of jacket and tie. A social club, where everybody knew everybody. In later days you'd see someone in his suit disappear into the toilets and re-emerge in jeans and a casual shirt for the club.*

In those days, none of the bars were owned by people from within the gay community: the gay 'crowd' would decide upon a venue — usually the lounge-bar of a swank hotel — and colonise it. Then, the management would see a lucrative and dependable clientele — 'we didn't drink beer,' says Joe, 'we drank gin or *parfait d'amour*'. If the management responded with a modicum of civility, the word would spread. Of course, this strategy did not always work: an oft-recounted episode in Durban gay folklore, for example, revolves around a set of particularly flamboyant men who, in 1959, attempted to take over the Ulundi Bar at the Royal Hotel, the poshest place in town. Their method, recalls Joe,

22

*was for a massive train of silly queens to flounce through the
Royal's lobby, enter the Ulundi, and send up any unfortunate
BMs ['baby-makers' — gay slang for heterosexuals] who were
there. Needless to say, the queens had outclassed themselves
this time, and the management would have none of it and gave
them a Royal kick in the arse.*

In the early 1960s, this pattern changed somewhat. In Johannesburg, for example,
as the Waldorf declined in influence, the bar at The New Library Hotel on Commissioner Street took over, promoting itself very much as a gay venue. In
Johannesburg in the early- to mid-1960s too, several gay-owned men-only dance
clubs came and went, the most well-known being The Farmhouse, out of town on
the road to Pretoria. Also in the 1960s, a gay man named Leo Smith opened a club
in his mother's flat in Rissik Street. While the bars remained straight-owned enterprises within hotels, the clubs — which were to epitomise the 1970s — were
exclusively gay business ventures.

In Cape Town and Durban, bar-life was more varied than in Johannesburg,
possibly because the passage of sailors — both those in the navies and those on the
merchant shipping lines — continued after the war ended. In Cape Town, for example, the equivalent of the Waldorf was the Grand Hotel, which was all-gay on
Friday and Saturday evenings from 5pm to 7.15pm. 'Robert', a businessman who
moved to Cape Town as a young man in 1958, remembers that

*everybody would go to the Grand, and you'd even find a sailor
or two there if he had a feel for that kind of thing. But then,
when the Grand closed at 7.15, the more adventurous bunch
would move on to The Delmonico on Riebeeck St, which was a
favourite sailor's pickup joint, a big Spanish building with a
band that was great fun. Or you would go to Darryl's or the
Navigator's Den down by the docks. It worked like this in those
places: first the prostitutes would come, then the sailors would
follow, and then the gays.*

First the prostitutes, then the sailors, then the gays. This sequence says much about
the marginal identity gay men, irrespective of class, had in society at the time.
Certainly, middle-class gay professionals like Robert patronised the dockside because of the possibility of sex and a fascination with 'rough trade' and men in
uniform. But, faced with the opprobrium of their peers, they also went to the water-
front because it was perhaps the only place they could be at ease once the Grand
closed. Buttoned-down and suited in the day, they joined the world of outcasts at
night. The fear of being rejected in their leisure-time, by the very society in which
they strove for advancement during their work-time, dominated many gay men in
those times — as it still does today.

In Durban, the same combination of prostitutes, sailors and homosexuals
could be found in the lounge of the Royal Playhouse, which had a very dramatic
setting: you walked up the broad sweep of front steps into an interior courtyard,
which had, Joe remembers,

a sky of spangled searchlights and a gallery with a restaurant on either side. There must have been 100 tables all told. Right next door was The Mayfair, which was all-gay on a Saturday night, so you'd shuttle between the two. [The Playhouse]... had a very uneasy mixture of a third each queens, sailors and tarts. You'd be at a table with several queens and there'd be sailors at the next table. It could be dangerous, of course. But it could also pay off.

There was clearly a code to be observed with sailors, and you had to be careful. Joe recalls that

the Royal Navy was always a better bet than the South African Navy. They wanted a good time and they didn't ask you for money. The South African chaps, on the other hand, were terribly paid and in need of finance, and, if they didn't bop you on the nose, they made no bones about asking you for rent.

Even in smaller port cities, sailors played a significant role: in Port Elizabeth in the 1950s, for example, the bar at the Palmerston Hotel, patronised mainly by prostitutes and sailors, became the only public venue in the city where gay men were welcome.

Once the sailors made friends with on-shore gay society, they were assured not only of some extra pocket-money, but hospitality and entertainment too. In Durban, for example, there was an 'entertainer' who had Sunday night soirées that always included a half-dozen sailors. There, remembers Joe, 'you'd find queens of shall we say the lower order dishing the dirt. And you'd find sailors either sitting around awkwardly or serving drinks.'

Those 'entertainers' who did include sailors in their soirées were looked down upon by others: in Durban, while the 'lower orders' — hairdressers and the like — went to one 'entertainer's' home, the more respectable went to another's. And in Cape Town, there were famous fancy 'do's' at the home of a gay couple in Constantia — jacket and tie and invitation only — as well as more ramshackle, open-ended affairs in the northern suburbs. All the 'entertainers', however, went to great pains to be discreet, 'to protect the safety of our guests', as Joe tells it.

Another oft-told piece of Durban lore involves one of the flamboyant 'Ulundi' set, who danced naked in the garden at a party, which resulted in a complaint from the neighbours, a visit from the police, and ensuing arrests and shattered lives. 'That,' says Joe, 'simply was not on. In those days we were allowed to do our own thing provided we behaved. So we behaved.' Certainly, this ethos required a fair amount of self-censorship on the part of the 'entertainers' themselves. Hannah remembers, for example, that

Gay women, and particularly butch gay women, were not welcome at many gay male parties, because the men thought that we would attract unfavourable attention from the neighbours. So if you were butch you were ostracised, even though who they

24

were trying to kid I do not know. The neighbours always knew exactly what was going on anyway.

Hannah, an 'entertainer' in her own right in lesbian circles, also took her own precautions: 'As long as there were no men present, the women felt safe from the law too. If the cops raided us we had a perfect excuse: we were having a kitchen tea.' 'Lucille', an accountant, explains the reasons for such intricate deception:

> *You have to remember, these were the 1950s. A girl was expected to sit with her knees tightly crossed until her wedding night. These were the days when a girl might be fired if she was so much as having an extra-marital affair. So you can imagine how beyond the pale a gay life was. Our lives were ruled by fear.*

Gareth concurs:

> *We lived by stealth. We'd look at the flamboyant queens who didn't give a damn, and while we might secretly envy them for their freedom, we thought they were silly, foolish things — and a great danger to us. At all costs we had to remain hidden!*

So strongly did Jackie feel this that, when the false rumour spread around the staffroom that she was having an affair with a colleague, 'I just got into my car and thought, "I'm going to crash this car and end it all," because it was so horrible, so terrible, that someone knew.'

Cottages, health clubs and café-bios: The cruising scene

A significant part of gay life in the 1950s and early 1960s — perhaps even more significant than now, given the lack of other options and the extent of social opprobrium — revolved around cruising. And, as is the case today, the cruising scene was the place at which closeted homosexuals, men who have sex with men but do not identify themselves as gay, came into contact with the gay subculture.

There were, of course, the public areas — Park Station in Johannesburg, the Esplanade and Albert Park in Durban, the Burg Street area, Gardens and Sea Point Promenade in Cape Town. 'The Wall', along Sea Point's promenade, and Graaf's Pool, the all-male swimming area, have together remained South Africa's cruising mecca. By day Graaff's Pool tended to be an unusual mix of older Jewish men (obeying the religious diktat of single-sex bathing) and younger gay cruisers and socialisers; by night it became the busiest gay place in town.

As well as the outdoor cruising areas and the public toilets — the most famous of which in Johannesburg was the vast City Hall 'cottage' — there were indoor locations that, as *loci* of sexual commerce, became very important gay meeting places: the 'health clubs' and the café-bios.

In Johannesburg, there were two 'health clubs': the London and the Atwater, both of which were active from the late 1950s into the 1960s. In their research into these, Galli and Rafael (see 'Johannesburg's "Health Clubs"', in this volume) report that they ostensibly existed to provide 'health services' — like massage and sauna — but were largely patronised by men looking for homosexual encounters. Galli and Rafael's informants are disparaging about the clubs — they use words like 'filthy', 'rat-infested' and 'sleazy dump'. But, for five pounds, one could spend the night — in the baths, parading the corridors, or in private cubicles with beds. Because of their 'health-club' cover and their privacy, they were, according to Galli and Rafael, frequented by 'closettes', an 'older crowd' who were not integrated into more open gay society. As with all cruising venues, a large proportion of married or bisexual men patronised the 'health clubs', while the more open younger people went to the bars. As with gay culture abroad, 'the baths' became an important gay meeting place, but they have never been as central here as in Europe or the United States. In 1993, there were only two such commercial ventures catering to gay men, both in Johannesburg. A third, in Cape Town, was run out of a private suburban home.

The café-bios were very important white cultural institutions in the 1950s and 1960. These were, according to one of Galli and Rafael's informants, 'ordinary cinemas where you could eat, smoke and have it off while watching a movie.' They were very popular with working-class teenagers, and so became patronised by gay men looking to buy sex. Joe recalls that in one downtown Johannesburg block opposite the City Hall on Pritchard Street there were three café-bios:

> There certainly wasn't a gay scene inside. It was very rough and straight, with kids drinking and smoking. But if you were interested in that sort of thing, you'd hang around outside and catch them as they were going in or out. Then you'd whisk them off to the City Hall to do business.

In Johannesburg at least, 'rent-boys' (also then known as 'LK numbers', after a well-known property rental agency called LK Jacobs) had a very specific social assignation: they were usually teenage Afrikaner boys, either from the working-class suburbs to the south and west of the city, or from outlying country areas. Joe recalls that

> a great deal of rent came from Newlands (a working class sub-urb), and I'm convinced the culture was passed from one boy to another in the schools there — it became known that this was an easy way to make some extra pocket money. There was a famous drive-in cafe in Newlands, and some gay people would go there to pick these numbers up. But this was too close to home, and the rent-pieces might be with someone who they didn't want to know, and so it was safer to wait for them to come to your turf — Park Station.

In Cape Town, the 'rent' was also often working-class Afrikaner boys, but there was, in addition, a large population of coloured sex-workers, who did much business both with married coloured and African men and with white clients. Most of this activity took place in the Burg and Loop Street area and was, interestingly, an important gay meeting place even for those who were not looking to buy sex: one

26

of Lewis and Loots' informants, an Afrikaner from out of town, reports that he 'started talking to the Muslim boys who were renting. That's how I became aware of the gay scene.' (See 'Moffies en manvroue', in this volume.) This was in the 1970s, but older gay men report that such interaction was happening as early as the 1950s.

From Bantry Bay to Hanover Street: Neighborhoods, race and class

As with the Joubert Park/Hillbrow area in Johannesburg from the 1940s onwards, Cape Town also developed several proto-gay neighborhoods in the 1950s. White gay men, for example, tended to congregate around the Atlantic seaboard, in Sea Point and Bantry Bay. The greatest attraction was — and continues to be — the cruising area. As was the case with 'Radclyffe Hall' and other blocks in Hillbrow, whole blocks in the Sea Point area became 'gay residences', one of the more well-known of which was Peps (now the very upmarket Bantry Court) in Bantry Bay. Robert, who took a room there in 1958, remembers:

> It was like a big family. There were about 50 flatlets, and 46 of them were occupied by gays. We were in and out of each other's business all the time, and we'd congregate down by the water, at a circular paved area we called The Bullring. If there wasn't anything else on on a Saturday night, you can be sure there'd be a gathering down there. I made great friends at Peps. If you were ill, seven or eight people would pop in to give you chicken soup. If there was a party, word spread like wildfire. Eveyone knew that Peps was a bit odd, but we were never bothered.

While white gay men gathered around Sea Point, coloured gay men became very much part of the texture of District Six, particularly along its main road, Hanover Street, where many gay men rented rooms and socialised by going on 'salon crawls' — visiting the many gay hairdressing salons. Gay life thrived in District Six, and in other coloured neighborhoods like Athlone, Woodstock and Salt River. Unlike the parallel white culture, however, the participants were working class and the bonding point was drag. Salon madames like Joey Costello held 'Drags', as the parties were known, at which famous female impersonators like 'Eartha Kitt' and 'Kewpie' would perform. The Drags were highly ritualised affairs, with half the participants in drag and the other half in men's clothing. Later, once they were publicised by *Drum* and *Golden City Post*, they became splashy affairs at places like the Kismet Theatre in Athlone. (See Chetty's 'A drag at Madame Costello's', in this volume.)

Within the coloured communities of the Cape Peninsula there were also, starting in the 1950s, renowned all-gay drag sports clubs, like the District Six Net-ball Team which participated in the women's league, frequently (and not surprisingly) sweeping up all the awards. These netball teams, like the drag-per-formers, have been a constant in Western Cape coloured culture, and have their latest incarnation in the Lavender Hill Netball Team, which was competing on the Cape Flats in the early 1990s.

The history of 'moffie life' in Western Cape coloured culture is perhaps South Africa's richest and most untold, and there are several possible reasons why gay life flourished and was tolerated in these communities. According to Chetty, one answer may lie in the tradition that the annual Cape Coon Carnival has to be led by a moffie, and that 'mocking and subverting the conventions of gender and sexuality are very much part of the ritual.' There are other possible reasons. One is the influence of the Muslim Cape Malays in the region: while the Koran explicitly condemns male homosexuality, many gay Muslims maintain that their culture has always implicitly tolerated it as a preferable option to heterosexual adultery. Another possibility is that sexual dissidence is more tolerated in a hybrid, creole society like that of the coloureds than in supposedly coherent societies with strong patriarchal mythologies and traditions, like those constructed by the African and Afrikaner nationalist movements in South Africa.

Except for the commercial activity around Burg and Loop Streets, there was very little interaction between the coloured and white gay communities in Cape Town. Robert and Joe both remember that there would, occasionally, be a coloured man at a party, usually the 'affair' of a white man, and, in Joe's words, 'tolerated on sufferance'. And, despite the fact that there were white people involved in the 'shebeen-scene' in neighborhoods like District Six in Cape Town and Sophiatown in Johannesburg, there is little evidence of white people at the moffie drag parties at salons like that of Madame Joey Costello.

Nevertheless, before the apartheid clampdown of the 1960s, there clearly was some interaction — the most obvious indicator being that the *moffietaal* slang of the coloured community became the accepted lingo of white gay people too in the 1950s, first in Cape Town and later in other parts of the country. Even Johannesburg women like Ellie and Jackie, who had little interaction with any gay men, white or coloured, remember the infiltration of words like 'nora' and 'dora' and 'hilda' into their clique's vocabulary in the late 1950s.

Even within the white gay subculture, class boundaries were rigidly defined. It appears that middle-class men found it far easier to enter a gay subculture than working-class men: because they had space, because they had economic independence, and because they had access and exposure to education which offered them alternatives to the heterosexual paradigm. While it is more than likely that working-class gay white men had their own social structures, they are defined by the middle-class gay subculture only marginally as 'rent' or 'rough trade' — labels that assign to them the role of the 'other'. As the subculture expanded in the 1970s and 1980s, however, this was to change somewhat.

The relationship between class and sexuality among women appears to be different. Perhaps because there was an imperative for working-class women to work — and thus leave home in many cases — there has always been a substantial working-class component to South Africa's white lesbian culture. Although this study was unable to find working-class women active in the 1950s and 1960s, many of the middle-class women interviewed mixed socially with working-class women. And there were, at the very least, two clubs in Johannesburg largely frequented by white working-class lesbians: Chick Venter's establishment, described above, and another club, Spiders' Web in Jeppe Street, which ran for a while in the early 1960s.

If there was a black working-class lesbian culture in the 1950s and 1960s, it remains inaccessible — to this study at least. There is, however, the interesting biography, published by *Drum* and *Golden City Post* in 1955, of Gertie, a cross-dressing lesbian gangster from the Cape Flats who had many 'girlfriends'. (See 'Lesbian gangster', in this volume.) At the time, Gertie claimed to have a lover, for over a year, who 'does not know that I am a woman.' Such a scenario seems unlikely, and it can be assumed that, even if there was no black lesbian subculture in which Gertie participated, there was at the very least a group of 'heterosexual' women who were quite prepared to play along with the charade.

Nevertheless, despite evidence of the existence of working-class homosexual activity in both black and white communities, the formalisation of homosexual subcultures into a gay movement after the Forest Town raid of 1966 was an entirely white middle-class initiative, informed by the style, ideology and particular concerns of this sector of the population. Only in the 1980s did black men and women begin to play an active role in gay politics.

Two
'Men at a Party' and the Law Reform movement

'Mass sex orgy' in Forest Town!

'350 IN MASS SEX ORGY!' blared the *Rand Daily Mail* on Monday 22 January 1966. That weekend, police had raided a large gay party in Forest Town, a quiet and respectable old suburb to the north of Johannesburg. Nine men had been arrested for 'masquerading as women' and one for 'indecent assault on a minor'. Two years later, the South African Police was to report to a Parliamentary Select Committee investigating homosexuality that, to their 'disgust' and 'repulsion', police officers had found 'a party in progress, the like of which has never been seen in the Republic of South Africa...' (See Retief's 'Keeping sodom out of the laager', in this volume, for a full account of the official response.)

Joe, who was there, recalls that 'it was the biggest party we had ever had, very glamorous and very uncontrolled'. It was clearly an 'A-list' gay do, organised by three socialites who shared the house. But, says Joe,

> the hosts made sure everyone would be there by even circulating maps at the New Library bar. That's how everyone knew about it. And that was the party's downfall: it was well-known that Priscilla [the police] would hang around the New Library to pick up information about the gay scene. So of course they found out about it.

In the style of South African gay parties since the 1940s, the Forest Town bash was a 'bottle-party': guests would arrive with bottles labelled with their names, which would then be stored behind the bar. The raid began when a police sergeant managed to persuade one of the hosts to sell him liquor. Immediately, the police arrested the handful of drag queens who were present: when they were unable to prove that they had arrived at the party — which was, after all, private and thus beyond the ambit of the law — in men's clothing, they were taken off to the police station and charged with masquerading as women in public. The rest of the party-goers were held at the Forest Town home for a few hours, photographed (which in itself was a severe form of intimidation, given the enormous fear of disclosure) and released.

Prior to the Forest Town raid, in the 1950s, there had been periodic 'swoops' on public places, the most infamous being at the Esplanade in Durban in 1956. There had also been frequent raids on parties, usually because of complaints of 'disturbing the peace'. The 1966 raid, however, was the largest, most organised and most publicised the police had ever attempted. Why this happened in 1966 remains a mystery: gay life had not become significantly more public in the mid-1960s, and, before the raid, there had not been a visible increase of police interest in the subculture. Retief offers the most plausible explanation: led by Prime Minister Verwoerd's clampdown on the liberation movements and his formalisation of apartheid, the South African authorities were consolidating Afrikaner 'Christian

30

National' control over the country, expelling from the laager anything that was deemed threatening to white civilisation.

The choice of a raid on a sophisticated gay party in Johannesburg's plush English-speaking northern suburbs lends substance to this theory. Although this study has been unable to find documentary evidence, gay men who were active at the time recall that, in Johannesburg, Afrikaans cultural and religious organisations were agitating about the fact that wealthier Jewish and English men were corrupting their youths: most 'rent-boys' were young Afrikaners, often fresh in from the *platteland*, and most of their clients were wealthier English-speakers. If this is true, an interesting connection could be made with black homophobia in the 1980s and 1990s: the nationalist notion that homosexuality is a decadent, upper-class import 'contaminating' the purity of a mythologised — either Afrikaner or African — race.

Whether or not the police deliberately targeted Johannesburg's liberal northern suburbs, the impression following the raid was definitely one of decadent, immoral high-living. Newspapers fixated upon the fact that prominent professionals, doctors and lawyers were present at the 'sex orgy', and, reports Retief, the police head office immediately sent a circular to all SAP divisional commissioners warning that 'there are indications that homosexuality and gross indecency is being practised between male persons throughout the country and that offenders are now pursuing an organised *modus operandi*.' The conspiracy-rhetoric is typical of the times: Nationalist control over South Africa was consolidated through the construction of bogeymen, and to the black conspiracies, communist conspiracies, English conspiracies, Jewish conspiracies, could now be added the 'queer conspiracy'. With the very same rhetoric as it had already deployed in the 'fight against communism', the SAP now recommended that informers be used to infiltrate 'queer parties'.

The authorities, however, were faced with a problem: while sodomy as well as a range of other 'unnatural' offences was illegal according to the common law, gay men could only commit statutory offenses when in public: this meant masquerading as women or soliciting at cruising spots. If, then, the authorities were to enter private homes and crack down on this organised ring of 'queer parties', they would not have the necessary legislation behind them: apart from picking up a few drag queens, as they did at Forest Town, they would have to leave empty-handed.

Thus, after much consultation with the police, Verwoerd's Minister of Justice, PC Pelser, proposed draconian anti-homosexuality legislation to the House of Assembly in March 1967. The motion was deferred and then proposed again in 1968, when, as an amendment to the Immorality Act, it sought to make male and female homosexuality an offense punishable by compulsory imprisonment of up to three years. This would have had the effect not only of bringing lesbians into the scope of the law, but of making homosexuality itself statutorily illegal, whereas previously, only public male homosexual acts had been regulated by statute.

'Everyone Pitched In': The Law Reform Movement of 1968

Following the proposal of anti-homosexuality legislation, a wave of panic swept through South Africa's homosexual communities, particularly among lesbians, who had previously been ignored by the law. Jackie recalls:

> *We were terrified. There was a rumour that women would not be allowed to live together. I remember going absolutely cold and thinking, how are we going to live if we can't live together?*

Gareth started looking at the possibility of immigration: 'We feared a witch-hunt, and all my friends were packing,' he says and, in fact, at least six of his acquaintances actually did leave the country. The terms of the legislation were so harsh that Pelser was prevailed upon to refer the matter to a Parliamentary Select Committee, which was charged with hearing evidence on the nature of homosexuality and proposing final legislation a year later. The Select Committee published notices calling on members of the public to submit evidence, giving assurances that all evidence would be confidential: the point being, of course, to encourage homosexuals themselves to testify.

Almost immediately, a small group of gay professionals, led by prominent gay advocate, began organising in Johannesburg and Pretoria. An 'action group' was formed, later formalised into the Homosexual Law Reform Fund, known euphemistically as 'Law Reform'. Law Reform's task was very simply-defined: to raise the R40 000 needed to retain a firm of attorneys to prepare evidence and lead the case against the proposed legislation before the Select Committee. Gay people were asked to make contributions and to submit testimony not to the Select Committee directly, but to Law Reform's lawyers: in this way, Law Reform could control and coordinate the evidence being presented to the Select Committee while at the same time guaranteeing the confidentiality of those who gave evidence.

By April 1968, the Law Reform group was already engaged in frenzied activities throughout the Pretoria-Johannesburg area, holding house-meetings to explain the purpose of the organisation and raise funds. On 3 April, Joe attended one such meeting:

> *We were told that this was a crisis, and so we had to forget our differences and pull together. It was very impressive, very factual and non-hysterical, and the stress was on pragmatic, co-ordinated action.*

The following week, on 10 April 1968, Law Reform called a public meeting at the Park Royal Hotel in Joubert Park — the first gay public meeting ever held in South Africa. It was publicised by word of mouth and by very discreet pamphleteering in the bars. About 100 people attended. There was strict screening at the door — to prevent intrusion by either police or the media — and, once more, gay people were urged to give money and submit evidence through Law Reform's legal team.

The campaign was run by a core of roughly 20 people. Meetings were held almost every evening, and the organisation spread until there were informal Law

Reform cells all over the country, with core activists addressing house-meetings set up by sympathetic acquaintances. There were three major subcommittees: the Legal Committee, responsible for co-ordinating testimony and preparing representations to be given to Parliament; the Data Committee, responsible for collecting a body of research on the nature of homosexuality; and the Fundraising Committee, which was the point at which most people became involved. Joe, who was secretary of this committee, notes that,

> *fundraising drove the whole thing. The fundraising lists were the link between the grassroots and the organisers, and fundraising parties were the places where people met.*

By September 1968, when the Parliamentary Select Committee's report was published, a total of R27 000 had been raised. Alexis Preller, one of South Africa's pre-eminent artists, donated a painting worth R1 000, and dozens of people held parties at which the hat was passed around, or gambling evenings at which a percentage of the take was donated to the fund. Said Hannah, host of several parties:

> *Suddenly, gay life flourished and there were more parties than ever before. People seemed to forget their differences, and everyone pitched in. People were meeting with people they would never have previously passed the time of day with. Suddenly differences were suppressed.*

Ironically, the threat of repression galvanised the gay subculture, creating community as never before. Joe also noted another difference:

> *You found that the latest subject of conversation was not likely to be the latest hairdo, but how you could get letters out in bulk. And I think for many people it was empowering: for someone who has been nothing but a little queen serving in a shop to find herself now actually working to put pressure on the government to respect gay rights. I think it opened a window in many individual lives.*

Despite the fact that 'the little queens', as Joe calls them, pulled their weight with fundraising and envelope-licking, the organisation was far from democratic, and was tightly run from the top by the committee. While there were several women involved it was also very much a male environment. As with The Mattachine Society and the Daughters of Bilitis,[8] the homophile movements a decade earlier in the United States, this was a professional organisation aimed at influencing lawmakers rather than organising gay and lesbian people themselves.

Gay and lesbian South Africans organising against the proposed legislation in 1968 might well have found the ammunition they needed within this country's own liberation movement: as gay activists in the United States used the liberation ideology of the civil rights movement, gay liberationists in South Africa might have found their manifesto within the African National Congress' Freedom Charter (as they did successfully two decades later), with its invocation of rights for all and its forceful salvos against discrimination. And they might have used, as a model for action, the anti-apartheid Defiance Campaign of the 1950s.

But several forces militated against this: firstly, and most obviously, the Freedom Charter and its authors were banned, and there was an enormous stigma, in white South Africa, to left-wing politics. Secondly, the middle-class white gay men who began organising in 1968 had little access to black homosexuals beyond illicit meetings in cruising places. These black homosexuals might have introduced South Africa's own liberation struggle into the gay rights movement, but, in the late 1960s, they barely existed themselves as an organised or even informal entity. Thirdly, as Retief notes, the authorities themselves had defined homosexuality as a white problem, ignoring even the possibility of black homosexuality; not wishing to complicate things, the Law Reform movement responded in turn.

Fourthly, and most importantly, the Law Reform movement was narrowly defined around a single issue: its aim was to prevent the proposed anti-gay bill from becoming law. As such, it was self-consciously — and, in terms of its own goals, appropriately — accommodationist in its approach. In fact, the explicit decision was taken not turn the issue into a 'political' battleground, and the Committee decided against calling upon the white parliamentary opposition to enter the fray: not even Helen Suzman, Parliament's lone advocate for human rights, was canvassed. According to Joe, the thinking was that

> if we launched a political attack against the government, we would be shot, because we then would have given the National- ists the opportunity to behave like the great moralists of the country and make the opposition look like Sodom and Go- morrah. And so we focussed all our attention on the National Party itself. We worked, in a way, within the National Party.

Law Reform's greatest coup in this respect was the retention of Advocate Dawie de Villiers, a government supporter and Nationalist hero for having successfully de- fended South Africa's case for retaining control over South West Africa at the World Court in the Hague in 1965. Joe remembers that

> it was comforting to know that somebody so high-profile and so close to the government was on our side. I think that was a major reason for Law Reform's mobilisation successes. People were impressed. They thought, 'well, if De Villiers is on our side, we can't lose.'

'Keeping our dirty habits off the street': The effects of the Law Reform movement

In June 1969, gay patrons of the Stonewall Inn bar in Greenwich Village, New York, rioted after a police raid. The 'Stonewall Rebellion', as it became known, heralded the beginning of a grassroots gay liberation movement in the United States. In South Africa, the late 1960s saw unprecedented gay and lesbian activity. But, unlike the United States, this activism was not radical or mass-based.

In response to the threat of criminalisation, some gay South Africans — urban, white and middle-class — had organised themselves for the very first time, not surprisingly very much the way gay Americans had in the 1950s: quietly and professionally, attempting to protect themselves by carving a niche within apartheid South Africa while not disrupting the status quo.

And on these terms they were successful. The evidence the Law Reform movement presented, particularly in the field of psychology, persuaded the Select Committee to drop the legislation. Instead, only three amendments to the current law were proposed. The first was that the age of consent for male homosexual acts was to be raised from 16 to 19; designed to prevent 'child-molestation' by protecting teenage boys. The second was to outlaw dildoes. And the third was the infamous 'men at a party' clause, which criminalised any 'male person who commits with another male person at a party any act which is calculated to stimulate sexual passion or to give sexual gratification.' Most absurd was the definition of a 'party': 'any occasion where more than two persons are present'. Clearly, this was designed to give the law precisely the teeth it needed when raiding parties such as the one in Forest Town in 1966.

These three amendments were passed into law in March the following year, 1969, and despite the fact that they ranged from the discriminatory to the downright ridiculous, they were widely hailed as a victory for common sense. An editorial in the *Cape Times* stated, for example that

> *Witchhunts directed against those thus afflicted* [with homosexuality] *would make the republic look ridiculous in the eyes of civilised people everywhere, apart from the gratuitous suffering it would have caused. At first sight the Select Committee appears to have produced humane, common-sense provisions for dealing with a problem that is as old as Western Civilisation.*[9]

In South Africa in 1969, even sympathetic liberal commentary saw the need to protect 'innocents' from the 'problem' of homosexuality. The *Cape Argus* wrote, for example, that

> *the essence of the approach... was that innocent members of society must be protected against the effects of homosexuality without penalising homosexuals for deviations from social norms they could not help.*[10]

The *Bloemfontein Friend*, however, felt compelled to point out to its readers that the law 'does not imply that homosexuality between consenting adults will be permitted [because] it continues to remain an offence under common law',[11] and, in Parliament, Minister Pelser warned that, contrary to some interpretations, the new law in no way condoned homosexuality: there would be 'no relaxation' in the legal position concerning homosexuality, and while there were moves in other countries to legalise homosexual practices, 'this we cannot allow.'[12]

The message from the authorities was clear: the status quo remained. The Law Reform movement had not, in fact, been successful in reforming the law. Rather, it had simply staved off even more repressive legislation. And, with its three new provisions, the law had actually tightened its grip on the freedom of gay people. In fact, following the passing of the law, Law Reform's legal counsel advised that gay society proceed with renewed caution, as any gatherings could be construed as 'parties' under the new legislation, and even dancing could be viewed as an 'act calculated to stimulate sexual passion': gay clubs that offered dancing could thus be charged with inciting people to illegal activity.

Nevertheless, gay people felt immense relief after the panic and rumours that had spread earlier in the year about laws forbidding two women to live together and mandatory three-year jail sentences for people caught at gay bars or parties. And, according to those who were active at the time, there was a palpable sense of personal victory: 'We had done it ourselves,' says Gareth. 'We were threatened and we fought back and won. For the very first time. It felt great!'

But despite the ebullience, the Law Reform movement collapsed as soon as the Select Committee published its findings. Joe recalls that even at the Park Royal Hotel public meeting following the publication of the Select Committee report in September 1968, attendance was down by over 50%:

> *It was very sad indeed. The whole thing just seemed to evaporate. Everyone went back to their little cliques and bridge clubs. All the mixing and interaction and socialising just ended.*

For the urban gay men who were involved, in one way or another, with Law Reform, the experience had provided a remarkable opening: common ground — in the form of a shared threat — had been found with gay people other than those in one's immediate social circle, and there had thus been the stirrings of a potential gay collectivity. But Law Reform was unable to serve as the basis for an ongoing gay movement for the very reason it had been successful in the short-term: it was a narrowly-defined, single-issue campaign aimed at blocking potential legislation rather than at building an enduring gay and lesbian community.

Law Reform's lack of democratic process meant that, once the leadership burnt out, there were no eager young turks with a sense of ownership of the movement ready to take over. Essentially, the small group of professionals who motivated Law Reform were not interested in much more than maintaining the status quo: they did not necessarily feel that the situation before Pelser's proposed legislation in 1967 was intolerable, and so, once things were perceived to have returned to this status quo, they did not see much more to fight for.

Nevertheless, despite Law Reform's instantaneous evaporation and the sense that things had gone 'back to normal', the passing of the amendments to the Immorality Act did have a profound — if not immediately perceptible — effect on gay society. Even though there were undoubtedly sporadic raids after 1969, it appears that the authorities changed tack considerably. The 1968 enquiry into homosexuality had proven to the police that the extent of homosexuality in South Africa meant it was impossible to eradicate.

A different fight for freedom

Rather than attempting to wipe homosexuality out, the authorities now simply sought to minimise its social effect, and thus their campaign focussed on public places: toilets were closed early, popular cruising venues were more rigorously patrolled and subjected to perpetual sweeps. The effect was to move the subculture indoors, into bars and clubs which, contrary to the expectations of Law Reform's counsel, were left alone. It seemed, says Joe,

> as if the intention was to segregate us from society, to prevent 'normal' people from coming into contact with us as much as possible. So as long as we kept our dirty habits off the street we were safe.

Ronnie Oelofsen, who opened the Dungeon club in 1969, says that 'as long as there were no minors on the premises and you were not selling liquor, you were safe. The only time I have ever been raided was when I showed a banned movie one Sunday night.' And Hannah, who owned and ran a club in downtown Johannesburg in the early 1970s, remembers the regular visit from a vice squad colonel assigned to keep an eye on her:

> He would come by every now and then for his bottle of whisky. He said he had no objection to the club because he preferred to know that everyone was under one roof, rather than at Zoo Lake or Joubert Park getting beaten up.

Keeping the queers indoors not only meant keeping them under control — it also meant keeping them out of sight of religious conservative lobbies who had precipitated the anti-gay legislation in the first place. Although this severely curtailed the freedom of movement of gay people who cruised, it also had another unexpected — and perhaps more positive — effect: it formalised gay culture, creating as never before gay venues that became safe and dependable community meeting places for those white men and women who were allowed in. Certainly, it also stratified gay society: those who were black or who could not afford either the entry-fee or the risk of being spotted in a gay place were left, quite literally, out in the cold. But, indoors, a new phase of gay community began.

Three
Expansion of a subculture: the gay 1970s

'Bloody Sweaty Queers': The disco scene

The flourishing of gay commercial life in the form of clubs and bars was accompanied, in the case of Hillbrow in Johannesburg at least, by the formalisation of an area where gay people had always lived into a clearly identifiable 'gay neighbourhood', with gay bars, gay businesses, and a new level of tolerance from other inhabitants. As the neighborhood grew, the authorities decided to view Hillbrow's densely-populated flatland too as a 'gay venue' of sorts, choosing not to apply the same pressure on its streets as they did on other outdoor areas.

The 1970s were boom years in South Africa: even as blacks in the country became more politically marginalised by the entrenchment of apartheid (the fuse finally blowing in 1976), white South Africa experienced unprecedented economic growth, resulting in even higher standards of living. Which meant more expendable income, and thus a boom in the leisure industry, gay and straight alike. Clubbing, always more costly than nipping off to the pub for a drink, became the vogue. The new economic climate also meant that a higher number of young white people were able to leave the confines of family and become part of an urban gay subculture.

This had important consequences for the demography of gay society: for the first time, significant numbers of Afrikaans men and women, often coming in from the rural areas, joined the subculture — not only in Johannesburg, but also in Bloemfontein and Pretoria. Even in provincial hubs like Pietersburg, Potchefstroom and Welkom, small gay subcultures developed. With its high concentration of civil servants and army personnel — relocated people without direct family connections — Pretoria had always had a large, overwhelmingly Afrikaans, gay population; in the 1970s this population formalised into something of a subculture, an indicator being the establishment of the capital's first exclusively gay venue, which opened in the early 1970s and is still running as Club Equusite.

Equusite, located on the top floor of a double-story building in the 'motortown' part of the city (meaning that the area is deserted at night), has become, over the years, Pretoria's gay community centre: by the early 1990s, a gay restaurant and even a gay church were housed within its confines. In those days, it was known as the *spookhuis* (ghosthouse), and habitués called themselves *spoke* (ghosts), because, as one regular told a researcher from the Human Sciences Research Council, '*wanneer alle ander ordentlike mense al slaap, dan loop die spoke rond*' ('when all other respectable people are asleep, then the ghosts walk about').

Another informant added: 'Everybody spook[s] at the spookhouse. I suppose because in a certain sense its the ghost in the closet, you see, and it's coming out of the closet as well.'[13]

The demographic changes in gay subculture led to a heightened openness, in Johannesburg as well as Pretoria. 'Andre', a bank clerk who moved to Hillbrow from the Western Transvaal, aged 17 in 1971, puts it like this:

A different fight for freedom

When an Afrikaans boy from the platteland comes out of the closet, he has to leave his home and family in a very big way. Just to be gay he has to fight all that conservative Afrikaner moralism and Calvinism. He is expelled, in a way. So he finds a new family among other gays in the city. And he has nothing to lose by being open — he's lost it all already. I find this very different from some my English gay friends who grew up in Jo'burg. They are still very much part of the life where they come from, so first of all they have to be more discreet and second of all they've got a foot in both camps.

For many English-speaking suburban gay men, the rupture was not so radical, and they did not need to become entirely part of a subculture. While there was certainly a need for secrecy in the army and the civil service, many other Afrikaner gay men coming to the cities in the 1970s immersed themselves entirely in the gay subculture, thus strengthening and formalising it.

Another reason for the flourishing of gay life in the early 1970s was the fact that these were the halcyon years of the gay rights movement in Europe and North America. While there was no attempt to establish a similar rights movement in South Africa in the 1970s (with one notable doomed exception, which is explored below), the idea of a 'gay life', revolving around clubs, bars and neighborhoods, was being imported into South Africa by gay people who had travelled abroad and experienced the exhilaration of Amsterdam, New York or San Francisco.

In the first couple of years of the decade, then, South African cities saw the arrival of the 'gay club': The Stardust in Durban, Wings in Cape Town, and, of course, that flagship of gay nightlife in Johannesburg, the Dungeon or 'Big D'. There had been gay dance venues previously — like the Farmhouse, the Hideaway and the Midniter in Johannesburg — but these new venues were unusual: because of their size, because of their longevity (most lasted for the better part of a decade, and the Dungeon is still running) and because of the new openness they embraced.

The Dungeon advertises itself as 'the longest-running club in South Africa': it opened just weeks after the passing of the Immorality Act Amendment in 1969 and has not been dark a single weekend since. It is situated in an incongruous castle-like building in downtown Johannesburg that was opened by Paul Kruger at the turn of the century. In the early days, its decor befitted its name, and chains and skeletons adorned the walls. Over the years, however, owner Ronnie Oelofsen has filled it with an eclectic mélange of posters and artifacts: shirtless torsos riding into the sunset, AIDS education posters, religious iconography (including a very prominent Star of David) and even a blown-up autographed photo of Foreign Affairs Minister Pik Botha wishing the 'Big D' the best of luck! The Dungeon is still unlicensed — patrons bring their own bottles and deposit them at the bar — and, unlike the other gay clubs that have emerged briefly during its tenure, it has a rather naive atmosphere vaguely reminiscent of a high-school dance. The Dungeon, says Joe, 'was always a clean place; the kind of place you took your date to, not the kind of place you went to camp.'

In the early 1970s, the club was open four days a week — Sunday was Movie Night, and 300 people would regularly attend. Being unlicensed meant it did not have to obey segregation laws, and even in the early 1970s, there was a smattering of black men: usually transplanted Malays from the Western Cape who found in The Dungeon the only welcoming Johannesburg venue. (Black gay activist Simon Nkoli disputes this, and recalls having been turned away from the venue in the early 1980s.) Very significantly, the Dungeon has always attracted a large lesbian clientele: the club continues to be at least 50% female.

The Dungeon's clientele is also predominantly Afrikaans, and Oelofsen attributes this to a tradition he impulsively started on the club's opening-night: the inclusion of a set of *sakkie-sakkie*, (Afrikaans folk dancing). From 1969 to the present day, the disco music is interrupted nightly for hits like Nico Carstens' *'Outa in die Langpad'*. Another tradition Oelofsen started in the club's first year was the drag competition, and, in 1970, the first Miss Dungeon was held. Oelofsen recalls:

> It was wonderful, quite unlike anything we'd ever had before. All the contestants and the judges went off to the revolving restaurant at the top of Hillbrow tower — in full drag! Then they came back and did the show. They had to walk the ramp and answer questions like, 'What would you do if you were a real woman?' Of course, the style then was very kappies-en-rokkies — it was like having a bunch of Afrikaner huisvroue on stage! Now things have become more professional and sophisticated.

That the Dungeon has only been raided once in its 24-year life — and then only for showing a banned movie in 1969 — is the result not only of the management's strict rule-keeping, but also of a conscious attempt to maintain friendly relations with its neighbours and the authorities. Every year, for example, Oelofson gives his venue to a group of inner-city town councillors to host a senior-citizens' party: the blue-rinse set take their tea under the posters of bulging crotches, and the Dungeon is left in peace.

The Dungeon soon outlived its competition — most notably The Midniter, a hippyish gay club in Anderson Street, and The Hideaway in Berea. Through the 1970s, it became the 'old faithful' foil to funkier clubs with more drugs, more adventurous music and more camping — like the Anaconda, Mandys (which was to be the scene of a momentous raid later in the decade) and Blood Sweat and Tears (known in the vernacular as 'Bloody Sweaty Queers'). These clubs were almost exclusively male, but one or two, like Square One in Joubert Park, were co-owned by lesbians and had large female clienteles too. Hannah, one of Square One's owners, notes, however, that

> the women were always more difficult than the men. They were more irregular, and always trouble. They'd be the ones to do the drugging or have a quick little brawl. They were always showing off.

40

A different fight for freedom

The Pinking of Hillbrow: The Butterfly and the T-Bar

The bar scene had continued unabated since the 1960s: in Johannesburg, Rocky's at the Continental and The New Library were the most popular until the opening, in the early 1970s, of The Butterfly at the Skyline Hotel on Pretoria Street in Hillbrow. Almost immediately, this became the jam-packed neighborhood watering hole of Hillbrow's fast-growing gay community. 'Jock', a gay man who lived in Hillbrow at the time, remembers that

> it was always full. People would walk in there on Saturday at noon with their Checkers bags filled with ice-cream and butter and stuff. The idea would be just to have a quick drink. But you'd get involved. You'd stay until late on Saturday night. And so you'd always see people leaving the bar with soggy Checkers bags.

It was a notoriously rough place, particularly by the door, which, after the demise of Park Station as a pick-up venue, soon became Johannesburg's premier 'rental area'.

What The Butterfly was for gay men, the Together Bar — or T-Bar — was for lesbians. It opened around 1974, in Hillbrow's seedy Hilton Court Hotel, and was, says Julia Beffon, who was to frequent it later in the decade, 'every girl's answer to The Butterfly'. The T-Bar remained Johannesburg's number one lesbian pub until 1989, when, according to Beffon, 'the management decided to upgrade it and kicked the women out. Later they tried to get the women back, but there was a complete boycott of the place.' While several other lesbian bars flared briefly during the 1970s and 1980s, none were as popular or as enduring as the T-Bar and, since its collapse in 1989, nothing has replaced it.

As with The Butterfly (and earlier lesbian hang-outs like Chick Venter's and The Spider's Web), the T-Bar had a 'rough' reputation: 'There were lots of tough types,' says Beffon. 'Once, after I beat someone at pool she went and ripped my car up.' The bar, run by the hotel management and not by lesbians, was grimy, unkempt and roach-infested, but it had a regular clientele from all walks of life.

All walks of white life, that is to say. For in the 1970s, both bars were exclusively white. Nevertheless, what was notable is that, despite their edginess, they were not the 'preserves' of particular cliques or styles within the white lesbian and gay subcultures. By the 1970s in gay meccas like New York and San Francisco, there were already leather-bars, bulldyke-bars, clone-bars, drag-bars, working-class bars, etc. In Johannesburg, where the options were limited, you went to The Butterfly or the T-Bar no matter who you were or what you were into. The stratification took place within. Recalls Beffon:

> While the tough types had knife-fights round the pool-table, the corporate ladies from the Northern Suburbs would be clustered together at a table doing their own thing. And so many school-girls! It was the one known place for gay women, so if you were coming out you headed straight there. The butch thing was

*also incredibly strong there. The crowd was overwhelmingly fe-
male, but there'd be a few gay men, usually drag queens.*

And Graeme Reid, who frequented The Butterfly in the late 1970s and early 1980s,
remembers that there was a specific, highly-stratified geography to the place:

*In one corner there was Houghton, in another Doornfontein,
somewhere else Melville, and opposite them the Southern Suburbs. It was always jam-packed, and the trick was to find your
place in society — or your aspirations — and stay there. Of
course, if you were socially mobile, you could position yourself
between Houghton and Doornfontein and enjoy the best of both
worlds.*

Of course, in the still-segregated 1970s, this geography did not include Soweto,
Eldorado Park or Lenasia. But an article in *Exit* (South Africa's gay newspaper —
see below), published upon The Butterfly's closure in 1987, speaks of a 'quiet
revolution' that took place during the 1980s:

*Not only did some of the tougher crowd vanish, but it became
more multiracial. In the early days, even the barmen were all-
white, and only the cleaners were black. Now there are blacks
on both sides of the bar.*[14]

And while there were no black women at the T-Bar in the 1970s, Beffon recalls that
in the 1980s, 'you would see lots of Indian and coloured women.'

Indeed, as Hillbrow itself transformed, so too did these two bars. However,
with the exception of a Hillbrow bar called Madame Jo-Jos, which existed briefly
in the early 1990s, black lesbians have not been able to lay claim to another space
since the closure of the T-Bar in 1989. In contrast, by the time The Butterfly moved
upstairs and changed its name to The Skyline in 1987, it was almost exclusively
black. While white gay men moved on in the early 1990s — first to Connections
down the road and then to Champions in Braamfontein — The Skyline continued
to play a vital role as the only predominantly black gay venue in what was by then
a predominantly black neighbourhood.

As Hillbrow was to become a 'grey' area in later years — a white neighborhood where black people could live, illegal but unprosecuted, in relative safety
— it became a 'pink' area during the 1970s: a heterosexual neighborhood (most of
the residents continued to be pensioners, young single heterosexuals and newly-ar-
rived immigrants) where gay people could live in relative safety. It was the
pioneering presence of gay people living in Hillbrow that turned the area into a
tolerant 'liberated zone' of sorts, laying the ground for it to become Johannesburg's
first deracialised neighborhood in the 1980s. The irony of this is that as soon as it
did deracialise, most of the white gay people moved out, and those who remained
were enveloped by the new multiracial culture; Hillbrow has thus entirely lost its
gay flavour.

Alex Robbertze, a white gay man who moved to Hillbrow in the early
1970s and still lives there, laments the passing of those days:

A different fight for freedom

When I started living in Hillbrow, I used to go to a gay butcher, a gay tailor, a gay greengrocer. There were gay or gay-friendly restaurants all the way up and down Pretoria Street. So you felt safe. You didn't really care. We'd often walk with linked arms or even kiss on the street. I wouldn't dare to do that now. That whole scene's gone now.

'About parties, not politics':
Gay support networks in the 1970s

But the 'scene' that had sprouted in Hillbrow stopped way short of explicit political organisation. Pieter Bosman, who was later to found GASA, the national Gay Association of South Africa, recalls:

People would talk about the need to organise ourselves like in America, but no-one really did anything about it. Literature was very difficult to get hold of. One bookstore in town, Butch Berman, had the odd gay book: word would spread and everyone would rush down there. On the whole, though, our gay reading consisted of Gordon Merrick novels and those physique pictorial volumes. And if someone brought anything in from overseas, it was usually porn.

The only local attempt at establishing a gay rights movement in the early 1970s took place at the University of Natal in Durban, and its short life says much about the difficulties facing such attempts at that time. In April 1972, a symposium on homosexuality was held on campus, at which a member of the Students' Representative Council, Mark West, announced the formation of the South African Gay Liberation Movement. In a statement to the press, West said: 'I believe, as do my followers, that homosexuals should come forward and demand their rights. We should not be forced to meet in dark bars.'[15]

This was the first time in South Africa that a gay person had publicly placed gay rights within a framework of human rights and used the word 'liberation'. Not surprisingly, the authorities responded swiftly and, immediately following this announcement, the police began an investigation into the fledgeling movement.

Three weeks later, West announced that he had been forced to sign a statement disbanding the Movement after a visit from the police, who had 'explained' to him that, as sodomy was a common-law offense, the Movement would be breaking the law by inciting people to illicit activity.[16] Even though the anti-sodomy laws were 'sleeping' and seldom applied, this brief incident illustrates just how effective a deterrent they could be: the authorities had no qualms using them when needed to keep gay organisation in check.

Nevertheless, by mid-decade, other more successful attempts were being made to create a gay community broader than simply the bars and the clubs. Interestingly, these attempts took place in Durban which, of South Africa's three principal cities, had the least developed bar and club scene and nothing approaching the 'gay neighbourhoods' of Johannesburg and Cape Town. In 1976, a gay man called Bobby Erasmus founded South Africa's first gay organisation since the Law Reform days of 1968: the fancifully-named Gay Aid Identification Development and Enrichment, or GAIDE.

The organisation started out as a social club, and soon branched out into social support services. Office space was rented in the centre of town, a telephone information and counselling line was started, and a monthly newsletter was also distributed to all members. Stephen Roche, who joined GAIDE in 1977 and later went on to found GASA's Natal Coast branch, recalls that the organisation was

> *very dynamic. It got the job done. What was most remarkable was how open we were. Our meetings were held in Committee Room Three in City Hall, slap bang in the middle of everything, and we were never harassed.*

GAIDE members were recruited through get-togethers and parties. Echoing what people say about Law Reform's impact on the gay community in 1968, Roche notes that the organisation

> *provided alternative milieu for the community, drawing together a greater cross-section, as opposed to the self-selected cliques going to the bars and clubs. GAIDE cut right across class, and there were people ranging from high-powered professionals to post-office workers.*

GAIDE did not cut across race. Very significantly, however — and quite unique in the history of male-dominated South African gay organisation — GAIDE did boast a high percentage (40%) of active women involved on both a social and organisational level. Roche attributes the success of GAIDE to the presence of a few powerful personalities but also, very significantly, to the fact that:

> *it was about parties, not politics. At that point we didn't fuss about whether or not we were going in the right political direction, we just got on with it. The politics was covert rather than overt: it had to do with providing people with a safe place in which to test themselves, with providing role models for coming out, and with bringing people together on the basis of common need and a commonly-shared oppression.*

Unlike the ill-fated Gay Liberation Movement launched on Natal University's Durban campus four years previously, GAIDE neither sought nor received any publicity. Erasmus realised that the success of his organisation would be in the establishment of a support structure for gay people rather than in that of a political action group. Not only were the authorities more likely to tolerate this approach, but gay people themselves proved more receptive.

The tension between activist and social support functions has characterised South African gay organisation ever since. Since the late 1960s, in the United States and Western Europe, the two functions have always managed to co-exist. In South Africa, however, the experience of GAIDE — and every popular gay organisation that followed it — is that, in the creation of a formal gay subculture, activism has had to play a secondary role to social support. This lack of diversity is possibly due to the small number of gay people who have been prepared to 'go public' as leaders, but it is also due to the level of political oppression in South Africa: any talk of 'rights' was regarded with suspicion not only by the authorities, but by the conservative white gay community itself, which eschewed any identification — either overt or implicit — with the broader liberation struggle. But even in the largely black gay organisations of the 1990s, which have embraced strongly liberationist politics, the tension between political activism and the maintenance of social space still exists, as shall be seen below.

Very importantly, despite an unprecedented level of gay activity in places like Hillbrow, the 'space' that gay South Africans had claimed within larger society in the 1970s was fragile and new. Abroad, the gay liberation movement of the 1970s was built on nearly three decades of gay life in San Francisco, New York, London or Amsterdam. By 1972, when the New York-based Gay Liberation Front organised the first Pride March, there were already in place a plethora of formal and informal support-structures. Of those who had already availed themselves of these structures, a small number were now 'ready' to take to the streets. In South Africa, on the other hand, support structures consisted of a handful of bars and clubs, where the emphasis was more on the finding of sexual partners — always a primary need — than on building community. Thus, more politicised gay South Africans found themselves in a dilemma: on the one hand there was the urge to join a growing world-wide gay rights movement, but on the other, there was the need to build community in South Africa first with the establishment of social groups and structures. Nearly 20 years later, this need still exists.

Perhaps unintentionally, GAIDE did play a political function, largely due to the work of a heterosexual Durban psychologist who was involved with the organisation — Leonie Woolfson, whose masters thesis on lesbianism was based on the case-studies of several Durban women.[17] In late 1978, at roughly the time of GAIDE's disintegration, Woolfson's work received much coverage in the national media, and, at a large public meeting on the University of Natal campus, she called for an end to the repression of homosexuals.[18]

GAIDE collapsed in 1978 when Bobby Erasmus emigrated — yet another example of South African gay organisations' dependence on powerful leaders, and these leaders' failure to set in motion a broadbased movement. GAIDE's newsletter, however, had subscribers all over the country, and, in the next few years, similar initiatives were to sprout in the Transvaal and the Cape. These tended to be smaller in scale and purely social rather than also providing counselling services.

In Johannesburg in 1978, a sudden run of plays with homosexual themes prompted journalist Henk Botha to start South Africa's first commercial gay magazine, *Equus*. The magazine had a circulation of about 3 000, and was distributed at gay venues and even, for a while, through the Central News Agency, South Africa's largest commercial publications distributor, which was fooled at first by the 'For Ladies Only' strap on the cover. *Equus* was glossy in appearance, and, while it included fiction, gay interest articles and advertising for gay venues, its *raison*

45

d'être was clearly the male photo-spreads. It folded, however, after only six issues — because of financial problems exacerbated by the Publications Control Board banning several issues of the publication as 'undesirable'.

At roughly the same time as *Equus*, several newsletters circulated, based on the GAIDE model. The most successful was also the most unlikely, *The Gaily Male*, published by a group of gay Afrikaans men in the remote Northern Transvaal town of Potgietersrus. The home-printed publication consisted of personal advertisements, some terrible short-stories, and pornographic pictures with the offending body-parts inked out. *The Gaily Male* functioned as a pen-pal club, primarily for Afrikaans men in the far-flung platteland, but, in 1981 and 1982, the newsletter organised two weekend social get-togethers in the Waterberg, attended by more than 200 people each from all over the country. It was at these weekends that the members of many of the small social groups first met each other and hatched the idea of a national gay organisation.

From 1979 to 1981, the preferred form for these social groups was the 'supper club'. The first of these was formed in Johannesburg in 1979 and called itself, jokingly, the Azanian Men's Organisation (it later changed the name to the Alternative Men's Organisation). In 1981 another group formed in Johannesburg, calling itself Unité, consisting of men and women. And in August of that year, a group of Cape Town men started the 6010 Supper Club in Cape Town. John Pegge, one of the founders, recalls:

> *We would hire a restaurant once a month and take it over. The motivation was to make a space. We were mainly middle-class white men who had contact with Western Europe and America, and we saw the value of social organisation outside of the bar and the club.*

The late 1970s: 'Sensuality and defiance' — and backlash

Perhaps because of this new level of social activity from 1979 onwards, public censure of homosexuality seemed to increase. In July 1979, for example, four students were expelled from the Potchefstroom Teachers' Training College for 'homosexual activity'[19] and, two months later, rugby hero Naas Botha prefigured society's later response to AIDS by publicly saying that 'I do not see any place in society for the homosexual... I think it is a modern-day disease and our duty is to cure the disease'.[20] The following year, more anti-gay invective was to be found in the media when the Nederduits Gereformeerde Kerk announced it would be debating the homosexual problem. That year too a sensational murder trial put homosexuality into the public eye: Dr Desirée Smith had killed her husband and his lover upon coming home and finding them *in flagrante delicto*. Smith was acquitted on the grounds of having mistaken them for intruders: in a flood of articles explaining the trauma of women who discover their husbands are gay, the media treated Smith with sympathy and her victims with disdain.[21]

Most alarming to the gay community, however, was the fact that, after a decade of hassle-free existence, gay nightclubs were being targetted and raided; the authorities' pact to leave gay clubs in peace, made in 1969, seemed to collapse, probably because of the incredible popularity of clubs such as The New Mandy's and Zipps in the late 1970s, even among heterosexual clubbers, and the rampant and defiant sexuality these clubs celebrated. Gay people, writes Jimmy Beaumont,

> *were perceived as being the arbiters of style, fashion and music taste. Their clubs set the pace for others to follow. The 'dark disco' of the era was blatantly sexual; it throbbed with sensuality and defiance; every song was distinctive, and a skilled DJ could manipulate his audience like a pied piper, building up rhythm till the dance floor exploded in a frenzy of whistles, shouts, passion and naked, sweating torsos. 'Cruising the Streets' by the Boystown Gang became a classic, with its hard porn lyrics ('Up against the wall, you asshole; you too, cunt' and 'Stuff that big sausage in me...') and a pelvic beat that invited, or insisted on, dancefloor intimacy.*[22]

Gay identity, says Beaumont, was 'more obvious and blatant' in such clubs, particularly 'in the drug use, which filled venues with happy people and the smell of stale socks'. Although the grounds for the raids were always drug-swoops, liquor-busts or searches for minors, it was clear that their real reason was to curb this defiant new sexuality. At a raid at The New Mandy's over the Christmas holidays in 1978/9, for example, patrons were manhandled, photographed, verbally abused, and kept locked up in the building until morning. There were a few black gay men present at the club, and they came in for the harshest treatment. Many South African gay people refer to the 1979 Mandy's Raid — and not the 1966 Forest Town Raid — as South Africa's 'Stonewall'. This is because clientele, and particularly the drag queens, fought back (there are stories, perhaps apocryphal, of police officers with head-wounds incurred by high heels), and also because it was this raid — and a subsequent one the following year at the same club — that, more than anything else, prompted some gay people to move beyond the 'social support' model and begin talking of rights once more.

In the next two years, there were several more raids on Mandy's and other Johannesburg clubs and, in direct response to this new clampdown, an expressly activist gay organisation, Lambda, was launched at a large party at Club 2001 in Johannesburg in late 1981. Like GASA which was to follow it, Lambda attempted a difficult balancing act: to be an activist organisation aimed at protecting the rights of homosexuals while at the same time remaining 'apolitical'. Its founder and chairman, Alex Boyiatjis, made the following public statement: 'We are not aiming to run protest marches or set ourselves up as militants but we don't want to be a silent minority any longer.'[23] The contradictions in this statement were to plague and finally wrack the growing gay political movement for the rest of the decade.

Four
The 1980s: gay rights and gay politics

GASA: The birth of a national organisation

In many respects, the early 1980s signified an opening-up for South Africa, socially as well as politically. At the beginning of the decade, President P.W. Botha began instituting his 'reform' programme (balancing it, however, with heightened repression) and, in the aftermath of the Soweto upheavals, a massive upsurge of black liberationist activity swept through the townships. For the very first time since the National Party came to power in 1948, there was a tangible sense that the decades of Afrikaner Calvinist rule were coming to an end, and that the strict apartheid packaging off of people would give way to a more liberated and integrated society. It would be hyperbolic to call the early 1980s a 'Summer of Love' equivalent to the 1960s in Europe and North America. But at least in South Africa's urban centres, the very tenets of apartheid Calvinism were being challenged. Those years saw the beginnings of deracialisation and the establishment of anti-apartheid countercultures that questioned, vociferously, the religious and political restrictions of the previous 40 years.

White urban gay men, having consolidated their subculture in the 1970s, participated in this new counterculture and, by 1982, were ready to assert themselves politically. But, as we shall see, the failure of gay politics in the 1980s was that it was overtaken by the march of black liberation in those same years, and that it was unable — or unwilling — to align itself in any way with that march. Nevertheless, between 1982 and 1984, GASA, the Gay Association of South Africa, had formed a national organisation that constituted, for the very first time, something approximating the kind of gay grassroots movements to be found in Western Europe and North America.

Certainly, these roots were very much within only one sector of South African society — white, middle-class men. And certainly, there were dilemmas over political involvement and crises over poor leadership and management, both of which ultimately led to the organisation's downfall. But, during its active years, GASA facilitated a groundswell of gay activity that focussed the gay community and provided a basis for the more radical and politically explicit lesbian and gay activism that was to follow it.

GASA was formed in April 1982 out of three Johannesburg organisations: Lambda, the political group formed two months previously, and AMO and Unité, two 'supper clubs'. All three groups had been insignificant local initiatives, but within months, the new organisation had established nine branches across the country. By May 1983 there were over 1 000 paid-up members, and interest groups ranging from sports clubs to religious societies to support and counselling services. There was also *Link/Skakel*, the monthly newspaper that was to become *Exit*, and regular public get-togethers — 'Gay Days' and 'Jamborees'.

48

In October 1982, for example, only six months after GASA's founding, more than 3 000 people attended a Gay Jamboree at the Transvaal Country Club in Kyalami. While the focus of this Jamboree was entirely entertainment — live music, dancing, braais (barbecues), competitions, even mud-wrestling — it was an implicit political act. 'This is the first time in South Africa that gay people in this country will be gathering outdoors en masse for a day of fun and enjoyment,' reported *The Star*.[24] And, it must be said, The Kyalami Jamboree attracted at least three times as many people as the Pride Marches — more explicitly political acts — that have characterised public lesbian and gay life in the 1990s. Nearly three years after that first Gay Jamboree, in May 1985, GASA held a convention at the President Hotel in Johannesburg; to the usual fairground activity was added a symposium, with speeches on gay rights and gay activity in South Africa, and a gay art exhibition. Like its organisers, the convention was almost exclusively white and male. But, with its mixture of culture, academic debate and social events, it was a public exploration into the nature of gay life in this country the likes of which has not been repeated since.

In 1983, GASA opened its national office in Hillbrow, and its bank of large picture-windows, on the first floor of Burton Court, decorated with the GASA logo which included a pink triangle, soon became a local landmark. Alex Robbertze remembers:

> *There were worries that stones would be thrown at the windows, but it never happened. Once, someone suggested that we throw open the curtains and kiss for all of Hillbrow to see, and we did just that. We would often look out of the windows and see men, obviously out-of-towners, just standing there and looking up and pointing, as if they were tourists visiting a national monument!*

The following year, GASA-6010 in Cape Town opened a community centre in the city, from which it was to run its counselling service, and GASA Natal Coast opened its offices in the Berea Centre in Durban. Several interest groups also developed and affiliated themselves to GASA, the first one being the Religious Fellowship Workshop, which held its first service in December 1982, and later transformed into the still-active Gay Christian Community. A group of gay Jews within GASA formed Yachad, and there were also groups, in the early years, for married gays and parents of gays. Gay organisations also emerged on two campuses in 1983, the University of the Witwatersrand and the University of Cape Town. Perhaps the most successful 'interest group' affiliated to GASA was TOGS, the Transvaal Organisation for Gay Sport: in July 1984, an astonishing 1 000 people turned out to watch an all-gay rugby match between Pretoria and Johannesburg at the Rand Afrikaans University. TOGS has persevered long after GASA's demise: it still exists, and has over 200 members.

Also in 1984, Ann Smith, a GASA president and later its International Secretary, formed a women's interest group in Johannesburg. She explains:

49

*I was one of the few women in GASA, and I was constantly
being asked to bring other women in to the organisation. But it
was painfully clear to me that the reason women didn't join up
was because it was a very male world, and they did not feel
welcome. So my lover and I set up the group with the explicit
intention of creating a safe space, within GASA, where women
could be with one another and discuss their issues.*

The group lasted for only a few months, and Smith believes that the problem was
ultimately one of class: she says the professional and working-class women she
brought together within her home were incompatible, and the initiative collapsed.

At roughly the same time, in 1983, another lesbian group, unaffiliated to
GASA, emerged at the University of Cape Town. LILACS (Lesbians in Love and
Compromising Situations) was an offshoot of the gay students' association on campus and the product of feminist consciousness-raising groups in the 1970s. That too
collapsed after a couple of years, but in this case, report Armour and Lapinsky,
because of tensions 'between those members who favoured serious political debate
(including feminist and political content) and those wanting only to jorl'. (See 'Lesbians in love and compromising situations', in this volume.) Several other lesbian
initiatives — like Sunday's Women in Durban and the GLOW Lesbian Forum in
Johannesburg — have faced similar problems, as shall be explored below.

The social aspect of GASA was undoubtedly its major draw-card. People
joined because of the parties, the get-togethers, the 'Members Only' Sunday evenings at Jamesons Bar, the free passes into clubs. Henk Botha, one of GASA's
founders and later editor of *Exit*, believes that

*GASA worked for one reason only: it provided people with a
way of getting together. Before, you could meet friends and sexual partners only through the bars. Now, you could also meet
them at GASA get-togethers — and not only at GASA parties;
also at GASA meetings, sports gatherings and the like.*

GASA's founders also believe that the *Link/Skakel* newsletter and the counselling
service — later to become GAB, the Gay Advice Bureau, which still operates as an
autonomous body — were also crucial mobilising tools: they provided a link to the
urban subculture for isolated gay men. In 1982 and 1983 GASA thrived particularly
in provincial towns where there was no competition from bars and clubs —
Welkom, Bloemfontein, Kimberly, East London, Port Elizabeth, Pietermaritzburg
— and in these towns, the organisation was purely social in nature.

GASA and the politics of the 'apolitical'

While GASA's white male constituency might have been ready for a more public
social life, it remained politically conservative. Says Henk Botha,

*For this reason, GASA made it quite clear that it was apolitical
and wouldn't enter the political sphere. Because that was a
minefield. That's why we grew so quickly. If we had taken a*

political line, we would have collapsed much earlier than we did.

GASA's avowedly 'apolitical' stance was a major attraction. Ironically, it was ultimately the reason for its collapse: it attempted to remain outside the political fray at a time in South Africa's history when this was untenable. It was thus ousted from the world gay community and destabilised by a growing anti-apartheid and black gay movement within South Africa.

For GASA's architects, being 'apolitical' meant two things: firstly, remaining non-aligned in broader South African politics, and secondly, following a moderate, non-confrontational and accommodationist strategy. Among its 11 points, the GASA Mission Statement, drafted in 1982, stated that the organisation aimed to provide a 'non-militant non-political answer to gay needs'. A recruitment ad in *Link/Skakel* underscored this: 'Remember, GASA is not a militant organisation planning protest marches through the city streets, and your membership will not imperil your privacy.' The antipathy towards a 'political' label, we see, was directly linked to fear of exposure.

Nevertheless, GASA's Mission Statement encompassed several explicitly political functions, including 'uniting all gays under a democratic banner to offer an identity and foster confidence and self-respect amongst gays', 'changing the distorted, prejudice and uninformed image held by the broader public' and 'encouraging law reform by setting a positive example to the authorities and the non-gay society.'[25] And, within months of its formation, GASA faced its first political challenge: in November 1982, a 'lesbian scandal' erupted in the South African Railways Police and a witchhunt followed: the Railways Police Commissioner, Lt-Gen Hannes Visagie, announced that gays were 'not welcome' in the force. After a five-month investigation, four women and nine men were dismissed and a further 60 officers resigned of their own accord — presumably to avoid disclosure.[26]

GASA faced a dilemma: its mission statement required it to challenge this 'distorted, prejudiced and uninformed' action, and yet it was 'apolitical'. There was also little advocacy for lesbian issues within the organisation. Thus, when the scandal broke, GASA failed to respond: in fact, that month, a GASA member justified the lack of response to a newspaper by saying, 'If we started waving banners, we would only increase the animosity towards us.'[27]

Finally, largely due to the work of Ann Smith, GASA issued a statement that 'lesbianism is not illegal' and that 'the dismissal or forced resignations of women because of lesbianism is a flagrant case of discrimination against women, as it involves moral issues which are not legal ones.'[28] The issue had been highly contentious within the organisation, and GASA's activities went no further than writing a letter to the SA Transport Services and issuing a media statement. GASA defended this 'soft-pedalling' in a *Link/Skakel* editorial:

> *An organisation which has only about 1 000 members is highly vulnerable to official censure. Had GASA made representations on a political level, we may well have been annihilated.*[29]

Over the next couple of years, GASA did make occasional public statements. When the police raided Scants, a gay club in Johannesburg in October 1984 and arrested seven people, GASA objected publicly. The following year, Minister of Transport Hendrik Schoeman received a pair of cufflinks at a function in Springs and said 'cufflinks are things that moffies wear'. When asked to elaborate, Schoeman quipped that 'moffies are guys who sleep in pink pyjamas and keep their gloves on when courting.'[30] Once more, GASA objected, and Schoeman retracted his statement and apologised.

There is no doubt that through these public utterances the organisation played a watchdog role, increasing its public profile while keeping homophobia in check. But GASA's salvos were erratic, eccentric, and rather arbitrary: the organisation deliberately shied away from taking up the cudgels in a more direct and ongoing way, as such a policy would have forced it into a more confrontational role, and, in the repressive 1980s, might have jeopardised its legality. GASA's primary motivation for remaining 'apolitical' was, in the words of Ann Smith, that

> we saw that in this country, political protests were immediately banned, and if we were banned, not only would we discredit the gay movement, but we would not be around to provide vital services to gay people.[31]

'Not really welcome and we knew it': Black men in GASA

GASA's political conservatism was not only hampering its ability to act publicly according to its own mission statement, it was also causing internal dissent among its membership. This rift was exacerbated when Simon Nkoli, a black man with a background in anti-apartheid liberation politics, joined GASA in 1983. Nkoli, who was simultaneously active in the radical Congress of South African Students (COSAS), recalls that he had fought from the start for a more activist gay politics in GASA. As one of only a handful of black men in GASA at the time, Nkoli also rubbed up against discrimination within the gay community GASA claimed to represent:

> The best thing about membership was that, apparently, your little pink card got you into clubs at discounted prices. I got my Link/Skakel in the mail, and it was a feast of possibility: the Dungeon, The Butterfly, Mandys. I tried Mandys and they said 'no blacks'. The Dungeon. 'No blacks.' I showed them their ad in Link/Skakel: 'All GASA members welcome at a discount.' 'I'm a member of GASA,' I'd say. 'Yes,' they'd reply, 'but you're black. What if the police come?' The only place I managed to get in was somewhere in Jeppe Street: I was the only black person there and I felt so intimidated that I never went back.

Because GASA did not seem to take black recruitment and issues very seriously at all, Nkoli decided to form a black interest group within the organisation. He obtained an interview with *City Press*, the black Sunday newspaper, in August 1983, giving his personal address and calling upon black gay men to contact him; within a week, he says, he was 'deluged' with responses, and arranged a special meeting: 82 people attended. Nkoli recalls:

> *What was fascinating was how different their language was to the white middle-class members of GASA. They said things like 'we have to fight for our rights! We have to mobilise!' They were ordinary people, mainly in their early 20s, and most joined GASA immediately. We decided to meet every second Saturday of each month, and it was an instant success. Once we had a fundraising party in Soweto and more than 200 people showed up. We would also go to shebeens together, and, at Lee's Place in Orlando East, we started the first gay shebeen, where we met every Sunday, joined by one or two of the more progressive white GASA members.*

But problems began as soon as these newly-organised black gay men started meeting in the GASA offices in Hillbrow: there were complaints that the black people meeting there every Saturday were making too much noise, and that this was endangering GASA's lease of the building. It was also proposed that GASA limit the number of black people allowed to enter because of the danger of theft. A member of the GASA executive at the time recalls that

> *the white GASA members were mad as hell: these black kids would come in, drink all the booze, light fires in the middle of the office to cook their food, make a noise, and leave a helluva mess! I have to say that the grievances against this new group of members were legitimate. But perhaps they could have been more sensitively dealt with. There was a different way of doing things, and, if we really wanted black people in the organisation, we should have been more accommodating.*

The above point is critical: irresponsible as the black group may well have been, there was little tolerance for — or understanding of — these new members, who were undergoing the exhilaration of coming out much as GASA's white members had in the 1970s. The great difference was, however, that whereas white gay men from the 1970s onwards had several meeting places to choose from, black gay men were still unwelcome in the bars and clubs. And even if they were permitted to enter, most did not have the financial means to do so. While some gay-friendly shebeens did exist in Soweto, these were unstable and capricious, and so Nkoli's group within GASA was their only option. Also, unlike their white counterparts, most still lived with their families and thus did not even have private spaces in which to explore new-found sexual liberation. GASA's offices thus came to serve the social function for these men that The Butterfly, Mandy's and Zipps served for their white comrades.

According to Nkoli, the new black members were 'incredibly offended' by the proposal to limit their entry to the GASA offices. They decided not to meet there any more, gathering rather in Soweto in people's homes on a rotating basis.

But, Nkoli maintains, 'the damage had been done: almost as quickly as they had joined up, the black members resigned. They were not really welcome, and they knew it.'

The extent to which black people were unwelcome was made clear to Nkoli during a hiking-club trip to Pretoria later that year. Upon arrival at the venue it was discovered that it had a whites-only policy (this was 1983, after all, and the Separate Amenities Act was still in full force). Rather than leaving in outrage, however, the white GASA members went in anyway, instructing their four black comrades to wait in the car. Nkoli disobeyed, however, and entered. In the ensuing ruckus, GASA came under much fire from some of its own membership. And while the association took a policy decision to avoid segregated venues in the future, Nkoli claims he was suspended from the organisation: the grounds being that he had broken the law and thus placed GASA in jeopardy.

What particularly galled black members, says Nkoli, was that

> GASA was using us to blacken up its image. Every time there was a function in a private house, the picture would be taken with the few darkies prominently displayed, and would be sent overseas.

Earlier in 1983, GASA had applied for membership of the International Gay Association, but was turned down after intense lobbying by the Scottish Homosexual Rights Group (SHRG). SHRG took issue with GASA's 'apolitical' stance — how could the organisation claim to be 'non-racist', it asked, if it did not actively oppose apartheid? SHRG accused GASA's white gays of having 'sold out to the authorities in return for the police ignoring the (segregated) gay bars and discos'.[32] GASA was thus given a probation period: a year in which to prove it was truly non-racial.

But rather than fully integrating into GASA, Nkoli and the few remaining black members remained, in his words, 'affiliated but separate', and, in May 1984, they formalised themselves into The Saturday Group. According to Nkoli,

> our main reason for existence was to provide counselling for black gay people trying to come out, but we were completely nonracial, and we had white members and even, for the very first time in a South African gay organisation, some black women. We had a telephone counselling service, and we would also pay house-visits when asked. We also organised parties — a birthday party, for example, would became a major gay event.

In Durban, GASA Natal Coast also claims to have attempted to bring black people into the organisation. Stephen Roche of the Natal organisation maintains that, unlike the situation in Johannesburg's townships, there is 'no visible gay activity whatsoever' in Durban's sprawling townships of Umlazi and KwaMashu. Of South Africa's three major cities, Durban remains alone in not having any form of organised black gay subculture. Nevertheless, McLean and Ngcobo claim that *isingqumo*, the gay slang that is spoken in townships on the reef, originated in Durban. Linda Ngcobo also noted before his death that

> *there was definitely an African gay network in the Durban townships. When I used to go down there, I always became involved in the life of shebeens and house-parties. It was very closed, though. You had to be Zulu to get access. But I was Zulu and there was no problem.*

Clearly, then, the perception of no gay activity in Durban's townships has been a function of organised white gay subculture's inability to penetrate these townships; there was no Simon Nkoli to facilitate the interaction and, very importantly, the war that has wracked these townships since the mid-1980s has made residents particularly suspicious of outsiders. GASA Natal Coast did attempt, briefly, to make contact with Durban's more accessible gay Indian subculture. Says Roche:

> *In around 1986 GASA was approached to judge a drag show at The Airport, an Indian nightclub in the Butterworth Hotel. We discovered that this was very well-run, and that, although it was largely straight, many gay Indian men went there. So we raised the possibility of a gay night at The Airport. But it never happened, I think because of the immense closetry in the Indian community.*

Roche and several Indian men who grew up in Durban all believe there has never been an exclusively gay Indian space in the city; once more, without the critical primary socialising function of a bar or a club, political mobilisation remains impossible. In the 1990s, Roche, who teaches at the largely-Indian University of Durban-Westville, facilitated a gay and lesbian support group on campus; in 1993, this group had an informal membership of 20, seven of whom were Indian men and three Indian women.

Murderer or hero?: The Nkoli affair and its aftermath

The large response first to Nkoli's letter in City Press in 1983 and then to The Saturday Group in 1984 proved that the growing homosexual community in the townships was ready to become part of a gay organisation. But, almost immediately following the formation of The Saturday Group, Nkoli was arrested after a rent boycott demonstration in his home-township of Sebokeng, and held in custody for two years before being charged, with 21 other prominent United Democratic Front activists, with treason. As soon as Nkoli was arrested, The Saturday Group fell apart. In the very month of his arrest, GASA was admitted into the International Gay Association; the way GASA was to deal with his arrest, however, was not only the reason for its expulsion a year later, but, ultimately, for the disintegration of the movement.

GASA leaders are adamant to this day that Nkoli had been a minor player in the South African gay movement in the years before his arrest, and the evidence suggests that they are correct. Nevertheless, he became a *cause célèbre* after his arrest: the confluence of his open homosexuality and his imprisonment as a soldier against apartheid made him immensely appealing to liberation-oriented gay organisations around the world. In Nkoli, gay anti-apartheid activists found a ready-made hero. In Canada, the Simon Nkoli Anti-Apartheid Committee became a critical player in both the gay and anti-apartheid movements. Through Nkoli's imprisonment, too, progressive members of the international anti-apartheid movement were able to begin introducing the issue of gay rights to the African National Congress. The highly respectable Anti-Apartheid Movements of both Britain and Holland, for example, took up Nkoli's cause, and this was to exert a major impact on the ANC's later decision to include gay rights on its agenda.

But while Nkoli was being celebrated by the gay world abroad, he was at best ignored and at worst abandoned by South Africa's own gay movement. GASA claimed not to be supporting him because of his minimal role in the South African gay movement and because of its 'apolitical' constitution. The real reason, however, was that Nkoli's politics were intensely threatening to the organisation's conservative white membership, who feared that any support of Nkoli would be construed as support for the illegal liberation struggle. They did not, on the whole, support the anti-apartheid cause in the first place.

Publicly, GASA tried to ignore Nkoli's imprisonment. But, by 1986, when he was formally charged with murder (he was acquitted during the ensuing trial), the pressure of his international support and the fact that his few supporters within GASA had mounted a vigorous letter-writing campaign to gay organisations worldwide protesting GASA's hypocrisy, forced the organisation to deal with the matter. In August 1986, GASA leader Kevan Botha announced, at that year's International Lesbian and Gay Association convention, that his organisation had withheld support for Nkoli because he had been charged with common-law murder and GASA could not sanction criminal activity. This statement was a revealing indicator of how entrenched GASA was in the apartheid perception of extra-parliamentary activity as criminal activity rather than as the only available means of black protest and resistance. It only further served to alienate GASA from both the international gay movement and the growing body of progressive gay activists at home.

In a hard-hitting response to GASA's 'apolitical' defense, gay Hillbrow priest and Nkoli confidante Father Don Dowie wrote, in *Exit* in 1986, that the 'apolitical' label was nothing more than an excuse used by GASA members to skirt the race issue:

> *We are involved whether we like it or not, and to adopt a self-consciously apolitical posture is in itself a political declaration and will be seen as such by blacks, if we achieve a standoff in the persecution and harrassment of gays at the expense of our wider social commitment.*

Blacks, said Dowie, stayed away from GASA precisely because

> *to many blacks, a concern by blacks in gay affairs seems frivolous, irrelevant and divisive. They will only allow credibility to*

*the gay cause if we can show them that they matter to us and
that we are prepared to defend their right to be human.*

Dowie's comments were remarkably prescient: in the years to come, senior officials
of both the African National Congress and the Pan Africanist Congress were to
dismiss gay issues as bourgeois frivolities and irrelevancies. His comments were
also symptomatic of many gay South Africans' growing discontent with GASA's
'apolitical' label. In 1986, impelled by Nkoli's involvement in the Delmas Treason
Trial and by President P.W. Botha's declaration of a State of Emergency, progressive gay South Africans began forming explicitly political organisations in direct
opposition to GASA.

But by the time the Nkoli affair reached a head in 1986, GASA as a national organisation was in state of collapse anyway. According to its executive, the
row over its politics was the least of its problems: it had over-extended itself and
had been mismanaged, and was in deep financial trouble. Already, in July 1985, it
had 'unbundled' its single largest asset, *Link/Skakel*, which was now set up as an
independent newspaper, *Exit*. In August 1986, GASA dissolved as a national organisation, and was replaced by the 'Gay Forum', a network of 35 gay organisations
that had its first conference in Welkom the following month. Later, this body was
known as the 'Gay Alliance'; it never took root, however, and was replaced by two
local networks, The Johannesburg Forum and The Cape Town Forum, in the late
1980s.

After the national collapse of GASA, GASA Rand did continue in Johannesburg, as did two other regional branches of the association: GASA-6010 in Cape
Town and Gasa Natal Coast in Durban. In October 1986, Gasa Natal Coast held the
first of its annual Gay Pride National Festivals. In the style of GASA's large gatherings since the Kyalami Gay Day of 1982, this event — which was to be repeated
annually in Durban until 1991 — was more of a festival than a march, and consisted of a fairground during the day and cabaret and competitions at night
culminating in the inevitable Mr Centrefold. More than 1 000 people attended the
first Durban festival, and, in the years following, average attendance was around
600. Like GASA in the rest of the country, GASA Natal Coast was overwhelmingly
white and — despite the experience of GAIDE in the mid-1980s — overwhelmingly male.

Despite the continuation of regional GASA branches working along the
old-style support-group/gay festival lines, the Nkoli affair and the spiralling political situation in South Africa prompted a new kind of lesbian and gay politics. In
1986, a new black group appeared on the scene: the Rand Gay Organisation,
founded by Alfred Machela in April of that year. Machela claimed that his organisation had over 300 members. In August 1986, the RGO was admitted to the
International Lesbian and Gay Association. It was never heard of again, and
Machela now lives in Stockholm.

Also in 1986, in direct response to the imposition of the State of Emergency in June, a group of white gay anti-apartheid activists in Cape Town — some
of whom had had leadership positions in GASA-6010 — formed Lesbians and

Gays Against Oppression (LAGO). Although this group numbered barely more than a half-dozen, their prominence within the anti-apartheid structures of the Western Cape, coupled with the fact that they were the first to fold gay rights issues into the anti-apartheid struggle, meant that they were to have an immense impact on the South African gay rights movement.

Directly challenging the 'apolitical' nature of GASA, a LAGO pamphlet, distributed widely at anti-apartheid rallies in the Western Cape, stated that the group was formed to 'situate the lesbian and gay struggle within the context of the total liberation struggle'. LAGO also made a point of supporting gay political trialists — Nkoli as well as Ivan Toms, the conscientious objector who had been a founder-member of both LAGO and the banned End Conscription Campaign (ECC).

Toms' much-publicised battle with the SADF proved to be an important mobilising point for left-wing gay politics in South Africa: not only because the South African Defence Force deliberately used his homosexuality to smear him, but because the ECC requested him not to publicise his homosexuality. This demonstrated the persistent homophobia of the military establishment and also the reluctance of anti-apartheid organisations to deal with gay people in their midst. Also, with its presence at rallies in the Western Cape and its pamphlets, LAGO challenged the 'homophobic ethos' of supposedly democratic organisations based on the principles of non-discrimination. LAGO lasted 15 months before being re-placed by OLGA, the Organisation of Lesbian and Gay Activists, which was to play a vital role in lobbying the African National Congress.

'AIDS Panic Overstressed'?
GASA-6010, the gay movement and AIDS activism

Despite the new presence of LAGO in Cape Town, GASA-6010 remained strong. Even more so than in Johannesburg, Western Cape gay politics was acutely divided between those who were interested in political activism and those involved in social support services. The activists who had left GASA-6010 to form LAGO in 1986, however, had always been a minority in the organisation. When 6010 was formally constituted in July 1982, it defined its functions psycho-socially: 'to promote the gay individual as a respectable member of society, and to allow the gay individual a better opportunity to evolve as an integrated and respectable member of society.'[33] A 24-hour telephone counselling service was set up and, since then, 6010 (it was to affiliate with GASA and become GASA-6010 a year later) has concentrated almost exclusively on counselling and social support services.

John Pegge, one of 6010's founders and the director of its counselling services, explains:

> *Facilitating the coming-out process has always remained 6010's primary function. We have defined ourselves as a social service organisation precisely because this is the critical first step towards the development of a gay identity. Only once gay people have come out and feel comfortable with their sexuality, can they become involved in more explicitly political activity.*

Pegge notes, however, that the 'single most difficult aspect of coming out since the 1980s has been the spectre of AIDS.' In 1984, GASA-6010 set up an AIDS Action Group and, since 1987, GASA-6010 has also run primary health care clinics at its community centre, staffed by volunteer medical personnel and receptionists. By 1993, the HIV-clinic, was offering testing, counselling and post-test treatment, and was the only one of its kind in South Africa catering specifically to gay people. Since 1987, GASA-6010 has also conducted extensive safer-sex outreach in Cape Town's bars and clubs, and has held annual AIDS Candlelight Memorials.

GASA in Johannesburg played down the threat of the AIDS epidemic — while it published a safe-sex poster in 1983, the first mention of the epidemic in *Link/Skakel* was a headline blaring 'AIDS PANIC IS OVERSTRESSED'.[34] GASA-6010 thus became a shrill voice in the dark. Pegge, Isaacs and Miller have written that, because of the government's inadequate AIDS policy,

> *AIDS prevention and care would fall upon the limited, politically fragmented resources of a gay minority itself. With the lack of a central powerbase, including no sense of political and legal identity... a perceived sense of state alienation and a social context of pervasive oppression, the task of achieving such a strategy for the gay minority was and remains awesomely difficult.*[35]

Added to these problems is the fact that state and non-governmental bodies alike have decided to play down the 'gay' aspect of the epidemic in an attempt to persuade heterosexuals that they are at risk. While this might make sense in terms of promoting a safer-sex programme for the wider population, it means that there is little funding and materials specifically for gay people.

The representation of AIDS in the media in the mid-1980s says much about the perceived role that homosexuals have played in the spread of the epidemic: before 1985, the epidemic was characterised as 'The Gay Plague'; in March of that year, however, newspapers began reporting black HIV-cases in Soweto, and mediaspeak immediately transformed 'The Gay Plague' into 'The Black Death'. One newspaper ran the following headline: 'Gay Plague Spreads to Townships'. Even though the article gave evidence that one of the people with AIDS discovered in Soweto was a heterosexual man believed to have brought the virus from Zaire, the next paragraph read: 'AIDS is mostly prevalent in homosexual groups and Soweto has its own gay community, some of which have had contact with white gays.'[36] The imputation was clear: black gay men who moved between the white gay subculture and the townships were responsible for importing the epidemic into heterosexual black society.

As with the other GASA branches, 6010's organisational structure was predominantly white and male. But because it was located in the Western Cape, where there is a large coloured gay subculture, its client services were — and continue to be — heavily patronised by coloureds, who are less likely than whites to have access to private medical and psychological care. Pegge estimates that at least 60% of 6010's average 1 000 clients a year are coloured. Very few of these coloured clients move from being clinic visitors to being members of the organisation, and this, as we shall see, became a major reason for the establishment of the largely-black ABIGALE in 1992.

6010 (it reverted to its original name after GASA's collapse) still exists: it has remained a powerful regional initiative precisely because its role is so special-ised and narrowly defined around counselling and HIV-treatment.

'Every gay here is a criminal': Law Reform revisited

While GASA-6010 and GASA Natal Coast continued to function regionally, the collapse of the national organisation in 1986 made space for two new forms of gay political activity. The first found the notion of single-issue gay politics to be unten-able in South Africa, and attempted to bring gay rights issues into the broader human rights struggle: this was characterised first by LAGO, and later by OLGA and GLOW in 1989. The second, looking back to the 1968 Law Reform movement, insisted on fighting specifically for the reform of laws that discriminated against homosexuals.

In April 1985, after President PW Botha decriminalised interracial sex as part of his reform programme, he asked the President's Council (a nominated mixed-race upper house of Parliament that replaced the whites-only Senate in 1983) to investigate the Immorality Act. The Council set up an Ad Hoc committee and in August 1985 put forward its recommendations. The committee equivocated on the subject of homosexuality, suggesting that 'more thorough investigation' was re-quired on three issues: 'the possible widening of the criminal prohibitions on gay conduct to include gay women'; how society should 'express its abhorrence to ho-mosexuality'; and what 'programmes of rehabilitation or forms of punishment would be desirable.'[37]

Panic, of the type experienced in the mid-60s, set in once again in gay society; explicit in this ruling was the sentiment that homosexuality was abhorrent, requiring rehabilitation at best and punishment at worst. And so, as in 1968, a law reform movement was launched, this time called the National Law Reform Fund (NLRF). It aimed to make submissions to the President's Council, 'to present every scrap of evidence to convince the authorities that gays exist and that they can be (and to a large extent are) worthy members of the community.'

In Johannesburg, an alliance of 20 organisations formed a fundraising in-centive called Benefit; at its launch in March 1986, human rights advocate Edwin Cameron put the case for this new activity most succinctly:

> The shocking truth is that many gays in South Africa have to a great extent been living a dream that is in fact a legal night-mare. The simple fact is that male gays in South Africa have no legal right to practise their gayness. Almost every gay here this afternoon is, according to South African law, a criminal.

A different fight for freedom

The message was clear: the 'victory' wrought by the law reform movement in 1968 was a hollow one, and a gay subculture had flourished in the 1970s and early 1980s only because the authorities had chosen to ignore it. Said Cameron:

> We exercise the freedom we think we might have in South Africa not by right but by favour, by indulgence. We are dependent on, at best, the goodwill of the police to meet and act as we do; and at worst we are dependent on their blind eyes, their lack of knowledge or their inefficiency.

As in 1968, middle-class gay white men responded with alacrity to the possibility of their freedom being abrogated. However, now there was a tradition of public gay gatherings — established by GASA — upon which Benefit could draw. Benefit's March 1986 launch at Shaft 8 at Crown Mines outside Johannesburg took the form of a large gay festival, attended by 1 200 people, and was replete with fairground activity, live entertainment and competitions.

Unlike 1968, however, there was not the same government focus: PW Botha's campaign to smash anti-apartheid resistance overtook all else and the gay issue was forgotten. The NLRF had raised R59 000 by January 1987, but had nothing to spend it on: it was thus transformed into the National Law Reform Charitable Trust. Three trustees were appointed, and it was decided that this money would be used in future to 'market gay lifestyles' and to intervene, in any possible way, in the gay law reform struggle in South Africa. Of the R59 000 raised, however, only R10 000 was spent, and there was much dissatisfaction within the gay community: talk abounded of misappropriation of funds.[39]

Also unlike 1968, there was the sense of a 'larger struggle' even within the NLRF's activities. Although the NLRF and Benefit were entirely white middle-class organisations, Cameron's keynote speech in March 1986 employed the concept of 'freedom', explicitly referring to the critique of white gay culture that had been developed through the Simon Nkoli controversy: that white gay South Africans were 'living a dream', looking after their material interests and comforts while ignoring the issues of discrimination and oppression — their own, and that of others around them.

An electoral 'victory' and the end of an era

This critique of self-interest reached a head in 1987, when the white parliamentary elections were to prove to be a watershed for South African gay politics. At the same time as the growing anti-apartheid movement called for a boycott of these elections, *Exit* called upon gay voters to exercise their power through the ballot box. Every candidate in the election was asked whether he or she supported gay rights, and, in constituencies where there were significant number of gay voters, candidates from all parties scrambled to join the gay rights bandwagon. 'Yes' responses were received from 23 candidates of the liberal opposition Progressive Federal Party and from ten National Party candidates.

It was a fascinating display of gay political power, and in largely-gay Hillbrow, National Party candidate Leon de Beer won the seat from Progressive Federal Party veteran Alf Widman: de Beer had made much noise about gay rights, while Widman had equivocated. Recalls *Exit* editor Henk Botha:

> *Like most gay people in the constituency, I would never have voted Nat. But it was an exciting moment for us. Here was this handsome, charming man, and he was talking in favour of gay rights. It was the first time any candidate was prepared to stand up openly and support gay rights.*

By 1987, Hillbrow was rapidly integrating, and already had a significant black population. De Beer, as a member of the pro-apartheid governing party, was taking a stand on this issue too. If gay voters defected in droves to the National Party, it was not only because de Beer was charming, handsome and pro-gay: it was in part because he represented a party trying to contain and manage the deracialising process.

Exit trumpeted that gay voters in Hillbrow could 'sway power, even to a candidate like Leon de Beer who represents an unpopular and repressive party, if he comes out strongly enough in favour of gay rights.' While the paper claimed to 'want every privilege afforded to whites to be extended to our black brothers and sisters,' it was unrepentant: 'we will use any vehicle to campaign for gay civil liberties, even if it means resorting to the whites-only democracy of South Africa.'[40] Gerry Davidson, *Exit*'s current editor, notes in her history of the publication that 'to many, the message was clear: white gay rights were the only ones *Exit* (and by extension the GASA elite) was interested in.' (See 'Exit', in this volume.)

For the first time white gay South Africans behaved like an organised political minority, and the effect had been felt. There was immense power to that. But this was 1987. It was no longer possible to maintain a gay civil liberties struggle separate from the larger struggle for racial equality. Ironically, the greatest moment of victory for single-issue 'apolitical' gay politics was also to be its death-blow. The GASA era was dead.

Five
Lesbian and gay subcultures in the 1990s

From 'Dark Bars' into the streets: Opening up space

Since the collapse of a largely white, politically conservative GASA and the emergence of a black gay subculture in the late 1980s, there has been a radical shift from the 'apolitical' and accommodationist single-issue politics that characterised gay life from 1968 onwards to an assertion of gay rights as human rights — equivalent to all the others being fought for at this time of profound constitutional and social change in South Africa. From 1988 onwards, a complex of lesbian and gay organisations that may be described as 'charterist' developed: charterist, because they aligned themselves ideologically with the adherents of the ANC's Freedom Charter and because they set about developing their own Charter of Lesbian and Gay Rights.

This new politics was heralded first by LAGO and OLGA in the Western Cape, small groups of white activists within the liberation movement. Then, as black gay South Africans identified a movement in which they might participate as equals and obtain services specifically appropriate to their circumstances, more mass-based largely-black organisations were founded: first GLOW in Johannesburg in 1988 and then, four years later, ABIGALE in the Western Cape in 1992. The new alignment has also included lesbian-feminist organisations like Sunday's Women in Durban and student groups at the English-speaking universities.

The standard-bearer of this new politics is the annual Lesbian and Gay Pride March, organised by GLOW, which has taken place in Johannesburg every year since 1990. In the 1960s, gay men and lesbians embraced either in dark parks or behind bolted doors. In the 1990s, some are beginning to embrace, defiantly, on the streets in full view of the national media at the annual march. In 1968, that first public meeting of Law Reform at the Park Royal hotel was strictly controlled to prevent unwanted entry by police or the media; in 1992, the police are called out to protect lesbian and gay marchers and the media is encouraged to record them. In 1966, police raided a party and arrested nine men for 'masquerading as women' in a private home in Forest Town; in 1992, the Pride March is led by drag queens.

In 1972, when University of Natal student Mark West tried to found a Gay Liberation Movement because 'we should not be forced to meet in dark bars', he was subject to police harrassment. In 1992, many gay men and lesbians still choose to meet in dark bars, but now also have the opportunity to establish a public political identity outside of these bars and on the street. A pride march, as a moment of public expression, is the perfect analogy for coming out of the closet: out of those dark bars and dark corners of dark parks into the full glare of sunlight and television cameras. As such, it best symbolises the new gay liberationist politics in South Africa.

In organising the march, GLOW has quite self-consciously fused two traditions: certainly, there is the carnivalesque tradition of the annual New York Pride

March or Sydney Gay Mardi Gras, but there is also South Africa's own tradition of the anti-apartheid protest march. And, by invoking these two traditions, the march has managed to bring into the public view an unprecedentedly wide cross-section of lesbian and gay people.

The march is growing slowly in size (from 1 000 marchers in 1990 to nearly 2 000 in 1992) and in representativeness — even though the majority of marchers are still white men, the number of black participants has increased from 5% to 25%, and about 40% of marchers are women. Nevertheless, it can in no way be seen as a microcosm of the totality of homosexual experience in this country: powerful though it is as an annual public expression, it is no more than a surface manifestation of the aspirations of a small group of people, black and white, who have embraced a new liberationist politics. South African lesbian and gay communities remain, on the whole, invisible to the public eye, still subject to their characterisation as 'unapprehended felons' by the law, sinners by the church, and deviants by society in general.

However, a look at lesbian and gay activity in the 1990s demonstrates a growing openness and increasing diversity in the face of this opprobrium. This can be seen, firstly, in the very architecture of public lesbian and gay spaces. In Johannesburg in the 1970s, gay bars and clubs put up rolls of barbed wire outside their cloistered premises to keep police out and made a point of stopping unfamiliar faces at their dungeon-like doors and asking them if they were gay. Now, although there is a downturn in commercial gay activity (there is nowhere near the number of gay venues as there was in the early 1980s), those that do exist are far more open. Champions, opposite the station in busy Braamfontein, spills out onto a large apron of grass, a public park in fact, and when the weather is fine this park becomes an outdoor extension of the bar, in full view of passersby. Likewise, a new lesbian venue in Rosebank, Harlequins, is located on the premises of a college and has big sliding glass doors rather than blackened portholes; outdoor cafe tables rather than steps leading down to a dingy basement.

Some clubs have diversified their activities, becoming 'community centres' of sorts rather than simply places to dance, drink and get laid. A case in point is Club Equusite, Pretoria's longest-running gay club where, on a Sunday afternoon in the early 1990s, you could see between 30 and 60 gay men and lesbians clutching Bibles as they climbed past the dancefloor with its smell of stale beer and cigarette smoke from the night before, up to the Lace Restaurant on the second floor. Here, with a few basic rearrangements of the furniture and a few deft reinterpretations of the Scriptures, the Rev Hendrik Pretorius has built South Africa's first and only registered gay church: the Reformerende Gemeentes van Gelykes in Christus (Reforming Congregations of Equals in Christ). Pretorius, who resigned publicly from the staunchly Calvinist Dutch Reformed Church at the Lesbian and Gay Pride March in 1990, has put into place a veritable queer vicarage, with deacons, elders, pastoral counselling and even gay marriages.

The church, like the nightclub in which it is housed, is participatory theatre: people come together to define common values, to act out their beliefs and to bond into a community. Certainly, the values defined at Saturday night's rave might be in direct opposition to those defined at Sunday afternoon's church service, but, insist the congregants, they are not mutually exclusive. Says 'Louwrens', a deacon of the church:

> *Clubs have become of necessity the only safe spaces where gay people can gather. But, often, being gay means dancing and drinking and having sex. That's how society has decided we are, so that's how we behave. But we have other needs too, spiritual and political, and there's no reason why the club, which is the only space we have, can't also be used for these needs.*[41]

And clubs are not the only space where this new openness and diversity can be seen. In the townships, precisely because of the lack of space and the closeness of humanity, gay parties and shebeens, when they do exist, are always in full view of the neighbours. In kwaThema, a township outside Springs on the East Rand, gay men meet publicly and outdoors in at least five shebeens and hold Miss GLOW competitions for all at the community centre (see below). In Soweto, a gay catering company, staffed by gay men takes care of weddings and funerals every weekend: while stolid and churchy mourners or celebrants gather in the living-room, the gays rule the kitchen, turning their work into an assertion of public identity that cannot be avoided. Linda Ngcobo's funeral, at the Phiri Hall in early 1993, is perhaps the best example of this new township openness.

And in sport, another leisure-time activity of vital importance as a gathering space, particularly for lesbians, there has also been a shift. In the 1950s and 1960s, closeted lesbian activity took place beneath the jolly-hockeysticks facade of the soccer and hockey teams. In the early 1990s, though, the womens' softball league games at Bezuidenhout Park and Sturrock Park in Johannesburg constituted perhaps the largest outdoor gatherings of lesbians to be found in South Africa. In softball at least, the sporting women are no longer as closeted: large groups of lesbian friends accompany the players and picnic during proceedings.

In the women's softball league, there are white and some 'coloured' teams; given the popularity of soccer in black communities, however, the women's soccer league, which also has a strong lesbian flavour, is predominantly black. Unlike in softball, the teams themselves are racially mixed, and there are also three well-known township teams with predominantly-lesbian membership: the Mamelodi Sundowners from Pretoria, and Leeds United and the Soweto Women's Soccer Club or 'Gloria Team' from Soweto. But, given the newness of open lesbian culture in the townships, it is perhaps not surprising that the words of a member of the Gloria Team echo those of white women like Jackie and Hannah four decades previously: 'It is just so difficult to expose yourself that even there it is not always safe to come out to women you suspect are also gay.'[42]

In the Western Cape, the latest permutation of the famous District Six Netball Team, black men in drag who participated in the netball league in the 1950s and 1960s, is to be found in the Lavender Hill Netball Club on the Cape Flats. More conventionally, TOGS, the Transvaal Organisation for Gay Sport, competes every weekend with other members of the Transvaal Road-Runners Association. Says Jonathan Selvan, head of TOGS Roadrunners:

> *The presence of our members in the Transvaal Road-Runners Association has a profoundly political effect. The TOGS club is one of the backbones of the association, and everyone knows it is gay. And so, at every single road-runners meeting, TOGS puts forward a gay title. You could say we have our own gay march every weekend ... the presence of gay athletes helps break the stereotyped gay image. Of course, there are campy people in TOGS and they are very welcome — sometimes they are even our best sportsmen. But there are also a lot of regular guys. Our political message is that gay people can be sportsmen, and good ones at that too.*

It is worth restating here that, in a society where homosexual activity remains criminal, merely gathering for social or support reasons does constitute a profoundly political act. And so there is implicit politics in the sports teams; in the religious groups (not only Pretorius' church but also the GASA-era Gay Christian Community and Yachad, which still operate in Johannesburg); in the counselling and support services, like 6010 in Cape Town and the Gay Advice Bureau in Johannesburg; in the Cape Town Women's Centre, which existed briefly during 1992; in the gay-initiated HIV-support groups like Body Positive, Friends For Life and, most recently, the Gay Mens' Health Forum, formed in 1992 by Simon Nkoli.

Whatever their 'apolitical' claims, even the monthly PAWS parties, held on a rotating basis at private homes and spread by word of mouth through Johannesburg's white gay community, have a political function. So too the Spring Ball, which took place in 1990, at which 200 lesbians, including many older women, attended a party at Durban's Westridge Stadium. So too the Durban-based 'Company of Friends', a group of older women who got together, raised money by running a bar in a private home, and set up a corporation to buy a property on the South Coast to which they would all retire.

Much of this new openness is, of course, a product of the times. Certainly, there is evidence, since the unbanning of the liberation movements, that South Africa's censorship apparatus, relieved of the responsibility of 'protecting' South Africans from subversive political material, is trying to justify its continued existence by clamping down on homosexual material. Retief reports that a Cape Town lesbian and gay book distributor, Otherworld Books, is continually harassed. And, in early 1993, two safer-sex videos were banned, largely because of the explicit gay sex in one. Nevertheless, the unbanning of the liberation movements and the inevitable process of change since 1990 has meant a total collapse of the Afrikaner Calvinist hegemony that governed South Africa for five decades.

With the collapse of such stringent controls and the entry into a phase of 'transition', new space has been made for open lesbian and gay activity. It is no coincidence that the first pride march took place in 1990, just months after the unbanning of the liberation movements: it was a product of both euphoria at the possibility of a new dispensation and the practical fact that, since the ending of the States of Emergency that lasted from 1985 to 1990, protest marches were once more legal. While the new liberationist gay politics has its roots in the 1980s, and was set up in direct response to the 'apolitical' line of GASA and the moral imperatives of joining the broader anti-apartheid struggle, it is significant that this new politics only found popular support at the very moment of the collapse of the apartheid regime. It is as significant that this shift came about at the very moment black homosexual activity began to formalise into a flourishing township gay subculture.

'A rhythm of joy': Lesbian and gay subcultures in the townships

It is a November Saturday afternoon in kwaThema in late 1990, and it could be any weekend afternoon township party: 1970s disco sounds scratching through the static of an over-extended hi-fi system, the orange-and-white striped marquee in the yard, the plates of *pap* (stiff maize porridge), the laughter, the hostess barking genial orders from her chair. Look closer, though, and you'll notice that the guys are dancing with each other, vogueing a home-brew version of black gay American dance styles. In a corner, two women have salvaged a quiet space from the revelry to embrace, and on the *stoep* a group of teenage boys are earnestly discussing outfits for the next drag show.

The reason for the party is a meeting of the kwaThema chapter of GLOW. Over 20 years after those first, clandestine meetings of Law Reform in 1968, when white middle-class professionals got together to oppose legislation criminalising homosexuality, a group of young black gay men and lesbians party, on a township street, within full view of neighbours who pop over for a drink, and even send their children round for an afternoon of festivity. The hostess is a woman in her late 40s named Thoko Khumalo: she has a gay nephew and has declared herself to be Ma GLOW, 'the mother of the gay people'. Her home is a gay shebeen, a haven for the township's lesbian and gay youth. Of all the Reef's townships, kwaThema has, rather unexpectedly given its low-key and peri-urban nature, the largest and most visible gay population. This, says Simon Nkoli, is because 'kwaThema gays and lesbians have a place to go — Ma Thoko's.'[43]

British Sgxabai, an early black member of both GASA and The Saturday Group, began organising kwaThema in the early 1980s. He died in November 1991, of wounds incurred from a family feud over his sexuality — further proof that, despite the relative tolerance level in the township, being openly gay can be fatal. A year before his death, Sgxabai spoke of 'the early days' in kwaThema:

> When I first came out, being gay was unusual. But I knew a few people, and... got people to organise at my place. We'd make parties. There were about 30 of us. I'd invite guys from Daveyton and Kathlehong too. We'd march in the streets and we didn't give a damn. It was the early 1980s, and groups of us would walk defiantly through the streets of the township. It was the time when that disco song, 'I am what I am' was on the hit

parade and that gave us strength. We were confronting the com-
munity to take seriously the words of a song they all listened to
on the radio.[44]

McLean and Ngcobo describe the homosexual subculture that developed around the mines, and one of McLean and Ngcobo's older informants, Junior, recalls being in an all-male *stokvel* (credit union) in the early 1970s in which there was much homosexual activity. Based on his experience, Junior started an explicitly gay *stokvel*, the Jikaleza Boys, in 1991. (See 'Abangibhamayo bathi ngimnandi' in this volume)

From the early 1980s, there have been the traceable beginnings of gay organisation in the townships. With the advent of Simon Nkoli's black group within GASA, shebeens like Lee's Place and Mhlanga Rocks in Soweto became gathering places for gay people: just as white gay men 'turned' bars into gay haunts in the 1950s, black gay men were now transforming specifically-chosen shebeens into township gay hangouts. As with the bar-owners in the 1950s, the shebeen queens saw in this new clientele a regular and dependable source of income, and encouraged their patronage. As soon as gay people in a township had an identifiable place to go, more crept out of the closet. By 1993, Lee's Place and Mhlanga Rocks had closed down, but several others had emerged in townships around Johannesburg: Big Mike's in Soweto, the Swazi Inn in Thembisa and The Bold in Sebokeng. Parallel to this, as the cities began to desegregate, some previously-white gay venues started attracting increasingly black clienteles.

Nowhere, however, has a gay community become as much part of an African community's fabric as in kwaThema — aided in no small way (until her unexpected death in mid-1993) by Thoko Khumalo's vociferous sponsorship. Not only did the gay kids patronise Ma Thoko's, but they have 'taken over' several other venues in the township too: at a shebeen called Three One, for example, gay patronage is encouraged and welcomed. Says Lucky, one of kwaThema's gay youths: 'We bring Three One much business. Whenever we are there, the place comes alive. When we go out, our togetherness makes a rhythm of joy.'

As early as 1989, only months after its formation, the kwaThema GLOW chapter decided to transform the township's annual Penny-Penny Guy Fawkes Day at the kwaThema Community centre into a much-publicised Miss kwaThema GLOW drag competition. The youths rehearsed for months, more than 200 people came to watch, and the proceeds were donated to GLOW. Comments one participant: 'It wasn't just the gay people who came. Everyone knows that we are the best entertainment to be had in kwaThema and they love watching us.' Drag shows have become the central bonding point of gay township life, and it is the annual Miss GLOW finals, at which the winners from all the chapters compete, rather than the annual Pride March, that is the highlight of the black gay calendar on the reef. A precursor to Miss GLOW, organised by Linda Ngcobo, took place in 1987 and then, in 1988, the first Miss GLOW was held at the Mhlanga Rocks shebeen in Mofolo, Soweto. They have taken place annually ever since, and the last two — at Soweto's Ipelegeng Community Centre in 1991 and Champions Bar in 1992 — attracted around 30 entrants and over 1 000 spectators each.

68

A different fight for freedom

Most of the kwaThema chapter, like most of GLOW's 200-odd black membership, is under 25: evidence of the youthfulness of the budding township lesbian and gay subculture. Sgxabai explained this youthfulness:

People are freer now there's the pride of being oneself. Today's kids are more independent; more inquiring. I'm sure it had a lot to do with the independence that came with the liberation movement and the upheavals of the 1980s.[45]

McLean and Ngcobo note that the 1976 uprising had a similar impact on gay people of Sgxabai's generation, because it

shook society to its roots and, as a profound rupture of traditional hierarchies, had the effect of splitting young people from the roots and conventions of their elders. Suddenly, young people found themselves in opposition to many things their parents stood for — and this meant challenging not only conservative politics but all conservative mores.

Thus the current township gay scene has its roots in a generalised youth rebellion that found expression first in 1976 and then in the mid-1980s. And, once a white gay organisation took root in the 1980s and a collapse of rigid racial boundaries allowed greater interaction between township and city gay people, ideas of gay community filtered into the already-existent township gay networks. A few gay men and lesbians, like Nkoli, moved into Hillbrow. As the neighborhood started deracialising, they began patronising the gay bars and thus hooking in to the urban gay subculture — despite this subculture's patent racism. GLOW's kwaThema chapter was founded, for example, when a group of residents returned from the Skyline Bar with a copy of *Exit*: 'When we saw the publicity about this new non-racial group,' explains Manku Madux, a woman who, with Sgxabai, founded the chapter, 'we decided to get in touch with them to join.'

'Homosexuality is un-African': Homophobia and Black Consciousness

As gay township activity has become publicised, a backlash of sorts has emerged from the black nationalist tendency within the liberation movements, claiming, in the words of a much-quoted banner outside Winnie Mandela's kidnapping and assault trial in 1991, that 'Homosex Is Not In Black Culture' and that it is a decadent white contamination of black society. According to this particular strain of nationalism, homosexuality has been imported into black communities by inhuman labour systems, perverse priests, and white gay activists looking to expand their constituency and the validity of their cause. This ideology has its roots in the patriarchal notion that colonialism emasculated or feminized the black man, and therefore locates much of Black Power, quite bluntly, in the penis: in a remasculation, or reassertion of black virility.

While it is incontestable that the colonial project was emasculating, this ideology has had serious consequences for the politics of gender and sexuality

69

within South African liberation movements. Not only does it find homosexuality untenable (the image of an effeminate, limp-wristed 'stabane' — a man who wishes to be a woman — is obviously intensely threatening), but it also tends to negate the possibilities of female resistance and liberation, relegating women to the roles of mothers and wives of comrades rather than allowing them to be comrades themselves. There is thus more than a little irony to the fact that the most infamous avatar of the 'Homosexuality is un-African' ideology is Winnie Mandela, a woman who managed to use her Mother-of-the-Nation-and-Wife-of-the-Leader status to become an independent leader in her own right.

During her trial, a large part of Mandela's defense was predicated on the assertion that she was 'saving' black youths from the homosexual advances of white Methodist minister Paul Verryn. She buttressed this defence with the implication, made manifest in the words of the poster displayed outside her trial, that homosexuality was a condition alien to black society.

Mandela was not the first senior ANC official to code homosexuality as un-African: in 1987 National Executive Committee-member Ruth Mompati told the British publication *Capital Gay*, 'I cannot even begin to understand why people want gay rights. The gays have no problems. They have nice houses and plenty to eat. I don't see them suffering. No-one is persecuting them.'[46]

Quite apart from her blatant homophobia (in the same interview she asked, 'Tell me, are lesbians and gays normal? It is not normal. If everyone was like that the human race would come to an end.'), Mompati was giving expression to the notion that homosexuals do not need special rights because they are already well-off: in short, white. She could not accept that there might well be homosexuals living in those very oppressed black communities she had committed herself to liberate. Her comments created a storm of protest in the progressive British Anti-Apartheid Movement, and, a few months later, statements by other ANC officials attempted some damage control. Later, in 1991, largely due to the lobbying work of the Organisation of Lesbian and Gay Activists in Cape Town, the ANC Constitutional Committee included a clause specifically outlawing discrimination on the basis of sexual orientation in its draft Bill of Rights. The ANC Bill of Rights now entrenches 'the right not to be discriminated against or subject to harassment because of sexual orientation'.

Nevertheless, despite an angry open letter by GLOW to the ANC denouncing Winnie Mandela's homophobic defence, the ANC did not specifically condemn her defence, even though the draft Bill of Rights had already been published. This was not only because, at the time of her trial, Winnie Mandela was briefly rehabilitated within the ANC (Nelson Mandela had recently been released from prison and they were not yet separated), but also because, despite its commitment on paper to sexual equality, the ANC was not yet ready to assert that homosexuality might well be an organic part of African culture rather than an unpleasant reality imported by decadent white society.

In the 1990s, the leaders of two other liberation movements rendered the ideology behind this reticence explicit. Asked by *Exit* magazine in 1991 whether the Azanian Peoples' Organisation (AZAPO) had a policy on gay rights, national publicity secretary Strini Moodley responded: 'At this present time AZAPO does not consider homosexuality a priority. It seems to us that this phenomenon is largely affecting the more affluent sections of the community.'[47] As with Mompati's statement, Moodley expressed not only homophobia (the fact that homosexuality 'affects' sections of a community much as an epidemic might) but also the notion that this was an affliction to which the 'affluent' were particularly prone, much like consumption in the 19th Century.

The subtext of Moodley's statement was made even clearer in 1992, when Pan-Africanist Congress Secretary-General Bennie Alexander said that

> *homosexuality is un-African. It is part of the spin-off of the capitalist system. We should not take the European Leftist position on the matter. It should be looked at in its total perspective from our own Afrocentric position.*[48]

Alexander is not denying that homosexuality exists in African communities; rather, he is asserting that where it does exist it is a spinoff of apartheid capitalism. And in this assertion, he is aided and abetted, perhaps unwittingly, by a line of thought that runs through left-wing South African labour historiography: that the homosexual activity rife in mining hostels is the product of — or response to — the migrant labour system, the very cornerstone of apartheid capitalism. Men sleep with men in the hostels, the interpretation goes, because the hostels are unnatural prisons in which they have been wrenched away and cordoned off from their families and communities to work as slaves for the white economy.[49]

'Circumstantial homosexuality' is a reality in mining hostels as much as it is in prison, and there is much worth in the work that academics such as T Dunbar Moodie[50] and Patrick Harries have done in documenting the play of sexuality in these slave-quarters. Harries, in particular, recognised the subversive and pleasurable possibilities of these homosexual relationships, writing that they

> *reflected a forceful rejection of employers' demands that miners invest their libidinal energies in their work and that they value the virtues of sexual restraint. The homosexual relationship contradicted the imposed morality of industrialism and established an alternative propriety. These gender relationships provided workers with their own sense of hierarchy and status and with their own indices of prestige, power and pride. Bukhontxana (thigh-fucking) gave men a sense of security, upward mobility and self-worth in the constrained world of the colonist.*[51]

But McLean and Ngcobo take issue with the notion that mine-sex stopped at thigh-fucking, documenting accounts of less-ambiguous penetrative anal sex too. They also document, for the first time, the workings of African homosexuality outside the mining compounds, and they criticise Moodie for 'falling short' by making male sexuality on the mine seem to be *rather too much like a mechanical and necessary substitution for heterosexual life in a situation where there are no women. [Moodie] makes no real concession to the fact that some men may in fact have enjoyed sex with other men or might even prefer it to having sex with women.*

The analysis of circumstantial homosexuality has been subsequently used — by people like Alexander — as a metaphor for all that is wrong and unnatural with an undeniably heinous system. The fact that formal gay activity in the townships only took place after the establishment of white organisations like GASA, and that the anti-apartheid activists who have impelled the ANC to take on issues of sexual equality are almost exclusively white only lends substance to the ideology.

But it is entirely wrong to suppose that homosexual activity in the townships is a recent phenomenon, imported by white gay activists and 'dinge queens' (gay slang for white men who desire black men); indeed, black gay men and lesbians protest that such an analysis robs them of the agency for their own desire. Despite the recent upsurge of a township gay scene, homosexual activity — if not lesbian and gay organisation — has existed in black societies from long before the advent of formal white organisation, and certainly predates the founding of GLOW in 1988 or of Simon Nkoli's Saturday Group in 1984. As early as 1955, for example, *Drum Magazine* reported that the Cato Manor shantytown, outside Durban, was the place 'Where Men Are Wives'. According to Chetty, 'within the shantytown, *Esinyameni*, the Place of Darkness, was identified as the centre of Sodom where at one time colourful marriage ceremonies frequently took place.'

In Cape Town there has been an identifiable and public black gay subculture since at least 1950: although this subculture is rooted in coloured communities, it has always included a few African men: Chetty, for example, cites the case of David 'Lulu' Masikana, a famous African drag queen who participated in the Cape Carnival in 1963. Indeed, in the 1950s when apartheid was just beginning to be institutionalised, the distinction between 'African' and 'coloured' was almost negligible, particularly in the Western Cape. Hybrid though their roots may be, coloured people are embraced as Africans by some of the very adherents of Africanism who decry homosexuality as 'un-African'. Bennie Alexander, for example, comes from the very same hybrid stock as the coloured moffies that Chetty proves to be so integral a part of Western Cape culture: if they are 'un-African', so is he.

Western Cape history notwithstanding, there is also some evidence of rural African homosocial activity that exists independent of the migrant labour system and that is entrenched in traditional tribal hierarchy: the Lovedu Rain Queen in the Northern Transvaal is a hereditary leader who keeps as many as 40 wives. There is some work being done on the phenomenon of lesbian sangomas, and there has also been some documentation of an instance of lesbianism in rural Southern African culture: the 'mummy-baby' relationships that anthropologist Judith Gay recorded in Lesotho, in which relationships between young girls and slightly older ones include a form of sexual initiation and the basis for a lifelong support structure outside of heterosexual marriage.[52] Gay Africanism, a discourse only in the very early stages of development in South Africa, maintains that it is the censure of homosexuality that is a colonial import, brought to this continent by missionaries, and that there is irony to the fact that latter-day Africanists have assimilated this Judeo-Christian biblical propaganda and reconstructed it as pre-colonial African purity.

Whatever its roots, however, it must be conceded that homosexuality is as taboo in many African cultures as it is in many Western cultures. But the some-times-violent censure of homosexuality within black cultures must not be confused as evidence for the non-existence of homosexuality: the very fact of censure indicates that it exists.

Six
Lesbian and gay politics in the 1990s

Sexual Politics and the politics of liberation

The ideology of the new alignment of liberationist lesbian and gay politics is perhaps best expressed by a manifesto, drafted by GLOW, which has been used for the annual Johannesburg Pride Marches. The manifesto calls upon 'All South Africans who are Committed to a Non-Racist, Non-Sexist, Non-Discriminatory Democratic Future' to:

— *UNITE in the fight for the basic human rights of all South Africans, including lesbians and gay men.*

— *MOBILIZE against discrimination.*

— *ASSERT the role of lesbians and gay men in the current process of political change.*

— *CONFRONT South Africa with the presence of its lesbian and gay community.*

— *DISPEL MYTHS nurtured by years of discrimination and stereotyping.*

The manifesto then goes on to issue ten 'challenges', including a challenge to Parliament to 'decriminalise homosexuality'; a challenge to the law to 'recognise longstanding lesbian and gay relationships by giving them all the benefits afforded heterosexual couples'; a challenge to political organisations 'to support a Charter that protects lesbian and gay people from discrimination'; and a challenge to the liberation movement 'to embrace the struggle for lesbian and gay liberation as part of its commitment to free society from all forms of oppression'.

Immediately, we note not only a shift in rhetoric (the use of words like 'confront' and 'challenge', and the embrace of concepts like 'non-racist', 'non-sexist' and 'non-discriminatory'), but also of targets. This new agenda calls, as did past gay agendas, for legal reform and the dispelling of myths, but it also confronts the current process of political change head-on, calling upon lesbians and gays to 'assert their role' in this process and challenging the process, too, to take cognisance of the need for lesbian and gay rights. In fact, by challenging the liberation movement directly to 'embrace the struggle for gay and lesbian liberation', this new movement sets itself up in direct dialogue with organisations like the ANC in a way that the white gay organisations would have found untenable a decade earlier.

Certainly, there is strategy as well as conviction behind such an approach: just as the Law Reform movement of 1968 positioned itself 'within the National Party' because it saw that as the best way of gaining results, the new lesbian and gay liberation movement is positioning itself within the broad anti-apartheid coalition because it understands that the ANC will be the future government and it recognises, as no gay movement has before, the value in courting this sector.

74

This approach has paid off. Running parallel (and largely due) to the shift in lesbian and gay politics, the African National Congress has included gay rights in its pantheon of human rights, thereby bringing the call for gay liberation into the mainstream of political activity in South Africa. More recently, other political parties have followed the ANC's initiative in proposing specific constitutional protection for gays and lesbians, and in 1993, the multiparty negotiating forum approved a draft constitution that included a clause outlawing discrimination on the basis of sexual orientation.

There are several reasons for the ANC's acceptance of the principle of equality for gay people, firstly and most importantly, the dogged insistent lobbying of the Cape Town activists in LAGO and OLGA. Perhaps OLGA's most important symbolic action on this score was to apply, in 1989, for affiliation to the United Democratic Front, the broad-based coalition of grassroots movements that led the anti-apartheid struggle in the 1980s. A member of the Western Cape UDF Regional Executive, who was present at the meeting at which OLGA's application was considered, remembers its impact:

> Sheila Lapinsky was a well-known activist in the region, but when she entered the UDF meeting with this OLGA application, there was a range of responses, from giggles to disbelief. I think most of the regional executive saw this gay thing as a 'white thing'. But they dealt with the proposal seriously and responsibly, and I think it helped enormously that OLGA's people, like Lapinsky and [Ivan] Toms, had such credibility as comrades. And so OLGA's application was accepted, for moral and strategic reasons: moral, because OLGA motivated the worthiness of its cause, and strategic, because the whole point of the UDF was to make its constituency as broad as possible.

Another major reason for this new-found acceptability of gay politics was Simon Nkoli's coming out during the Delmas Treason Trial: as Nkoli records in his memoirs, his interaction during the trial with senior UDF officials like Popo Molefe and Terror Lekota had a major impact on their thinking. And, while work of local lesbian and gay activists aided the cause within South Africa, ANC members in exile were being exposed to what the PAC's Alexander calls 'the European Leftist position on the matter'. Liberal European notions of gender rights and the political legitimacy of gay rights had immense impact on senior ANC lawyers like Albie Sachs and Kader Asmal, who have hence become gay issues' strongest lobbyists within the ANC. And the storm that surrounded Ruth Mompati's homophobic statements to *Capital Gay* in 1987, coupled with the fact that many of the British and particularly Dutch Anti-Apartheid Movement's most committed officials were gay, persuaded many senior ANC officials in Europe of the moral imperatives of equal rights for gays and lesbians.

Nevertheless, given the evidence up to 1993, it would be premature to suppose that the lesbian and gay movement can be assured of support from a future ANC government. Official ANC support of gay issues has been at worst grudging and at best half-hearted; the Winnie Mandela issue being a case in point. While senior ANC office-bearers have sent messages of support to the annual Pride Marches (including one from secretary-general Cyril Ramaphosa in 1991), they have evaded repeated invitations to address or participate in the marches. Support on paper might be acceptable, but open and public identification is not. One senior ANC official explains that 'while the leadership might have accepted gay rights, the people have not. We have to be conscious of this. Our priority at the moment is winning an election.'

Indeed, while high-profile activists like Nkoli might be able to remain within the ANC as openly gay people, grassroots members of the ANC continue to work within a liberation culture that remains profoundly sexist and patriarchal. Thulani, for example, is a member of the kwaThema GLOW chapter and student activist on the East Rand. He recalls:

> When I was a member of my school's Students' Representative Council in 1987, my comrades were suspicious because I didn't have two or three girlfriends like the rest of them. So the rumour went round that I was gay, and they tried to expel me.

Since that experience, he has remained outside of ANC youth structures because 'I am scared I will encounter the same problems.'[53] In the early 1980s, Nkoli, who was on the regional executive committee of South African Students, encountered similar problems, also arising from the fact that he did not have the requisite status as a womaniser. Once it was discovered he was gay, a special meeting of the entire region was called to discuss the issue. He managed to retain his position because of his credentials and the support given to him by one or two friends who were, by then, national leaders of the student movement.

As gay issues gain credibility and lesbian and gay comrades come out, this situation is slowly changing: even if ANC leaders do not show public support for the pride marches, the ANC's official position has forced the organisation to at the very least consider the issue. The ANC journal, *Mayibuye*, has featured the issue quite prominently[54] and local branches have sent contingents and banners to the pride march, adopted resolutions condemning the homophobia in Winnie Mandela's trial, and arranged for meetings to be held with lesbian and gay activists. Most of these, however, are urban branches with large white memberships: while the Yeoville or Observatory branches of the ANC might be considering the rights of homosexuals, the issue remains unspoken within the township structures of the organisation.

Nevertheless, a milestone event occurred in late 1992, when Funeka Soldaat, an ANC Youth League activist in Khayelitsha, outside Cape Town, joined ABIGALE and facilitated interaction between the organisation and the Youth League. Thami Magelana, a Youth League leader in the township, recalls that

> Funeka suggested a meeting to discuss the issue of homosexuality. And it was fascinating to hear the youth ask questions once they got over their initial shock. And as a result they have committed themselves to help Funeka be open and fight for the

rights of lesbians and gays. They actually said they would give help in terms of organising lesbians and gays in the township and encouraging them to be open and accepted by the community.[55]

Since then, ABIGALE has been working hand-in-hand with the ANC in Khayelitsha, and, by mid-1993, the organisation had recruited dozens of new members in the township.

The new style and ideology of the lesbian and gay liberation movement in the 1990s has also vastly increased media exposure of homosexual issues in the country. In the 1950s and 1960s, as noted previously, the public image of the homosexual swung between the freak-show drag queen and the criminal child-molester. The 1968 Parliamentary debate over whether homosexuals should be further criminalised, widely reported in the media, only underscored this latter image. In the 1970s, media coverage was characterised by sensational exposes of the sordidness and sadness of supposedly 'gay' life, which was seen to be both dangerous (repeated accounts of 'gay murders' have graced the pages of South African newspapers since the 1940s) and decadent, particularly as the druggy and oversexed club-scene blossomed at the end of the decade. In the 1980s, this picture of danger and decadence was tinged with the new colour of retribution, with 'tragic tales' of gay 'AIDS Victims', even though, with the advent of GASA, the media did begin to give a 'political' angle to gay stories rather than simply consigning them to the 'human-interest' pages.

Certainly, the 1990s have seen a fair share of the kind of sensationalism that has characterised the coverage of homosexuals since the 1950s. With a recent spate of cruising-related murders in Cape Town and at the Zoo Lake and Emmarentia Dam in Johannesburg, violent death has become, once more, an over-used trope for the dangers of gay existence. And, after the first pride march in 1990, both the Sunday papers and TV newscasts were filled, not unsurprisingly, with images of the most extravagant drag queens present. But, since 1990, there has been an astonishing change in the nature of coverage, particularly on national television.

Following the 1992 march, both Agenda and Newsline, the news magazine programmes of TV1 and CCV-TV respectively, broadcast in-depth documentaries on homosexuality in South Africa with a respect that would have been unheard-of a couple of years ago. Gay rights was dealt with as a political issue worthy of serious debate rather than as a 'humour-piece' served to lighten up the regular diet of riots, upheaval and violence. Furthermore, attempts were made to present images not of freaks or perverts, but of people who just happen to be attracted to members of the same gender. The Newsline documentary highlighted images of couples at the March holding hands or embracing rather than images of drag and excess, and, according to a senior programmer at TV-news, the Agenda documentary on gay relationships 'went out of its way to find normal-looking couples who your average viewer would be able to identify with.'

There is an obviously loaded ideology behind the very notion of the search for a 'normal-looking' gay person. Certainly, the domesticated 'straight-acting' gay couple is a remedial and positive image of homosexuality in a society saturated with images of queens and child-molesters. But it is also a safe image, easier to digest precisely because it is less threatening to the patriarchal and conservative gender-role values upon which this society is built. Nonetheless, there has been a clear attempt to give 'free and fair' coverage to homosexual issues. This is a response not only to the new high profile of lesbian and gay politics (through the pride march), but also to the fact that this politics has, since the unbanning of the liberation movements in 1990, gained a new respectability on the left — and thus a new legitimacy.

Support vs activism:
Internal dilemmas of the lesbian and gay movement

Despite these advances, there was, in the early 1990s, nothing approaching the national network that GASA was able to cobble together in the early 1980s. During the late 1980s, there was an unsuccessful attempt to coalesce all the progressive lesbian and gay groups into an organisation called the Congress of Pink Democrats; more recently, the groups have realigned in a campaign to develop a Charter for Lesbian and Gay Rights. This too has been largely unsuccessful, for a major division exists within this new grouping of progressive, explicitly political organisations: the division between the social needs of members and the political imperatives of fighting for rights. Thus this new alignment is fluid and unstable, and is wrought by the very same dilemmas that have hobbled gay organisation for decades in South Africa. As formal gay South African organisation moves from its small white middle-class enclave into the broader society, and as it becomes more political in its demands and approaches, it faces precisely the same dilemmas that existed during the GASA years: how to provide effective public advocacy for sexual equality while at the same time providing for the more basic needs of its own constituency.

This dilemma is highlighted by GLOW's experience. Taking its lead from OLGA in the Western Cape, GLOW was founded on two principles: to 'build a gay and lesbian organisation that was nonracial and democratic in character' and to 'call on the gay and lesbian community to organise against all forms of discrimination'.[56] Almost immediately, this new agenda appealed to two very different communities: a city-based group of older largely-white activists on the one hand, and a township-based group of young black people on the other.

The former group became involved because, like those activists who had formed LAGO in Cape Town two years previously, they were disenchanted with the 'apolitical' line of mainstream gay organisation and wished to marry the gay rights movement to the larger human rights struggle in South Africa. Certainly, in this lot were to be found black activists like Simon Nkoli and, later, Tanya Chan-Sam. But the majority of GLOW's new black members — and thus the majority of GLOW itself — are young people for whom the organisation has a primarily — and much needed — social function. These are people who, despite the relative upsurge of gay venues in the townships and the fact that blacks are more welcome than before in gay bars in the city, still find in GLOW gatherings one of the only 'safe places' to 'be themselves'; to meet friends and romantic partners. In this way, they bear a striking resemblance to the white gay men who joined GASA in droves in the early 1980s — with a couple of major exceptions.

Firstly, the fact that these black people, unlike GASA's white members, come from a highly politicised culture and environment, where words like 'struggle' and 'rights' are part of the daily lexicon, means that they are amenable to the liberationist politics that GLOW embraces, even if their primary interest in the organisation is social. Secondly, unlike their white predecessors in GASA, much of GLOW's black membership is of the African urban working-class. For gay people, human rights means, first and foremost, the right to privacy. This is difficult enough for white middle-class people who have the means to live independently, but it is almost impossible in the township where economic conditions and cultural norms dictate that most young black South Africans, gay or straight, remain within the walls of their overcrowded family homes. The political space of an organisation like GLOW is thus fraught with personal and social needs.

The division between 'activist' and 'support' functions is complicated by racial issues; by the fact that many black gay people recently out of the closet often feel alienated by the social ethos and intellectualism of the activist groups. Medi Achmat, a working-class coloured woman from Cape Town, explains why she and a few others founded ABIGALE in 1992:

> Black and coloured working-class people didn't feel at home in GASA because it was so white and middle-class. Then OLGA came along, and we didn't feel at home there either. Even though they were part of the United Democratic Front and strictly anti-apartheid, they were still white and middle-class. Black people who went along found it too intellectual. No-one in OLGA took the time to explain the basics. It was all politics and no support. And so we decided to start ABIGALE as way of introduction for black people who have never before been part of a gay organisation.

As with the GLOW, which always links its Annual General Meetings to the far more popular Miss GLOW competition, ABIGALE makes a point of disguising more explicitly political or organisational activity as social gatherings. Says Achmat:

> Our members, particularly the coloureds and blacks, don't want to sit in meetings. They want to socialise, and they have no space for this. So we have get-togethers, like bring-and-braais, and then everyone comes. Then in the middle of the festivities we'll have a meeting. And it doesn't matter if they're drunk. Actually it's better. That way we get more out of them!

This activist/socialising division should not, however, be viewed solely as a black-white split. Kleinbooi notes, for example, that his feelings of alienation from the largely-white Gay and Lesbian Association (GALA) at the University of Cape

Town had more to do with a difference in political culture than with the fact that whites wanted to be 'political' and blacks 'social'. In fact, Kleinbooi's experience was the very opposite: GALA's political activism, he maintains, was merely the cover for social activity from which he felt alienated because it was white and middle-class. Similarly, many political activists in organisations like GLOW and ABIGALE make no bones about the fact that these organisations do serve very important social functions, and that only assume more activist roles after they have taken care of more immediate psychological and social needs.

The GLOW Lesbian Forum is a case in point of the primacy of support functions over activist ones. The group was founded from a lesbian-feminist perspective and was intent on providing a safe space for women as well as lobbying for lesbian issues within a male-dominated organisation. But perhaps because of this very male domination, it became a place where lesbians — particularly young ones just out of the closet — could find support and seek mentors. Kim Berman, who was involved in setting up the Forum, comments that

> *we had no option but look after the immediate needs of our members; women who were very traumatised by having been rejected by their families. Almost every black teenager in the group had made at least one suicide attempt, and there was nowhere to refer them to. And so we became their support-structure, a sort of Lesbians Anonymous. Of course this is critical work. But it meant we had to put more expressly political concerns on hold.*

The history of Sunday's Women, a Durban-based organisation of white women formed in the tradition of the American lesbian-feminist consciousness-raising groups of the 1970s, is fraught with similar dilemmas. The group started meeting in March 1989 because, says founder Leigh Phipson,

> *when I graduated from university and started working, I panicked a bit. I thought, how was I ever going to meet anyone? I wasn't into Images (a Durban bar frequented by lesbians), and I wanted an informal group of friends. So I set up Sunday's Women as a reading group for women, but also, very importantly, as a place where I could meet future girlfriends.*

For over two years, Sunday's Women met twice-monthly at 'bring-and-share' gatherings: around 25 women would meet, eat, socialise, and then take part in an issue-based discussion. The group was very successful, and brought out a high-quality monthly newsletter which, by 1992, had over 80 subscribers. But the conflict over political versus social functions dominated discussion from the outset, and eventually, once Sunday's Women decided to align itself formally with progressive organisations and take part in the pride marches, several members left the group. The social aspect of Sunday's Women was, in fact, a major contributor to the group's eventual collapse in July 1992. Says Phipson:

The problem was, a lot of our members became involved in re-
lationships, and when these broke up, it became too painful for
either one or other member of the couple to come to meetings.
Or on the other hand, a lot of women would join Sunday's
Women just to meet lovers. And as soon as they coupled off,
that was the last we saw of them.

ABIGALE seems to have been more successful in fusing social support and activist
functions. Even though its 100-strong membership is largely-male, it is led and run
by a lesbian couple, Achmat and her lover, who see themselves as *'die moffies se*
ma's' (the moffie's mothers). According to Achmat,

most of our members have been cast out, so they are looking
for family, and the thing that binds them to ABIGALE is com-
mitment to family. And so we are trying, unlike our own parents
and all the parents of our members, to be good mothers.

Achmat acknowledges that this maternal assignation places a lot of difficult emotional pressure on her: her inner-city apartment, for example, has become
something of a doss-house for ABIGALE members from the Cape Flats who need
sanctuary — or just a place to crash after a night at the club. ABIGALE plans to
establish a shelter and skills-training programme for Cape Town's gay men and
lesbians who are either homeless or unemployed or both: that, says Achmat, will
take some of the pressure off her and Trish. And, she adds,

any good mother's job is to teach her children how to care for
themselves and each other. I make a point about teaching
ABIGALE members to kiss and hug each other, to be affection-
ate. That way, they can begin to take over some of the support
work I do.

Like the 6010 group before them in Cape Town, the ABIGALE activists see this
social support work as a vital primary stage in lesbian and gay organisation, and
maintain that more explicitly political work can only take place after it has been
done: ABIGALE, says Achmat, is

not really a political thing. The idea is to make people feel
comfortable, to give them support and space. The political iden-
tity will follow later, only once they have taken care of basic
needs can our members become political activists.

Conclusion: 'We want people to feel free'

Despite Medi Achmat's description of ABIGALE as 'not really a political thing',
the group had become, by 1993, South Africa's fastest-growing and most strident
gay action group, and was beginning to become involved in more direct political
activism. In April 1993, ABIGALE picketed Strawbs, Cape Town's most popular
gay club, because of provable instances of a racist door policy.

The Strawbs controversy is proof that the racism Simon Nkoli experienced
in gay clubs in the early 1980s still exists: even after the collapse of formal apart-

heid, racial divisions continue to dominate lesbian and gay communities just as they do all aspects of South African life. While the possibilities of cross-racial communication are greater, black people remain marginal to the formal white sub-culture, and insofar as there is now a township gay subculture, this exists parallel to — rather than integrated within — urban gay life.

One consequence of the continued racism of the white gay subculture is illustrated by the widely-held perception within it that the annual pride march is a 'black affair', even though, in 1992, a full 75% of the participants were white. Publicity campaigns in gay bars like Champions and Connections have revealed that the majority of white gay men who participate in Johannesburg's mainstream commercial gay subculture stay away from the march because they find it 'too political', too closely linked to the ANC, and — quite bluntly — too black. For many white gay people, then, 'black' and 'political' are conflated in a perception that links current-day gay activism to black liberationist politics: this liberationism not only heightens their fear of disclosure, but, through its association with the aspirations of South Africa's black majority, runs counter to their own deeply-entrenched conservatism.

But while most white middle-class gay people stay away, so too do most black working-class gays and lesbians. And this points, most strongly, to the dilemma in which current progressive lesbian and gay politics now finds itself: its expressly liberationist ideology alienates the conservative white gay subculture while its expressly political profile does not talk directly to the interests of recently unclosetted gay men and lesbians from the townships who need social space and support.

Perhaps this dilemma will resolve itself with the diversification of activities that will inevitably accompany the maturation of lesbian and gay subcultures in South Africa. It would be unrealistic to expect all these subcultures — the sports groups, the activist groups, the religious groups, the bar and shebeen scenes — to find common ground before having established themselves, firmly and irrevocably, in their own respective rights.

But that just leads to another dilemma. On the one hand, this country's lesbian and gay subcultures have not yet matured to the point of being able to constitute an effective, coherent and united political minority. But on the other hand, because South Africa is at a moment of profound constitutional change, there is the urgency for that kind of united lobby to make its presence felt right now, as right now is when the terms of a future South Africa are being negotiated, and whatever rights are negotiated in this window-period of transition will see South Africa well into the next century.

In May 1990, only months after the unbanning of the liberation movements, ANC constitutional lawyer Albie Sachs spoke at an OLGA press conference in Cape Town and said:

> *What has happened to lesbian and gay people is the essence of apartheid — it tried to tell people who they were, how they should behave, what their rights were. The essence of democ-*

racy is that people should be free to be what they are. We want people to feel free.

Sachs' sentiments are, three years later, still not entirely shared by his own comrades, not to mention the other parties sitting around the negotiating table. Neither are they shared by most of the other major opinion-formers in the country: in this overwhelmingly religious land, not even the more liberal English-speaking churches have taken an unequivocal stand supportive of homosexual rights. At this putative moment of concern for the rights of all South Africans, any call for gay rights sounds shrill, self-interested and with the potential to detract from the larger struggle for democracy. Even in Sach's own formulation — 'people should be free to be what they are' — one can hear the cadences of a liberalism that seems rather frivolous when compared with the more pressing issues of the powerless, landless, economically underprivileged black majority.

How, then, to resolve all the above dilemmas? Certainly, a partial answer is to be found in the agreement at the constitutional negotiations, to protect gay people in a future Bill of Rights. An equal rights provision in a new democratic constitution could provide the basis for local government allocating funds and space for community centres; or the basis for airtime on public television; or, most important, the basis for a review of laws that discriminate against homosexuals. All of the above would not only raise public consciousness about the issues facing gays and lesbians, but might also serve to activate an effective national political minority out of a disjointed range of subcultures. We might see, once more, the power of 'the gay vote' as experienced in the 1987 white Parliamentary elections, except this time with a broader base and sounder political agenda.

In the meanwhile, the bonding-agents of community — the sports clubs, counselling centres, religious groups, bars, clubs and social networks — will continue to make space. And activists from within this community will continue to organise slowly-growing pride marches, lobby political parties, recruit members and make noise. There might not be a 'gay moment', as there was in 1993 in the United States, with a President courting 'the gay vote' and nailing his colours (albeit falteringly) to gay issues, but there are — and will continue to be — a series of 'gay moments' in which homosexual South Africans assert themselves: on sports fields, in shebeens, in industry, in academics, in the law, in the media, on the streets. There will continue to be moments, growing slowly in number and less fraught with the anxieties of disclosure, in which lesbian and gay South Africans will be able to imbibe Sachs' 'essence of democracy' and feel safe enough to be 'free to be what they are'.

Which brings us back to Phiri Hall on Saturday 13 February 1993. Linda Ngcobo's funeral was one of the only expressions of true democracy I have ever experienced in this hitherto undemocratic land. For there, even as they paraded their difference before an intimidating crowd of swaying congregationists, hundreds of gay people asserted, incontrovertibly, that they were part of a community: part of the community that had come to bury Linda Ngcobo. They took up their rightful place in the hall, at the microphone, beside the coffin, beside the grave. And thus they made sure that Linda Ngcobo — their Linda Ngcobo, the gay Linda Ngcobo, the activist Linda Ngcobo, the drag-queen Linda Ngcobo — will live and breathe freely in a future South Africa. What a tragic and ironic shame that Ngcobo himself won't be here to see it.

Notes

* Unless otherwise noted, all quotes are from personal interviews held between January and May 1993.

1 For an excellent synthesis of this debate, see Martin Duberman, Martha Vicinus and George Chauncey Jr. eds, *Hidden From History: Reclaiming the Gay and Lesbian Past* (Penguin, 1991), Introduction.

2 *Natal Daily News*, 23 July 1956.

3 See John D'Emilio, 'Gay Politics and Community in San Francisco Since World War II', in *Hidden From History*, p459. D'Emilio deals with the construction of gay communities in the United States more extensively in *Sexual Politics, Sexual Communities: The Making of a Homosexual Minority in the United States, 1940-1970* (Chicago, 1983). An excellent account of the makings of gay community in Britain is to be found in Jeffrey Weeks, *Coming Out: Homosexual Politics in Britain from the 19th Century to the Present* (London, 1977).

4 See Allan Berubé, 'Marching to a Different Drummer: Lesbian and Gay GIs in World War II', in *Hidden from History*.

5 For an account of how this has worked in South Africa, see Gordon Isaacs and Brian McKendrick, *Male Homosexuality in South Africa: Identity Formation, Culture and Crisis* (Cape Town, 1992).

6 See Elizabeth Lapousky Kennedy and Madeline D Davis, 'Boots of Leather, Slippers of Gold', in *The History of a Lesbian Community* (New York and London, 1993). The Canadian documentary film, *Forbidden Love*, also offers a vivid portrait of North American lesbian communities in the era, particularly in Vancouver.

7 *Sunday's Women*, September 1990.

8 D'Emilio notes that these organisations cultivated an image of middle-class respectability and worked for social change through 'the good offices of professionals. They saw their task primarily as one of educating the professionals who influenced public opinion and only secondarily as one of organising lesbians and gay men.' (*Hidden From History*, p460)

9 *Cape Times,* 19 March 1969.

10 *The Cape Argus,* 18 March 1969.

11 *The Friend*, 19 March 1969.

12 *Rand Daily Mail*, 26 April 1969.

13 Quoted in Willem and Evanthe Schurink, 'Some Characteristics of the Homosexual Subculture as Reflected by a South African Gay Club', paper of the Human Sciences Research Council, p11. The Schurinks have done an astonishing amount of work on gay (largely white and Afrikaans) subcultures in South Africa. See also 'Die Gay Assosiasie van Suid-Afrika: 'n Sociologiese Beskouing' (HSRC:1986); 'Gayness: A Sociological Perspective' (HSRC: 1986); and *AIDS: Lay perceptions of a group of gay men* (HSRC: 1990).

14 *Exit*, July/August 1987.

15 *Natal Daily News*, 20 April 1972.

16 *Natal Daily News*, 18 May 1972.

17 Leonie Woolfson, 'Aetiological and Personality Factors Relating to Homosexual Behaviour in Adult Females', Masters thesis, UNISA, 1975.

18 Just under three years later, at the beginning of 1981, a second report into lesbianism was to be published, this time by W.J. Schurink, *Gay Vroue: n Sosoiologiese Verkenning van die Leefwyse van n Aantal Lesbiers aan die Hand van Outobiographiese Sketse*, (HSRC, 1981). Coming from a state research organisation, the report unexpectedly offered some particularly enlightened

conclusions: most notably that lesbians had a very high self-image and level of self-acceptance. Both the Woolfson and the Schurink reports are based on extensive interviews with white women; in 1992, however, a Ph.D thesis (C Potgieter-Theys, 'The Gender Construction and Social Identity of Black South African Lesbian Women', University of Cape Town, 1992) dealt explicitly with black lesbians.

19 *The Star*, 21 July 1979.
20 *The Star*, 1 September 1979.
21 *The Star*, 28 May 1980.
22 WJ Beaumont, 'Thoughts on Gay Pop Culture in South Africa', unpublished paper, 1992.
23 *The Star*, 9 January 1982.
24 *The Star*, 28 October 1982.
25 *Link/Skakel*, December 1982.
26 *The Star*, 4 April 1983.
27 *Rand Daily Mail*, 8 November 1982.
28 *The Star*, 4 April 1983.
29 Cited in *The Star*, 1 May 1983.
30 *The Star*, 29 November 1985.
31 *Weekly Mail*, 12-18 October 1990.
32 *Capital Gay*, cited in *Link/Skakel*, September 1983.
33 'GASA-6010 Turns 10", *Exit*, August/September 1991.
34 'AIDS Panic is Overstressed', *Link/Skakel*, No 0110, February 1983.
35 John Pegge, Gordon Isaacs and Stephen Miller, 'Networking: A Prevention and Care Strategy for the Gay Minority in South Africa', paper presented to the Xth International Conference on AIDS, Montreal, 1991, p1.
36 *The Star*, March 1985.
37 *The Star*, 14 August 1985.
38 Reported in *Exit*, March 1986.
39 By 1993, the fund had accrued to more than R120 000, and, in that year, the trustees made over the assets to a new trust which will focus on lobbying the constitutional process to ensure a lesbian and gay equality clause in South Africa's new constitution.
40 *Exit*, June/July 1987.
41 *Weekly Mail*, 13 September 1991.
42 Kim Berman, 'Lesbians in SA: Challenging the Invisibility' in M Krouse and K Berman eds, *The Invisible Ghetto: Lesbian and Gay Writing from South Africa* (COSAW, 1993), pxvii.
43 This and all following information on kwaThema was originally reported in 'Township gays find a haven at Ma Thoko's', *Weekly Mail*, 10 November 1990, and 'Will British Sgxabai be the gay Biko?', *Weekly Mail*, 22 January 1991. 'Ma Thoko' died unexpectedly in 1993.
44 *Glow Letter*, April 1992, p2.
45 *Glow Letter*, April 1992, p2.
46 *Capital Gay*, 18 September 1987.
47 *Exit*, December 1991.
48 *Work In Progress (incorporating New Era)*, no 82, June 1992, p13.
49 See Charles van Onselen, *The Small Matter of a Horse* (Ravan Press, 1984) for an account of another form of homosexuality in black all-male societies. Van Onselen documents the way members of a gang in the 1920s practised homosexuality as a way of community bonding.
50 T Dunbar Moodie et al, 'Migrancy and Male Sexuality on the South African Gold Mines', in *Hidden from History*.
51 Patrick Harries, 'Symbols and Sexuality: Culture and Identity on the early Witwatersrand Gold Mines', *Gender and History*, 2:3, p333.
52 J Gay, '"Mummies and Babies" and Friends and Lovers in Lesotho', in E Blackwood ed, *Anthropology and Homosexual Behaviour* (Haworth Press, 1986).
53 *Weekly Mail*, 10 November 1990.

54 See Mbali Mncadi, 'The Right to Choose: Gay and Lesbian Rights', *Mayibuye*, July 1992.
55 From video footage taken by Zackie Achmat and Jack Lewis.
56 Graeme Reid, 'A Brief History of GLOW', unpublished paper 1992.

TWO —
Where we stand:
Moffies and the laager

'Unapprehended felons':
Gays and lesbians and the law in South Africa

Edwin Cameron

Assertion, evidence and inference: holding homosexuals to the law

CASE ONE: The white policeman and the black youth

Assertion: If the law falls upon you as a gay man, you may lose your job, your family and perhaps your future.

Evidence: In 1965, a white policeman from a farming town in Natal, nearing 50 and with 27 years' service in the South African Police, had a fallout with his wife. She threatened to leave him. He took off in his car on an alcoholic binge. On the outskirts of Pietermaritzburg he drove up to a group of black men. He told them he wanted a woman. One of the men, a youngster of 15 or 16, then got into the car with him. The policeman undid his fly buttons and lay on top of the boy. He put his penis between the boy's legs and was later seen, as the court put it, 'going through the motions of sexual intercourse'. He was arrested and arraigned in court. He lost his job and his pension. His wife started divorce proceedings against him. A magistrate sent him to jail. Two Supreme Court judges suspended the jail sentence. The fact that the young boy was black was not considered to be an additionally aggravating circumstance and they saw grounds to be merciful. The policeman did 'not normally behave in this way'. He did not set out to pervert the morals of a young person. It did not appear from the evidence that he had a 'tendency to perversion'. What happened was 'a temporary aberration', and all the 'quite appalling consequences which have resulted' were enough of a deterrent against future repetition.[1]

Inference: The law often treats gay conduct as a monstrosity. You may not find either mercy or understanding if the law catches you performing a homosexual act.

89

But will mercy and understanding be enough to ensure that gays and lesbians stand level legally with their fellow South Africans? Given the law's history of homophobia, built-in legal guarantees seem to be needed.

CASE TWO: Lesbians and jilted husbands

Assertion: To describe someone as a lesbian is defamatory under South African law. To be called a lesbian is an actionable insult which diminishes a woman's name and reputation in the eyes of 'right-thinking persons'. It can be punished with a civil action for damages.

Evidence: A wife left her husband. She moved in with a woman friend. Another friend phoned her former home. The husband answered. The friend asked to speak with the wife. The husband replied: 'Haven't you heard that she is staying with that bloody lesbian [*daardie donderse lesbian*]?' He made it clear he was referring to the woman friend who then sued the husband for defamation. She won. The official report of the case does not say what became of the woman friend and the wife.[2]

Inference: The law still regards gayness as an insult. So don't try to 'out' someone unless you have proof. If a jilted husband tries to bite his wife and her lover with words, they can bite back by suing him. He will lose — unless he can prove the lesbian claim in court. But the only certain winner in the legal battle will be prevailing legal bigotries — and the only certain loser, lesbian and gay pride.

CASE THREE: Cross-dressing in public

Assertion: If you are a man, don't go out dressed up in drag: if the court finds that you had criminal intent in doing so, you may be convicted under an obscure statute that prohibits disguises.

Evidence: On a May evening in 1965, three young Johannesburg men (the court records their race as 'coloured') were out walking on Bezuidenhout Street. They were all in drag. One, aged 19, was arrested. He immediately gave the arresting policeman his correct (male) name. The judges noted that he was 'psychologically aberrated, had a feminine voice, wore his hair in a feminine style, and was wearing female clothes and make-up when arrested'. At least one policeman, as well as the young man's lawyer, thought that he might in fact be a woman and not a man. The judges conceded that his only motive may have been 'to satisfy some feminine instinct or urge, or perhaps to save himself from the embarrassment or inconvenience that his feminine characteristics, such as his voice, would cause him.' But they held that since the young man's 'disguise' had been so effective, and in the absence of an explanation from him, he must have intended illegally 'to conceal his sex and pass himself off as a woman'.[3] Under the old law he was therefore guilty of a crime. The judges' ruling about drag made it necessary for Parliament, in 1969, to add the requirement of criminal intent before dressing in drag becomes an offence.[4]

Inference: Most judges seem to have little knowledge or experience of drag queens. And when confronted with them, they make no attempt to conceal their ignorance with even a semblance of humour.

Current laws

South African law has never treated lesbians and gays kindly. As far as both crimes and non-criminal issues are concerned, the law's approach has been to punish and to exclude.

Modern South African law finds its roots in Roman law. There, homosexuals were barred from legal practice — sharing this fate with gladiators (an unseemly occupation), and those suffering from physical handicaps such as deafness or blindness. Roman criminal law expressly prohibited 'unnatural practices' between men.

In the Roman Dutch common law (which flourished in pre-Napoleon Holland and from which South African law has evolved) only male/female sex acts which were directed to procreation were permitted. All other sexual acts — whether between men or between a man and a woman — were cruelly punished. Any gratification of sexual lust in a manner 'contrary to the order of nature' was a crime. Thus male/female sodomy and sex acts with animals were grouped together with male/male intercourse as 'crimes against nature'. Even solitary masturbation was, according to some, a 'punishable misuse of the organs of creation'. Historical authority indicates that in Roman Dutch law sexual acts between women were probably also criminal.[5]

As far as sexual conduct between humans — as opposed to sex with animals — is concerned, most of these prohibitions are no longer enforced in South African law. But one anomaly remains: male-male sexual acts are still criminal.[6] Anal intercourse between two men is still a crime. As recently as 1967, two judges in the Eastern Cape held that mutual masturbation between two men is criminal as an 'unnatural offence'.[7]

The problem is that no one knows what other male-male sex acts (like kissing or fondling) could conceivably still be held criminal.[8] Fortunately, recent statements by judges (who interpret the common law) have shown a strong distaste for expanding any of these categories.[9] In a 1990 case, a judge remarked that 'society accepts that there are individuals who have homosexual tendencies and who form intimate relationships with those of their own sex,' and that the courts had to take this into account in enforcing the existing criminal provisions.[10]

Progressive judicial approaches to sexual orientation were consolidated in a breakthrough judgement of the Cape Supreme Court in September 1993, where two judges condemned the fact that sodomy was still a crime, and urged the acceptance of homosexuality as a normal variant in society.[11]

Sexual acts between two women are not criminal. But in 1988, the tricameral Parliament extended the existing prohibition on 'immoral or indecent' acts between men and boys under 19 to those between women and girls under 19.[12] Newspapers avidly exploited the homophobic scare by sensationalising the first prosecution under the extended provision: the *Sunday Times*' headline was 'Women who prey on little girls'.[13]

91

The under-age sex prohibition discriminates against gays and lesbians as the heterosexual age of consent is 16 and not 19. Nineteen is considerably higher than in most Western European legal systems. What is more, the heterosexual under-age prohibition relates only to acts involving intercourse and to soliciting or enticing an under-age boy or girl 'to the commission of an immoral act'. The homosexual prohibition by contrast covers any 'immoral or indecent act'. The effect is that merely committing or attempting to commit a heterosexual sex act without intercourse with an under-age boy or girl is not punishable unless there is solicitation or enticement.[14]

One of the most curious provisions still on the statute books in South Africa, and perhaps one of the most curious statutory crimes anywhere, is section 20A of the Sexual Offences Act. This provision, inserted after a Parliamentary investigation into gays which was prompted by a police raid on a party in Forest Town, Johannesburg, in 1966, makes a criminal of any man who commits with another male person *at a party* 'any act which is calculated to stimulate sexual passion or to give sexual gratification'. The provision defines party as 'any occasion where more than two persons are present'.[15]

Some of the results of this enactment have been comical. They include a solemn decision by two judges of the Supreme Court that 'a party' did not come about when a police major, visiting a well-known gay sauna in Johannesburg to entrap gay men, barged in on a cubicle where a couple were having sex, and turned on the light. They jumped up and ran out as soon as the major appeared. The Court — in a liberal decision — held that the two men's jumping apart when the major switched on the light meant that no 'party' came about. The decision and its outcome — the accused was acquitted — is a happy illustration of the absurdities that enforcing such laws unavoidably leads to.[16]

These laws are seldom enforced. On the contrary, most Attorneys-General (the chief regional law enforcement executives of the Department of Justice) have indicated in private that they will not prosecute gay adult men who have gay sex in private or who 'party' at gay venues. But the criminal prohibitions as well as the discriminatory age of consent have a severely negative effect on gay men and women's lives.[17] Even when not enforced, such laws reduce gay men and women to what one writer has called 'unapprehended felons'.[18]

Apart from creating misery and fear, a few of the more obvious consequences are to legitimate or encourage blackmail — recent newspaper reports describe a 'blackmail gang' terrorising gay men at known cruising spots by posing as policemen and demanding 'fines'[19] — entrapment, violence ('queer-bashing'), as well as what lawyers call 'peripheral discrimination' such as refusal of facilities, accommodations and opportunities.[20]

Revulsion and reform

It is now widely acknowledged in South Africa — at least officially — that racism and sexism are irrational and unacceptable. But opprobrium toward gays is still everywhere. It is countenanced in the media, in employment and in social attitudes.

This often reflects obviously biased and selective reliance on Judeo-Christian Biblical doctrine and history.[21]

The traditional attitude of intolerance towards gay sexual conduct seems to be deeply ingrained in our legal history. All sexual acts not directed at procreation, even those between men and women, were prohibited under our common law, but our legal system has pronounced these non-homosexual crimes obsolete. But by a historical anomaly — one which cannot be rationally justified — the common law crimes targeting gay men have been preserved.

It is undeniable that negative attitudes to women and blacks are found in academic texts and court judgments. But these do not compare with the widespread and emphatic disapproval and even revulsion displayed in many past court cases towards gays. Instances abound where judges denounced homosexual conduct as a defilement and abomination of human nature — and thus as immoral and depraved. They have used words like 'filthy' and 'disgusting' to describe male-male masturbation. In more recent times, they have described gayness as a disease or mental disorder.[22]

It is striking that in many of the prosecutions involving gay men, it is difficult to establish whether one of the parties was under-age: the mere fact that gay sex took place was sufficient to trigger the judges' expressions of morality and revulsion, even where no element of exploitation or abuse was present. Even supposedly liberal critics of the legal system saw gays as a 'third sex'[23] — as if sexual orientation had anything to do with gender; as if one is any less a woman for being a lesbian or any less a man for being gay.

Abroad, more enlightened current attitudes regard homosexuality as a natural variant of sexuality unlinked to any pathology[24] — a part of what Susan Sontag calls 'the ineradicable variousness of the expression of human sexuality'.[25] Research has shown that homosexuality is encountered not only across all classes and sectors in any single culture, but in most cultures historically. It also occurs in the natural world outside human society.[26]

Unlike those who experience discrimination on the grounds of their sex or race, gays and lesbians face an additional source of social blame in that it is often claimed that sexual orientation is contagious, or subject to alteration (especially in adolescents) by corruption.

Gay men in particular are accused of child-abuse, with its associated implication of contamination and infectious spread of the condition. These beliefs are irrational — but that does not diminish their power to reinforce prejudice and discrimination. In 1987 the Committee for Social Affairs of the tricameral President's Council issued a Report on the Youth of South Africa in which homosexuality was categorised as part of the problem of promiscuity (along with 'extra-marital sexual intercourse', 'prostitution' and 'living together'). Homosexuality was classed as an 'acquired behavioural pattern' and 'a serious social deviation' which was damned as 'irreconcilable with normal marriage'; it was one of a range of 'evils' to which 'promising young people' fell prey.[27]

On the brighter side, even while recent court decisions have branded homosexuality a sickness, these have, ironically, been relatively enlightened: they represented a step forward from the homophobia and self-indulgent moral censure which preceded them.[28] They recognised that sexual orientation is not a matter of individual choice or of moral blame and took into account recent research that it was a product of physiological or genetic factors. Most recent judgments involving supposed 'unnatural offences' between men go even further — they express implied or increasingly explicit distaste for the common law prohibitions.

But the overall pattern of our legal tradition and legal precedent (the system by which judges follow the decisions in previous cases) provides no safe basis for freedom from irrational discrimination against gays and lesbians.

Gays and lesbians are specially vulnerable to irrational and unjustifiable discrimination, exclusion and stigma. They are a necessarily deviant minority (like left-handers) whose votes cannot force through political change. They are exposed to powerful historical and cultural forces of distaste and rejection. Unlike gender and colour, their defining characteristic is not obvious, immediately or at all. And sexuality itself, despite much recent progress, remains for many a taboo area, replete with repression and suppression.

The case for special constitutional protection for gays' and lesbians' rights to non-discrimination is therefore strong, and was recognized in 1994.

Constitutional protection against discrimination

In the pre-1994 constitutional negotiating process, four parties proposed bills of rights accepting that gays and lesbians require a measure of constitutional protection from discrimination: the African National Congress (ANC), the Democratic Party (DP), the Inkatha Freedom Party (IFP), and the National Party, which adopted the proposals of the Law Commission (a government-appointed body of lawyers and judges which considers law reform). But their means to the end of equality for gays and lesbians differed in important practical ways.

Oblique protection: the Law Commission approach

In its initial draft Bill of Rights the Law Commission suggested that, along with women, children and disabled persons, gays and lesbians constitute a 'natural group'. The common characteristic of these groups is that they have been assigned their distinctive status by nature. Governmental discrimination against these groups should thus be prohibited. But beyond this, the Commission claimed,

> [f]urther protection ... is not a problem which should be solved by a bill of rights. ... The proper place for introducing a prohibition on discrimination by one individual against another, or, for example, by an employer against his employees, etc, is in a civil rights charter or civil rights legislation.

In its original draft, the Law Commission protected the right to human dignity and equality, *which means there shall be no discrimination on the ground of race, colour, language, sex, religion, ethnic origin, social class, birth, political or other views or any disability or other natural characteristic.*[29]

In its later Interim Report on Group and Human Rights, the Commission's redraft included a provision guaranteeing 'the right to equality before the law'. This right expressly proscribes legislative, executive or administrative conduct from favouring or prejudicing 'any person' on the grounds enumerated above, including 'disability or other natural characteristic'.[30]

On 2 February 1993, the National Party government published its constitutional proposals. These adopted the law commission's formulation giving special protection against discrimination on the basis of 'natural characteristics'.[31]

This approach protects gays and lesbians, but does so obliquely — which gives rise to a number of problems. First, the reach of the protections afforded all groups, gays and lesbians included, is limited to state action. This would not outlaw many of the most pervasive forms of discrimination — which take place by private persons and corporate institutions. In addition, there is a drafting problem: the formulation implies that 'natural characteristics' are 'disabilities': thus only 'disabilities' which are 'natural characteristics' will be protected.

But more importantly, the Commission assumes that judges will interpret the concept of 'natural characteristics' to include sexual orientation. Because of our system of legal precedent and judges' expressions of distaste and revulsion for gays in the past, this could prove wrong.

In failing to be explicit about sexual orientation, this approach runs a further risk. This is that associated provisions in the Bill of Rights (for instance, clauses which depend on what 'natural characteristics' means), or clauses in other human rights documents or codes (such as an unfair labour practice definition dealing with employment) may be held to exclude sexual orientation.

Express protection: the 1994 Constitution

By contrast to the Law Commission, the draft bills of rights of the ANC, the DP and IFP (KwaZulu) expressly made discrimination on the ground of sexual orientation unlawful. In article 8 of its final draft (February 1993), dealing with gender rights, the ANC proposed:

(1) Discrimination on the grounds of gender, single parenthood, legitimacy of birth or sexual orientation shall be unlawful.

(2) Legislation shall provide remedies for oppression, abuse, harassment or discrimination based on gender or sexual orientation.

(3) Educational institutions, the media, advertising and other social institutions shall be under a duty to discourage sexual and other types of stereotyping.[32]

The KwaZulu/IFP proposals were as follows (clause 10(a) — Equality):

All citizens of the State of KwaZulu/Natal have equal social dignity, shall be equal before the law and shall share an equal right of access to political, social and economic opportunities irrespective of sex, race, colour, sexual orientation, language, traditions, creed, religion, political affiliation and belief, and social and personal status.[33]

The Democratic Party's Article 2 proposed this:

2.1 Every person shall have the right to equal treatment, and there shall consequently be no discrimination, whether direct or indirect.

2.2 Discrimination means unjustified differentiation. Differentiation on the ground of race, ethnic origin, colour, gender, sexual orientation, age, disability, religion, creed or conscience shall be presumed unjustified unless it is part of a rational programme intended to remedy substantial inequality.[34]

These formulations have the considerable virtue of expressly naming sexual orientation as a condition protected against discrimination, and they were approved in the wording of South Africa's 1994 interim constitution.

But the drafts which preceded the 1994 constitution were not uniform. The ANC draft, for instance, mentioned sexual orientation in one subsidiary clause, that dealing with gender rights, but nowhere else. Its main clause entrenching equality, clause 1, referred to race, colour, language, gender, or creed, political or other opinion, birth or other status — but it avoided sexual orientation.

This approach gives rise to problems of its own. Was the intent of the ANC drafters to create separate categories of those protected against discrimination? Are special prohibitions to apply in the case of some conditions (gender and race) but not others? Since sexual orientation (along with single parents and those born outside marriage) was mentioned only once, would some leeway be allowed for these kinds of discrimination?

As a mere matter of drafting, it was mistaken to include sexual orientation in the category of 'gender' — since the two have no intrinsic connection.

Perhaps the drafters of the ANC draft bill were sensitive to possible controversy. Protecting gays and lesbians from discrimination could evoke opposition — either from within the ANC or from opposing negotiating parties. For this reason they may have felt it wiser to mention sexual orientation in the gender clause but not elsewhere.

But the ANC's Policy Conference in May 1992 expressly endorsed the concept of non-discrimination towards gays and lesbians. A strategy of circumspection in relation to the ANC's own supporters was therefore unnecessary. The ANC may have more need for caution in regard to a negotiating opponent such as the National Party — but even there it is doubtful whether burying sexual orientation in a subsidiary clause could deflect attention from the fact that gays and lesbians are given some protection from discrimination. And if that protection is to be given

— as it now has been — then there can be no reason for it not to be given equally with other protections on the ground of race, colour, language, gender, or creed, political or other opinion, birth or other status. This, fortunately, is the approach reflected in the country's 1994 interim constitution.

The effects of constitutional protection: 1994 and ahead

Whatever the answers, adequate constitutional protection of persons discriminated against because of sexual orientation would entail at least the following:

1. Decriminalisation

This would involve abolishing the common law 'unnatural sexual offences', the common law crime of sodomy, and removing sodomy from those provisions of criminal procedure which give special powers of arrest and force against men suspected of sodomy. It would also entail abolishing section 20A of the Sexual Offences Act 23 of 1957 ('men at a party'), and making the age of consent uniform for hetero- and homosexual acts.

2. Legislative enforcement of non-discrimination

This would have to be targeted particularly at employment, tenancies, provision of public resources, and insurance — where there is mounting evidence that gay men are blacklisted for insurance regardless of medical status.

3. Rights of free speech, association and conduct

This would entail prohibiting discrimination in public decency laws and in what publications are permissible, and in the right to disseminate information and views, as well as equal rights of commercial association — for instance in bars and clubs. (The right to dress in drag would obviously have to be included.)

4. Permanent domestic partnerships

Genuine recognition of non-discrimination on the ground of sexual orientation would entail granting appropriate formal recognition to permanent domestic partnerships. Partner benefits in pensions, medical aid, immigration and insurance would have to follow, as well as rights of intestate inheritance. Where one partner loses the capacity to make conscious choices (of particular significance to the gay community in the AIDS epidemic) the remaining partner's standing should be recognised, either automatically or through a 'living will' document or power of attorney. There should further be no discrimination in the fair assessment of fostering capabilities in regard to adoption and child care.

Notes

1 *S v S* 1965 4 SA 405 (N) (the policeman and the young black boy).
2 *Vermaak v van der Merwe* 1981 3 SA 78 (N) ('*donderse lesbian*').
3 *S v Kola* 1966 4 SA 322 (A) (dressing in drag may constitute an illegal 'disguise'). See p122 below.
4 *Prohibition of Disguises Act 16 of 1969.*

5 *R v Gough and Narroway* 1926 CPD 159 (this decision ensured that the historical crimes which targeted men having sex with men, which the judges still regarded as 'abhorrent', would continue to exist in our modern law).

6 *R v Curtis* 1926 CPD 385 (masturbation between two consenting male adults is a crime).

7 *S v V* 1967 2 SA 17 (E) (masturbation between two men is still a crime).

8 *R v Baxter* 1928 AD 430 (the gay sex acts here were 'of so disgusting a nature' that the Chief Justice had to 'refrain from repeating them').

9 *S v Matsemela* 1988 2 SA 254 (T) (liberal judgment on sodomy).

10 *S v M* 1990 2 SACR 509 (E) (liberal statement on social acceptance of homosexuals).

11 *S v H*, review judgement of Cape Provincial Division, 6 September 1993 (breakthrough decision deploring crime of sodomy and urging acceptance of gays); *S v K* 1973 1 SA 87 (R, AD) (homosexuality as a mental disease).

12 *Immorality Amendment Act 2 of 1988.*

13 *Cape Times,* 14 November 1989 (lesbians and under-age sex); *Sunday Times*, 19 November 1989 (lesbians and under-age sex) and 18 October 1992 (gay-bashing).

14 *Sexual Offences Act 23 of 1957.*

15 *Immorality Amendment Act 57 of 1969.*

16 *S v C* 1987 2 SA 76 (W) (gay saunas and 'parties').

17 *Norris v Republic of Ireland*, case 6/1987/129/180, Judgment of 26 October 1988 (European Court of Human Rights).

18 Richard D Mohr, *Gays/Justice — A Study of Ethics, Society, and Law* (Columbia University Press, 1988).

19 *Sunday Star*, 18 October 1992 (gay-bashing).

20 *Sunday Star*, 1 November 1992 (gay men blacklisted by insurance companies).

21 *Bowers v Hardwick* 478 US 186 (1986) (Unites States Supreme Court).

22 *Baptie v S* 1963 1 PH H96 (homosexuality as a mental disorder); *R v C* 1955 2 SA 51 (T) (homosexuality a 'biological condition which it is very difficult to cure — very difficult indeed').

23 Barend Van Niekerk, 'The Third Sex Act', *South African Law Journal* 87, 1970.

24 Dennis Altman, *The Homosexualization of America* (Beacon Press, 1982); Gordon Isaacs and Brian McKendrick, *Male Homosexuality in South Africa — Identity Formation, Culture and Crisis* (Oxford University Press, 1992).

25 Susan Sontag, *AIDS and its Metaphors* (Penguin, 1989).

26 *Saturday Star,* 1 August 1992 (gay orientation may be physiological); *Star,* Wednesday 5 August 1992 (homosexuality may be genetic); *Sunday Star Review*, 26 February 1989 (gay orientation may be genetic or biological); *Time Magazine,* 9 September 1991 (gay orientation may be genetic).

27 President's Council, *Report of the Committee for Social Affairs on the Youth of South Africa*, Government Printer, Cape Town, 22 May 1987.

28 *S v Mafuya* 1972 4 SA 565 (O) (because homosexuality is a problem which those suffering from it ought to be helped to overcome, homosexuals should if possible not be sent to prison).

29 Law Commission, *Project 58: Group and Human Rights*, Working Paper 25 (1989).

30 Law Commission, *Interim Report on Group and Human Rights*, August 1991.

31 South African government, *Proposals on a Charter of Fundamental Rights*, 2 February 1993.

32 African National Congress, *A Bill of Rights for a New South Africa — A Working Document by the ANC Constitutional Committee* (Centre for Development Studies, University of the Western Cape, 1990); African National Congress, *Ready to Govern — ANC Policy Guidelines for a Democratic South Africa*, adopted at the National Conference 28-31 May 1992; African National Congress, *Draft Bill of Rights — Preliminary Revised Version*, February 1993.

33 KwaZulu Legislative Assembly, *Resolution: Constitution of the State of KwaZulu/Natal*, 1 December 1992.

34 Democratic Party, *Draft Bill of Rights*, May 1993.

Keeping sodom out of the laager:
State repression of homosexuality in apartheid South Africa

Glen Retief[1]

And who can deny that this was also the canker that afflicted the Biblical Sodom? No, Sir, history has given us a clear warning and we should not allow ourselves to be deceived into thinking that we may casually dispose of this viper in our midst by regarding it as innocent fun. It is a proven fact that sooner or later homosexual instincts make their effects felt on a community if they are permitted to run riot... Therefore we should be on the alert and do what there is to do lest we be saddled later with a problem which will be the utter ruin of our spiritual and moral fibre.
Justice Minister PC Pelser, speaking in Parliament,
21 April 1967[2]

Apartheid's war on sexual dissidence

There is a long history that remains as yet unwritten of the repression and regulation of sexuality by the apartheid state during its 40-year hold on power. The details of this hidden war on sexual dissidence are dispersed and confused, the stuff of gossip stories, wildfire rumours, toilet wall graffiti and sensational press reports. Those in the trenches of the continuing war are the visible rule-breakers: street-walkers, gays who cruise for sex, sex-shop owners and pornography merchants. Struggles with vice cops and moral crusaders determine the tenor of their day to day living. For respectable society, on the other hand, the repression continues to be taken for granted. Regular stories in the newspapers of police round-ups of sexual undesirables come and go without public protest. Moral policing is regarded simply as another part of South African law enforcement — as normal and unremarkable as speed traps or parking fines.

The acceptance of sexual policing as just another aspect of everyday life allows the whole subject to be treated as historically and politically unimportant. Consequently, research and writing about the repression of sexual minorities in this country are virtually nonexistent. Although there are isolated exceptions to the rule, in mainstream and progressive histories alike, sex as a site of political struggle simply does not feature.[3] It is as if the Immorality Act had never been passed, as if the police had not spent decades trying to stamp out nonconformist eroticism. Such selectivity generates double standards. When draconian legislation is talked about, the Police Act and the Terrorism Act are mentioned, but the Sexual Offences Act, which allows for jail sentences for men who do nothing more than kiss in public, is invariably overlooked.

In fact, far from being a political irrelevancy, sex has been an important area of concern for successive generations of National Party governments. Racist legislation and iron-fisted rule have, since the earliest days of Nationalist government, gone hand in hand with an obsessive interest in sexual policing. This policing has been based on the values of Christian Nationalist apartheid ideology: the need to keep the white nation sexually and morally pure so that it had the strength to resist the black communist onslaught.

Sex laws drafted and consolidated during the heyday of apartheid in the 1950s and 1960s prescribed tough penalties for a range of sexual offences. Apart from notoriously criminalising interracial sex, the Immorality Act of 1957 (later renamed the Sexual Offences Act) also made everything from prostitution, to soliciting for immoral purposes, to sex with "idiots" illegal and punishable by prison sentences of up to six years. In 1985, the racial provisions of the Act were altered but all its other provisions were kept intact.

Even the limited bourgeois freedoms of sexual speech and association allowed in the advanced capitalist countries of Western Europe and North America have never applied in South Africa. A quarter of the way into the last decade of the twentieth century, the South African Publications Board today still routinely censors any representations of sex or any sexual views that stray too far from what is defined as moral within a narrow, conservative world view. In practice this means, among other things, that anything with the sole purpose of providing sexual stimulation — such as sexy pictures or writing — is undesirable and hence illegal. The line between desirable and undesirable may have become blurred in recent years, but the underlying principle has stayed the same. South Africans may play soccer or rugby for the fun of it, bake *koeksisters* (sweet confection) because they taste delicious, or listen to Mango Groove because it gives them intense pleasure. Yet sexual material can never be enjoyed for its own sake.

100

Such authoritarian and anti-sexual policy, which aims to control and curb what South Africans are allowed to see, feel and think, is out of tune with government rhetoric about a new South Africa in which freedom of choice is to be enshrined and cherished. The National Party government is at last moving away (at least in theory) from its obnoxious policy of unilaterally deciding the political destiny of 35 million black South Africans. Yet, without much fuss, the Publications Board and the vice squad continue to play paternalistic moral guardians to 40 million people, telling them what they may or may not know about sex, which pleasures they are allowed to enjoy and which they must be protected from.

If the targets of morality legislation have been many, it is also true that homosexuals have been singled out for attack in numerous instances. The general erotophobia of the authorities has not been even-handed with regard to sexual orientation. Homosexuality has been treated as inherently sick and immoral. Gay men, lesbians and bisexuals have consequently been regarded with official hostility.

'Men at a Party': The gay threat to white civilization

Concerted attacks on the gay community in South Africa date from the Verwoerd premiership in the mid 1960s. Despite occasional incidents of victimisation, there do not appear to have been any organised campaigns against homosexuality during the early years of Nationalist rule. It seems, from later police reports, that gays were invisible enough for the state not to regard homosexuality as a serious problem. A 1968 police report, for instance, mentions that 'the South African Police has dealt with various forms of homosexuality over the years. [However] it was regarded as isolated.'[4]

The Nationalist government 'discovered' the gay subculture in the latter half of the 1960s and, in a flurry of panic, proceeded to launch a vigorous legislative campaign against it. The trigger of the campaign was a police raid on a house in Forest Town, in the northern suburbs of Johannesburg in January 1966, where to their disgust and repulsion police officers found:

> ...*a party in progress, the like of which has never been seen in the Republic of South Africa. There were approximately 300 male persons present who were all obviously homosexuals... Males were dancing with males to the strains of music, kissing and cuddling each other in the most vulgar fashion imaginable. They also paired off and continued their love-making in the garden of the residence and in motor cars in the streets, engaging in the most indecent acts imaginable with each other.*[5]

The news that gay parties were alive and well in the Republic of South Africa sent shock waves through the white establishment. The South African Police head office immediately sent a circular to all divisional commissioners warning that it appeared that homosexuality and gross indecency 'is being practised between male persons throughout the country and that offenders are now pursuing an organised *modus operandi.*' The circular went on to recommend that informers be used to infiltrate queer parties and that effective action be taken.[6]

The police also recommended to Minister of Justice, PC Pelser, that the laws be tightened in order to enable stringent measures to be taken against homosexuals.[7] Meetings were held between police and justice department officials, and it was decided to take the issue to parliament. Motivating the need for some kind of tough action against the newly discovered homosexual danger, Pelser told the House of Assembly in 1967 that, if unchecked, homosexuality would bring about the utter ruin of civilization in South Africa. Invoking the decadent ghosts of the ancient Mediterranean, he begged legislators to forget neither Rome, where weakness had become lechery and disgusting revelry, nor Sparta, where homosexuality had been a cherished ideal. Formerly glorious civilizations were lying in the dust and South Africa should beware of a similar fate. The canker of Sodom had to be sliced out before it ruined the moral fibre of the nation.[8]

The appeal to the integrity and survival of the (implicitly white) South African civilisation fell on receptive ears. These were, after all, the years of the famous white baby boom, when white mothers were being encouraged to breed faster than their black counterparts so as to prevent the white minority's shrinking into obsolescence. Not a single voice in Parliament challenged Pelser's notions; instead, United Party and National Party MPs alike debated the steps necessary to contain 'sexual perversion'. Liberal voices — pointing out that anti-gay laws constituted a serious infringement of fundamental human rights — were either silent, or simply missing.

A select committee of parliamentarians was established, at Pelser's request, to look into the matter more closely. The report of this investigation, the only serious policy-making initiative to ever come from the government on the question of homosexuality, was published in 1968 and makes for entertaining, if horrifying, reading. Perhaps the most memorable section is the report of a police detective in Pretoria who went undercover, tracked down some lesbians and gay men, and tried to find out everything he could about the lesbian and gay community. A few 'insights' from the cloak-and-dagger operation: queers usually occupy flats which they keep very neat and which they furnish fashionably; all true homosexuals drink excessively; a 'dilder' is a rubber object that the 'butch' lesbian utilises. And, rather appropriately, '[In homosexual speech] uniform members of the police are known as "morons".'[9]

The central point of debate in the Select Committee deliberations was whether or not homosexuality was infectious and could endanger the country's youth. The tug-of-war was between the law-and-order lobby, which was convinced that homosexuality was spreading because older men and women were seducing teenagers,[10] and the psychiatric lobby, which felt that a homosexual orientation was an ingrained psychosexual disorder that ought to be dealt with medically and not by means of prison sentences.[11]

A gay action group, formed in the aftermath of the party raid, paid legal and expert witnesses to make representations. The anti-criminalisation lobbying was not wasted, since the committee was talked out of the idea of new laws aimed at gay sex in general. However the committee did go ahead with reactionary recommendations relating to gay parties, sex with teenage boys, and dildos. Any sexual acts between men at a party were to be banned; the age of consent for male homosexual acts was to be raised from 16 years to 19; and the manufacture or distribution of any article intended to be used to perform an unnatural sexual act was to be prohibited.

A striking feature of the Select Committee report is its white male viewpoint: whenever homosexuality is talked about, it is white gay men who are used as examples, and lesbians and black gays enter the discussions as afterthoughts. Apart from a brief debate about whether homosexual sex across the colour bar should be banned, and about whether interracial relationships occurred in the gay community[12], black gay culture is never mentioned. Lesbians are assumed to exist in lesser numbers than homosexual men and to be an evil because they are completely unproductive.[13] Women are discussed in terms of their sexual activity, looks and butch role-playing. The MPs were rather worried about the sizes, shapes and attributes of the different kinds of 'dilders' used by lesbians — 'Is this instrument of normal or abnormal size?' a United Party member wanted to know.[14] Perhaps the eventual decision to ban unnatural articles was representative of a general anxiety about the penis being made redundant.

The recommended amendments to the Immorality Act were passed into law in 1969, amidst much mutual back-patting between the government and the opposition for having dealt with an unpleasant issue so smoothly and effectively. The immediate consequences of the legislation have never been fully documented, but there is evidence of a clampdown on outdoor cruising places and routine police surveillance of clubs, bars and parties during the 1970s.[15] So as to remind gay people of the law, police would also conduct random raids, bursting into a party or club, grabbing people who were kissing or dancing together, and bundling them into police vans. Photographers would line people up against the wall and snap pictures of as many faces as possible while cops took down the numbers of the cars parked outside. The ultimate threat was that one's identity would be leaked to the newspapers. Exposure could have meant unemployment, social isolation and vitriolic abuse wherever one went.

The 1980s: From policing to censorship

In more recent years, police have stopped the constant harassment of gay bars and social gatherings and have kept a lower profile with respect to lesbian, gay and bisexual communities. Since the 1980s gay bars have operated without attempts being made to close them down, and despite initial hostility, authorities agreed in 1990, 1991 and 1992 to allow a lesbian and gay pride march through the streets of Johannesburg. It goes without saying, perhaps, that tolerance has been greater in the metropolitan centres of Johannesburg and Cape Town than in the small towns of the platteland. For instance, in the claustrophobic eastern Transvaal town of Nelspruit, where I grew up, the local cops still turn up at the occasional gay party to check out the patrons.

The relaxation of control in the large cities probably indicates that police realise that trying stamp out all homosexuality is a waste of time. Nevertheless, repression of gay life continues in South Africa on a number of fronts. Rather than attempting to prevent gays from meeting and having sex, the more recent strategy has been to wage a low-intensity war on them. This type of repression raises the costs of being gay and attempts to ensure that homosexuality is kept out of the sight and mind of the general public.

One powerful weapon in the state's hands is censorship. While it is true that a great deal of heterosexual writing and erotica has come under the South African censor's axe, the censorship of gay material has been disproportionately severe. Magazines and books widely available in other countries are regularly banned here, simply because they assume that there is nothing wrong with homosexuality. As recently as January 1992, the Directorate of Publications could declare the popular US gay magazine, *The Advocate*, to be illegal because:

> *The sexual practice of homosexuality is promoted as normal and natural, satisfying and right, and this attitude would be regarded as blatantly shameless and repulsive by the [reasonable] reader.*[16]

Lesbian and gay publishers and book importers thus face an uphill battle for survival. Otherworld Books is an independent book company, based in Cape Town, catering chiefly for the lesbian and gay market. A serious, upmarket enterprise, it imports books on sexual theory, history, politics and culture. During 1991-92, Customs House in Cape Town confiscated every shipment of books bound for Otherworld, claiming possible contraventions of South African censorship laws. From time to time, customs police drop by Otherworld's premises and scan the shelves for suspect titles. Offending books are forwarded (after endless delays) to the Directorate of Publications, which has indeed ruled a number of them undesirable. Publications that have been banned include lesbian feminist theoretical tracts, anthologies of gay history and irreverent writing about lesbian sexuality.[17]

This homophobic censorship hurts gay people because it blocks the influx of liberating and radical ideas into the lesbian and gay community, stifling debate and interfering with valuable intellectual growth and consciousness-raising. The strategy is a familiar one, until very recently directed primarily at the democratic and socialist movements: ban protest literature, and protest will go away. However, as in the case of popular struggles for nonracial democracy, demands for an end to the oppressive sexual system in South Africa will not disappear because the state makes them illegal. Silenced people have a tendency to strike back. What has developed among lesbian and gay people in response to censorship has been an elaborate informal distribution network which facilitates the sharing of pornography, banned gay literature and radical works of theory.

Moral panics: Child abuse and other myths

Another weapon in the state's arsenal is moral panic. One of the most tenacious myths about homosexuals is that we reproduce ourselves by corrupting the young into our sick and evil ways. And the most virulent manifestation of this myth is the figure of the 'child-molester': the drooling old man who hangs around playgrounds, promising little boys sweets if only they will become homosexuals so that they can have sex with people like him. During the 1980s and on into the 1990s, police skilfully exploited this stereotype to launch a number of attacks on the South African gay male community.

In the three months between June and August 1988, detectives from the police Child Protection Unit (CPU) arrested more than 60 adult men and teenage boys in what quickly came to be seen as a countrywide net against child abuse and a fight against the alarming rise in child violations.[18] Thick front page newspaper headlines proclaimed 'CHILD SEX RIFE IN CITY'[19] and 'JONG SEUNS IN SEKSNET' (Young boys in sex net).[20] Public hysteria mounted, fed by police claims that they were uncovering child sex rings and that the arrests represented only the tip of the iceberg.[21] Sensational reports of the discovery of more victims broke one after the other in waves, confirming the perception that South Africa was facing a surging tide of immorality and perversion. Child abuse experts, Members of Parliament, and police spokespeople demanded drastic action: one suggestion was a jobs blacklist aimed at keeping known molesters away from children.[22]

Almost exactly a year later, the Cape Town Child Protection Unit conducted its own regional dragnet, in a dramatic swoop on gay clubs in the city. Motivated by the CPU's discovery that 16- and 17 year-old children were frequenting gay bars, police conducted a one-night operation on 26 August in which they arrested two suspected child molesters in their homes and interrogated male sex workers and gay club-goers. Journalists from *The Argus* appear to have been invited along to watch the whole operation: the next day's edition contained a full-page colour feature, replete with juicy details and photographs.[23]

In both the above cases, police spokespeople drew explicit links between homosexuality and child abuse, encouraging the idea that gay men were child-corrupters. In the 1988 scare, police in Durban told the press that

> child-abusers haunt venues like video arcades, where homo-
> sexuals pick up young boys. They bribe the boys with small
> amounts of cash and buy them food. They are then taken to
> hotels or flats and sexually assaulted.[24]

Captain Leonard Solms, the man behind the 1989 Cape Town swoops, was even more explicit. At a 1990 Dutch Reformed Church conference, entitled 'Chaos Around Eros', he told delegates that sexual abuse of boys by men was a much bigger problem in Cape Town than other South African cities and that 'if we don't do something, we will have many homosexuals in the next generation.'[25]

It is beyond the scope of this account to attempt a detailed analysis of the child sex ring scares and their social impact; still less so an analysis of the power dynamics involved in the relationships between the men and boys who were arrested. More research needs to be done in order to establish how consensual the relationships were, and whether the role of the police was purely homophobic or whether in fact a degree of protection was offered to children. A few preliminary comments about the scares need, however, to be made at this point.

Firstly, the scapegoating of gay men is both unfair and misguided considering that the vast proportion of child abuse is heterosexual and happens within traditional families. The vulnerability of children to rape stems not from the malevolence of evil sex perverts, but from the structured disempowerment of children in our society which makes sure they are seen and not heard, even when they are being mistreated.

Secondly, although the legal age of consent for homosexual acts is 19, it is misleading and inaccurate to talk of men who have sex with fully consenting 17 or 18 year old youngsters as being child molesters. Since the age of consent for heterosexual acts is 16, it is discriminatory to prosecute gay men who have relationships with 16 to 19 year-olds. Moreover, in the child abuse scares, the police failed to draw crucial distinctions around the age of the children involved or around the degree to which the younger man had sought out the sexual contact. The general assumption appears to have been that intergenerational sex between men was by definition bad and abusive and had to be stopped.

Considerable qualitative evidence in fact suggests that it was the police — and not the molesters — who were the abusers in 1988 and 1989. In at least one case police unnecessarily and intrusively arrested a suspect at his place of work;[26] in another case, a 38-year-old man gassed himself rather than face prison and public derision after police questioned him in connection with his 17-year-old lover.[27] Heather Regenass, a social worker connected at the time to the National Institute for Crime Prevention and the Rehabilitation of Offenders, recalls clearly that most of the cases involved young men in their late teens, and that the teenagers concerned were aware, streetwise people rather than innocent victims:

> *I have no doubt that the whole scare was an exaggeration, if not a complete fabrication. At the time the South African Police's image had been harmed by revelations of abuses under Emergency regulations. Gay men were easy targets; the police could arrest 'child molesters' and appear the heroes of the community instead of the villains.*[28]

Gay conduct as public nuisance

A third strategy used by police to justify repressive measures directed at lesbian, gay and bisexual people has been to treat homosexual activity in public places as a nuisance and to charge transgressors with sexual offences ranging from public indecency to sexual assault to immoral soliciting. Periodic station swoops, toilet patrols and the like are pursued with the aim of discouraging sexual contacts between members of the same sex. Because of the relative prominence of the gay male cruising culture, most of the victims have been men; but reported incidents of lesbians being arrested in bars and public places indicate that women are also affected. One woman who granted me an interview was arrested in a Durban gay club a few years ago, while kissing another woman. In the police station she had to deal with the crudest kinds of sexism and homophobia. A male police officer went so far as to leer down her shirt and tell her that all she needed was a good fuck — and that he would release her if she let him do the honours.[29]

As in the case of moral panics about child abuse, police attacks on public expressions of homosexuality attract considerable publicity and media attention. When police launched a crackdown on gay cruising at the Durban beachfront, the Natal *Sunday Tribune* published a prominent feature article entitled 'DURBAN'S BEACHES A GAY PARADISE'.[30] The article consisted largely of a sympathetic interview with the chief of the Durban Vice Squad, Anthony Ludick, who explained that homosexuality was disgusting and the public should not have to be exposed to it. 'Any man would be naive to allow his son to go into a public convenience unattended,' he said. 'He could well be subjected to a disturbing and distasteful experience.' In July 1989, when police arrested 69 men at various railway stations in the Cape Peninsula, the *Cape Times* unproblematically reported the police view that 'PUBLIC OUTRAGE SPARKS STATION HOMOS SWOOP'.[31]

For the police, lavatory sex is a social problem; for many gay and bisexual men, it is the only sexual opportunity available in contemporary South African society. The great irony in the vice squad's moralism regarding 'public soliciting' is that the police do absolutely nothing to stop the most common and damaging 'soliciting' of all — the everyday and abusive sexual harassment of women that occurs on the streets, in the supermarkets, at bus stops and railway stations. When straight men loudly and intrusively tell women in public that they want to go to bed with them, they are not branded nuisances and delinquents. Yet gays who make consensual sexual contact in public places are somehow regarded as serious threats to public peace and order.

Repression can be formal or informal, and the lack of official support when lesbian, gay and bisexual people are victimised can be as much of a problem as the overt hostility. It would be unfair, on the basis of the limited information available, to make generalisations, but preliminary research findings about police practice give cause for serious concern. In September 1992, the Institute of Criminology at the University of Cape Town organised a lesbian/gay/bisexual phone-in day about the issues of policing and violence.

Among the horrifying incidents reported was the story of N, a black gay man who was found guilty of petty theft after spending two months awaiting trial in prison unable to afford his own bail.

Upon being admitted to prison, N asked the wardens to place him in a single cell because he was gay and known by the some of the other prisoners to be so. The wardens refused to believe him because he did not look gay. He was thus placed in a large cell with 40 inmates. He was confronted by a gang who demanded to know if he was gay. He denied the accusation but was still gang-raped four times. He told the officers at the prison, who removed him from the big cell and placed him in a smaller one with two other men. He was told that he should forget about the incident unless he wanted to make things worse for himself.[32]

Another caller — J, a gay police officer — told of being beaten up and harassed by police doing the rounds at a railway station toilet: J was having oral sex with another man in a toilet cubicle when plainclothes police burst in (he identified them by the police torch that they were carrying and by the fact that he later saw a police van parked outside). The police proceeded to assault him severely, breaking facial bones and drawing blood. After beating him up and verbally abusing him, they left in the police van. He assumes he must have been recognised because he later received hate mail, death threats and sexually explicit anti-gay jokes at his place of work. He also received abusive anonymous phone calls.[33]

Straight courts to gay men: Don't get fresh with us

It is not only prejudiced police and prison warders who give licence to hate crimes against lesbian, gay and bisexual people: the South African judicial system has also played a significant role in legitimising the most vicious and brutal kinds of anti-gay violence. In Cape Town alone there have been at least 13 'gay murders' in the past three years. Typically, these cases involve gay men picking up sexual partners who kill them and then take any microwave ovens, hi-fi sets, video recorders or valuables they can lay their hands on in the victim's apartment. When they are arrested and have to appear in court, their defence is often that they were sexually harassed by the deceased, who they thus killed in self-defence.

Not all judges have bought the argument: in the case of renowned author Richard Rive,[34] evidence suggesting that the murder was premeditated swayed the judge into finding the killers guilty. However, in a worrying number of cases, judges have allowed the defence of provocation to form the basis for an acquittal[35] or, in some cases, mitigating circumstances.

The dangers inherent in this logic are illustrated in the case of George Herrera, a Parow restaurant owner who picked up three male hitchhikers in central Cape Town in August 1990. According to the defendants, Herrera took the three of them back to his flat for drinks. They had previously been smoking dagga and mandrax, and so the combined effect of the drugs and alcohol made them drowsy. At some stage two of them became dimly aware that Herrera, now naked, was stroking the third's genitals. Both men rushed to their friend's assistance; one restrained Herrera with a belt and the other strangled him with a telephone cord. The third defendant went to the kitchen to get a knife and proceeded to stab Herrera to death while his two friends lambasted him with an empty Coke bottle.[36]

In the Supreme Court murder trial which took place a year later, the defence claimed that the three killers had acted in the heat of provocation. They had acted mechanically and irrationally and now had the deepest feelings of regret and remorse. The only thought in their minds had been to restrain the deceased.[37]

In his verdict, the judge accepted their version of events, saying they had been clearly provoked by sexual molestation and had acted in the heat of the moment. The judge also said: 'One cannot but express one's concern that these men do not appreciate the risks they take.'[38] The implicit message was that if gay men get fresh with straight men, it is their own fault if they get stabbed, chopped up or strangled. Riaz Jeppie, who stabbed Herrera with the knife, got off on culpable homicide with a seven-year jail sentence, three years of which were suspended. His companions were each found guilty of assault with intent to do grievous bodily harm, and were sentenced to two years and 18 months respectively (in each case, half their sentence was suspended).

Cases like the above cannot help but confirm gay people's worst fears about the criminal justice system: that it is prepared to turn a blind eye to attacks. It is not surprising, considering its track record, that few gays are naïve enough to regard the law as their protector. State and juridical homophobia is justified in terms of uplifting the moral basis of society, but its real effect is to cheapen and dehumanise gay life.

Conclusion: State repression and the end of formal apartheid

State repression of homosexuality has not affected all sectors of the lesbian, gay and bisexual community identically. More research is needed to ascertain the precise ways in which lesbians and black gays have been affected by multiple forms of social oppression; how the threat of rape has kept lesbians from public cruising; how enforced poverty and segregation has inhibited the development of a commercial black gay subculture.

In South Africa, government homophobia has historically been expressed in the context of an apartheid belief-system which holds that South Africa is a country under siege and can only survive if it maintains its sexual purity and moral solidarity. Homosexuality is perceived, within this framework, as a threat to the nation, deserving of eradication and attack. As Law and Order Minister Adriaan Vlok, reacting to the 1988 homosexual sex ring scandal, told the Pretoria Members of the Order of Christ:

> *The young people of our country are not only being threatened by revolution. There is also the attempt to break down our moral standards and to destroy our future, our youth... Those who have any hope for a good future in our country, for all our citizens* [regardless of race], *will find comrades in the South African Police.*[39]

With the ending of formal apartheid and the shift away from 'total onslaught' mentality, perhaps an opportunity will arise for South Africans to relax a little. Still, early signs are that the current National Party government wants to piece together a multiracial conservative consensus around national values such as Christianity, hard work, and sexual morality. Such initiatives, tempting though they may be for people hungering for some sort of stability in their lives, must necessarily be opposed by those wishing to build a climate of freedom and opportunity. Old-style morality, with its out-groups and stigmatised sexualities, is ultimately incompatible with the goal of a diverse and free society. All of the participants in the current constitutional bargaining say they espouse the goals of individual rights and freedoms. Freedom of sexual choice is a value that they must not be allowed to forget.

Notes

1 This essay was made possible by research grants from the Human Sciences Research Council and the Institute of Criminology at the University of Cape Town. See Glen Retief, '"Policing the Perverts": an exploratory investigation of the nature and social impact of police action towards gay and bisexual men in South Africa', Human Sciences Research Council and Institute of Criminology, 1993.

2 From the *House of Assembly Debates*, Cols 1405-6.

3 The absence of any discussion of the issue can be observed in such mainstream histories as Christopher Saunders and Colin Bundy, eds, *Reader's Digest Illustrated History of South Africa* (Readers Digest, 1988). Revisionist or progressive works have largely focused on race and class oppression, as in Alfred Stadler's *The Political Economy of Southern Africa* (David Philip, 1987) and S Marks and S Trapido, eds, *The politics of race, class and nationalism in twentieth century South Africa* (Longman, 1987). South African feminist historiography is a newly developing field, and generally sexuality has not been its central focus, as in Cheryl Walker, *Women and Gender in Southern Africa* (David Philip, 1990). What has not to my knowledge ever been attempted in South Africa is social history along the lines of Jeffrey Weeks's crucial work, *Sex, Politics and Society* (Longman, 1981), which surveyed changing attitudes towards sexuality in Britain since 1800.

4 Submission by the South African Police to Parliamentary Select Committee 7 of 1968. Quoted in the *Report of the Select Committee*, p11.

5 Submission by the South African Police to Parliamentary Select Committee 7 of 1968. Quoted in the *Report of the Select Committee*, p11.

6 Circular dated 1 February 1966. Quoted in *Report of the Select Committee*, pp17-18.

7 Letter dated 10 February 1966. Submission by the South African Police to Parliamentary Select Committee 7 of 1968. Quoted in the *Report of the Select Committee*, p18.

8 Speech in Parliament on 21 April 1967. From the *House of Assembly Debates*, Cols 1405-6.

9 Submission by the South African Police to Parliamentary Select Committee 7 of 1968. Quoted in the *Report of the Select Committee*, pp20-21.

10 Submission by the South African Police to Parliamentary Select Committee 7 of 1968. Quoted in the *Report of the Select Committee*, p63.

11 Memorandum compiled by the Cape Town branch of the Society of Psychologists and Neurologists of South Africa and the Department of Psychiatry of the University of Cape Town, Submission by the South African Police to Parliamentary Select Committee 7 of 1968. Quoted in the *Report of the Select Committee*, p82.

12 Submission by the South African Police to Parliamentary Select Committee 7 of 1968. Quoted in the *Report of the Select Committee*, p36.

13 See interview with Maj. FAJ van Zyl of the South African Police. Submission by the South African Police to Parliamentary Select Committee 7 of 1968. Quoted in the *Report of the Select Committee*, p34.

14 Submission by the South African Police to Parliamentary Select Committee 7 of 1968. Quoted in the *Report of the Select Committee*, p38.

15 See Mark Gevisser, 'A Different Fight for Freedom' in this volume.

16 Letter from the Directorate of Publications to Leon Linz, dated 21 January 1992.

17 Personal communication, Moira Edmonds, 7 September 1992.

18 *The Star*, 21 August 1988.

19 *The Argus*, 18 June 1988.

20 *Rapport*, 14 July 1988.

21 *The Argus*, 16 August 1988.

22 See reports in *The Star*, 21 August 1988 and the *Sunday Times*, 21 August 1988.
23 *The Argus*, 27 August 1989.
24 *The Argus*, 16 August 1988.
25 *The Argus*, 18 May 1990.
26 Anonymous telephonic interview with the arrestee, 4 September 1992.
27 *Cape Times*, 16 August 1988.
28 Personal communication, 16 September 1992.
29 Personal communication, 5 February 1992.
30 *Sunday Tribune*, 1 July 1990.
31 *Cape Times*, 5 July 1989.
32 Telephonic interview, 4 September 1992.
33 Telephonic interview, 4 September 1992.
34 *State v Suleiman Turner* Cape Town SS 127/90.
35 *State v Guss Davey* Cape Town SS 285/91.
36 See statements by Langenhoven and Sookool in *State v Langenhoven et al.* Cape Town, SS 163/91.
37 Statement by Sookool in *State v Langenhoven et al.*
38 Judgement by Tebbutt J, from SS 163/91.
39 *Rapport*, 18 July 1988.

Three —

Making space: Queer societies

A drag at Madame Costello's:
Cape moffie life and the popular press in the 1950s and 1960s

Dhianaraj Chetty[1]

Out in the media

Carnival Queens

Leading the annual December Coon Carnival through the streets of Cape Town, the Moffie Queens[2] present an image of fantasy, hilarity and desire. Image is all-important — artifice used in defiance of the natural body's limits. The real Carmen Miranda would be proud of such a tradition. Heels, frills, fish net stockings, hairy armpits, trashy jewels: these say something about world the queens (and perhaps their audience) wish to inhabit. Never camera shy, the queens always enact the rituals of being outcast. What do we make of these images; what do they say about us?

The Moffie Queens may well be a small part of gay culture in South Africa. But they represent a particular kind of self expression and identity. For their audiences they are part of a line-up of freakish spectacles. They are almost inhuman, representing a kind of humanity and desire that is grotesque, unspeakable — and titillating. The first two pictures in the picture insert may well say it all: 'Yvonne de Carlo' (figure 1) is confident, brazen, baring her shapely thighs for the world's indulgence; 'Carmen Miranda' (figure 2) is the exemplar of drag, hyperfemininity and wanton sexuality. Yvonne, perhaps, is the glamour queen we all secretly want to be; Carmen, juxtaposed with the dwarf, that other classic figure of derision, is perhaps the oddity we love to mock.

115

Another portrait of Yvonne, from the same series, was initially published in *Drum* magazine in January 1962, alongside a beaming portrait of the leader of Cape Town's drum majorettes. The issue under discussion was whether real women or their moffie substitutes were what the carnival needed. Yvonne was adamant: 'What the carnival needs is more glamour: that means more moffies.'[3] *Drum* and the *Golden City Post* were sister publications with national editions and circulation, specifically targeted at black readers. In their heyday, the 1950s and 1960s, they were immensely popular; they were the biggest-selling publications among black South Africans. *Drum*, particularly, attracted the cream of black intelligentsia among its writers. So significant was its influence and its ability to capture the *zeitgeist* of urban black life that the 1950s renaissance in black culture is often referred to as 'The *Drum* Era'.[4]

The fact that these two very popular publications adorned their pages with moffie drag queens throughout the 1950s and 1960s says something about just how fascinating readers found them. Both publications appeared to thrive on the thrill of the scandalous and the salacious — in short, something close to the contemporary tabloid. The irony is that in their search for bestselling scandal, they captured some rare moments and images in the history of a gay and lesbian community. The Bailey's African Photo Archive, which holds all the photographic material commissioned for *Drum* and the *Golden City Post*, and from which these photos have been selected, is thus an unusual — and partly unwitting — repository of South African gay and lesbian culture and history.

Drum and, to a greater extent, the *Golden City Post*, carried a series of stories in the form of quasi-sociological investigations into the gay and lesbian community of Cape Town. *Drum* often picked up news stories from the *Golden City Post* and ran them as particular 'case-studies'. The result of this publicity was, of course, a skewed vision of gay and lesbian culture and life: those featured were often the most outrageous and most celebrated of Cape Town's coloured moffie drag queens. The coverage began in the early 1950s and stories of a similar genre were still being reported in the mid 1970s.

The story of Gertie, a lesbian cross-dresser who lived as a male gangster (reprinted on page 128), is a superb and unusual example. Though replete with contradictory messages and incomplete in many ways, it is nevertheless a sensitive and colourful biography. For example, Gertie never speaks of what motivates her attraction to women: that she has 'girlfriends' is simply presented as a matter of fact. Likewise, what compels her to be the 'butch' is unspoken: all we learn from her testimony is that she has little but contempt for 'typical women'. (In August 1969, *Drum* ran a similar feature, about Rookmoney Naidoo, a Durban woman who proudly declared, 'I Changed My Sex'.)

Gertie's story and the perennial focus on Cape Town's drag queens prompt us to ask two questions: why was this community of sexual dissidents based in Cape Town, and why on earth did South Africa's two most popular black publications choose — in a remarkably conservative era — to devote so much of their coverage to so obscure and marginal a community?

116

A drag at Madame Costello's

Why Cape Town?

The reports of gay life covered by the *Golden City Post* and *Drum* focused overwhelmingly on Cape Town. At around the same time, Sophiatown and 'Fietas' in Johannesburg were also known for the presence of gays and lesbians, but Cape Town is implicitly acknowledged, in the coverage, as the real epicentre of black gay and lesbian culture. Through *Drum* and the *Golden City Post*, Cape Town's gay 'aristocracy' became nationally familiar personalities. Perhaps less fortunately, their names and images came to represent 'the moffie' in an already-homophobic popular imagination.

Gay life in Durban is given no more than a couple of mentions: in 1955, the *Golden City Post* reported that the shanty-town of Cato Manor was the place 'Where Men Are Wives'. Within the shantytown, an area called Esinyameni (Place of Darkness) was identified as the centre of 'Sodom' where at one time colourful marriage ceremonies between men frequently took place.[5] The only documentation of gay life on the Reef is a series of photographs of a Moffie Show at the Bantu Men's Social Centre, but it appears that all the performers were Cape moffies on tour.

There is no doubt that the coverage in *Drum* and the *Golden City Post* reflected a reality: within Cape coloured communities there has always been a highly visible and socially developed moffie subculture. Gays and lesbians gathered at shebeens and clubs all over the city — like Aunty Josephine's, a well known venue in District Six — and the centre of their world seemed to be Hanover Street in District Six, where many gay men had lodgings. Of this community, the majority was coloured, and there appear to have been few, if any, African moffies. The papers focused on them on rare occasions. In 1963, for example, the *Golden City Post* carried the story of David 'Lulu' Masikana, 'a real man' who had worn a woman's 'step-in' for 232 days because he couldn't undo the fasteners of the garment he put on for the carnival. David, or 'Lulu the Queen' as he was better known, was up on charges of robbery. The magistrate was terse in his judgement: 'You are too effeminate even to get cuts.'[6]

More than anywhere else in South Africa, aspects of gay life like crossdressing and drag seem to have taken root in the coloured working class communities of the Western Cape. One possible answer for the prevalence of gay culture lies in the city's popular traditions. For example, the Coon Carnival — which was for many years a major cultural event — was led by a moffie, and some accounts suggest that it included a whole troupe of moffies. Social historians of the region have documented the moffies' presence, but have not offered much of an explanation of their role in popular culture or in their communities.[7] The Cape carnival, like its counterparts elsewhere, was an opportunity to perform and act out personas that would not normally be socially acceptable. Mocking and subverting the conventions of gender and sexuality are very much part of the ritual. In Cape Town, this seems to have made the general public more tolerant.

Literary drag

In *Drum* and the *Golden City Post*, the descriptions of this marginal world in Cape Town are filtered through the eyes of reporters — some with more perception and literary ability than others. Their writing registers a range of attitudes — from poorly concealed voyeurism and vitriol to paternalistic empathy. They reflect the ambiguities of a period when popular culture in the cities was becoming highly Americanised — a trend reflected in moffie life.

The 1950s was also the era when the divas and 'strong men' of Hollywood cinema were beginning to make a major impact on popular concepts of gender in South Africa. The drag queens and the popular media's apparent obsession with them should be seen within this context. The tabloids took Hollywood's fantasies to grotesque and parodied extremes.

In *Drum* and the *Golden City Post*, the freakishness of homosexuality was set against an image of what men and women really should be. In 1951, for example, an article in *Drum* entitled 'How Men are Made' publicised Boy's Clubs as models for what wholesome male (heterosexual) leisure culture for black men should be. The idea was to keep black men from straying into 'loitering, gambling, thieving and other criminal tendencies' in the cities. Providing a sanitised alternative to the world of ghetto life, the clubs were venues where black youth would be prepared for 'healthy citizenship'.[8] Loyalty, comradeship and team spirit were the essence of this new man. This was the stuff of missionary dreams and social reformers.

A few years later, in 1955, *Drum* carried the story of Gertie's fall from grace into the demi-monde of homosexuality, crime and delinquency (see figure 16). This was one of the newspaper's first major 'exposés' of queer life, and it presents a sharp contrast to the wholesome conventions of masculinity and femininity which otherwise constituted the regular diet for readers. Later that year the stars of the 'All Male Non-European Revuette and Minstrel Show' were pictured adjusting their make-up and tossing their skirts.[9] Then, in January 1956, the *Golden City Post* introduced its 'Moffie Confessions as Social Documents' series, with 'Linda Darnell' as the picture of camp refinement, seated at a piano in diamanté and taffeta. The commentary didn't quite match Linda's regal pose:

> *They lead a lonely and bitter life. Their only constant companions, their own kind — their only solace, what they find at the bottom of a bottle. Too often they face the danger of becoming drink sodden wrecks who burst into tears at the slightest provocation.*[10]

In the same month the *Golden City Post* ran a story supposedly aimed at 'tackling a major social evil': 'boy brides in gaol'. In this instance, circumstantial homosexuality amongst prison inmates was the issue. The same year, in its profile of 'Heddy Lamarr', the *Golden City Post* was almost earnest in revealing 'the strange emotional currents which can turn a human being into a social outcast'.[11]

118

There was something of a missionary zeal to this coverage. In 1966, for example, the paper ran a story about 'Doris Day' (Harold Blaauw in his other life), who had attempted suicide and was rescued by the Rev Charles Slingers, who effectively exorcised Doris of the evil which possessed him. Both of them are captured on the *Golden City Post*'s front page, with the reverend holding the repentant Doris's bra![12] The Doris Day stories, which had been running since 1963, were pure invention. George Knowlden, alias 'Gina Lollabrigida', settled the score, by claiming that Blaauw was holding moffies up for ridicule. As an aside it is worth noting that 'Gina' described her occupation thus: 'I break down walls for a construction company.'[13]

Other stories were within the camp horror genre. In August 1959, the *Golden City Post* carried the tale of a white Cape housewife who alleged that her husband had been kidnapped by moffies. The report speculated on the possibilities that a whole moffie empire might be unearthed in the search for the him, but was, at least, candid enough to admit the more likely possibility — that the hostage was a moffie to begin with who had left his wife by choice: 'Is this man living entirely as a woman all the time somewhere in the peninsula because he feels this is his way of life?'[14]

The hostage story followed on an earlier exposé that revelled in revealing a trend of migration to the Cape by moffies from the rest of the country.[15] Some of them had even managed to penetrate the city's social elite. This aristocracy of moffies was known to have marriages of convenience, money and status; a far cry from the usual 'streetwalker' with whom moffies were usually identified. In response to public hostility, some moffies justified their move by saying that Cape Town was the most tolerant place to be. By the late 1960s, after the 1966 police raid on a gay party in Johannesburg and the proposed anti-homosexuality laws of 1968, there was even talk, in the pages of the *Golden City Post*, of legislation and intensified policing to curb the homosexual menace.

But from the previous decade and well into the 1960s, the *Golden City Post* had been an active participant in Cape moffie culture — by organising the annual Moffie Queen competition at the Kismet Theatre in Athlone.[16] This was a good example of the media generating its own news, with the *Golden City Post* providing readers with blow-by-blow accounts of dynastic struggles in the fight to become 'Moffie Queen'. In January 1964 *Drum* devoted two pages to one of the battles, with commentary from well known observers: 'Kay Kendal' (figure 7), 'Marie Antoinette' and 'Zelda'.[17] Again, in June 1967, 'Piper Laurie' (figure 8) and 'Kewpie Doll' (figure 15) were the centre of attention in a similar struggle splashed on the *Golden City Post*'s front page.[18]

The event was always a huge success. For both reporters and audiences, this was the ultimate moffie spectacle: gay men living out their fantasies of femininity in public. And the *Golden City Post* played into the stereotypes of queeny bitchiness in the way it reported on the event: 'What, That Old Queen? Revolt Against the New Queen of the Moffies' the headlines read in 1959, when 'Ada Garcia' was elected Moffie Queen, much to the outrage of her younger and more

119

beautiful opponents.[19] The whole event was always a great laugh — and also, concurrently, an opportunity to appreciate the genuine dancing and performing talents of the contestants.

As it became clearer, in the 1960s, that the moffie scene was a smash hit in the pages of *Drum* and the *Golden City Post*, *Golden City Post* even decided to 'invent' a moffie columnist, 'Aunt Sammy', who was often 'on the scene' for the magazine. Aunt Sammy did in fact exist. She was a well known shebeen-queen, but, according to those who knew her, she was barely literate. Clearly, one or more of *Drum*'s more adventurous writers was engaging in their own experiment of literary drag.[20]

Moffie drags

Just as Gertie, the only lesbian featured in the pages of *Drum* and the *Golden City Post* in the early years, conformed to the fixed stereotype of the bulldyke, so too did the images of moffie life, whether in text or pictures, conform to a fixed range of possibilities. The moffies were inevitably in drag; they were effete, theatrical, tragic or comic. Alternatively, they were cast as social pariahs, wallowing in self-pity and praying for sex change operations. The pictures of a typical 'moffie drag' provide a sense of lives lived between these two powerful stereotypes. The photographs were all taken by Ian Berry at a private party at Madame Costello's house in Davidson Street, Woodstock in December 1958. Some of them were published in *Golden City Post* that month and some in *Drum*'s January 1959 issue (see figures 3-14).

What makes these photographs unusual is that they were not taken at a public competition of the type run by the *Golden City Post* at the Kismet in Athlone, but at private house-party — a moffie drag. Nevertheless, *Drum* did play a particular role in this house-party: even though it was private, the magazine 'set' the event up by paying for the food and liquor. As with the Kismet events, then, the popular press was engaged in the project of constructing a 'moffie' spectacle for its readers.

Madame Costello, or Joey, was an older queen well-known on the circuit, and her home was a regular venue for drags. She was renowned for her operatic talents, and was a regular face in the papers. In 1955, she produced the 'All Male Non-European Revuette and Minstrel Show'.

Monthly drags of this type were also held at popular venues like the Ambassador Club. Cards would be printed and pamphlets would advertise revues like the 'Gay Fifties'. Here, a standard entirely different to the performances at places like the Kismet prevailed. In the intimacy of the house parties, moffies described and acted out the internal codes of their 'community'. These were clearly not casual affairs, but neither were they put on specifically for the titillation of heterosexual observers. Despite the fact that they were, in a sense, 'set up', these photographs tell a far more complicated story.

As the photographs demonstrate, 'drags', as the parties were known, were elaborate performances of ritual and style, celebrations of romance and fantasy.

120

Figure 1. 'Yvonne de Carlo' poses for *Drum*, January 1962. Photographer unknown.

Figure 2. 'Carmen Miranda' and a dwarf at the Coon Carnival. 1957. Photograph by Barney Desai. Other photographs from the sereis were published in *Drum*, March 1957, under the heading 'When Coonland Goes Crazy'.

A drag at Madame Costello's
photographs by Jan Berry

Figure 3. Madame Joey Costello in the kitchen

Figure 4. The scene in Madame Costello's living room

Figure 5. 'Linda Darnell'

Figure 6. 'Linda Darnell' and partner

Figure 7. 'Kay Kendall'

Figure 8. 'Piper Laurie'

Figure 9. 'Ginger' (left) and friend

Figure 10. 'Rita Ricardo' and partner

Figure 11. 'Rita Ricardo' and friends

Figure 12. On the dancefloor at Madame Costello's

Figure 13. On the dancefloor at Madame Costello's

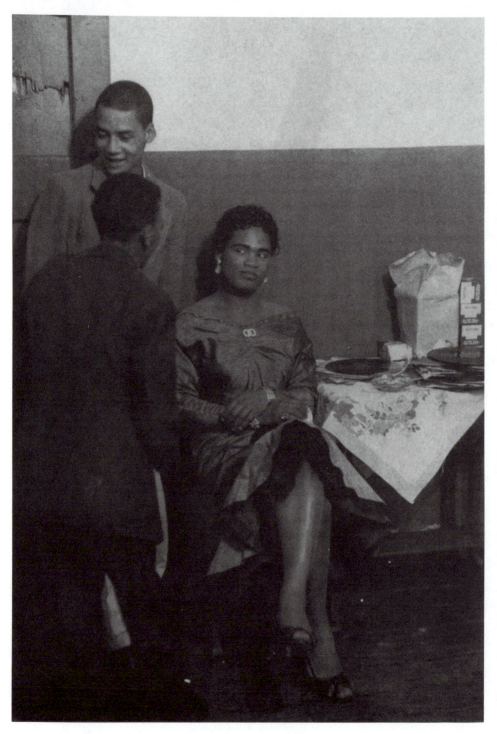

Figure 14. Taking a break

Figure 15. 'Kewpie Doll' poses for *Drum*, January 1968. Under the photo appeared the following quote: 'People should not try and interfere with our sect. No-one can change us'. Photographer unknown.

Figure 16. Gertie Williams poses for *Drum*, April 1956, with her family.

One couldn't just be a moffie, one had to look the part. And, in looking the part of their female icons, the 'girls' invested much in the quest for womanhood. The subjects of the pictures are at once demure, flirtatious, coquettish and playful. These are not images of pathetic or pitiful people, of 'lonely and bitter' lives finding 'solace' only 'at the bottom of a bottle'.

In contrast to the pseudo-psychological 'common sense' that informed the reportage on gay life in the period, the pictures show a remarkable empathy and sensitivity to the subtleties of camp, and the feeling of the imaginary world created at the drags. 'Rita', a friend of 'Eartha Kitt' (murdered in 1959), captures something of the true pathos of life in between the real and imaginary worlds:

> There are many of us in the town. Our numbers grow... we meet often. Some sneer at us. Some understand. But we just adjust ourselves to the conditions. Our world is real. We cannot exist otherwise.[21]

Style and images of the self have always been crucial aspects of gay and lesbian life. Style is about the politics of the personal in these pictures, and, in the 1950s, a certain style gave Cape Town gay life its own blend of camp. Elaborate costuming, make-up and stage-names added up to a certain aesthetic. In just the same way as camp practitioners of the 1980s looked to Madonna and Grace Jones for inspiration, in this era it was the cinema that provided icons. Gay men became 'Capuccine', 'Doris Day', 'Eartha Kitt', and 'Lena Horne'. In a report on the upcoming election for Moffie Queen in 1967, for example, the following entries were noted:

> Mitzi Gaynor of Maitland Salon; the pert and proper Miss Perkins of District Six; Liverpool Lily of the Seven Steps; Miss Hayley Mills of Woodstock; Miss Anita Ekberg of Rochester Road; dark and curvaceous Shirley Bassey of Sir Lowry Road.[22]

Sometimes, however, the role-playing became even more staged. Amongst the most celebrated of the public performances was the 18th Century theme ball held at the Ambassador Club in 1967. Kewpie Doll/Cappucine was the toast of the evening which began with the procession through District Six and Woodstock of a horse-drawn carriage loaded with Marie Antoinette look-alikes.[23]

Role playing was a finely crafted art form for the gay men who came into public view. The characters wanted to be appealing as 'women'. The costumes, the make-up and all the other devices gays and lesbians use with such power and creativity allowed these men to re-imagine themselves outside of the conventions imposed by a world of heterosexist images. But this is an ambiguous step: the camp and cross-dressing which these men took so seriously might have been about flouting convention, but it was also about appropriating the available vocabulary of sexism. On the dancefloor in Madame Costello's lounge we see 'men' dancing with 'women'; we seldom see 'men' dancing with 'men' or 'women' with 'women'.

That images of cross-dressing are subversive is evident in the rage and hostility they provoke and in official attempts to censor them: for years, for example, masquerading as a woman was an offence for which gays were intermittently prosecuted.[24] What could possibly be dangerous about wearing clothes meant for another gender? Oddly, it suggests that marginal and persecuted men could be more powerful by posing as women. In 1965, *Drum* and the *Golden City Post* covered the case of John 'Joan' Kruger, Edward 'Edna' Hobles and Mohamed 'Sonia' Kola who were found guilty of masquerading as women. Their friends Muriel and Sharon had taken the most extreme measures to avoid persecution, at least from the law: both had sex changes.[25]

The regulars at drags were seemingly uninterested in the other identities of their female icons, except for their one dimensional public image as vampish movie queens. True enough, their acting out of sexual identities in drag was a transgressive act, but it was far from being anything like a mockery of heterosexual convention. They wanted something undefinable which only straight women could access. In a bitter retort, Joan, one of the accused in the 1965 case of unlawful masquerading, revealed a part of that desire: 'If I wanted to dress like a woman just for kicks, I would have done it only once — not all the time.'[26]

In one of its investigations in 1956 the *Golden City Post* visited a drag. The reporter's first impression of the assembled company barely conceals a sense of terror — the terror of being confronted with something subversive.

> *Their powder heavy faces and the blue evening frock one wore added to the grotesqueness of everything. ...the party took on an almost nightmarish quality... there was not one REAL woman present... As the evening lengthened, all restraint vanished. It was easy to see why a drag is a necessity in their lives... At times I tried to tell myself that it wasn't real: that it was all part of a horrible dream, but the blaring music; the gaily festooned room; the two bitter girls in the corner; the frenzy of desperate longing let loose by the amount of liquor they had consumed, showed to what extremes they would go to, for a time, to be what they longed to be.*[27]

Clearly, the author here is reinforcing the picture of a life that is both depraved and dangerous. While there is no doubt that this picture is being painted to conform to stereotypes, there was a high level of crime and alcoholism within and around the moffie community. Gertie Williams' story gives some indications of the role drugs played in her social world which was clearly defined by an ethos of criminality.

Crime was a part of ordinary life for some. In a celebrated case, Doris Day was kidnapped and knifed by thugs from District Six in 1966 only days after her celebrated exorcism at the hands of Reverend Slingers. And the beloved Eartha Kitt was killed by her lover. Whether or not the moffies were themselves criminals, there is no doubt that an ambivalent relationship existed between gays and gangs, particularly in District Six. The Scorpions, the Globe Gang and the Casbahs were very much a part of life. It was not uncommon for gang members to demand sex from gay men, and in exchange for their favours, gay men were inducted into a network of protection and patronage. Sexual violence, it appears, was the consequence if a gay man refused to comply.

From recollections of the period it is difficult to tell clearly whether the relationship was entirely exploitative or if some gay men encouraged it. Those moffies who had the protection of local *skollies* (thugs) were in the best position to challenge homophobic violence. At the same time, they could be easy prey. It is equally unclear why gangsters, who generally embody the most malevolent image of masculinity, were so keen to be involved with gay men. Was it just a matter of easy sex? If that was the case, why did they not prey solely on female prostitutes?

The hair salons

What becomes a legend?

In mid-1992, after trying to piece together this gay network of the 1950s and 1960s using reporters' recollections, I stumbled upon a member of the Cape Town crowd in Johannesburg. A maze began to unravel which led to a tour of some of the Cape Town's lesser-known hairdressing salons, in which were to be found some of South Africa's finest talents from the 1950s, who for all these years have remained as hairdressers in their working-class neighbourhoods.

In the main, the gay men who did fall under the scrutiny of the papers, or as some would suggest, turned the media spotlight on themselves, came from working class backgrounds and were the mainstay of the city's hairdressing industry. The beauty business was their natural niche. According to one self-proclaimed authority, 'their delicate hands and generally frail personalities forbid any intrusion into highly demanding operations such as woodwork, building or truck driving.'[28]

In the 1950s and 1960s, the Hanover Street area of District Six had a whole cluster of hairdressing salons around which gay life revolved. 'Salon crawls', in which one would while away the day visiting the various establishments, were popular social outings. In other ways, the beauty business gave gays the opportunity and means to create for themselves a world of femininity. Though some were taken up by the contemporary obsession with 'the sex change operation', most were content to look and act the part of their icons, in every way possible.

Since the forced removals of 1976 and the destruction of District Six, these salons are now to be found dispersed all over the Cape Flats — from Kensington to Mitchell's Plain.

Kewpie

The star performers in the 'moffie revues' of the 1950s and 1960s continue to use their stage names. Kewpie, (see figure 15) also known as Kewpie Doll and Capuccine, was one such star. Kewpie remains a legend in the coloured working class area of Kensington in Cape Town, although this *enfant terrible* of the moffie drag scene in the 1960s is now more sedate and even a little maudlin in his later years.

His salon still has pride of place on the street and, at 7 p.m. on the day in 1992 when I visited him, faithful male customers were still coming in for their haircuts.

Like its owner, the salon had a sense of faded glory, a mixture of kitsch and decay: this was not the world of track lighting and hi-tech. While we talked, two younger acolytes were preparing for a night at Tots, the favoured Wednesday evening venue for the coloured gay crowd. Both were perfectly cross-dressed in well fitted jeans, blouses and accessories.

Like most of his generation of gay men, Kewpie grew up in District Six, in a family of six children who went to local schools like St. Philip's and the Berlin Mission School. His mother, a housewife, is remembered especially for her tolerance of his sexuality from its earliest expressions. Kewpie wanted to be a dancer and began ballet classes at an early age: he was, in fact, trained in ballet at the University of Cape Town, destined for a career before the lights. Parental pressure, though, put a hold on these ambitions.

It was nevertheless acceptable within the close confines of District Six for Kewpie to start cross-dressing at an early age. When his parents moved from the area, he stayed on, working as a clerk during the day and running a hairdressing business from home. Around 1954, Kewpie moved into what is now Kensington to set up his salon, the first in the area. It was a major achievement for a drag queen who was already vivacious, in the news, and on the move.

Kewpie reminisced about other characters desperate for media attention in the 1950s; characters who regularly claimed to be committing suicide, having a baby or something of the kind, and who are now married with children. Two such examples are Doris Day and Rita Riccardo (who was at Madame Costello's drag — figures 10 and 11).

Piper Laurie

Piper Laurie (see figure 8), another of the legendary figures of the period, is also a hairdresser — in Mitchell's Plain, the sprawling coloured township to which many former inner city residents were forcibly removed. Piper, who turned 55 in 1992, is remembered as a true diva in his youth, and our first encounter was in perfect keeping with that reputation: he was curled up in bed with innumerable poodles. When we met again he was attending to the constant stream of Mitchell's Plain matrons in his salon.

Like Kewpie, Piper was a District Six boy. He was talented enough to make his way to Trafalgar High, amongst the most prestigious of coloured schools at the time, but left after standard eight. Piper — or Ismail Hanif as he was then — was the eldest of nine children. His mother was a housewife and his father worked for the municipality as a labourer. The family was devoutly Muslim, and Piper was very much a member of the faith. While his father was less accommodating of Piper's early expressions of gay identity, his mother and the rest of the family acknowledged his difference at an early age.

Piper made a point of his sexuality and what he thought of gender roles at school by insisting on doing needle-work classes. While still at primary school he

124

dyed his hair red, and by the age of 14 was using make-up regularly. At about the same time he entered the world of gay sex, usually picking up white men in the city. At this time the sexual economy of Cape Town was located around the old station, Burg Street (the main cruising area for men) and Loop Street for female prostitutes. Gay prostitutes often dressed in drag and had a regular supply of clients from ships in port. A number of the prostitutes lived in nearby Woodstock.

Aside from hairdressing, Piper had a varied career. He too was a ballet student to begin with. Early on, he spent three years working as a dancer for the celebrated Eoan Group. The Group, which emerged from within the coloured community, became a focus of 'high culture' in the city with their performances of ballet, opera and musicals. But even in the world of the arts, Piper's 'difference' got him into trouble: men dancing in dresses were unacceptable to the coloured cultural elite, and he was eventually dropped from the dance troupe.

For a time in the 1950s, Piper performed with a touring revue company, African Jazz and Variety. African Jazz went on to become Shebeen and then African Follies, and Piper gained quite a reputation as a dancer, working with Dolly Rathebe, Rose Mathys and Miriam Makeba, all of whom belonged to the same company at various times. In the black music world, it appears, gay people were generally respected and supported. One show Piper remembers especially from the 1950s was 'High Note', an all-male revue in which the dancers were almost all gay men from Cape Town. Some of the city's finest — Linda Darnell, Carmen Miranda, Yvonne de Carlo and Tilly Millin — were featured.

Piper spent some time in Durban and, with another well known drag-queen hairdresser, Sandra Sassman, created something of a stir. They shocked the conservative city with their openness: they were in full costume all the time. While the anti-drag laws were never enforced in Cape Town, in 1964 in Durban Piper was arrested and fined for 'masquerading'. Piper maintains that he and Sandra introduced drag to Durban: they organised performances at well known local clubs — the Himalaya Hotel and Pelican in Durban, and the Kismet in Pietermaritzburg.[29]

Bobby

Bobby, another of Kensington's hairdressers, was, like Piper and Kewpie, also at the heart of the District Six scene in the 1950s. He too came from a devoutly Muslim family of nine children. The family's acceptance of his sexuality is immediately visible in the confidence with which he relates to them: to his battery of nieces and nephews he is 'Aunt Bobby'.

As with Piper and Kewpie, Bobby had an authoritative father and a mother who seems to have been very supportive of her son: there is a definite fondness in his memories of her 'ironing my stiffies' — stiffies being the nylon petticoats, like figure belts, essential for the well-dressed girl's skirt.

Compared to his peers, Bobby was a little slow in gaining experience with men, but at 16 he started his first very tentative relationship. There was precious little space in District Six for young people to experiment with sex. Not only were the homes small and overcrowded, but, in a strict Muslim family, any premarital sexual activity was strictly taboo. As everywhere, however, spaces were found: in District Six it was a park, locally known as the Green Curtains, where gay and straight men met furtively for sex. It was here that Bobby met his first love, a straight man with a heterosexual public life. He kept Bobby on the side — behind the Green Curtains.

By 19 Bobby had left school and started work as a hairdresser. He worked in this trade for 12 years and then for seven years in the metal industry, where he recalls no harassment.

When he began hairdressing, Bobby also began his experiments with drag: when on the circuit, he became 'Dolores Grey'. He soon got to know that lesbians and gays gathered at 'hops', neighbourhood parties known to be good for cruising. Later, Ma Philips' house, a boarding house where a number of gays lived, became a frequent venue for 'drags'. The Drill Hall and the Dry Docks area were also frequent haunts.

Bobby's second lover, who stayed with him for ten years, was married with children and shuttled between his male lover and his family. Bobby's family eventually accepted the relationship, and this was not too unusual in his community. The religious taboos on pre-marital sex made the availability of gay men as sexual partners appealing for straight men. If sex with young women was hard to come by, aside from prostitution, then effete gay men were a good enough substitute. But that did not mean the relationships were only about sex: many of them — like Bobby's — lasted much longer and could be called serious gay relationships. Such relationships, which often co-existed with conventional marriage, are still well known in the Cape Malay community.

In the confines of District Six and on circuit, gay characters always attempted to keep up appearances. Good seamstresses, like a Mrs van Graan from Athlone, are well remembered for their efforts in this regard. Escorts would arrive by taxi to pick up their partners for the evening. Children would stand by and applaud as the vamp made her appearance in full costume. Movie premieres were especially competitive events. And when the Eoan Group did its first American musical in the early 1970s, Bobby remembers buying dresses on sale at Foschini with Milly Perkins for the event.

Bobby is now semi-retired but still very much a part of the small, older gay community in the neighbourhood.

Conclusion

This is a small slice of life in 1950s and 1960s Cape Town. It was by no means the dominant form of gay life in the period or in the city — that fuller picture has yet to emerge. In a sense this is 'pre-revolutionary' gay life and culture. But, in their own way, these moffies created a culture worth celebrating. They sustained that essential element of queer culture — subversion. Masquerading as a woman meant subversion, but those involved engaged in the process to a greater or lesser extent.

Their lives in the context of their own communities is a dimension not easily visible in these brief sketches, but it is possible to sense the ambiguity of their position. For some, acceptance by family and community came with time: for others acceptance has meant sympathy for an outcast.

For all of them, ordinary life, whether in the hair salons or the factories, was turned into something else. Hair, sequins, frills and masks of feminine guile made life bearable and memorable. No doubt there was pain in their lives, but the vagaries of the popular press — at least for a time — allowed them the freedom to dream.

Notes

1 Archival research assistance by Marie Human, curator of Bailey's African Photo Archives.
2 'Moffie', coined in the coloured communities of the Western Cape, has become the South African equivalent of 'queer', 'faggot' or 'flikker', with extremely derisive connotations. Nevertheless, particularly among coloured gay men themselves, it has been reappropriated, with some pride, as a term of self-identity: it is in this spirit that this essay uses the word.
3 *Drum*, January 1962.
4 *Drum* was a weekly feature magazine; the *Golden City Post* a weekly newspaper. Both still exist — the *Golden City Post* as the Sunday *City Press*, and *Drum* as a popular magazine with local editions all over Africa.
5 *Golden City Post*, 15 May 1955.
6 *Golden City Post*, 1 September 1963, p6.
7 See, for example, Shamil Jeppie, 'The class, colour and gender of carnival: Aspects of a cultural form in inner Cape Town, circa 1939-59', paper to History Workshop Conference, University of Witwatersrand, February 1990.
8 *Drum*, November 1951.
9 *Drum*, September 1955, p51.
10 *Golden City Post*, 29 January 1956, p1.
11 *Golden City Post*, 29 January 1956, pp16-17.
12 *Golden City Post*, 25 September 1966, p1.
13 *Golden City Post*, 24 November 1963, p24.
14 *Golden City Post*, 30 August 1959, p1.
15 *Golden City Post*, 14 June 1959, p2.
16 *Golden City Post*, 24 September 1967, pp1-3.
17 *Drum*, January 1964, p42.
18 *Golden City Post*, 18 June 1967, p1.
19 *Golden City Post*, 13 September 1959, p1.
20 *Golden City Post*, 14 June 1964, p8.
21 *Golden City Post*, 5 July 1959, p1.
22 *Golden City Post*, 18 June 1967, p1.
23 *Golden City Post*, 9 July 1967, p14.
24 See Cameron in this volume for a fuller discussion of this law and its application.
25 *Drum*, September 1965, pp3-6. See also p90 above.
26 *Drum*, September 1965, p4.
27 *Golden City Post*, 12 August 1956, p4.
28 *Drum*, October 1976, p47.
29 *Golden City Post*, 11 July 1965, p1.

Lesbian gangster:
The Gertie Williams story

Excerpted from Golden City Post and Drum
Edited by Dhianaraj Chetty

Editor's note: What follows are two extracts, the first from the *Golden City Post* in 1955 and the second from *Drum* magazine in 1956. Both appeared without bylines, and are about Gertie, a cross-dressing lesbian gangster from Cape Town. For an analysis of the style and content of these articles, see Chetty's 'A drag at Madame Costello's'. See figure 16 in the photo section for a photograph of Gertie, published in *Drum* in April 1956.

Golden City Post, September 1955

The amazing true confession of a South African coloured girl who lived for five years as a man begins in *Post* today. It is the story of 'Johnny' Williams, told by Gertie Williams, who became a member of a gang of boys, a boy caddy, a handyman and later a deck-hand on a trawler.

We publish the story exactly as it was written, because it is a sincere, although at times grim, human document. A medical certificate, which the writer handed over to *Post* states that although Williams has all the physical attributes of a woman, 'she shows mentally, a marked tendency to be identified with males, even to the extent of having girl friends.'

My life as a man

A few weeks ago I appeared in the Wynberg, Cape Town Court, with another man. We were charged with theft. Later in the day a newspaper report said that I had disguised myself as a man. The report also mentioned that I had worked on the trawlers. We were sentenced to two months, which was suspended for three years.

We had been found guilty of stealing my grandfather's watch and some of his clothing.

I was not playing the fool when I disguised myself as a man. I did it because I hate to be a woman.

I was born in Wynberg, Cape Town, 25 years ago, and was baptised Gertrude by the Minister of the local Dutch Reformed Church. My Ma and Pa and Grandpa were regular church people. They got me into the Wesleyan Primary School. In Sub A I stole the teacher's money. He was very angry about the whole business, so he called the police. My mother must have spoken to them because soon after that trouble I was transferred to Battswood Primary School. During playtime I always mixed with the boys and played marbles, cricket, rough football and top-top. The other girls used to call me '*Galla man*' and tomboy — I just couldn't worry.

I did have a few other girl friends but they were older than myself. Together with Marty, Alida, Dola and Margaret, I *draaied stokkies* [bunked school] and passed the time smoking tea leaves in the park. At night I used to hang around with the girls at a café. They used to go out with men and I was always sent to the shebeen to get drinks for them. The girls taught me to drink wine and I liked it. Afterwards Marty's mother got to know about our doings and told my mother. Was she angry! Added to this, the minister told my mother that I was ducking Friday night rehearsals of the girl's choir. Ma was also told that I used to come to practice *lekker gefire* (dead drunk).

Reformatories

A policeman picked me up at home and took me to the Place of Safety near Prince George's Drive. For a week I lived there and then they sent me to Riviersonderend, about two hundred miles from Cape Town. I thought I was going to a school, but instead landed up on a farm outside a town. On the farm I had to look after the children of the farmer and also do kitchen work. My duties were not too hard, but I was very lonely and longed very much for Cape Town. Everything was quiet on the farm and there was nothing exciting to do — except when I stole a bit of wine from the cellars.

After three months I decided that I had enough of farm life. Late one night when all were asleep I made my break. It was a long way back home but I decided that if I followed the railway line I would get there. Back home in Wynberg, I spinned a line to Ma. I told her that the farmer had come to town for two days. Ma didn't believe me so she made enquiries. I hardly had time to look around when I was arrested, and sent off to a farm near Caledon. The farmer and his wife met me at the station with their horse and cart and took me to their farm where I was to spend more than 13 months of my life. My hair was bobbed and I wore a man's shirt and khaki shorts.

From the start the farmer noticed that I wanted to do the harder work with the menfolk. He didn't mind and the *nooi* (madam) in the kitchen did not trouble to give me women's work. I worked with the men in the field. We cut corn and dug and tilled the land with spades and forks. No man could show me up because I kept up with them no matter how tough the work was. In the evenings, at *challe time* (knock-off time) all the workers were given a horn full of wine — I also got my share.

That was the best thing about the farm. I was also very happy that the men did not believe I was a girl. The only work I did not like on the farm was milking the cows.

Although the farmer was kind to me I started getting lonely again. One day I ran away but only got as far as Caledon when they caught me. When the farmer asked me why I had done this, I told him, 'Baas, the big days will soon be on in Cape Town. All the bands and Coons is walking in the streets and I wanted to go there.'

A week later I vanished from the farm. I had it fixed up with a pal of mine who was a lorry driver in Caledon. Everything went well and I arrived safely in Wynberg. There was no welcome for me when I returned home. Ma again reported me and soon after that I was sent off to the Kimberley Home for Girls. I stayed at the home for four months and during that time did sewing, fancy work and cleaning out the dormitories.

The four months were soon over, and I was nearly 14 years old. From Kimberley I was sent to a girls' reformatory in another province, where I was to stay for five years. When the new batch of admissions was booked in, we were given uniforms. There we saw a few girls standing around and giving us a good look over. They discussed us amongst themselves.

After I had finished washing, a longtimer, Doris X, came up to me and said, 'You'll be my girl friend.' I answered back very quickly: 'I am a man myself, so you'll have to forget about it.'

I then told her that I was an old jail-bird, and then they agreed to let me be a 'man'. The few of us who were 'men' sat at table number one, and we were the big shots of the place. The girls all respected us. They were not allowed in the shower room when we were there.

After a week at the place, I fell in with a girl called Irene who worked in the kitchen. She was my 'girl friend' throughout the time I was there. Irene was doing a seven year stretch for murdering her baby and putting it in a shoe box. She was really a nice kid. There was a dagga plant growing in the garden that only a few of us 'men' knew about. Boy, did we have a nice time with the *boom* [marijuana] in our cells at night.

All of us were longing to get out of the place as soon as possible, and the visit of King George to South Africa was the finest answer to our prayers. Everybody got special remissions and I was among those pardoned. Free at last, I was put on to the train to Cape Town. When I saw the outline of Table Mountain I was as happy as when I smoked a pill of *dagga*. Everyone at home was glad to see me at home after four years.

On my return from the girls' reformatory, I spent a month at home and then I got a job in a shirt factory in Wynberg. Once a girl at the factory teased me and called me 'Gertie man'. One blow to her face was enough to shut her up, and also anybody else who would speak about me. While I was working at the factory, I met Arthur. He used to hang around at the same corner as I did. He also belonged to our gang, the Flying Tigers. We were together for over six months, but although I was very fond of him, things just didn't click. I didn't like too much romance.

One day, near New Year I heard that Arthur was going out with another girl. On New Year's Day I picked him out and we had a terrible quarrel. I told him straight: 'Arthur, we are finished.' On the same day I decided that I would change over completely and become a man. This is what I had planned out in the reformatory. I left the factory, took my savings out of the post office, and bought myself a shirt and a pair of slacks. After that I went to a tailor and had a special suit made for myself. I like a long cut coat, two tickey pockets, two back pockets, six belt hoops and a 24 bottom.

I left the Flying Tigers and joined up with the 44 Boys. From now onwards I was Johnny Williams and this was the end of Gertie. No more dresses, no more lipstick and powder, no more Gertie. My Grandpa was very worried about me. My mother strongly objected, but I told them it was no use. I wanted to be a man, and nothing was going to stop me. So they called the *predikant* (preacher) to speak to me. He said: 'Gertie my girl, it's a sin to play man when you are a woman.'

I said, 'If it was a sin, then God would have shown me the sick bed.' He gave up after speaking to me for a long time. On the corner with the gang I smoked *dagga* and drank lots of jupe (cheap wine). We gambled and had fights with other gangs. My favourite fighting style is with a buckle belt. Once, while we were in a gang fight, one of the opposition was about to give Attie a coward shot from behind. I let go my belt on his head and he was soon bleeding down the neck. I'm not afraid of a fight. I can stand my ground with the best in the business. Our gang also hung around a cinema in Wynberg. We had lots of fun teasing the girls when the lights went off inside. Some time ago when we were fooling around with the girls in the bio, one of the dames screamed so loud that the ushers chucked us out and the manager barred us from entering again. We also had fights outside the place because some of the other fellows who had dough didn't want to stand us for a show. Once while we were all in a bar having a *dop* (drink) of jupe, one of the opposition boys made a dirty remark. He called to his friend 'Hey, here is Galla-the-man-woman.' He looked at me and called me a moffie. I didn't wait long. Before you could say District Six I grabbed an empty beer bottle and knocked him over the head. After that the ructions started. Now I am barred from the bar, too.

Now we go to another bar. I remember it was there that the barman lost one pound against a friend of mine when they had a bet that I was a woman. The barman would not believe it until I showed him. He told me to come in next week again. When I came back he organised a bet with another man for five pounds saying that I was a woman. This man also didn't believe it and lost his money. The barman, who was very happy with himself, gave me ten bob. I used to do odd jobs to get extra money. Sometimes I used to go to a golf club, where I got a job as a caddy. At other times I broked [sic] (hawked) with vegetables, and when the season was not so good I used to go around doing handyman jobs like building small walls. At one time I used to prepare the cricket pitch of the Cape and District Six Sports Ground. But all these jobs were too few to keep me going, so I finally decided to try my luck on the trawlers.

I decided that hanging around Cape Town wasn't going to do me any good. So I went out to get a job on the fishing ships. I got a job in Hout Bay catching crawfish in a dinghy with a net. Nobody suspected me. They all took me for a man. Later I got on a trawler and we went out for about three weeks.

Whoo! It was hard on the trawler. I did all kinds of work: ice-packer, deck hand and collection boy. At one time my hands were full of blisters and bled from all the rope pulling and handling of the rough, prickly crawfish. But I didn't squeal. I was ready for anything at any time. On board the trawler I always wore pyjamas under my outfit so that when I undressed at night none of the other members of the crew could see my body. When I used to have a wash on deck I always had a big towel around my shoulders, which would cover me.

When I got back and collected my pay, which was about 15 pounds, I bought wine and dagga with it and did a bit of *smokkeling* (ran a shebeen). My business did not last for long because I drank up most of the profits, so I had to go back to the trawlers. Everything was smooth on the boats until I borrowed a nice blue suit from one of the crew without asking him. I thought I would return it to him the next day but he immediately reported me to the police for theft. When the cops came around to my place they asked grandpa where Johnny Williams was. He said that there was no Johnny Williams, but that he only knew Gertie. The fellow whose suit I did borrow was shocked when I appeared and my pa told him that I was a woman. The police did not believe it until they had me examined. The police told me to come to court in a dress. I didn't like the idea very much, but could do nothing about it. I put a dress in a carrier and when I got to the court I went to the lavatory and changed into it. The magistrate sentenced me to one month, suspended for two years. I went back to the lavatory and dressed up again in men's clothing.

Back in Wynberg I started having a romance with a married woman. We were happy together until Mrs M, who has a *smokkelhuis* (shebeen), told her that I was a woman. Then she moved out of the area. Anyway, I don't have to worry. I have got a nice friend now who lives in Sea Point. We have been together for over a year. She does not know that I am a woman. But I will lose her too when this story is read by thousands of people in Cape Town.

Arrested again

Five weeks ago a friend and I were sitting outside the window of my grandpa's room. I saw grandpa go to the cupboard and take out some rice. He forgot to lock it again. We decided to steal his pack of clothes and also a watch. We got 25 shillings for the suit and 12 shillings and six pence for the watch. We were in paradise for the next two days. With the money we bought four bottles of jupe and ten *kartjies* (scrolls) of *boomdagga* (best marijuana) and we had a hot party with the 44 Boys on the veld. When the CID came to our house to investigate the theft I confessed. Both of us were sentenced to two months suspended for three years.

Now you all know the story of Gertie and Johnny Williams. I also want you to know that when the first fruits of the season come to town I make wish before I eat them. My wish is that God must make me a man. It is the only thing I want most in the world. I hope He will grant me that wish, for I never want to go back to being a woman.

Drum, April 1956

Behind the rugged front of Gertie Williams' life is the sensitive suffering of a person who feels misplaced in her sex. Gertie Williams is the Cape Town girl discovered by *Golden City Post* who refuses to remain a girl in the teeth of Nature's dictates and society's raised eyebrows. She prefers the rough and tumble of life as a man — and you can throw in all the hard work and horse-play life as a man means. She says:

> *All my gang are men, and the only feeling I have towards women is the same feeling any regular man would have. But to be with the silly creatures all the time and to listen to their foolish chatter, I would never be able to bear. If I cannot be in the company of men, I would rather be dead. My earnest prayer each night is that God would be merciful to me and change me completely into a man. If it could be done by any operation, I would gladly risk it as no pain could be too severe if it meant the fulfilment of my desire.*

But this he-baby doesn't find it easy all the way. First she has to prove her 'manliness' all the time, and that means scrapping with the roughest Cape Town can give. Then she has to hide her womanliness. That is tricky. It takes her quickly from job to job; it makes her sneak away from places where she is known too well; she sometimes has to lie herself out of embarrassing situations.

She was a gardener for a time, a golf caddy, a cricket groundsman, a trawler fisherman and a bricklayer. The only thing she won't do is housework. Yes, Gertie boasts too that she does her share of the fighting in one of the top gangs in Wynberg. How tough can a girl get! And she found a girlfriend for herself more than once. When at a dance thrown by a local football team, Gertie suddenly grabbed a girl and danced with her. Out on the balcony they went, into the moonlight. After the dance Gertie took the girlfriend home. And since then she 'went steady' with the girl, even when she discovered that Gertie was no man. Gertie says she charmed her into accepting the state of affairs. But frustration and deep longing remain with her always. And she's always afraid of the future. She says:

> *What the end is going to be, I don't know. There is no hope of marriage for us, and the raising of a family which I yearn for. We will have to spend the rest of our lives living like this, unless God is merciful and ...lets me become a whole man.*

133

Johannesburg's 'Health Clubs': *Places of erotic languor or prison-houses of desire?*

Peter Galli and Luis Rafael

In Johannesburg's city centre lies a forgotten relic of our past, the London Health Clinic (LHC). The building still stands in Nugget Street, just south of the railway, but the vagaries of time have left their marks: in front of what was once a glamorous swimming pool — inlaid with fine mosaic but now empty and covered with a layer of grime — are two rusty deck-chairs, a poignant reminder of the time when there were those who languished in the sweetness of sensuality. Behind these chairs are the broken window panes and dark interior of a forgotten space.

It wasn't always like this. There was a time, between 1955 and 1965, when the LHC in Johannesburg teemed with life and activity. Which is not to say that it was always looked upon favourably. One of its former patrons, Jeremy, described it as 'a bloody Chinese laundry with dirty cream stucco and a tall chimney on top. The inside was very old, very tatty, with lots of white tiles.' Another of its patrons, Rupert, was even less flattering. He recalled that 'it was a filthy place, old, and infested with thousands of cockroaches. The plaster was falling off the walls and there was moss growing in the steam-rooms.'

The LHC wasn't the only 'health club' available in Johannesburg at the time. Rupert also mentioned an equally popular venue, a sauna opposite the Carlton Hotel in central Johannesburg, the Atwater:

> This was such a meat-rack — a sleazy dump — on the first floor of a broken-down building. It was painted black and noncommital pictures of landscapes and the like were scattered all around.

134

Still, the health clubs remained a popular alternative to the other facilities then available to gay men, and were one of the few outlets for the relatively safe expression of gay sexuality. Because the health clubs were important in the general circuit of gay life, we decided to record people's recollections. Our intention was not merely to transcribe people's memories of their experiences: we wanted to record their stories critically. Our article, however, is anecdotal rather than empirical.

The heyday period of the 'health clubs' was also the height of the apartheid era, the time of Strijdom and Verwoerd, when the visible gay scene was one occupied by white men only. Our respondents were white men who are now in their sixties and seventies and would have been between 18 and 28 at the time. These men came from middle-class backgrounds and were able to afford the costs of such activities, out of the reach of many poorer whites. The three men whom we quote at length were all professional people: one was a health worker, one worked for a large financial institution and the other owned his own communications business.

Many of the men active at that time were either reluctant to comment or were no longer alive. The most logical place to find suitable men to interview was through the Johannesburg support network for elderly gay men. Although this group caters for a large body of such people, we were told that it would not be able to help us, as many of the group members were still 'in the closet' and a study of this nature 'might destroy their relationships with their families'. This was despite assurances of complete anonymity. Only one person from this group was willing to share his experiences with us. This left us with only one option: we had to find our sources in the existing gay bars and clubs. This proved to be a tricky enterprise. Few older gay men frequent these places, and those we found were often suspicious of our motives, assuming we were either rent-boys or con-artists.

The 'health club': A displaced signifier

The name 'health club' is, of course, a euphemism; one of those terms that stand for a concept to which it bears little resemblance; a displaced signifier. The LHC and its cousin The Atwater ostensibly existed to provide 'health services' such as massages and saunas, but were largely patronised by men looking for homosexual encounters. Rupert recalled that:

> During the day [the London Health Clinic] served the purpose of a health club for [straight] men, but after 5 o'clock it cleared and the pleasure-seekers moved in.

There was an explicit division between day-time and night-time functions: the day being the domain of the male straights, the night of the gays.

And it was clearly their after-dark functions that kept these establishments going: In 1959, for five pounds — the equivalent then of the cost of an expensive meal in a good restaurant — a patron could stay the night. As Rupert said:

> This wasn't cheap. People went there and paraded in the corridors, but any action took place in the cubicles. It was common

*for people to stay over. The sheets were changed in the cubicles
where we slept and the towels were reasonably clean.*

Despite the unflattering descriptions, the establishments were run efficiently. They
were, after all, money-making enterprises that depended on the fluctuations of the
user's pocket. According to Rupert, there was always a rush period at the start of
the month when people had just been paid.

Rupert recalled that the Atwater fell under the control of the indomitable
presence of 'an ungainly slob who was overweight. But she [he] saw that the towels were reasonably fresh and that the coffee flowed freely.'

'Like going to a peach tree': The social context

The 'health clubs' were not the only meeting places for gay men, but existed alongside other activities as one of many choices in a wide spectrum of venues.

There were the bars. Mark told us that, in the early 1960s, there were
already exclusively gay bars, like the New Library and the Waldorf. And some
clubs — like that of Leo Smith, who opened a social club in his mother's flat in
Rissik Street in 1965 — offered an alternative to the health clubs. Mark said that:

*Leo's makeshift club was so successful that he opened the first
club in the same area... a few years later he closed this and
opened the Iron Butterfly in Berea in about 1967.*

Other popular outlets for sexual gratification also existed. 'Cottaging', procuring
sexual partners in public toilets, was probably the most widely utilised. One of the
centres of this activity was the Johannesburg City Hall toilet — which Jeremy
described as 'One vast loo that was open 24-hours a day, buzzing with life. That's
where the desperate went to when they couldn't get anything at the clubs.'

Equally popular and very similar, involving the exchange of commodities,
was the rent scene, centred around Johannesburg Station and Joubert Park. Mark
related how he 'used to spend hundreds of hours driving round the station looking
for a pick-up.' These pick-ups were inexpensive: before the Republic in 1961,
Jeremy informed us, a rent would cost half a crown or 2s 6p — far less than the
entry fee of the London Health Clinic — and thus available to a far greater section
of the population.

And, according to Mark, there were far more rent boys then than there are
now. However, none of the respondents were aware of any rent-boys at the health-
clubs, as the five pound entrance fee would probably have precluded this. Having
paid the entry fee, patrons were not expected to part with any more money.

Another alternative to the health club scene was the tea-room bioscope, or
cafe-bio. Mark said:

*There were three or four of these, which were ordinary cinemas
where you could eat, smoke and have it off while watching a
movie. But this was basically a rent scene and they centred
around Hillbrow and town.*

136

So popular was this alternative that Jeremy described it as 'like going to a peach tree and looking at which peach one wanted to pluck.'

More sophisticated than all this was the closed circuit of the Johannesburg dinner-party scene, proclaimed by Rupert to be 'the essential thing'. There was a highly organised party system in Johannesburg's northern suburbs and, indeed, it was the raid of one of these parties in Forest Town in 1966 that brought homosexuality into the public eye by provoking intense police and parliamentary opprobrium and leading to the 1968 Parliamentary Select Committee enquiry into the 'problem'.

Place of celebration for 'closettes': The clientele

In order to determine the role of health clubs in relation to the other available options, we needed to determine if there was an overlap of people. Jeremy said that 'an older crowd' frequented the health clubs, as opposed to the clientele in the bars and clubs, who were more likely to be 'people in their late teens to their late 20s'. These older people were not fully integrated into mainstream gay society. Jeremy's opinion was that 'they were gay but they felt awkward with gay society.' Rupert also observed that 'usually, one met married guys in the saunas. Many of these were bisexuals.'

Insofar as the health clubs allowed their patrons free sexual expression, they represented a positive reappropriation of the joys of that sexuality. Jeremy said that those who might have had hang-ups about their sexuality were free to express their unencumbered sexual desires in relative security. And individuals were not alone — they formed part of a community united in a similar quest for sexual experience.

This sexual freedom existed simultaneously with the growing access and availability of drugs in the 1960s. Mark pointed out that:

> *Amphetamines were legal on prescription. Uppers were very popular. So was acid* [LSD]. *There were very good brands available then: Hawaian Blue, California Sunrise. They were freely available and contributed to the La Dolce Vita lifestyle that we seemed to live.*

Drugs and sexual liberation were closely connected at the time, although this connection should not be exaggerated.

At the same time, however, all the respondents emphasised that this sexual freedom existed within a prejudiced heterosexual society that did not easily tolerate deviant forms of sexual expression. As Jeremy said: 'Police surveillance was always a big thing in those days and we always had to be on the watch.' Given the circumstances, it may well be argued that this sexual liberation was really a ruse, an illusion perpetuated within the walls of the 'health clubs' but shattered by the censure that existed as soon as one left the premises.

These manifestations of sexual expression, after all, were not accepted by straight society, particularly given the restrictive legislation enforced by the Calvinist National Party government in power since 1948. Hence the need to contain these behaviours within a structure that would effectively hide them. The very architectonic structure of the LHC, a fort in miniature, reinforced the hidden and repressed nature of these sexual expressions. Jeremy said that:

> *The club had a swing door so that only one person could enter at a time. Should priscilla* [the police] *raid, by the time they had all entered we would have had enough time to be engaged in healthy activities... We felt secure within the club.*

It is no surprise that such a protective structure attracted, by and large, 'closettes', those who could not inhabit that other gay world and who lived dual lives, in secrecy and fear.

Thirty years later: What has changed?

Now, 30 years later, how different is the 'health club' scene? In order to find out, we visited the two venues that operate in Johannesburg. The first place, a long-standing venue, catered for an eclectic crowd; the clientele ranged in age and in class, and, although the majority was white, there were black men there too. This contrasted with the complete absence of those not designated white in the scene between 1955 and 1965. At any one time during our Saturday visit there were at least 30 people at the club, and the centre of activity was the steam room, which was always full. Some of the older men kept turning the steam on very high, clouding the room and reducing any sort of visibility. But the place offered other, equally steamy, attractions. Each visitor was given a separate cubicle with its own bed and locker. Many of the visitors stayed the night.

Another of its attractions, catering for the more adventurous, was the 'black hole', a dark orgy-room always filled with men. When they wanted a break, patrons would lounge, with their towels around them, on the barstools sipping coffee, coke or a Castle beer. This was no different from what it had been in the LHC, where, our respondents told us, patrons would use the communal 'bar' space for less-fraught interaction.

The second venue was run-down, with mould growing on the walls and on the floor. It was smaller than the first and included not only a steam room, but also a sauna and a gym. This reminded us of what had been said about the LHC, which offered 'legitimate' health services during the day. Although people were given shorts to wear, most walked around without them. Because there were no individual cubicles, activities tended to be public. Contrast this with the LHC where public nudity never occurred.

We met the owner of one of these venues, also believed to be the owner of the LHC, to gain more specific information about the scene in the 1950s and 1960s. He was, however, very reluctant to talk, denying any involvement with the LHC. Given the difficulties these places might have with the authorities, we understood his reticence.

Contradictory messages

That the 'health clubs' played an important role in the gay life of the 1950s and 1960s is unquestionable. But their very nature seemed to contain within it messages that were contradictory: they represented both liberation and repression. Liberation came with the patrons' freedom to express their 'illegal' sexual desires within the protective space of the 'health clubs', but there was repression in that this behaviour had to remain hidden behind the facade of legitimate activities.

These health clubs existed in a restrictive, moralistic society, where gay solidarity, as embodied by organisations devoted to gay causes, did not exist. Because of this they could be regarded as the closest thing to a community meeting place.

Today, after Stonewall, the AIDS scare, the formation of gay liberation organisations and three gay pride marches in Johannesburg, the presence of the health-clubs remains unaltered. What does this tell us? If they remain as popular today as they were then, given the easing of sexual mores, can they be said to still constitute a haven from a prejudiced heterosexual world?

Perhaps the growth of openly gay culture in Johannesburg has had a minimal effect on gay men's lives — particularly closeted men. Given the widespread censure of gay sex — it is, after all, still criminal in South Africa — perhaps the health clubs were, and still are, a necessary and perhaps even positive space for the reappropriation of some gay sexualities.

'Moffies en manvroue':
Gay and lesbian life histories in contemporary Cape Town

Jack Lewis and Francois Loots

Compelled by personal needs, gays and lesbians often challenge sexual mores, roles and stereotyping. Without any conscious political agenda, we expand the scope for free expression of a homosexual identity simply by being ourselves. Our personal confrontations with the straight world can produce a growth in consciousness making us spontaneously aware of how our mere openness as lesbians and gays can undermine and change anti-homosexual prejudice and intolerance.

What many of us want is quite simple: to find partners and be accepted as ordinary people, no different in status from heterosexual couples. However, our existence often seems to be a threat to the dominant moral and political order. What follows is the story of two couples — one gay and one lesbian — trying to live openly homosexual lives against the prejudices of family, religion, community and workplace. It is also the story of the acceptance that can be achieved through honesty and openness.[1]

Peter and Hennie

Peter and Hennie met in a nightclub — Studio 4 — in 1978. Peter was living at home in Steenberg, a traditionally coloured area marked by soulless blocks of flats

---

1 We have attempted to let Peter and Hennie and Trish and Derese speak in their own language, the vernacular of the Western Cape's coloured communities. We believe this language, a creole unique to the region, carries within it the expression not only of a wonderfully rich idiom, but also of a whole class and culture that is lost in translation. To our readers who are familiar with Afrikaans, we invite you to delight in the sheer inventiveness of this language; to our readers who are not, we ask forgiveness and refer you to the footnoted translations.

and small houses. *'Ek was die aand baie bored by die huis. Toe vat ek die laaste trein in Kaap toe.'*[2] He found his friends at Studio 4 and, later that evening, saw Hennie at the entrance, *'en ek sê vir my tjommie, nou daai man wil ek hê. Toe sê my tjommie, di's 'n straight boer, die man gaan jou skiet!'*[3]

Hennie's beard and glasses made him appear quite butch, and Peter was always turned on by straight authoritarian figures — to seduce them was a *''n moerse kick'*.[4]

That evening Hennie had been aimlessly roaming the streets and had landed up at Studio 4. He was not in the mood for company, but Peter was eyeing him and they started to dance. *'Toe ek hom eers sien dans, toe's ek gehook!'*[5]

Peter, classified coloured at birth, was born in 1955 and raised in Lakeside, a typical pre-Group Areas mixed community. With the imposition of the Group Areas Act in the 1950s, his family was forced to move to a two-bedroom council house in Steenberg. His father was absent and he was only to meet him once. His mother managed a cake shop, and he spent most of his childhood in his grand-mother's care. He left school after completing Standard 6 and, at 16, began work at the Simonstown naval dockyard, where he was to remain for 17 years. Recently, he opened a fast-food business operating from the home he and Hennie have shared for the last seven years in Maitland, a white working-class suburb that is rapidly deracialising.

Hennie, a white Afrikaner, was born in 1956 and went to school in the Transkei, where his father was one of the more enlightened missionaries of the Dutch Reformed Church. Hennie followed in his father's footsteps and, in 1974, enrolled at the Stellenbosch University seminary. After completing his Honours de-gree and meeting Peter he quit his studies, and now works for the Provincial Administration.

Trish and Derese

When Trish met Derese at a night school in 1985, the two struck up a cautious friendship. They arranged to meet one evening at the home of Derese's Aunt Miriam, who worked at the same factory as Trish. Derese had asked Trish for something to read and Trish, rather slyly, included a lesbian novel in the pile of books she brought over to Aunt Miriam's. The ploy worked, and when the conver-sation turned to lesbianism, Derese was her usual adventurous self:

> *Ek sit my hande so om haar en ek speel met haar nippels en ek check. Nee, sy stop my nie; so sy is 'n lesbian! En so't ons beginne.*[6]

---

2 I was rather bored at home that night. So I took the last train to Cape Town.
3 I said to my friend, now I would like to have that man. And my friend said, that is a straight 'boer' [farmer], that man will shoot you!
4 a big thrill.
5 Once I saw him dancing, I was hooked.
6 I put my hands around her like this and played with her nipples and I thought: No, she's not stopping me, so she is a lesbian. And that's how we started.

Despite many difficulties they have remained together for seven years. Derese now lives with her brother in central Cape Town and, for the first time, the couple is able to live an openly lesbian life.

Derese, a coloured woman of Malay heritage, was born in 1963 in 'Fietas', one of Johannesburg's mixed-race communities demolished by the Group Areas Act. At the age of two she and her brother were sent to live with their Aunt Miriam in Cape Town, while her parents worked in Johannesburg. She grew up in a strict Muslim environment — with Aunt Miriam and her uncle who worked as a cleaner for the city council. Her mother joined them a few years later and her father eventually followed. In 1977 the family moved to Mitchell's Plain, built in the 1970s and now the largest coloured township in the country.

Derese left school while in Standard 5 and spent eight years helping with house work before starting work in 1984. She had various low-paying jobs until she started working for a clothing wholesaler, where she remained for four years. She left her job recently to work for a community health organisation.

Trish, also classified coloured but from a staunch Christian background, was born in Steenberg in 1959. Her father too worked as a cleaner for the city council and as a machinist in a factory, while her mother worked as a char. When she was three, her family moved to Bonteheuwel, where they still live. Bonteheuwel was one of the first places to which coloureds were forcibly removed from District Six and other areas with the imposition of the Group Areas Act. Unlike Mitchell's Plain where the houses are spread out and slightly bigger, the township consists of rows of small semi-detached two-bedroomed homes.

Trish left school after completing Standard 7 and started working in a garment factory to support her family. She is currently on disability because of arthritis.

'Did you know he is queer?':
Growing up in a heterosexual world

There is a belief, not without foundation, that a gay sub-culture is more visible and tolerated within the coloured communities of Cape Town than elsewhere in South Africa. Hennie had heard of a gay sub-culture in the old Cape port community before the forced removals of the apartheid era.

> *Jy sal vind dat die mense in District Six, hulle het baie toler-*
> *ance gehad. Hier was moffie konserte in die ou dae in Wood-*
> *stock, wat die moffies op die stage gaan parade. En die mense*
> *book 'n hele hall en mense koop tickets om die moffies dop te*
> *hou en almal dress vir hulle op en stap op die stage rond!*[7]

Even in 1992, drag shows in clubs like Caesars, Cape Town's longest running gay club, were attended by mothers who had lovingly designed and sewn dresses.

---

7   You will find that the people in District Six were very tolerant. In Woodstock there used to
    be moffie concerts, where the moffies paraded on stage. And they booked a hall and people
    bought tickets to watch them. Everyone dressed for the occasion and walked around on stage.

The accommodation between gay and lesbian sub-cultures and the straight world has produced its own words and phrases. Peter recalls that when he was young, the word moffie (which has its roots in the coloured vernacular) was very common: adults would say, *'Nee, daa' gat ene, moffie karrentjie.'*[8]

Or, people would speak about a *'moffie gladys'*. There is a widely used gay alphabet which originated in Cape Town and is constantly being improvised *beula* (beautiful), *wendy* (white), *clora* (coloured), *priscilla* (police), *dora* (drunk), *natalia* (native), *greta* (greedy), *lana* (penis), *fatima* (fat), *mavis* (queen) and *bag* (butch).

Peter's childhood was populated by many gay men, and there was a relative tolerance of homosexuality. In Steenberg,

> *daar's baie openly gediscuss. Enigetyd dan sien jy hier kom ene verbygestap met 'n overall an, en die hare is in rollers en di's op pad winkel toe, en die klompie kindertjies agterna. Vir die kindertjies was dit altyd 'n novelty.*[9]

But this openness was restricted to a stereotype of the gay male playing a female role doing traditional female work:

> *'Jy moet nou vanaand oorkom, want my hare moet gewas wo'd'; 'Kyk hieso, my dogter hulle het 'n 21st of 'n wedding of 'n ding an'; 'doen hulle hare of kom help me'die sewing'.*[10]

As long as it was within this stereotypical role, an open gay sub-culture could assert itself. Homosexuality was not unusual: one family in the neighbourhood had five sons and five daughters — all gay. There was the local *Sunday special* when

> *jy shave en die hare is mooi en jy trek vir jou lekker an en almal is hier af na die veld toe. Nou sit en kyk ons nou hoe die five broers op die veld netball speel in hulle skirts en die five sisters hardloop rond op die sokkerveld. Daar was nog 'n klomp anders gewees.*[11]

Despite this relative openness in the older coloured communities, a lesbian sub-culture was not readily accessible. In Derese and Trish's more religious communities there were taboos against homosexuality and lesbians were seldom heard of. Trish relates that factory workers jokingly refer to a woman having sex with a woman as *sassa plattes*. She presses the palms of her hands against each other and explains that it means *plat teen plat* or *koek teen koek*.[12] A lesbian is commonly known as a *manvrou*, literally a 'man-woman'.

---

8 See, there goes one, moffie karrentjie. (Karrentjie is an old expression meaning queer)

9 It was openly talked of. At any time you would see one pass, dressed in an overall, the hair in rollers, on the way to the shop, and a group of kids following behind. For the kids it was always a novelty.

10 You must come over tonight, because my hair needs to be washed; look here, my daughter has a 21st birthday or there is a wedding; do their hair or come and help with the sewing.

11 You shave and you dress neatly and everyone goes to the veld (usually a dusty field). So we watch the five brothers playing netball dressed in skirts and the five sisters running around on the soccer veld. There were many others as well.

12 flat against flat or vagina (literally, cake) against vagina.

143

Trish, who grew up in a strictly Christian household and who was actively involved in a Christian youth group, remembers that while it was forbidden to talk about, there was a *moffie* in their road. His name was Mervin, he was very effeminate, and was very open about himself. One day, he caused a stir in the neighbourhood: *'Toe sê hulle: 'Het julle gehoor? Mervin is getroud met 'n man! En die ma staan nogal langesaan die bruid! Sy't 'n lang wit rok aan.'*[13] Despite the taboo, people spoke anyway.

In Derese's Muslim community gays were even less visible but, as a child, she did have contact with two gay men. One was a relative. He was very camp, *'en dan het die man altyd so die koekies en die trays aangedra by weddings. Dan sê hulle: "Hie' kom Sies Gammat." Nou Sies beteken Antie of whatever.'*[14]

Derese was attracted to the way he spoke, especially his use of slang. Even though he was derided by her parents for wanting to be a woman, Sies Gammat's presence taught the children something: *'toe't ons mos geweet wat is 'n moffie!'*[15]

It was through the other gay man she knew that Derese came to realise how actively *moffies* were censured in her community. Across from their house

> *was daar 'n groentewinkel. En daar't 'n outjie daar gewerk, Peter. En Peter't altyd 'n mooi voorskootjie gedra en so aan. En dan het die kinders hom altyd so gegooi met vrot tamaties en dinges. Dan sê hulle: 'Hie's Peter Eiebakkies'. Maak hulle nou gai van Peter en so.*[16]

'And she saw the red flames': Finding lovers

Due to the silence surrounding lesbians, the homosexual sub-culture tended to be restricted to males. Accordingly, gay men provided the only public image of homosexuality for Derese and Trish. The silence about female homosexuality was perpetuated in their first relationships. As a teenager Trish had a petting relationship with a girlfriend: *'ons twee het geweet ons vry met mekaar en daai.'*[17]

But they never spoke about it. Derese and Trish feel that the open hostility towards gays in their families led them to perpetuate their own silence in order to avoid discrimination and censure. When Trish first met a *manvrou* at age 17 she was incredibly curious and slightly scared.

Her brother was friendly with Candy, a known lesbian. He once brought her along to visit the family. Trish recalls her initial apprehension after being told:

---

13 And they said: 'Did you hear? Mervin is married to a man! And the mother even stood next to the bride who was wearing a long white dress!'

14 And then the man used to bring in caketrays at weddings. Then they'd say: "Here comes Sies Gammat." Now Sies means aunty.

15 so then we knew what a moffie was!

16 There was a greengrocer. And a guy called Peter used to work there. He always wore a beautiful apron and so on. Then the children always threw rotten tomatoes at him and things like that. Then they'd say: 'Here is Peter Eiebakkies!' [a nickname with sexual overtones] So they mocked Peter.

17 We two knew that we were petting and so on.

'"*Julle lol'ie met daai manvrou nie*". *Ek was eintlik bang. Hulle praat al klaar so van 'n moffie, nou hoe gaan hulle praat...?*'[18]

Fortunately, Candy ended up staying the night. Trish thought, '*nou right, hier's nou 'n manvrou. Ek wil nou kyk wa'van is die manvrou gemaak.*'[19]

Although she usually slept with her mother, that night she was determined to share the sleeper couch in the lounge with Candy. At last she was able to ask a *manvrou* about herself and talk about her feelings. So began her first affectionate friendship with an openly-identified lesbian.

As with Trish, Derese's first sexual contacts with women were secret adolescent curiosities. Even though Sies Gammat had made her aware of what *moffies* were, female homosexuality came as a surprise when, at 13, she first experienced it. Her new sexual awareness was a revelation. She had met a girl called Nadia and become attached to her. One night,

> *toe sit sy nou op die bed. Toe praat sy nou haar life history, van haar ma wat nou 'n prostitute is. Toe huil sy so en ek sit toe my arms om haar en ek comfort toe vir haar. En soos ek vir haar comfort, toe soen sy my. En toe vind ek uit ek hou daarvan!*[20]

When Derese started seeing Nadia, she was afraid of her family's reaction, not only because of homosexuality, but because of a general taboo on sexuality. Any intimacy between the two of them always involved manoeuvring around the restrictions of parental authority and sibling interference. Nonetheless, she and Nadia met often: '*en ons het seks gehet, en ons het aangehou seks gehet.*'[21]

One evening Nadia gave Derese a lovebite. Derese tried to conceal the evidence with a plaster, but her mother forced her to remove it, '*en sy sien die rooi vlamme.*'[22] Trying to escape, Derese ran upstairs to hide in a bedroom. But she was too slow.

> *...my pa agterna. En die hele familie kom sit nou daar by my. Ek dink: 'Oe Derese, nou moet jy 'n liegstorie uitdink. As hulle nou so angaan oor die lovebites, nou hoe gaan hulle nie an as hulle weet Nadia het vir my die love bites gegee nie!*'[23]

Her father was determined to get hold of the culprit: '*Hulle het my heel aand ge-crossquestion.*'[24] To avoid coming out, Derese blamed a fictitious boy. '*Toe sê*

---

18 'Don't fool around with that manvrou'. I was actually scared. If they talk like that about a moffie, then how will they talk...?

19 Right, here is a manvrou. I want to see what this manvrou is made of.

20 She was sitting on the bed. She was recounting the story of her life, about her mother who was a prostitute. She started crying and I put my arms around her to comfort her. And as I was comforting her, she kissed me. And so I discovered that I like it!

21 and we had sex, and we continued having sex.

22 and she saw the red flames

23 My father followed me. And the whole family came to sit next to me. I thought: 'Oh, Derese, now you have to make up a story. If they are performing like this because of lovebites, how would they carry on if they knew that Nadia gave them to me?'

24 They cross-questioned me the whole night

my pa: "Waar's die ou? Ek wil nou sy adres hê, ek gaan nou daai ou vrek maak". My pa gaan soek hom toe, maar my pa kry hom toe nie.'[25]

Derese continued to see Nadia, but learned from her family's reaction: *'Toe raak ek mos bewus dis verkeerd, verstaan jy? En dan het ons nog so seks gehet, ma' ons was baie op ons se nerves.'*[26]

Derese and Trish had no open lesbian subculture into which they could escape. Derese gives a coy smile: *'Vrouens moet alles meet onnerie kombers.'*[27]

But lesbians also cruise. Derese met another lover in a café. She had been drinking and went in to buy a breath-freshener. A woman approached:

> *En toe sê sy vir my: 'You're a heavy drinker?' Toe lag ek net. En toe sê sy: 'Are you a heavy smoker?' Toe sê ek vir haar: 'No'. Toe sê sy: 'Are you a heavy poker?'*[28]

Poking refers to smoking a (*dagga*) pipe, but Derese clearly had other things in mind.

> *Toe dink ek sy sê sekswise, poke ek? Toe sê ek: 'Yes'. Toe vra sy mos nou vir my of ek nie saam met haar die next Saterdag vir 'n drink by die Carobel wil gaan nie.*[29]

Trish feels that she was under greater peer pressure to behave in a heterosexual way. She had boyfriends, but always to avoid being marginalised as an outsider, *'om mense te laat kyk. Ek issie soos hulle sê: "Sy's annester, sy'tie 'n boyfriend nie, waars haa' boyfriend?"'*[30]

* * *

Peter and Hennie had easier access to other gays — men are not confined to the domestic sphere with its emphasis on the protection of virtue and the maintenance of appearances. There is a subculture of clubs and cruising spots which facilitates making and pursuing contacts.

As a teenager, Peter often went alone to the beach at St. James. One Sunday a man approached him:

> *maar net soos hy ankom wil ek nog uitbars van die lag, want hy't vir my toe net te weird gelyk. Hy't 'n mooi vel, mooi liggaam, alles, maar sy baaibroek was vir my net te hoog. Die*

---

25 Then my father said: 'Where's this guy? I want his address, I'm going to kill this guy'. My father went looking for him, but could not find him.
26 I became aware that it was wrong, you understand? We continued having sex, but we were very nervous.
27 Women must meet everything under the blankets (behind closed doors).
28 Then she said to me, 'You're a heavy drinker?' I just laughed. And so she said, 'Are you a heavy smoker? I said, 'No', and she said, 'Are you a heavy poker?'
29 I thought that she meant sexwise, do I poke? So I said: 'Yes'. And then she asked me if I would like to have a drink with her the next Saturday at the Carobel.
30 for the sake of appearances. I'm not the way they were saying: 'She's different, she does not have a boyfriend, where's her boyfriend?'

eerste ding wat ek in my kop angehad het, is: 'n man dra nie sy baaibroek so hoog nie![31]

The man, Edwin, had a different set of values, a different perception of privacy, something which took the young Peter by surprise:

Toe kom die ou reguit na my toe en hy kyk so vir my en hy sê vir my: 'Jy's 'n moffie en ek is 'n moffie en ek dink ons twee moet 'n Coke gaan koop, want ek het Brandy da' anderkant.' En ek skrik my gat af, want ek het dan net da' gelê. Hoe kan die fokken man nou sien dat ek gay is? Hoe kan hy met sikke goed daa' ankom. Ma' ek spring toe ook net op asof ek georder word en ek was toe saam, want immediately hou ek toe van die ou.[32]

Edwin was a few years older than Peter but more experienced and already light years out of the closet, and he became a mentor to the younger boy. He took Peter to Burg Street in central Cape Town, then a popular cruising spot. Peter was stunned:

hier's 'n plek waar jy net stap en dan stop 'n ou en hy tel vir jou op. Die mense het heavy gecamp daai tyd op Burg Straat, hulle't so uitgekamp op Green Market Square met hulle wyne. Dan sit hulle maar net in die kar en cruise en almal strol op en af.[33]

The cruising areas and bars around Burg Street were places where people from different backgrounds could mix freely. Peter was even picked up by the cop assigned to police the area!

Despite Hennie's initial apprehension about homosexuality, he was drawn to the rent boys around the Burg Street area, and says he learnt about the gay scene by chatting with the *Slamse laities* (Muslim kids) who worked the street. The cruising area was

soort van 'n outlet vir wat ek gevoel het... ek het een keer saam met 'n rent piece daar gegaan wat my 'n gat in die kop gepraat het met special student rates en ek weet nie watse kak alles nie.[34]

---

31 but as he approached I wanted to pack up laughing, because he looked just too weird. Nice skin, nice body, everything, but his bathing costume struck me as being too high. The first thing I thought was that a man does not wear his costume so high!

32 He came straight to me, looked at me and said: 'You are a moffie and I am a moffie and I think the two of us must buy some Coke, because I have brandy over there'. I got a hell of a fright, because I was just lying there. How can this fucking man see that I'm gay? How can he come up with things like that? But I just jumped up as if I were ordered and went along, because I immediately liked this guy.

33 Here is a place where you just walked and a guy would stop and pick you up. In those days people used to cruise heavily on Burg Street, they would camp out on Green Market Square with their wine. They'd simply sit in their cars and cruise people walking up and down.

34 The area was kind of an outlet for what I was feeling. Once I went with a rent boy who persuaded me with talk of special student rates and I don't know what other shit.

'She did not know if she should say son or daughter': Coming out to the family

Hennie's relationship with his father was an intellectual one, but they would also go jogging and practice rugby together. This bond led the 13-year-old boy to confide to his father that he felt attracted to boys. After overcoming his initial shock, Hennie's father sent him to a marriage counsellor who gave him

> *weird advice... Hy't my gevra, nou hoe masturbeer ek, en my aangeraai om liewer nie my hand te gebruik nie, omdat dit 'n homoseksuele manier van masturbasie was. Ek moet liewer op die bed lê en as't ware die bed stoot. En hy het my aanbeveel ek moet 'n botteltjie warm water saam met my bed toe vat, in my onderbroek druk.*[35]

Hennie complained and his father then arranged a meeting with a medical doctor, who turned out to be sympathetic and understanding. He did not claim to provide a 'cure', but strengthened the young boy's confidence:

> *Hy was die eerste persoon teenoor wie ek as't ware kon oop-maak en kon sê wat in my gedagte gaan, sonder dat daar 'n aura van vooroordeel in die lug gehang het.*[36]

Hennie feels that his homosexuality challenged his father's idea of masculinity. His parents were initially hostile to his relationship with Peter: not only sexuality, but skin colour and class were at the root of their difficulty in accepting their 'son-in-law'. Eventually his parents did acknowledge them as a gay couple: *'Na sewe jaar het hulle kom kuier. Toe't hy uitgevind die's nou 'n baie lang one-night stand en "Ek moet ma' nou gaan kuier hier".'*[37]

In contrast, both Peter and his family dealt with his coming out pragmatically. His mother and her friends would *jol* (party) with Peter, and they often went to a mixed club in Claremont. She had a friend, John, who used to go dancing with her. He would stay over at their house and share a bed with Peter. At one stage his mother started objecting to his regular visits, because she had heard that he was a *moffie*. This prompted Peter to come out. At first his mother was *befok* (furious) and blamed John. *'Toe sê ek nee: dis nie deur hom nie, niemand kan vir niemand so maak nie en dit was net altyd da'sô.'*[38] Feeling he had nothing to lose, he presented his whole family with a stark choice:

---

35 He asked me how I masturbated and advised me not to use my hand, because that was a homosexual way of masturbating. I should rather lie on the bed and kind of fuck the bed. And he recommended that I take a small bottle of warm water along to bed and put it in my underpants.

36 He was the first person with whom I could be open and say what I had on my mind without there being an aura of prejudice in the air.

37 After seven years they came to visit. Then he realised that this is a very long one-night stand and that 'I must just visit them'.

38 So I said no, it's not because of him, no one can make another person that way and it has just always been there.

Ek los dit up to julle, decide of julle vir my in die huis of uit wil hê, want niks het verander nie, ek is nog altyd dieselfde persoon, dis maar net dat ek met dieselfde seks kooi toe gaan. My ma het so lang tyd stil gebly, toe sê sy net: 'Wel die fact remain jy's nog altyd my...' Daar was so moerse lang pause, toe sê sy '... my kind.' Sy't nie geweet moet sy sê 'seun' of 'dogter' nie.[39]

Unlike Hennie's parents, Peter's family was quite nonchalant about his new lover when he took Hennie and another 'whitey' to meet his mother in her room behind a garage in Wetton. His mother handled the situation in her usual practical manner, asking: *'Nou wie van julle naai my dogter?'*[40]

Embarrassed, Hennie tried to stall her, but she persisted, and he had to confess. At this she calmly responded that she only wished to know how she should set the table!

Peter explains that for him it is important to be relaxed about one's sexuality; then people won't feel threatened. At the time of coming out Peter was contributing to the household financially. The primary concern was to clothe and feed everyone properly — being practical and not setting absolute standards was a necessity. Hennie is amazed at the contrast with his own family — when faced with such non-conformity *'is daar groot drama en dis studeerkamer toe.'*[41]

* * *

Trish and Derese, by contrast, lived in more repressive situations, not only because of their sexuality, but because of their gender. In a context where women are considered permanent minors in the 'protective custody' of a man, Derese's father had made it quite clear to her that she would leave the family home only upon marriage or death.

At one point, Trish's family pressurised her to marry a boyfriend. To head off their persuasions, she used his religion as an excuse — she is Anglican, whereas he was a Seventh Day Adventist. The family said that *''n vrou draai vir haar man.'* To which Trish responded: *'Nie **die** vrou nie!'*[42]

In Bonteheuwel, as in many other working-class neighborhoods, women often control the household. They manage the finances and raise children without much support from their husbands. Trish had a close bond with her mother and, in Standard 6, without any prompting, she started to bunk school to help out with the shopping, cooking and cleaning. Soon afterwards her mother fell ill and Trish left school to find work.

---

39 I leave it up to you, decide if you want me in the home or out, because nothing has changed, I am still the same person, its just that I go to bed with the same sex. My mother kept quiet for a long while, then she said: 'Well, the fact remains that you are still my...' There was a hell of a pause and she said '... my child'. She did not know if she should say 'son' or 'daughter'.

40 Now which one of you is fucking my daughter?

41 there is big drama and it's off to the study.

42 'A woman changes her ways for a man.' To which Trish responded: 'Not *this* woman!'

When her mother suspected that she might be having a relationship with Candy, she confronted Trish, who was reluctant to admit to it. Her brother squealed that Candy had been buying Trish presents. *'Toe sê my ma: "jou bastard, ek het geweet, jy wil dan nie vir my sê nie".'*[43]

Trish was deeply hurt by her mother's rejection, and stayed away from home for three months. At first she thought that she should resign herself to staying in the closet. But she realised that she had to help her family, and so returned, initially for short visits, allowing them to see that she was still the supportive daughter they knew. When Trish finally decided to move in with Derese, her mother scolded: *'Jy pak jou klere alweer vir 'n vroumens.'*[44]

But her mother has become less inflexible and now, even though she still disapproves, she tempers her judgement with comments like: *'Ek likes dit nie, maar julle jongmense smaak mos van sulke goed.'*[45]

'But you lied to me!': Religion

As a theology student, Hennie had ethical reservations about whether one could be a minister if homosexual. But his first sexual encounter with a young soldier on the Transkarroo train, *''n baie sweet experience'* persuaded him: *'Julle het mos vir my gelieg. Mense soos my pa het altyd vir my vertel dis so sleg en degenerate!'*[46]

His father, he has decided, works within a Biblical framework of ethical principles to which the flesh has to conform. Hennie argues that you cannot work with a non-existent 'soul', only with the physical needs of human beings. In doing so, religion can give support and assistance.

After Hennie and Peter moved to Maitland, a Dutch Reformed Church minister came to visit, and turned out to be an old classmate of Hennie's from the seminary. He invited Hennie for supper and, noticing a photograph of Peter's grandparents on the lounge wall, asked if there was a *'gesinnetjie'* (little family) he should also invite. Hennie explained his version of *'gesinnetjie'* and asked if he would still be welcome to attend church. The minister responded that although he could not keep anyone away from the 'word of God', he was concerned: *'Aangesien daar so min mans in Maitland is, sal hulle my nou kies vir die kerkraad!'*[47] (The men in Maitland mostly worked shifts and were thus unavailable for church duties.) Hennie took the minister's apprehension at this prospect as a licence to stay away!

* * *

In Trish's family home the walls are covered with religious images, including a Jesus clock inscribed with the words *The Immaculate Conception*; in Derese's fam-

---

43 So my mother said: 'You're a bastard, I knew it, but you don't want to tell me.'
44 There you go again, packing your bags for a woman!
45 I don't like it, but you youngsters like that kind of stuff.
46 But you lied to me. People like my father always told me that it's so bad and degenerate.
47 Since there were so few men in Maitland, they were bound to elect me to the church council.

ily home you are greeted by a *kaba* clock[48] on the wall and framed quotations from the Koran.

More than anything else, religious conviction has made it difficult for Derese and Trish's families to understand and accept their daughters as lesbians; in fact, both families use religiously-derived views on homosexuality to repress their daughters' sexuality and police their relationships.

Derese was forced to come out to her family after Trish's mother threatened to phone them. Her brother is also gay and they decided to come out together. They spoke to their father who advised them to pray, after admitting that *hy het ook gejol,* (he had also sown his wild oats), implying that being a homosexual means being promiscuous! Her father felt that he had failed in his duty as religious head of the household and would read passages from the Koran to the family condemning homosexuality. He even threatened that if she and her brother *'nie vir ons regtrek nie, dan soos die Koran sê, "Dan moet ek vir julle afskryf as my kinders".'*[49]

But Derese was encouraged by one particular Koranic verse read by her father to the family. She remembers it as saying: *'as jy op 'n age kom dat jy voel jy nie wil 'n homosexual wees nie en jy ruk jouself reg, dan vergewe God vir jou.'*[50] She argues that for straight Muslims, 'all sex before marriage is out, you can't be forgiven. But gays can be forgiven? So it can't be such a big sin after all!'

Trish's mother works within a similar biblical framework. She would leave a Bible open at verses which condemn homosexuality, but Trish refused to accept verses out of context. Despite the way that religion has been used to condemn all three of them, Derese, Trish and Hennie are all adamant that they have retained their belief in a God — albeit on their own terms.

'In and out like a thief': Race and place

Peter remembers that in Lakeside, where he grew up, *'colour was nie 'n issue nie. Die eerste keer wat ek nou geconfront was met die colour issue was toe ek uit die Lakeside area uitgegaan het na klubs toe.'*[51]

From the club he would accompany someone to a white area, but would be warned to be careful not to be seen by neighbours: *'En toe het dit vir my regtig omgekrap en uitgefreak om soos 'n skelm in en uit te move.'*[52] The hypocrisy of white gays who were happy to sleep with coloured boys as long as they were not seen came as a shock for Peter.

Racism affected his relationship with Hennie from the outset. Hennie was living in a flat in Vredehoek, a suburb close to the city centre, when he met Peter.

---

48 A photograph of the kaba in Mecca with a clock on it.
49 if we did not pull ourselves right, then, as the Koran says, 'I would have to write you off as my children'.
50 If at a certain age you feel that you do not want to be homosexual and change your ways, then God forgives you.
51 Colour wasn't an issue. The first time I was confronted with the colour issue was when I went out of the Lakeside area to clubs.
52 It used to upset me and freak me out, moving in and out like a thief.

151

The area was *boererig* (conservative) and they avoided the neighbours: *'Mens moet laat nag in en vroeg oggend uitsneak.'*[53]

After two years they moved in together in a flat in Sea Point. Here Hennie had to sign a contract stating that no non-whites, other than 'bona fide servants', would be allowed on the premises. Peter adds: *'Ek het mos goed na die master gesorg!'*[54]

Sea Point, a high density flatland and holiday area close to the beach, is a particularly gay part of Cape Town, and Peter used to check out the renowned late night cruising scene at the beachfront 'wall'. But, despite the area's reputed liberalism, he still had to sneak in and out of the flat. They thus lived in complete isolation.

Despite their efforts at unobtrusiveness they were soon in trouble. One night the police rapped at the door, as the neighbours had complained that: *'...daar's 'n moerse party aan die gang, daar's anderskleuriges hie'so en ek weet nie watte klomp kak alles nie.'*[55]

Then Hennie received a letter from the agency complaining that a bunch of coloureds were coming into the flat. He wrote back that 'you are a Jewish agency and ought to know better when it comes to discrimination.' Although the agency apologised, Sea Point's traditional liberalism proved to be rather superficial, and Peter and Hennie decided to move, buying a spacious two-bedroomed house in Maitland. Ironically, Maitland, traditionally a National Party constituency, was to offer them more opportunity to integrate into a community and become accepted as a gay couple. Hennie likes the fact that it is *''n matriarchal woonbuurt, want die mans bly nie daar nie. Hulle werk almal op die railways, skofte. Die vrouens run Maitland.'*[56]

By the time Peter and Hennie moved into Maitland in the late 1980s, it was, like many working-class white suburbs, already rapidly deracialising. One evening *''n antie met dieselarms'*[57] came to canvass for a conservative candidate in a municipal election. When Peter opened the door she assumed he was a servant and asked for the *'baas'*. When Hennie came to the door she asked him if he objected to coloureds moving in next door. Peter comments: *'Ek is soos die nag! Die kleurlinge mag in die huis wees, maar hulle moet net nie langsaan intrek nie!'*[58]

Together with racial restrictions came class issues. Whites would say Hennie is *verkaffer* (like a 'kaffir'), and that he *'gaan net soos 'n klomp hotnots aan.'*[59]

---

53 One had to sneak in late at night and out early in the morning.
54 I indeed took good care of the master!
55 ...there was a big party going on, that there were people of different colour here and all sorts of other shit.
56 a matriarchal area. The men do not stay there. They all work shifts on the railways. The women run Maitland.
57 a woman with diesel arms
58 I was like the night. The coloureds can be in the house, but they just should not move in next door!
59 behaves like a bunch of 'hotnots' (a racist term for coloureds, derived from hottentots)

On the other hand coloureds would sometimes say to Peter that he lived like a 'whitey'. Some whites looked at Peter as different from other 'non-whites', telling him that he was not like the other coloureds or blacks. Hennie and Peter always rejected this honourary white status and those who would bestow it. But they quickly learned how to assess people and their intentions, and are particularly scathing about *'liberals en sophisticated moffies wat eers vir my sê hulle het nie 'n problem met skincolour nie!* If you don't have a problem, then why mention it?'[60]

* * *

As Trish and Derese are both classified coloured they do not have to deal with overtly racist attacks on their relationship. But the apartheid definition of coloured encompasses a wide range of religions, cultures and hues, and Trish and Derese have found themselves victimized by another form of discrimination prevalent in coloured communities: the mutual antipathy between Muslim people of Malay descent and Christian coloureds.

Trish was used to working with Muslims and as a religious person always took an interest in their belief and customs. The women at work showed her how to tie a scarf in Muslim fashion and soon she was not only tying theirs for them but wearing one herself. At home, however, her mother advised: *'Los daai Slamse af, daai Slamse is nie vrinne nie.'*[61] Her attitude reflected a long tradition of Christians believing in Muslim *doekom* or witchcraft. She used to say, *'Die Slamse, hulle toor vir jou. Ek likes nie die slamse nie!'*[62]

Derese explains that for many Muslims, on the other hand, *'if you are not a Muslim, you are a Boesman, whether jy watter nasie is. Boesmans is nie mooi mense nie. Hulle het nie hare nie.'*[63]

'It's none of your business!': The workplace

For both Trish and Derese, work provided the opportunity to experience an environment free from the policing of family and religion. Here people could talk about issues unmentionable at home and identify each other.

Aged 15, Trish began work at a garment factory as a cleaner, and was soon promoted to machinist and elected as a union shop-steward. Over 300 women worked together in a virtually exclusively female environment. Trish maintains that amongst workers, teachers and nurses, lesbians become visible: *'Daar's honnerde!'*[64]

At Trish's factory, the women did not talk about *manvroue* until one started working there. Being a shop steward, Trish had an easy entrée to friendship with the newcomer, whose name was Lizzie. This was the first time that Trish had asso-

---

60 liberals and sophisticated moffies who start off by telling me that they don't have a problem with skincolour!
61 Leave those Muslims alone, those Muslims are not friends.
62 The Muslims, they use witchcraft. I don't like the Muslims!
63 If you are not a Muslim, you are a Bushman, whatever nation you are. Bushmen are ugly people. They do not have hair.
64 there are hundreds!

ciated openly with a *manvrou,* and she was most impressed by the fact that Lizzie only wore pants, and by the influence she quickly came to exert in the factory:

> *Sy was soos 'n mansmens en hulle't begin vir haar te anvaar.*
> *En sy was eintlik soos 'n sonstraal gewees. As sy nie die dag in*
> *is nie, dan lag hulle nie, dan gat hulle nie aan nie.*[65]

Lizzie became a mentor for Trish who began to think: *'Ek wil ook so 'n character wees. Ek wil nie hê die mense moet neersien op my nie. Hulle moet my as ver- missing sien as ek nie daar is nie.'*[66]

Trish's association with Lizzie led to much light-hearted bantering on the factory floor. Someone would shout *'Trish, sassa plattes!'* To which Trish would always respond: *'Wat weet julle? Julle moet dit try!'*[67]

Lizzie began a relationship with a fellow worker. Initially, there was hostil- ity and confusion, but Lizzie paid scant attention. And when the women sat together and asked the usual questions — 'now how do you do it?' — Trish was not going to explain either: *'Hulle't dit nooit verduidelik nie, dit was altyd net questions!'*[68]

The workers eventually came to accept Lizzie and her lover as a couple, saying *'daai twee is hulle eie grootmense.'*[69] Fellow workers lived through their stormy relationship, like the time *'toe een van hulle die ander gesteek het met 'n skêr. Hulle het 'n personal fight gehad. En 'n anner keer, toe fly die trouringe af by die venster.'*[70] Relating this incident, Trish becomes quiet and blushes, remembering that she and Derese also threw their rings away during a recent argument.

After a series of extremely low paid jobs in supermarkets and masala shops Derese ended up working for a clothing wholesaler. The pay of R500 a month was low but the environment better. Derese worked long hours with the boss's niece, Belinda, and before long a relationship developed. They did their best to conceal their affections, and were successful until *Antie* Valda, the office cleaner, observed them *vrying* (fondling) in the toilet. Within a day word was out and the boss was receiving complaints. He threatened to fire Derese if the relationship persisted. Der- ese responded that:

> *of ek 'n lesbian is of nie, dit is niemand se worries nie. Sy is*
> *haar eie groot vrou en ek is my eie grootmens. Wat ons in ons*
> *privaatgeid doen is niks van julle besigheid nie!*[71]

---

65 She was like a man and they began to accept her. And she was like a ray of sunshine. If she was not there on a day, then they did not laugh, they did not joke.
66 I also want to be such a character. I don't want people to look down on me. They should miss me when I'm not there.
67 What do you know? You should try it!
68 They never explained it either. There were only questions!
69 Those two are adults.
70 when the one struck at the other with scissors. They had a personal fight. Another time the wedding rings flew through the window.
71 whether I'm a lesbian or not is no one's worries. She is an adult woman and I'm an adult. What we do in private is none of your business!

The boss separated them, and Derese and her lover kept to themselves, secretly adopting a motto from the movie *Children of a Lesser God*: 'She spoke her love in silence and I answered with all my heart!'

But just as the storm appeared to have blown over, Trish's mother, in an attempt to separate the ongoing relationship between her daughter and Derese, complained to the boss about his employment of a lesbian. Evidently having taken to heart his lesson on the right to privacy, he responded, 'what Derese does in her private time is her business!'

* * *

At the Simonstown naval dockyard where Peter worked as a labourer, he quickly adapted to the dominant macho worker culture, *'trenchdigging en dagha mix en al die butch goeters.'*[72] He eventually progressed to signwriting and finally to the position of office clerk. Peter had no reservations about being openly gay at work. He recalls that there were 'closet-cases' in the dockyard, 'but I just couldn't give a damn. *Almal was seker van my, want ek het vir hulle net aware daarvan gemaak'.*[73] Because of his casual manner and self-confidence Peter found relations with fellow workers,

> *baie easy, van die labourers af tot die groot base. As ek sê ek gaan die hele day afvat, want my man is siek by die huis, dan is dit OK. Ek mean ek kan my job verloor het daardeur, maar ek het net gedink, I've got nothing to hide.*[74]

His first adolescent sexual experience was with a fellow worker, a 'blond, blue-eyed surfer' who asked him home. After too many tequilas they ended up *'in 'n gespieëlde-tile badkamer — die bad is vol foam en ons is in die bad met tequilas en alles. Fabulous! Dit was vir my incredible.'*[75] But he soon learned the rules of the game, when his workmate told him, 'If anybody finds out about this, I'll kill you,' and made it clear that Peter was not to so much as look at him unless the two were alone: *'Ek kon dit toe nogal nie verstaan nie, want ek was hopelessly en stupidly in love met hom.'*[76] The hurt and humiliation of having to deny his feelings in public clashed with Peter's openness about homosexuality and he decided to end the secret affair.

Peter was repeatedly overlooked for promotion, and gained permanent status only after 15 years. This, he feels, was probably the result of both race discrimination and veiled anti-gay prejudice, and finally prompted him to leave the dockyard.

---

72 Trenchdigging and cement mixing and all that butch stuff.

73 Everyone was sure about me, because I just made them aware of it.

74 very easy, from the labourers to the big bosses. If I said that I was going to take the whole day off because my husband was sick at home, it was OK. I mean, I could have lost my job because of this, but I just thought, I've got nothing to hide.

75 in a mirror-tiled bathroom. The bath was filled with foam and we were in the bath with tequilas and everything. Fabulous, I found it incredible.

76 I could not really understand it, because I was hopelessly and stupidly in love with him.

'I'm all the moffies' mother!':
The personal becomes political

Peter and Hennie keep what they call an 'open house'. When they lived in Sea Point, Peter's younger brother would visit for a weekend and bring friends along. These friends would return with more friends. Thus commenced the tradition that has continued in their larger house in Maitland, which has become a refuge for those who seek to escape, however briefly, their mundane existence at home. Some come to discuss their problems or are assisted in finding direction or a job. Others have run away from difficult conditions at home: alcoholic or prostitute parents or abuse. Children and teenagers visit because 'they get individual attention' and affection. They sit on Peter's lap and feel that someone cares, *'by die huis doen hulle nie sulke goed nie.'*[77]

In keeping an open house, Peter and Hennie have always felt that they carry a responsibility, and they make a point of meeting the parents of regular visitors. Some parents have become regular visitors themselves and tell their children: *'Nee fok, julle kan nou die naweek by die huis bly. Ons gaan nou self 'n slag visit.'*[78] For these parents gays are not a problem. In fact, *'niks is 'n issue nie, ons is net Peter en Hennie.'*[79]

In this way they have rapidly gained respect in Maitland. Peter has often been called to stop a fight or throw out a drunk boyfriend. And their public visibility and positive image as a gay couple has led to family members, friends, schoolchildren and parents becoming accepting and supportive. Hennie and Peter feel particularly proud that some of their wards have stood up against moffie bashing. Even though they had never discuss gay rights with the children, a group of regular visitors once *'defended ons se honour'* (defended our honour) when a gay boy was victimised at school. For their pains some of these boys were expelled.

* * *

Derese only recently moved away from her family: living more independently and openly has meant a tremendous amount for her and Trish. Trish visits regularly, often staying for weeks and only occasionally going home for a break. They hope to move in together permanently as soon as they can afford a place of their own.

Trish and Derese too have found ways of participating in an alternative gay and lesbian subculture: they helped to form a support group for lesbians, gays and bisexuals. For Trish, the group is has enabled her to meet other lesbians and gays and is a place *'waar ek net myself kan wees. Dit laat my lig sien op gay en lesbian mense. Hulle is net mense — soos ek nou.'*[80]

She has assisted in building the support group, because she feels it would be a good thing to help other lesbians escape the suffering she went through.

---

77 at their homes they don't do such things.
78 'No, fuck', you can stay at home this weekend. We are going to visit for a change.
79 Nothing is an issue, we are simply Peter and Hennie.
80 where I can be myself. It has allowed me more hope for gays and lesbians. They are just people — like me now.

Trish's efficiency provided the skills needed for her position as treasurer. Derese's outgoing personality meant she was soon elected as chairperson. She declares: *'Ek is al die moffies se ma!'*[81] They help organise *jols* and picnics, but they spend much of their time listening to worries and troubles, and providing comfort and advice. Derese laughs:

> *Ons act as 'n dating service. Ons is 'n pick up place. Is mos beter, ons gaan in op safer seks en alles daai. Ons sort uit of dit 'n one-night stand is en of hulle vir love gaan. En dis vir hoekom ons alles weet — hulle kom terug en sê! ... Toe sê ek, 'Julle foken moffies werk op my nerves nou'. Ma' ek wys hulle om te soen en mekaar vas te hou. Dis mos wat 'n ma doen!*[82]

* * *

Neither Peter and Hennie's 'open house' nor Trish and Derese's support group is expressly political. Hennie says that while laws and attitudes have certainly confronted them, they never thought of their behaviour in terms of a political statement, 'we only think of survival'. They feel, modestly, that by South African standards their difficulties and battles are comparatively minor ones relating to every day life, but, 'in a sense life is politics'. Despite their social concern, Hennie explains that he and Peter have not involved themselves in party politics: *'Ons was vulnerable. Enigeiets kan gebeur; jy moet net die neighbours aanstoot gee!'*[83] Instead they decided to create a space at home for people to be themselves. You start, he has argued for years, (in the words of the poet NP van Wyk Louw) *'by die kleindaad van goeie trou'*.[84] Derese's attitude is similar:

> *As mense vir my kuier dan wil ek hê hulle moet gemaklik voel, sien jy? Soes ons se support group, it's a political thing. Politics is soes as iemand vir my brood vra en ek share, di's politics.*[85]

---

81 I am all the moffies' mother!
82 We act as a dating service. We are a pick-up place. It's better, we go into safer sex and things like that. We sort out whether they are into a one-night stand or looking for love. And that's why we know everything about them — they come back and tell! Sometimes I say, 'All you moffies are getting on my nerves'. But I show them to kiss and hold each other. Isn't that what a mother does?
83 We were vulnerable. Anything could happen; you just have to provoke the neighbours!
84 With the small deed of good faith.
85 when people visit me, I want them to feel comfortable, do you understand? Like our support group, it's a political thing. Politics is like when someone asks me for bread and I share, that is politics.

Abangibhamayo bathi ngimnandi (Those who fuck me say I'm tasty):
Gay sexuality in Reef townships

Hugh McLean and Linda Ngcobo

Meet the Guys

This essay is based on interviews conducted in 1992 with 20 African men who have sex with other men. Their lives disprove the lie: 'Homosex is not in Black Culture!'[1]

Bongani* is about 30. We met him for the first time in the Skyline Bar in Hillbrow and have not seen him since.

Chris* is 22, from Moroka in Soweto. He works for Junior's catering firm when he can, and is a close friend of Linda's.

Fillie is in his twenties and unemployed. He lives with his hubby at his mother's home in Moroka, Soweto.

Jeffrey is 26. He is from Zimbabwe but now lives in Thembisa. We met him when he was having a drink in the Skyline with his colleagues from an interior decorating firm.

Junior is 39 and runs his own catering firm. His home in Jabulani Flats provides a meeting place for many young gays in that area of Soweto.

Kimberly is 22 and is from Mabopane, outside Pretoria. He is Odelle's cousin and a friend of Linda's.

Linda, that's the Zulu Linda, not the girl's name, was a teacher from Senoane in Soweto. He wrote this essay with Hugh. He died of AIDS-related complications in February 1993.

Abangibhamayo bathi ngimnandi

Lucky is 20 and from Soweto. He lives in a shack in the backyard of his mother's home. He would like to study law.

Martin is 17, and also from Soweto. He dresses in drag whenever he can. He used to go to school but was forced to leave because he is gay.

Mlungisi is 21 and lives in Meadowlands. He is unemployed.

Odelle from Mabopane is also 21. He is reigning Miss Glow 1992, and earns a living making dresses with his mother.

Pik[*] is 20 and from Soweto. His family suspect he is gay. He is afraid they will find out, for they support him.

Ron is 20 and from Daveyton. He is unemployed.

Ruben is 26 and from Sebokeng. He works for the Department of Education and Training in Vereeniging.

Shado[*] is 27. He is from Gazankulu in the Northern Transvaal but now lives in Tsakane. He is a National Union of Mineworkers shopsteward on a mine in the East Rand.

Sipho is 18 and a is school student in Soweto.

Stompie is 25. He is from Soweto and is unemployed.

Thami is 24 and is from Dobsonville in Soweto. He is unemployed.

Thebo is 24. He lives in Meadowlands and works for a legal firm in Johannesburg.

Trevor is 23 and is from a Township near Witbank. He works in a store.

* (not their real names)

Fourteen of these men are members of GLOW, the Gay and Lesbian Organisation of the Witwatersrand, but they could not be considered part of the same social circle. Not all of them know each other and some of them have never met.

Let's talk about sex, baby![2]

When particular forms of sexuality and human bonding are determined deviant, they give rise to social groupings and sub-cultures. Homosexual people organise themselves socially, to begin with, around a common sexual orientation. In this way, social organisation and sexual activity become linked. This essay is about both.

Heterosexuality is inextricably linked to the institutionalised social forms of the family, religion and the state. The domination of men over women; the oppression of youth by elders; the construction of masculinity; and the rule of the father are all elements that constitute patriarchy. Patriarchal rule stigmatises and represses homosexuality and whatever else it considers 'deviant desire'. Surviving and resisting this rule results in homosexual organisational forms both copied and different from institutionalised heterosexuality.

In this context, acts of 'sexual deviance' assume far more significance than mere bad manners. In the last 50 years they have become the markers which define another species. The sexual act is the specific event which constructs this species, with its own sets of behaviour, styles and forms of organisation. While this 'species' is not exempt from the divides of class and race, lesbians and gay men are

159

almost universally seen as 'other'. Our 'otherness' is located within a discourse, and it is this which defines our 'species'.

Much of what follows, then, is about *sex*. These men talk about sex proudly, bluntly and honestly. We have tried to do the same.

> *LUCKY: Abangibhamayo bathi ngimnandi. (Those who fuck me say I'm tasty)*

We have not censored what we have written from fear of confirming some people's worst suspicions or out of deference to other people's prudery.

This essay is a political intervention, an act of speaking for ourselves; it is not psychoanalysis or anthropology, nor does it catalogue museum objects. Most of the contributors are young men, all are open and willing to talk. We did not record the interviews and not everything we have written here is exactly as it was said. Some things we wrote down word for word, others we could never forget. This essay has been discussed with most who contributed and we are confident that nothing has been distorted.

Sex for beginners

Playing *mantloana* (housie-housie) can often be a lot more fun than parents ever imagine. The idea of sex and children scares grown-ups. Yet children, in their sexual games, are often less hung up, more tender and more passionate than their parents. They can certainly be less exploitative. Sex, in children's games, is not always explicit. Sometimes it is; and a desire for sex with another boy (even if he is supposedly playing mama) can be the whole point of the game. Then some boys just do it, and don't bother with the game:

> *LINDA: My first sexual experience was when I was about seven. We used to play a game with the other boys. Building houses. It would be nice if the government would play this game now and not some of the other games they are so good at. Anyway, we played mothers and fathers in these houses. I was always the mother. And we would try to do the thing that makes mothers and fathers.*

> *LUCKY: I was small then, when I discovered that I like other men. I only needed to have sex with my friends. I was always the dominator. This was when I was nine or ten. At this time we used to play far from our houses where people could not see us. We played in the long grass and in the reeds. We built houses out of grass and sticks. We'd play — I'm gonna be the mother, who's gonna be father? Then I would clean the house. My husband would go to work and I would wait for him. Most of my friends wanted to change: sometimes the father, sometimes the mother. Me, I didn't want to change, I just wanted to be the mother. I would wake up early and give my husband water in a tin. And I would kiss him hello and good-bye — just baby kisses.*

> *This one boy liked to be my husband. When we were in our house and about to go to sleep, he said to me: 'Strip off your clothes'. And he stripped off his clothes. 'We must do what mothers and fathers do'. Then he lay on top of me and he put his penis between my thighs.*

Children learn to come to terms with themselves and the adult world in their games. Lucky shows how much he has learned about men and women from the adult world: he cleans the house; he waits for his husband; he wakes up early to fetch water; he pecks him hello and good-bye on the cheek; he lies on his back for sex. A virtual catalogue of women's subordination and bondage to home and family. Yet Lucky does it eagerly and refers to himself as the 'dominator'. Given their role-models, it is understandable that young boys who are attracted to members of the same sex explore this attraction within the framework of heterosexual stereotypes, sometimes the mother, sometimes the father. This appropriation belies the 'naturalness' of the sharply defined male-female roles to which we are conditioned and points to their social construction, rather than their genetic pre-ordination.

Some boys discover their sexual attraction to other boys at a very young age and penetrative sex can be experienced even before puberty:

> *ODELLE: I discovered I liked men when I was nine years old. We were doing gardening at school. A certain boy seduced me. An impulse was sent to my nerves and we made love right there in front of the others. I enjoyed myself. But the first time I had real sex with another boy was when I was 12 years old. I oriented him with my feelings and he got inquisitive and we had anal sex.*

Some relationships, started at a young age, go on to last a number of years and display remarkable commitment and tenderness. They have the outward form of adult heterosexual relationships, but as sexual arrangements between young 'underaged' boys, they turn the world on its head.

> *LUCKY: He was very interested in me and we had a relationship for about two or three years.* [This is the same boy who liked to be Lucky's 'husband'.] *He used to call me every day. He would take me to his home and we would have sex. Sometimes he would give me 10c or 20c. All this happened when I was too young for sperms.*

Passing on knowledge

Sex is more often learned from older boys and men. In each case the early experience with an older male is related as positive and formative. We didn't find anyone who was 'made into a homosexual' by an older 'pervert'. Those who spoke about such experiences had either discovered their attraction to males and their bodies before, or recognised quite quickly when it happened that it was what they were after.

161

LUCKY: When I was still very young I met a guy in the Carlton Centre. He said that he had a contract at the SABC and he was looking for young boys. He was an older man, maybe 26 or 27, a black man from Port Elizabeth and he wore a tie and suit. He had a room in the hotel. We went up to his room and he gave me a kiss and said: Can you strip? I need to see your body. Then he touched my cock and he said: How would you like if you have sex with me?

CHRIS: There was a priest at a big church who used to like boys. We went and played there. He would take us into the dining room and tell us stories and to be careful of girls, things like that.

One day he said: 'Let me see your cocks'. We all undid our pants and took out our cocks. I liked it and was enjoying myself. He said to me: 'You look nice', because I was uncircumcised. Then he said he wanted to test something and he started to masturbate me. I thought, why am I doing this?

This priest taught me how to wank. He called it to 'skomora' or to 'shaya indlwabu'. When I was young I never stopped going to this priest. I don't see him now, he is an old man. But we began to have sex. He would say: 'First have me, then I'll have you.'

'Turn the other cheek'! For Chris, the relationship was important in helping him to come to terms with his homosexuality. The priest, for his part, was unselfish about the arrangement:

CHRIS: Then he organised me a boy of about 19 to fuck. We were both shy but the priest said to me: 'I am giving you a chance'. So this boy, first I fucked him and then he fucked me. We saw each other a few times. We called each other Ticket, this was our code word. If I saw him in the street I would say Ticket and he would answer Ticket, then we would just pass, no one would know what it meant. Now Ticket has a girlfriend and he is no more open with me, before he was coming to my place a lot.

Before the hostels gained their current notoriety in the townships, they were notorious among township residents for other reasons.

JUNIOR: People would say to the young boys: 'Don't go near the hostels, those men will grab you and smear you with Vaseline.'

Today things are different — you do not have to tell anyone to stay away from the hostels. But a while ago, such a warning was more likely to send some boys directly to the hostel gate to lurk about, hoping to be 'grabbed'.

JUNIOR: In the 1970's we would go to the hostels. Dzanibe always organised a lot of boys. He had a shebeen where he would drink with his friends.

When you went there, you knew you were going to be 'serviced'. We would sit there drinking. Then one would just tap you at the back. He would take a key from Dzanibe and we would go to one of the rooms. We were five guys, and we were all of us dispersed in various rooms.

We would enjoy that. These men were very secretive. They had wives. But they were very happy when the boys came. They would even wear Aramis. They would always be asking Dzanibe to: 'Bring us something new.'

The hostels were our own Skyline, we would go there to break the monotony.

There is a tradition of male 'marriage' which came from the hostels, and the ceremony is often more like a seminar on sex. Dunbar Moodie reports that 'the young "boys" of the miners are not merely sexual partners; they are also "wives" in other ways, providing domestic services for their "husbands" in exchange for substantial remuneration... There is in fact an entire set of rules, an *mteto*, governing this type of relationship, whose parameters are well known and enforced by black mine authorities.'[3]

*LINDA: At these marriage ceremonies, called **mkehlo**, all the young **skesanas** [those who play the passive role] sit on one side and the older ones on the other. Then your mother would be chosen. My mother was MaButhelezi. These things would happen in the hostels those days. They were famous.*

The older gays would chose you a mother from one of them. Then your mother's affair would be your father. Then your father is the one who would teach you how to screw. All of them, they would teach you all the positions and how to ride him up and down and sideways.

*Some Durban **skesanas** organised such a feast for me too. The main one was MaMkize — a famous **skesana**. He died of AIDS some years ago but people don't like to talk much about it now. MaMkize would organise an **mkehlo** to teach you how to sleep with a man. They would chose your mother, then you would have to sleep with your father with your boyfriend sitting outside the door.*

But having sex with another man is not always a thing that has to be learned. It comes more naturally than people think.

JEFFREY: The first time I went with a man, we went out to movies, had some beers, got pissed. Then he took me to his flat. I found I had the whole theory of love. I just took my straight experiences and put them into gay life. I had no problems at all.

Jeffrey is typical of someone who discovers he likes men 'later in life'. He recalls no early childhood experience with other boys.

In the last decade specifically, young people have learned more about homosexuality from *You* magazine and *Dynasty* than Diepkloof hostel. And with the variety of influences, the edges of the patriarchal template begin to soften and blur.

*LINDA: ...that famous **skesana** would organise an **mkehlo** to teach you how to sleep with a man... This doesn't happen now. You don't have to be taught these things. Now is the free South Africa and the roles are not so strong, they are breaking down.*

Inventing the skesana

*LINDA: A **skesana** is a boy who likes to be fucked.*

The stamp of patriarchy on the young mind evolves a simple logic: If I do not feel as other boys do, then I must be a girl. Among many young township boys who feel attracted to boys and men, this means the adoption of a persona. The young *skesana* is a noticeable type — she lives and loves to a particular code. From a blinkered heteronormal viewpoint, she is merely a boy behaving like a girl. From our viewpoint, the *skesanas'* behaviour illustrates precisely that 'girlhood' is a set of behaviours and not an inherent identity.

The social arrangement which establishes the *skesana's* persona and gives expression to her chosen sexuality is her love affair with a 'man'.

MARTIN: I think in a relationship the woman must attend to her man. Like a woman she must clean the house, and he must be treated like a man.

THAMI: There must be a 'man' and a 'woman' in a relationship. A man must act mannish in his behaviour and his talks and walks. But a female must be queenish in every way.

*LUCKY: When I have sex with him [the 'male partner' in a relationship], I don't wish to be satisfied. I only wish that he should get satisfaction. I don't tell him that I'm not satisfied. If I want to be satisfied then I will go to other **skesanas**, then we can be satisfied. But when I have sex, it is only with my lover, and I don't tell him about the other **skesanas**.*

So the *skesana* has a second sexuality: found in an outside liaison which does not rival the status of her relationship and involves 'sex' which is not always regarded as sex because it is typically non-penetrative.

The *skesana* feels compelled to adopt a persona which seems logical within the tyranny of sexual polarities. Yet in the face of the strong social taboos against such betrayal of manhood and society's harsh subordination of woman, there is something profoundly radical and courageous about a boy 'being a girl'.

Skesanas assert their female role with great determination and they themselves enforce their receptive role in sex. Society insists that women should be passive. Ironically, *skesanas* often have to dominate to assert their own 'passivity'.

LINDA: In the beginning he liked touching me; and he liked to masturbate me. And he wanted to be screwed in the thighs. But when I was about 16 I didn't want him to touch me. He was angry at first but later he understood. I told him: 'You can touch me, but not my dickie!' So he fucked me. I would come but not always — I was not frustrated though. I loved him and I wanted him to be satisfied. If I came I came. I think in all those years I only masturbated twice. I would have sex though with other skesanas.

This receptive role in sex should neither be confused with subordination nor dismissed as self-oppression. Remember that Lucky, who just wanted to be mother, was always the dominator. The *skesana* attains pleasure by flirting with power.

LUCKY: I would have sex with someone I don't know. I go to a tavern. If someone needs me, I'll take him, but I'll make sure he doesn't know I'm gay. My friend Filli taught me: 'If you pick up a man, lift up your legs and hide your cock between your thigh and your body. You can use your saliva for lubrication while he fucks you up the anus'. I can move like a real woman, take him up and down, up and down. I don't let him touch my cock and he doesn't know. I can even fuck him in the morning and he won't know.

The pride is evident. None of that can be regarded as passive.

LUCKY: My boyfriend didn't know I was a gay man for five months. You can see I'm a little bit fat so many boys don't know if I'm a woman or a man. My boyfriend is Mbuso. He lives with me at my home. He loves my mother. I think he got curious when he saw my friends. He would ask me many funny questions, like: 'Why are you friends with these people?' Then my mother told him that I was a boy. He was very surprised but he told me it didn't matter, he was in love with me. He was very curious at first but I never let him see my privates. Even when I bathed, he would stand outside and wait. I thought, if he sees me he won't love me again. He is straight.

Injongas

LINDA: An injonga is the one who makes the proposals and does the fucking.

Injongas are the active partners who service the *skesanas*, and they can be men or boys. When the *injongas* are around the *skesanas* are in great form. Many *skesanas* regard the *injongas* as straight, even those *injongas* who openly acknowledge that they like having sex with men. 'They're not gay, their boyfriends are!' was a remark overheard about the young, macho gumboot dancers who led the 1992 Lesbian and Gay Pride March through Johannesburg.

MARTIN: My male lover is not gay, he's just heterosexual. I am always the woman in a relationship.

Certainly, many *skesanas* see themselves as women. But the man who calls himself an *injonga* is someone who consciously adopts the role of a man who has sex with men. He is different from the 'accidental' homosexual, the *pantsula* (macho township guy) who sleeps with what he believes to be a hermaphrodite or with someone who pretends, and who he pretends, is female.

*ODELLE: I pick **pantsulas** up all the time by imposing a girl. I orientate in front, I mix passion with juicy seductions and finally he is all mine.*

Imposing a girl: Odelle would not 'propose her man' directly. His job is to propose her. However, the *skesana* clearly initiates the process. The *pantsula* is merely left with the formality of concluding the deal.

Some *injongas* are bisexual or may later adopt a predominantly heterosexual lifestyle, as did the childhood loves of Lucky and Linda. Other *injongas* are a permanent part of 'gay' township life and are indistinguishable from the *amafezela* or straight men.

Many *injongas* were *skesanas* once. This reflects the progression of an age-old 'man-boy' convention in homosexual arrangements, common also among township men who have sex with other men.

*LINDA: I mentioned the **skesanas** before. Most gay boys are **skesanas** when they are young. Then when you get older, like Masilo, you might change. Because you are without a relationship and you get no proposals. Then you turn to become an **injonga**. So people change roles when they get older.*

Moodie writes of a similar arrangement between 'married' men in the mine hostels: 'As the boy becomes "old enough" he might "wish to start his own family" on the mine, becoming senior partner... There was thus a biological period (somewhere in the middle of his twenties, it would seem, but also depending on the extent of one's mine experience) when a "boy" would become a man, unable to endure any longer his non-ejaculatory sexual role. This would be the end of the "marriage". Thus men who were sexually active with senior men in their youth took boys when they became "boss" boys themselves.'[4]

While Moodie may be right here, his otherwise groundbreaking article falls short on one major point: it seems to make male sexuality on the mine rather too much like a mechanical and necessary substitute for heterosexual life in a situation where there are no women. He makes no real concession to the fact that some men may in fact have enjoyed sex with other men or might even prefer it to having sex with women.

Moodie also typifies the view that sex between African men involves thigh sex and that anal penetration is rare and frowned upon. He states, for example, that 'sexual activity itself hardly ever involves anal penetration, but rather takes place externally.' This is effected, according to one of his sources, 'through the satisfaction of sexual passions by action between the thighs... actual sodomy is rare and is generally looked upon with disgust.'[5]

Thigh sex was widely practiced in Africa as an acceptable form of intercourse, primarily between young unmarried men and women. A 'despoiled' bride, if she was to marry at all, would fetch a low *lobola* for her parents. Thigh sex was thus a sensible alternative.

While this cultural precedent might explain the widespread adoption of thigh sex on the mines as a form of intercourse between men, it does not explain why, for most of the men we spoke to, sex is synonymous with anal penetration. We have indicated previously the interrelation between male sex in the hostels and gay township life. It would be nonsensical to argue that homosexual practice in hostels and townships had independent and unrelated lines of historical development.

A more likely argument is that the illegality and strong social taboos against sodomy make it unlikely that men will admit to it freely. Thigh sex may even have enjoyed a degree of promotion above anal sex, among *impis* and later in hostels, as a preferable form of sex between men.

It would be too far-fetched to imagine that anal sex is a recent discovery, or a phenomenon associated only with prisons and criminals already outside the law, and who would therefore not be concerned about engaging in illicit sex. The taboo against male sodomy must have something to do with the patriarchal conception that 'being penetrated' is somehow quintessentially female. The acclamation of virginity — unpenetrated womanhood — is in reality the sanctification of penetration, possession and masculinity. This charade is quite unconsciously subverted by *skesanas* and *injongas* who show that the quintessential male and the quintessential female can be put on like clothes.

We would suggest that for most African men who have sex with other men, sex equals anal penetration. Remember that *skesanas* who 'play with each other', even to the point of orgasm, do not consider this to be sex. Sex happens when *amanjonga wa kwabo baba-ayinela*, when their *injongas* penetrate them.

Attempts to sanitise sex between men by discounting the possibilities of anal sex is not only unnecessarily prudish and misleading, it is dangerous. In the AIDS era it is even more essential to speak about all sex practices in a frank and non-judgemental manner.

Imbubes and Mix Masala

*LINDA: An **imbube** is someone who goes fifty-fifty.*

Some *injongas* will confess that they actually also enjoy a receptive role in sex. They will not admit this openly and it would be disastrous if the *skesanas* found out.

SHADO: I was in love with my homeboy when I was young, for about two years. But now, even though I love women I am seeing this white man for about two years. I do not tell people that

I love men, but I will not let them say bad things about gays.
What I specially love is to be fucked.

There are those 'undecided *injongas*' who the *skesanas* would call *imbubes* or 'mix masalas'. An *imbube* tends to be treated either with mild tolerance as someone who can't make up his mind, or with the same irritation as someone who wants to play *morabaraba* (a board came played with bottle-tops) but doesn't know the rules.

*LINDA: I could never be an **injonga**. I don't think I can fuck but*
*I never gave myself the opportunity. Maybe I can be an **imbube**.*
*But most **skesanas** like strict role playing. And they will bully*
*you if you want different portfolios. And the **injongas**, they hate*
*the **imbube** life — or they say they do.*

*CHRIS: I am in a relationship with a **skesana**. His name is*
*Sello. I am an **injonga**, but my real secret is that I am an **im-***
bube.

Not all African men who have sex with other men know the moves in the *skesana* jive. For the moves are part of a particular sub-culture, and they are learned. The gender jive is strongly associated with the hostels and mines. Certainly, it is in part a caricatured reaction to patriarchy, but it is not a simple mirror image of power relations under patriarchy: it distorts, subverts and plays with domination, subordination and gender.

Some of the men reject rigid 'portfolios' in a relationship and insist that the partners must be 'free'. They show a degree of impatience towards 'men who behave like women'.

Hermaphrodites

ODELLE: The community is against us. They say it is an abnor-
*mal issue. They call us names like uTracy and **isitabane**, which*
means hermaphrodite.

It is widely believed in the townships that homosexuals are hermaphrodites. This is not only regarded as the explanation for the feminine 'voguing' of *skesanas*, but it is commonly regarded as a plausible reason why some men sleep with them.

LINDA: In the township they used to think I was a hermaphrodite.
They think I was cursed in life to have two organs. Sometimes you
*can get a nice **pantsula** and you will find him looking for two*
organs. You don't give him the freedom to touch you. He might
discover that your dick is bigger than his. Then he might be em-
barrassed, or even worse, he might be attracted to your dick.
*This is not what a **skesana** needs or wants. So we keep up*
the mystery. We won't let them touch and we won't disillusion
*them. Before, all **skesanas** wanted to have a small cock. Now we*
can relax, it does not matter too much and people don't discuss
cocks as much. I think it makes you more acceptable if you are a
hermaphrodite, and they think your dick is very small. The prob-

168

*lem is, the **skesanas** always have the biggest dicks. And I should know.*

> *For them, there must be some physical reason for being homosexual, you see. Then it is part of nature. It is not a man against God. Before, I thought I was a woman. Now I think I'm a man, but it doesn't worry me anyway. Although it used to cause problems earlier.*

A belief in hermaphroditism is a logical consequence of the polarity of gender in broader society. It provides the 'physical cause' Linda speaks of. This 'deformity' safely locates homosexuality within the catalogue of clinical disorders, thereby making it at least explicable and, to a degree, acceptable. That someone would chose to be a homosexual simply because he likes other men is unacceptable to most people because it questions the most basic patriarchal assumptions about men and women.

Coming Out

A mother from kwaThema speaks about the advantages that parents of gay children have over the parents of straight children:

> *Today gay life is the best life of them all. The gays have respect, they don't fight. They love each other. When they have a squabble they don't kill each other like **tsotsis** with knives. They solve it now now.*[6]

Many mothers are proud and accepting of their sons. Says the mother of Maboys, a friend of Lucky's:

> *This is my son; I just take him as he is. I am proud of him. He and his friends are free to come here.*

The lack of economic options and the pragmatic tolerance that can come from overcrowding and living in close proximity often result in quite settled arrangements. Many boyfriends are tolerated and even accepted at home.

> *CHRIS: My mother knows I am gay. When she found out she said I must go away. Now she just doesn't want me to get AIDS.*
>
> *MARTIN: My family said I was gay before I knew. They said: **Isitabane lesi**. They said this because I spent all my time in front of the mirror. Now they are quiet about it. My friends just accept it too. I came out when I was growing up. Everyone knew; they thought for me when I didn't think about myself.*
>
> *MLUNGISI: My mother understood; her uncle was also gay. All the others at home understood and accepted it. My friends who are understanding are okay, those who do not swear at me calling me **isitabane**. The community loves me for my hardworking household chores. They say if only I was a girl my mother would be proud.*

FILLIE: I live with my hubby in my mother's house. The people in the street don't mind. They say that as long as my parents accept it, it's okay.

Linda's mother had, in some respects, an unproblematic attitude to gender:

LINDA: I used to wear girls clothes at home. My mother dressed me up. In fact, I grew up wearing girls clothes. And when I first went to school they didn't know how to register me. I wear girls clothes now sometimes, but not so much. But I sleep in a nightie, and I wear slippers and a gown — no skirts. I like the way a nightie feels in bed.

His father, however, had other concerns.

*LINDA: My father had a problem. He is a **Mfundisi** in the church. So you can understand what is his problem. He doesn't mind me going with gays though. He just doesn't want me falling in love with church members. He says it will be degrading him.*

But coming out to family and friends can be quite hazardous.

LUCKY: My parents and my family were very against it when they found out I was gay. I think they saw from my friends. My mother was very curious about sex and she used to fight and yell at me. One day she was very angry and she threw me out into the street. For three days I was just in the street, they would not let me back in the house.

I was only in Standard 9 and I did not know what to do, so I went to the police station. At the charge office I explained that my mother has chased me out and I'm gay. They said they must see for themselves, they called each other and took me into a back room. There were three of them, one of them was a woman. They touched me and they wanted to see if I had two organs. After that they took me home to my place.

When we got home my mother took out all my makeup to show them and she complained that some of my friends were wearing dresses. The police were laughing but they told my mother: 'Leave him, there is nothing you can do'. One of the policemen took me outside, he said to advise me, but he proposed me. I said fine but I never heard from him after that. He was an old policeman, about 40.

So it was fine after that. My mother let me come back home and she has grown to accept it now. I even stay at home with my lover. My friends were very ashamed when I told them that I was gay. Some of them loved it and they asked many questions. Now it is different: all of my friends are gay. At first the community was against me, but later they said that if my parents understand then they have no problems.

170

How to get ahead by advertising

Coming out to families is only part of the process. Gays must also identify each other.

> *LUCKY: To know another gay in the township is easy. First of all there is the beauty, then the movement and the attire.*

> *THAMI: You can recognise them from their movement, their attire and their queenish actions.*

Skesanas of all cultures are intentionally noticeable. Their brazenness announces them as available to the less obvious *injonga* or the closeted *pantsula*. If you ask how gays are recognised in the township, it is the *skesanas* who will be described.

But dressing to attract attention is not the only way to pick up a man. Sometimes it can happen almost by accident:

> *CHRIS: One day I saw Jojo and we greet each other, Hi Hi! He was very happy and he said to me: 'Where do you stay and what are you doing on Sunday?' So on Sunday I went to pick up him and have some beers. I was at his place. He said to me that his mother loves me. I laughed and thought: 'You don't know what I'm after.' He said that he liked me, he respected me and that we should be friends. He said: 'I like you and I'll do anything for you.' I said: 'Okay, can you kiss me?' He said: 'No problem.' So we kissed and started romancing, and then he became a bit shy. But he said to me: 'It's very late now, you can't go back. You will have to sleep here.' So in bed he was responding very freely to me and I fucked him. When we woke up I looked at him and said: 'Hi Jojo'. He was a little bit shy and he said: 'Aish, yesterday I was drunk.' I just laughed inside.*

Many ostensibly straight men and boys are curious about sex with other men and are eager to try it. So while being 'out' may have its risks, it is definitely worth it.

> *ODELLE: I discuss my sexuality with all my straight friends. They are very supportive and very interested. I fell in love with a straight friend once. At first he just wanted to experience it, later he fell head over heels in love and oriented some of his friends.*

> *MARTIN: I talk to my straight friends about sex. They just take it. Most guys are curious about sex between two men. Many of the guys are willing to try it but they don't. They say: 'I'm going to see if he's going to suit,' and 'I'm going to taste that one and pass.' Many of my friends try it. I have tried it with my friend.*

It must be assumed that many men who feel attracted to other men either manage to suppress it or are confused and anxious about it. We met and spoke to Bongani

171

at the Skyline, a largely-black gay bar in Hillbrow. He was a bit drunk and talkative, and his words betray the secret pain of his hidden love for other men.

> *BONGANI: I don't like* **skesanas** *because I don't want them to know at home. I don't want to embarrass my family. I've got a girlfriend to shield myself. I only have sex with her once or twice a month and I use a condom. I'm scared of AIDS. I don't want someone to say I'm gay. Girls are bitches but in a way guys are more bitchy. It is difficult to get a boyfriend. You can have him tonight but he will disappoint you tomorrow. I have never succeeded to get a steady boyfriend.*

Pleasure and power — and pantsulas

'Pleasure and power do not cancel or turn back against one another; they seek out, overlap, and reinforce one another.'[7]

Pleasure and power heighten the act and the pursuit of sex. Not only is it pleasurable to exercise power, but it is pleasurable to evade power and to subvert it. Controlling pleasure also gives power. Picking up a *pantsula* can put a *skesana* on a panga-edge. But what a pleasure to pick up a straight man who claims he is looking for a woman!

> *LINDA: On a weekend I went to a shebeen with a lady friend of mine. I was in drag. I often used to do this on the weekends — many* **skesanas** *do it. We were inside. It seemed as if four boys wanted to rape us, they were* **pantsulas** *and they were very rough. One of them proposed my friend and she accepted. The others approached me one by one. The first two I didn't like so I said no! I was attracted by the third one, so I said yes to him.*
>
> *As we left the shebeen, my one said to me: 'If you don't have it, I'm going to cut your throat'. I could see that he was serious and I knew I must have it or I'm dead. So I asked my friend to say that she was hungry and we stopped at some shops. I went inside and bought a can of pilchards. I knew that the only thing the* **pantsula** *was interested in was the hole and the smell.* **Pantsulas** *don't explore much, they just lift up your dress and go for it.*
>
> *We all went to bed in the one room. There were two beds. The one* **pantsula** *and my friend were in one and I was in the other bed with this* **pantsula**. *The other two* **pantsulas** *were together on the floor next to the door on some blankets, I don't know what they were doing.*
>
> *Sardines is one of the tricks the* **skesanas** *use. We know that some* **pantsulas** *like dirty pussy, for these you must use pilchards, but not Glenrick because they smell too bad. Other* **pantsulas** *like clean pussy, for these you can use sardines. For my* **pantsula** *I bought pilchards because I could see what kind he was.*
>
> *So before I went to bed I just smeared some pilchards around my anus and my thighs. When he smelled the smell and found the*

172

*hole he was quite happy. We became lovers for some months after
that. He never knew that I was a man and he never needed the smell
again because he was satisfied the first time. He ended up in jail
because I think he stabbed somebody.*

In the townships, the *pantsula* is the archetypal macho figure. Many are
feared, others are respected for their style. The *pantsula* sees power as brute force.
For the *pantsula* looking for a fuck, the myth of hermaphroditism is a convenience:
he can regularly pick up *skesanas* and not have to deal with the anxiety of redefin-
ing his sexuality, especially to himself.

It is in the *skesana's* interest to uphold this myth. The mystery is a source
of allurement and a locus of control: keep him interested, keep him guessing. The
determination of the *skesanas* not to let their penises be touched during sex is the
mechanism through which the myth is enforced.

The double impetus of pleasure and power is violently evident in some
relationships.

> *LINDA: Oupa used to hit me a lot, he just becomes mad. He
> would accuse me of many things and hit my face in the wall. I
> took it as a symbol of his love. Many of us are beaten, with
> fists, sometimes even stabbed. First he beats you, then he fucks
> you then he says I'm sorry dear. It's like that.*

The dialectic in this relationship dictated that Linda had the upper hand in the end
and was less dependent on Oupa than Oupa was on him.

> *LINDA: Oupa came out in 1987, after three years in jail. I had
> different feelings but he still wanted me. I tried for months to
> patch things, but it didn't work out. Now he is working. He is
> married and he has kids. I was his first and his last male lover.
> I loved him very deeply.*

None of the men say much about violence when the subject is first broached. But
there is a shift of the eyes or a flick of the hand and then later, some of it slips out
and then a little more. Violence in relationships can be a lot more private than sex.
And violence in society is so endemic, so obvious that it can go completely unmen-
tioned. Clearly, the trangressive nature of their sexual behaviour makes lesbians and
gays particularly vulnerable to violence emanating from outside the relationship
too:

> *LINDA: Many of the **skesanas** are afraid of being raped, and I
> have been in some fights where we have had to fight back. But
> this is part of the experience.*

> *MARTIN: Many, many people want to hit me because I am gay.
> Some men were going to rape me once. They said: 'You look
> like a woman'. But I ran away. I have not really seen violence
> against other gays. There is not much violence against lesbians.
> Most people are afraid of lesbians because lesbians don't play,
> they just fuck you up.*

173

THAMI: I know of violence against lesbians. People think it is madness, how can a woman be in love with another. In fact they just need to be raped. That's what people think.

The relationship between violence and the power of certain human beings over others is direct in patriarchal systems. The violence against a woman in the home and a woman in the street is part of the same contempt — a contempt deeply rooted in a belief in the 'right of men to rule'. There is a direct cross-over in gay relationships: in domestic arrangements violence is dangerously close to passion and domination. In the street, homophobia is dangerously close to real aggression.

Marriage

LINDA: I was planning to get married in 1984, to my childhood sweetheart Oupa. With his parents and the help of my parents we had everything organised for the wedding. Things like the white wedding gown; my hubby's tuxedo suit; the wedding rings; the cookers — everything was in order.

Then something terrible happened. Oupa's aunt came to call him and his friends for help while I was there, saying someone down the street raped her. Oupa and his friends ran to those boys. There was a fight and Oupa stabbed one of them. He went to jail and the bail was R200.

The case was on the 12 April. I was so worried, even my boss knew what had happened. Then Oupa phoned at work to say the case was the next day. I had been a month without seeing him because in our custom the bride is not supposed to see the groom for a month before the wedding day.

Most of the men would like to marry their lovers. Marriage is what heterosexual relationships aspire to, and these men want the same for themselves. For them gay marriage would signify acceptance by normal society. They wish to be seen as normal and in this regard show no desire to be seen as 'other'. There is much talk of the many married gays who live in Pimville, a district of Soweto. And Fillie lives at home with his hubby to whom he is formally married.

These formal marriages do not represent the alternative to marriage that the *Mkehlo* parties do. The *Mkehlo* parties do not have the overtones of fidelity of these 'out' marriages. They are an 'in' homosexual festivity which make no attempt to reconcile with the straight world. Yet the 'out' marriages are no plea for acceptance. They are an insistence that gays should have the same rights as straights. Junior tells a story:

JUNIOR: There was an old man who was interested in a young boy. This young boy was me. There was a big age gap. But I had an affair with him for four years. Everyone loved me, even his wife and daughters. Whenever I used to visit him his wife would leave his bed and go to sleep with the kids.

174

> *Uncle Willie was a really loving guy and he used to satisfy me.*
> *His wife said to me: 'I'm happy if you're going to look after my*
> *husband. Just you maintain his dignity'. We were even preparing to*
> *get married, but I missed the date. I don't know why. I could have*
> *stayed with him.*

Uncle Willie's wife's acquiescence to this arrangement reveals either a love transcending patriarchal bounds or simply the acceptance that her husband may take a second wife should he wish to do so. Polygamy, after all, is quite at home under patriarchy. The general discourse around relationships and marriage is that of monogamy, fidelity and possession. But it is a discourse almost completely contradicted by actions in everyday life, where both partners commonly have other lovers on the side. Jealousy and fidelity need each other; they are shoes on the same monster. In this way, as with straight relationships, the accepted discourse is a smokescreen for what really goes on.

For these men seek, in their relations with their lovers, space for sex, companionship, independence from elders, and to be free from social stigma. These things are linked, in heterosexual relationships, to the establishing of a home and to achieving a measure of autonomy. Marriage is believed to be where these things happen, therefore marriage is what everybody wants.

The Economics of Sex

When Lucky's childhood lover gave him 5c or 10c, it was no tip, it was the enactment of a centuries-old tradition: the exchange of domestic services for patronage. While this would be common in homosexual relationships where there was a significant age gap and the 'senior' partner worked, it is interesting to see it at work among peers where the only imperative is gender roles.

In every culture favours are exchanged for sex. While there is often the pretense of a mutual contract, the power is clearly held by the partner who has the material surplus to exchange for emotional and physical services.

Patronage in heterosexual relationships is reinforced by women's oppression. In its crudest terms patronage is a mechanism for reproducing society by catering for a man's domestic needs and bearing his children while he goes out to work.

Even though gender roles in homosexual relationships are dictated by convention, they are often not permanent, and can be discarded when they fail to fulfil any function. A *skesana* does not face the overwhelming social and economic conditions which oppress women. She is free to play with gender, and by assuming other roles she can just as equally liberate as bind herself.

Economic hardship strengthens the hold of patronage in many relationships. Yet while the sugar-daddies have the cash, the *skesanas* often have the looks — and the power of being sexually desired. *Skesanas* may be economically bound to their patrons, but their patrons in turn may be emotionally bound to them. A middle-aged *injonga* who does not wield the same power over his *skesana* as a straight man over his wife would be just as adamant to know whether today's youngsters are really in love or just gold diggers. When Martin met his first lover, patronage asserted itself from the start.

> *MARTIN: The first gay I knew was Peter from the township. I saw he was a nice guy. He said I must come and help him clean the house. I discovered that I liked men after having sex with Peter. I was with him for three years. I didn't tell anyone about it.*

Selling sex is far neater, more direct, often more lucrative and it can be more equal. Linda tells of a trip to the mines.

> *LINDA: When things began to change in the hostels we went to the mines. There, there is still strong role-playing. But on the mines you don't do it for love — you do thigh sex for money.*
>
> *I'll tell you about a trip to the mines. I went with MaMkize in '83 and Oupa didn't know. We left on Friday and came back Sunday. We went to visit Dio in Carltonville. I remember, it was Kloof no 4 shaft. We were just going to make some money. MaMkize told me: 'You must take a towel of your own, some Vaseline; you charge R10 and you mustn't say no!'*
>
> *I was the youngest of four **skesanas** that time. When we got to the gate the **manshingilane** knew MaMkize but he asked if MaMkize would donate me for entrance. 'No, she'll talk for herself', said MaMkize.*
>
> *He was a big man, with a big tummy. And he told me that he loved me and not to be afraid. He took me to a special room at the back and he organised his own towel for me. Then he took off his trousers and he told me he was going to give me **inkuni**. Then he climbed on me and he used his saliva between my thighs. Afterwards he paid me R10 and he asked me to count him on my list. The other one at the gate then wanted me, but the big one said no, I was his. I think he was pleased with me.*
>
> *It was 8.30 and we went through. We met Dio. He was with the MaShangane group. They are the love ones. They are very ugly but they have big pricks. As we walked, the men called 'Dio, Sister, Sister!' They would come to make their appointments. I had 15 in my line that first night. They would come up to me and ask, 'How much? Can you take me now?' I would write down their name and say: 'You are after so-and-so'.*
>
> *Then we found a spot. We had our towels and our Vaseline. We were dressed normally but we wore bras where we kept our money. Then each one would come and when he is finished, he wipes himself with the towel. No one was rough. They were just jealous of my youth. I think they were after young blood, as I was about 16 or 17. They had no interest in cocks or anything, they just wanted to fuck your thighs.*

176

Saturday was fun day. There was a new group. Some from the previous night. Not Shangaans only. First they would have some drinks and if they wanted me I'd say: 'Find me at Dio's'.

At Dio's there were five of us. It was a hostel room. We put sheets up between the beds for curtains. The men would sit and drink in the centre of the room. Then they would come one by one behind the curtain. I had 24 that night and I was very tired. I think I made plus-minus R600. Most men just wanted to fuck and some of them liked kissing. But they were all very polite.

Afterwards all five of us went to the showers together. The men knew we were boys. They didn't think about hermaphrodites. On the mines its done openly with all the young boys. One of the younger men who had me liked to kiss me very much — he wanted to spend the night with me. And because I liked him I let him do it with no extra charge. So that was my trip to the mines.

Social Life

Skesanas commonly move around in small groups of close friends for company and safety. But they also enjoy the jibes and wolf calls from local *pantsulas*, point out one they may have 'had' and say irreverent things about his masculinity. On any Sunday, it can take the whole afternoon to track down a *skesana* who would have 'just left' minutes before you, as she moves methodically with her friends from one home to the next.

But as well as the impromptu gatherings in homes and the weekend township runabouts, there is also a strong network of more formal activity in which *skesanas* participate. *Stokvels*, for example, are revolving credit unions that are very popular in the townships. And gay *stokvels* not only generate cash, but provide a useful social function by helping to establish a sense of social cohesion and community.

JUNIOR: From 1974 to 1976 me and a friend used to do catering for stokvels. This stokvel was a group of about 15 men. And you won't believe, they were all jailbirds and ex-tsotsis. The stokvel was called: 'Where are the Women?', and I don't know why they ask because whenever the women came these men would chase them away. Anyway, they used to make means to seduce me and my friend.

I think they had experienced this thing in jail. Because they would never fight and they were not jealous. They had their plan worked out and they took turns with us, one week this one, another week that one. Both of us, we went through the whole 15, and there was not one fight. We were protected by these men.

And they were into everything, oral sex, fucking. You would find a real hunk saying: 'Please lay me'. Then he would want fifty-fifty. I think they learned this anal sex from jail. We went until '76, then things broke when the riots started.

177

In the early 1990s, Junior started the Jikileza Boys, a gay *stokvel* for boys and men mostly from Meadowlands and the Jabulani areas in Soweto. This *stokvel*, which closed in 1992, provided money in the event of death in a member's family. A funeral is a huge event in a township and it is extremely difficult to get together sufficient cash. As the membership for Jikileza was between R20 and R30 a week, some of the young school going members obviously attended on behalf of their extended families.

The *stokvel* was held on most Saturday afternoons and at a different member's house every week. This was to ensure that each member in turn had the chance to keep the proceeds from the sale of food and drink. There was usually a large crowd and non-members (who pay more for food and drink) were most welcome.

A *stokvel* is an open, public occasion. The Jikileza Boys, with its loud music and flamboyant members, was something like a travelling cabaret. For its members it was a mechanism for accessing extra cash and a space for finding partners, meeting other queers, dancing, drinking and fun. For its neighbours on a different street every week, it was an openly gay occasion which they were welcome to join. Not all Jikileza's members were gay; some of them were straight women. One gives her reason for being there:

> *I feel I can be comfortable with gays. I am myself. I am not chased by men. I enjoy to be with them.*

In addition to stokvels, skesanas get together for collective income-generating activities like dressmaking, hairdressing, and baking. Junior, for example, now manages a catering business and draws on a pool of about 30 young men to prepare meals and wait. They cater for night vigils, tombstone unveilings, weddings, *stokvel* parties—any township celebration. Opportunities for work are shared so that everyone can benefit. The catalysts for this form of income-generating activity are both social and economic, and the activity provides both social cohesion and a communal salve to unemployment and poverty. There is also a strong and often extremely effective component of peer-group teaching.

Gay clubs and taverns are also, by all accounts, quite vibrant in reef townships, and many are regularly attended on weekends by several hundred people. Like bars and clubs in town, however, they often seem short lived. The Mamelodi Club, the Eleganto Club (Pretoria Town), Big Mikes (in Molapo extension), Mhlanga Rocks (in Mofolo, one of the most famous), the Swazi Inn (Tembisa), and Ship A-hoy (Mamelodi) are but a few.

By far the most popular activity are the drag shows which require tremendous energy and skill to organise properly. The amount of interest and support from 'non-gay' township dwellers is astounding. There is something in the mental and emotional anatomy of a drag show which is hard to understand: what makes a crowd of gay men scream and cheer so for a bevy of other gay men doing their damnedest to look like women? It is too easy and too trite to ascribe this to conventional sexism. It is a sincere celebration of gender-inversion and it is taken very seriously indeed.

Abangibhamayo bathi ngimnandi

The attendance by a number of straight African woman at 'gay' functions is too significant to pass without mention. Many of these women say that they enjoy the company of gays because they feel unharassed as women and accepted as they are. The potential for a movement of the 'sexual fringe' to unhinge the most narrow and arrogant assertions of patriarchy is largely unrecognised. While *skesanas*, *injongas* and *imbubes* themselves may not be free from the shackles of sexism, there is no doubt that their very existence subverts and plays with the role ascribed to women in society.

AIDS

AIDS is not seen as a significant issue in these men's lives: their comments about it were often asides, and they spoke specifically about the epidemic only after much prompting. It will take much death and pain before this changes. While AIDS will only become fully comprehensible to people when those they know or love begin to die, much work needs to be done (not only among township homosexuals), to educate people about AIDS and HIV and to campaign now for effective care for people with AIDS. The following attitudes to condoms are as typical as they are alarming:

> **MLUNGISI:** *I do not prefer it, I like flesh to flesh.*

> **LUCKY:** *I hate it, I need the biological cock.*

> **SIPHO:** *I do not believe in condoms, I like flesh to flesh.*

Some of the men are unresolved and inconsistent in their use of condoms.

> **JEFFREY:** *I trust my partner, although he is a very active injonga.*

> **BONGANI:** *I use them but only when I sleep with a girl.*

> **KIMBERLY:** *I have trust in our love, if I'm with somebody else I use a condom.*

Others practice safe sex by avoiding penetration, and only a few use condoms on a consistent and informed basis.

> **STOMPIE:** *My partner penetrates me, so he wears the condom.*

> **RON:** *I do penetration. I wear a condom because of AIDS.*

Of the 20 men interviewed, 18 know about AIDS, nine have changed the way they have sex as a result, but only three consistently practice safer sex. Due to their association with GLOW, the people we interviewed were probably comparatively well-informed about AIDS. The figures for 'unconscientised' township dwellers must be even more frightening.

Politics and the ANC

It is difficult to pinpoint the time or specific event marking the emergence of a gay movement in black townships. It probably came about in recent years, due to a combination of events and factors. For younger gays, the recent gay pride marches and the existence of a gay character on *Dynasty* are usually cited as the events marking the emergence of this movement. For older gays it was the Soweto uprising of 1976.

> *LINDA: Gays are a lot more confident now in the townships. I think this happened from about 1976. Before that everything was very quiet. 1976 gave people a lot of confidence.*

The 1976 upheaval shook society to its roots and, as a profound rupture of traditional generational hierarchies, had the effect of splitting young people from the roots and conventions of their elders. South Africa's massive youthful majority questioned the authority not only of the state, but of teachers and parents, and pushed its own agenda to the fore. Suddenly, young people found themselves in opposition to many things their parents stood for, and this meant challenging not only conservative politics but all conservative mores. The 1976 uprising also opened the way for new allegiances:

> *LINDA: I remember when the time came to go and march and they wanted all the boys and girls to join in. The gays said: 'We're not accepted by you, so why should we march?' But then they said they didn't mind and we would go to march in drag. Even the straight boys would wear drag. You could wear what you like.*

Whether or not the above story is exaggerated, 1976 was the period when a gay movement emerged in the townships, and this period without doubt marked the beginning of a qualitative change in attitude, primarily among township youth, to whatever it was that deprived them of freedom. Thus, the fight for full rights for gays and lesbians became linked in the minds of young township homosexuals to the fight for national liberation and economic survival even if straight militant youths did not make this connection themselves.

And, as the African National Congress became the symbol of that struggle in the years following 1976, most of these men place their hopes for gay rights in a future ANC government.

> *SIPHO: The ANC is fighting for everybody's rights, we will be legalised and really established.*

> *RUBEN: I think that every one should be involved in politics, also gays. An ANC government will bring gay rights and must have support from gay people.*

There is much hope that the ANC will solve their problems, which they say are the following: we are not recognised, that we are subject to queer-bashing, and that we are illegal:

> *LUCKY: The main problem facing gays in South Africa is that people hate them. If gays were many then everything would be okay. Gays should be involved in politics. How will they get*

180

rights if they are not? Yes I think an ANC government will be better, but it is difficult to tell how.

There is also an understanding that gay people themselves must take up the issue if they are to be freed.

PIK: The main problems facing gays in South Africa are discrimination and racism. We must solve them by campaigning. I think an ANC government will make South Africa better for gays and lesbians because they believe in gender equality and non-sexism.

Not surprisingly, the right to marriage features high on many agendas:

LINDA: The thing that has done most for gays in the township are the marches we have had for gay and lesbian rights. These have been very important and I hope that we will be legalised with an ANC government. Then maybe we can even get married in Regina Mundi [Soweto's principal cathedral] and they won't be throwing in the teargas.

TEBO: I have kept a clipping that says the ANC supports gay rights. Nelson Mandela says gays should get married. One day we will be set free, and we will have our things to do. That's what I think.

However, some of the men are not so sure, and their comments reflect a general skepticism and the broader alienation they feel from society.

JEFFREY: I don't get involved in politics. I think it's a dirty game. I'm not sure if an ANC government will strengthen gay rights.

MARTIN: I think gays and lesbians should be involved in politics. But I don't have a hope about an ANC government. Most people hate us.

While the ANC's stated opposition to discrimination on the grounds of 'sexual orientation' deserves cautious acclaim, the real test for the organisation's commitment to lesbian and gay rights will depend on how actively it is prepared to defend these rights when they are attacked.

But, whatever the official ANC policy and practice, the emergence of a black gay and lesbian movement in the recent political era has given many black gays and lesbians the understanding that political mobilisation is necessary to win rights and freedoms. With the right approach to organisation, this understanding can be translated into enthusiastic and determined action.

Organising a township-based movement

The great strength of the Gay and Lesbian Organisation of the Witwatersrand (GLOW), founded in 1988, was that black homosexuals emerged as a political force. They brought with them some of the determination and courage of the huge struggles against the repression of the mid-1980s. The gay rights marches every year since 1990 — unthinkable before then — are adequate illustration of this. And the fact that GLOW's founder, Simon Nkoli, was one of the 22 accused in the Delmas treason trial — the corner-stone of the state's case against popular upheaval — provided GLOW with a political credibility which reaffirmed the link between the struggle for lesbian and gay rights and wider political struggles.

The gay rights movement after Stonewall[8], and the recent struggles against AIDS, gave lesbian and gay politics in the industrialised North a political edge. However, the adoption of what appears to be the style, social orientation and content of 'gay politics' in the West may not be entirely appropriate for affecting real change on the 'sexual fringe' in South African townships.

Gay organisation in South African townships has simple causes: necessity and survival. This is not to say that these imperatives are not at work elsewhere in the world. They are, particularly among working class lesbians and gays; but they are too often overlooked by more comfortable South African white gay and lesbian activists who have had exposure to the western discourse of 'gay politics'.

GLOW combines both the potential for a popular and strong township-based movement of enormous social weight and the potential for gay activism in the tradition of the best European and American models. This potential is not yet realised. GLOW's ideology and activities are unfortunately rather removed from the everyday life of its township membership. So while the organisation has working groups for media, action, gay men's health, education as well as a lesbian forum, its membership is organised around *stokvels*, clubs, drag shows, catering groups, hairdressing: anything that generates income and provides a safe social space. The working groups are essential and heartily approved of by the membership, but there are too many practical problems related to transport, communication, distance, dispersion and lack of money, to allow for real and consistent involvement by the bulk of GLOW's membership.

The future of a strong gay movement in South Africa depends on the extent to which present activism will become thoroughly township-based. Political issues are crucial, of course, but they cannot be forced on a membership which does not see the immediate reason for them. GLOW therefore needs to construct itself solidly on the activities of township gays (and too often invisible lesbians and bisexuals) and to build among them a conscious political core which can translate and extend these activities into a broad movement that will defeat homophobia, backwardness and bigotry.

Appendix: A Taste of Isingqumo

Minority groups, in the face of social stigma and the threat of open violence, often turn inward and develop mechanisms both for protection and maintaining cohesion. Stylised mannerisms and dress codes, common meeting places and ways of speaking are the hallmarks of gay sub-culture all over the world.

Men who have sex with men and form part of the township gay sub-culture on the Witwatersrand use *isingqumo*. *Isinqumo* without the 'g' means 'deci-

182

sions', and the *skesanas* say that the parole got its name because one must take a decision to use it. It is a highly developed hybrid slang which straights would have difficulty following. This, of course, is the whole idea. The vocabulary for *isingqumo* is extensive and colourful. Although *isingqumo* incorporates many languages and styles of speech, it works mainly through ideomatic corruptions of Zulu. The sophistication and pervasiveness of *isingqumo* is an indication of the developed nature of black gay sub-culture and its rootedness in South African Black townships on the reef.

As can be expected, there are many words for those things that are of specific interest to gay men. A group of *skesanas* could quite easily have a conversation like this:

> *1: Isiphukwana sake, kuyavuswa na?* (His cock, is it big?)
> *2: Maye.* (Yes)
> *3: Injini!* (Lie!)
> *4: Kuncishiwe.* (It's really small)*; or,*
> *5: Kuyapholwa.* (same meaning)

1. *Uphuku* in Zulu is the word for 'pole' or 'stick'; the suffix '-ana' is a diminutive; hence *uphukwana* is strictly correct for 'little stick', *isiphukwana* is the *isingqumo* variant. The word *vuswa* is the passive tense for 'woken up'. A literal translation is: 'His little stick, has it woken up?'
2. *Maye* is commonly used for 'yes' instead of *yebo*, which is standard Zulu. The Zulu word *maye!*, however, is an exclamation expressing shock.
3. The word *imbuqo* would be used in standard Zulu, and has the same meaning as 'taking someone for a ride'. *Injini* comes from the word 'engine'.
4. In standard Zulu *uncishiwe* is literally translated as 'not given'. It has the meaning of 'not talented'.
5. *Phola* comes from the word 'cool' in Zulu; *pholwa* is the passive tense. *Kuyapholwa* could be translated: 'It makes one cool'. Both *kuyapholwa* and *kuncishiwe* are very derogatory.

A straight guy is *ufezela* or *uphoqolo* or *umchakisana*. *Ufezela* is a Zulu word for a reptile which looks like a lizard; *uphoqolo* is close to the Zulu *phoqokile*, meaning 'broken'; *umchakisana* is close to the Zulu *chaka*, which means poor.

An old man or a father is *injubugane*, your mother and your grandmother are *mamburuza*, and if you go anywhere you, you don't *hamba* you *shaya* (hit), *gawula* (*tsotsi* word for 'eat'), *dwala* (*idwala* is a pit) or *bambelela* (hold on to something).

A white person is *udayi* (from dye); beautiful is *ublandi* (from blonde); ugly is *uncishiwe* (the same word for a small penis).

Isingqumo can get really useful when you're in a tavern eyeing men with your friends. You can say *Ngimfolela uphaba la kwakho* (I want the one next to you. Literally: 'I'll bend over — or line up — for him, your wing!'), or *Ubamba isicibi don't know!* (He drinks a lot. Literally: 'He holds on to the stream, don't know!' Don't know is used to mean 'very much'), and you can be sure that only *skesanas* and a few *injongas* will understand.

For something dangerous or really bad, *Kupholiwe!* (the other word for small penis) will put all the *skesanas* and most *injongas* on red alert.

As *isingqumo* is a rapidly evolving slang, much of it will either fall away or change in the next few years. The fact that most of the words are derived from Zulu point to *isingqumo's* origins among Durban *skesanas*. This would seem to indicate that a gay sub-culture was more developed in Durban from earlier on. On the other hand, it could be related to the intensely patriarchal nature of Zulu society and the greater need for secrecy. Many Soweto *skesanas* will insist that Durban *skesanas* are 'more closeted' than other gays.

Notes

1 The slogan on one of the posters in support of Winnie Mandela outside the Supreme Court while she was on trial in May 1991. See Holmes in this volume for a fuller discussion of the homophobia of Mandela's defence.
2 A popular American song in 1991, sung almost as an anthem by most of the men interviewed in this piece.
3 T Dunbar Moodie et al, 'Migrancy and Male Sexuality on the South African Goldmines', in Duberman et al (eds), *Hidden From History: Reclaiming the Gay And Lesbian Past* (Penguin, 1989), p413.
4 Moodie, p418.
5 HM Taberer, cited in Moodie, pp413-414.
6 Quoted in *Gay Life Is Best*, a documentary made by Zackie Achmat and VNS with ABIGALE and GLOW about the 1992 Gay Pride March. The woman, who attended the march, is a neighbour of MaThoko Khumalo, an older woman who has engendered a strong and highly visible gay subculture by opening her home to local gays and providing them with a space and a meeting place. Before she died in mid 1993, meetings of the kwaThema chapter of GLOW were held at MaThoko's and, every year, she brought a posse of her guys to the Lesbian and Gay Pride March. The fact that there are so many openly gay men in kwaThema is proof that coming out is facilitated by the presence of a safe refuge or haven.
7 Michel Foucault, *History of Sexuality: Volume I* (Penguin, 1990).
8 When gay men, lesbians, cross-dressers and transsexuals rioted for three days in New York in June 1969, after a police raid on the Stonewall Bar in Greenwich Village

Glossary

affair: the township gay word for a relationship
amafezela: straight men
ayina: fuck
imbube: those who switch between playing penetrative and receptive roles in homosexual sex
impi: traditional Zulu army
injonga: those who play the active, penetrative (butch or top) role in homosexual sex
isingqumo: gay township slang, literally 'decisions'
lobola: bride-price
manskingalane: guard
mantloana: housie-housie
mfundisi: elder
mkehlo: the marriage ceremony between men in migrant labour hostels
mix masala: those who switch between playing penetrative and receptive roles in homosexual sex

morabaraba: a board game similar to draughts, played with bottle-tops
mteto: the set of rules governing relationships between men in migrant labour hostels
now now: immediately
panga: a home-made township axe
pantsula: a township macho who dresses like a fifties mafioso
shaya ndlwabu: to masturbate
portfolio: one's portfolio is one's assigned role as either a skesana or an injonga
skesana: those who play the passive, receptive (femme or bottom) role in homosexual sex
Regina Mundi: Soweto's principal cathedral famous for anti-apartheid gatherings in the 1980s
skomora: to masturbate
Skyline: a gay bar in Hillbrow very popular with and frequented mainly by black men
stabane, isitabane: hermaphrodite(s)
stokvel: revolving credit unions, very popular in the townships
tsotsis: township thugs
tsotsitaal: literally, gangster language. The vernacular of the street in urban South African townships
uTracy: hermaphrodite

Five women:
Black lesbian life on the Reef

As told to Tanya Chan Sam

Editor's note: The following are five vignettes of women who are members of the Lesbian Forum of the Gay and Lesbian Organisation of the Witwatersrand (GLOW). The Lesbian Forum was specifically set up to provide a women's space within the largely-male organisation, and performs both social (coming out) and political (consciousness raising) functions for its members.

Bongie: True confessions of an amachicken

I am a 24-year-old lesbian. I live in Soweto. I started school here in Soweto but when I reached high school, my mother felt I should go to boarding school. So from the age of about 13, I was sent first to Swaziland and then to Nelspruit, in the Eastern Transvaal.

There I was! A city girl from Soweto stuck in a small platteland town. It was difficult and lonely at first, not just for me, but for all the out-of-town boarders. But the Nelspruit school was a girls' school, so we were lucky. There, the problem was understood and all the older girls were very nice and supportive, helping us younger ones to adjust. Not all of them: obviously there are people you don't get on with and others you will never be friends with. But often some of the older girls will help you to settle down.

So you will be friends and share things. Very often this friendship can allow you to hold hands, kiss, talk in whispers: because you are sweethearts or sweeties. Sometimes it is also called the *amachicken*, but that is the old word, and the girls don't like to use it too much. The *amachicken* are the younger girls who are looked after by the older ones. Many *amachicken* share rooms with the older girls. I myself had a sweetie, but my heart was broken when she had to leave school. She was very good to me. She was very tender in love.

186

I did love her, but I didn't think of it as lesbian. And I didn't only have one girlfriend. I tried to propose to another one... she had a boyfriend. He used to visit her at the boarding school, and I knew she had intercourse with him, but I still wanted her, so I approached her. She asked me if I was lesbian. And that was the first time I heard the word. She said she didn't mind being friends with me, but if I was a lesbian she would be scared of me. But if we could be *amachicken* then she wouldn't mind. You see, she meant just to kiss and hold hands and nothing further. But I wanted more. We did kiss and hold hands and such, but in the end we broke up because of her boyfriend. She didn't want to hurt him. I think it was through my relationship with her that I realised, for the first time, what it was I felt for other women.

At the school some of the teachers know about the whole *amachicken* thing, but they don't do very much to try and stop it. Some will say that sleeping with a woman is wrong, and they'll push you to find out if you've got boyfriends. This makes many of the girls scared that the teachers will find out about what really goes on between *amachicken*. So I used to lie and say yes, I have a boyfriend in Jo'burg. I think many of the girls did this.

In my family, only my sister knows about me. My mother doesn't know, but she always asks why I dress so butch — I never wear dresses, you see. I feel scared to tell her the truth, because I fear she won't understand. I'm also scared to tell my grandmother. Sometimes, by the way she talks to me, I'm sure she knows. She talks of women who live close with each other. Once I asked her what she meant, and she said 'not you, my child'. So she confuses me.

There are plenty of lesbians in the township, but most are in the closet. I'm very shy to approach them, because of what they might think. I also don't know anyone from school because all my schoolfriends live in the Eastern Transvaal. My happiest time was at school, because I could be with lots of girls there and not feel funny. Here in Soweto I only meet straights and its very difficult for me to find a lover.

In fact the last sweetie I had was at school. I was very much in love with her and wanted to stay with her. But she is from Natal and lives too far from here. I can't even visit her. I wanted to be with her forever. Even after we finished school we stayed in love and wrote to each other all the time. But because of the distance, well, we stopped writing.

I do wish for lesbians to come out and say 'yes, we are here!' I'm scared to do it for myself but I see many young girls being confused and I want to help. But how? Sometimes these *tsotsis* [gangsters] and these Jackrollers [a notorious Soweto gang] go out in gangs and rape women. The Jackrollers go particularly for lesbians, and when they catch one they say 'We'll put you right.' So it's really dangerous for a young woman living in the townships to be open as a lesbian. Or your parents could bring the priest for you. Then they will pray over you. I would hate that!

I do feel better when I go to the meetings of the GLOW Lesbian Forum. I feel so comfortable there because even if I say nothing, I'm still one of all the lesbians there.

Thandazo Alice Kunene: 'Stabane and all that'

My family does not discuss homosexuality, and if they do, they talk about *stabane* and all that. So maybe I was scared to face up and say I like girls better because then they would call me *stabane*. I knew that logically I couldn't be *stabane* because that is a hermaphrodite, someone with both male and female genitals. Yet I was afraid of the stigma and sadness of *stabane*. I laugh when I think of how confused I was as a teenager; I even went to the dictionaries and looked up the word *stabane* and learned the word 'hermaphrodite'. It fascinated me and yet I couldn't understand why.

It was only later, when I was older and I saw the word lesbian in a magazine that things became clearer. I remember the word almost jumped off the page! I thought for a long time about it because I knew I was one. Of course, I'm sure I had heard the word before but perhaps my ears were not yet open to listening.

I was born in Soweto and I've lived there all my life. I used to have plenty of boyfriends although I never had intercourse with them; they were nice Christian boys! I never had a close relationship with a boy, only with my female friends.

The first time I went for a woman it was for my friend Thembi. I was finished school. I was a young woman. We were in the church choir together. One day she came to sleep at my house and we did nothing, although I wanted to kiss her. I was very confused by my attraction to her. I still had a boyfriend who used to come to my house. My father knew him and approved of him. Thembi would suffer a lot when he was there. She would phone me all the time when she knew he was over.

Thembi is also in the church and my parents respect her. She is a divorcee: her husband used to batter her. She's a sweet somebody and I felt angry about her life. I wanted to be her friend because she had no other friends in the church. She never did anything sexual with me, but sometimes we would cuddle in the bed and she would kiss me good-bye. I know now that I was in love with her and I think she with me. But she never said the words and I didn't either.

My family knows nothing. But when someone phones me, my mother tells them to phone me at Thembi's, because I'm always there. I'm still seeing her, but as close friends now, because Thembi is very threatened by GLOW. I attend the Lesbian Forum now and she is too scared to say that she is a lesbian.

Through GLOW I'm beginning to learn about gay liberation. It started when I saw a programme on TV about the Winnie Mandela trial and GLOW. I became very interested in the case and I wanted to know more about this GLOW. Now I'm very involved in GLOW, but I only like the Lesbian Forum and the things they do. When there are men at GLOW functions they tend to take over and this is true for all of them, black or white. They only think of themselves.

And I must admit I do feel funny around some gay men. In my head I think *stabane*. And then I scold myself because that is wrong, but they make me feel funny when they dress like women and try to be like women.

I'm glad to be involved in lesbian and gay organisation. It must start to be more active in the townships because here is where we need it. The black community is very strict and they need to be educated about us. We are also people just like them. We must educate them about our rights just like the ANC educated us about our political rights.

Tilla Jantjies: 'I love that word, dyke!'

I was always a tomboy, a dyke. I love that word, dyke! It's me! I look at other women on the street and if they remind me of myself or look butch I think, 'What a dyke!'

I struggled very much with my sexuality as a teenager. I also had a boyfriend. God, I even slept with him. Only once. But even then men never really interested me. I only did it because my family and friends expected it of me. I conformed very much to what society dictates. I wish that I could have come to terms with my sexuality earlier and not wasted so much time angsting about who and what I was and where I fitted into society.

I was born in Pietersburg, in the Northern Transvaal, but I grew up in Reiger Park, the coloured township of Boksburg. I finished high school there, living with my grandparents, because my mother stayed in Pietersburg.

My family knows about my lesbianism. My mother knows but isn't very happy, and she still has this habit of introducing me to all of Pietersburg's eligible young men. I ask you! It took a while for all of them to accept it, but my aunts and uncles, who are really like sisters and brothers to me, were very supportive. They even knew when I was much younger. I always had some close girlfriend and would put my arm around her or wrestle with her. Sure, my family teases me: they've always called me a *manvrou*, a man-woman. I used to ignore them and think, '*Ag, hulle praat kak*' [They talk shit]. I could be what I wanted.

It was very difficult growing up in Reiger Park. It is a very conservative area — its politics straight Labour Party. You can just imagine. You can't move without everybody knowing your actions. But I had a *lekker* (enjoyable) group of friends who used to cover for me. They knew about me and my girlfriend and used to introduce me to other lesbians. I was too shy. We didn't want to go to nightclubs in the area, so we used to go clubbing in Kathlehong, the nearest black township. It wasn't nearly as dangerous as it is now. Easy by Night was *the* club. There was such a great vibe that I felt completely free and no-one bothered with us. It wasn't a gay club — just uninhibited.

The first gay club I went to was the Camel's Back, in Yeoville. My lover and I just sat at the bar and stared in the mirror in front of us. We were too scared even to look at one another. The whole place was filled with white women. I couldn't believe there were so many beautiful lesbians. I felt such a fool because my lover and I had dressed up. I was wearing a suit — I was very butch then! We sat the whole night until about 2 am because neither of us wanted to go, but at the same time we both wanted to get the hell out of there! I wanted to watch those women all night long and yet I was very frightened of them. It took a couple of days for us both to recover. We couldn't stop talking about the experience.

I go to Champions now, even though it's almost all men, because there isn't a lesbian club any more. I miss being only with women. It's a different atmosphere. I'd be too scared just to go up to a stranger and chat her up, but somehow, just being with other lesbians makes you feel closer to them. It's almost like when there are only women together there's a stronger flow of energy and warmth. That gets interfered with when there are men around. I don't know, maybe I'm being too romantic about women.

At work they know, too. There are two other lesbians who work with me, so I don't feel isolated. My boss is very open and supportive of us. People are bitchy and have phoned my office and told my boss I'm a lesbian. He called me in and told me not to worry, that my job wasn't in jeopardy. There are very few straight people like that.

I support gay rights wholeheartedly. It's time we said our say. I went on both lesbian and gay pride marches. It had me on a buzz for weeks. Now is the time to speak. South Africa has never experienced this degree of openness. If we don't make our voices heard we will be shut up for ever.

Zubeida: 'No-one wants a wife who talks politics and wears men's socks'

I grew up in Fordsburg in a conservative and staunchly Muslin family. It has taken me a long time to come to terms with what I regard as comfortable sexuality. As a Muslim girl growing up in such a community it is taboo to express any sexuality, let alone ideas about an alternative family. Muslim girls are covered from head to toe when they attend *Madressah*, the religious school. And even when they're not at *Madressah*, they're covered from head to toe in the conservative expectations of their parents and community.

Of course, there are many progressive Muslim people who raise children without these conservative and repressive hangups. But my family could never deal with my sexuality. Although my family, being Indian, regards itself as oppressed in South Africa, they would never support any liberation struggle. Certainly, politics was discussed in the home, but my parents always cautioned us not to get involved.

Their caution was in vain: when I went to university, I got involved in the Black Consciousness Movement and was exposed to the lesbian and gay subculture on campus. Not surprisingly, this was a time of intense conflict with my family and we had many heated political debates. By my third year I was dressing weirdly and insisting on staying in town and them not fetching me. It took ages before they conceded and let me be.

I moved into a commune and loved it at first. I met my first lesbian lover there, Dee. We moved out after a while into a flat. My parents weren't very happy about either living arrangement, but, ironically, they preferred the flat to the commune because at least there would be no men there. Dee and I had separate beds for show. I was very closeted.

At the time I was getting involved with a man. At first I just didn't think about it. Both relationships were attractive to me. I passed Dee off as a flatmate and him as a friend. But Dee found out eventually. I had been miserable about telling her, and it affected our relationship terribly: she was outraged that I had not told her.

I've had other relationships with men and women. Now I try to be as honest as possible from the beginning. It's extremely difficult, because many potential friends and lovers are put off by my bisexuality. I've been told this. It is even difficult to discuss bisexuality in GLOW. I don't wish to categorize myself or others and certainly don't want to place value judgements on anyone. Why is one not allowed to fall in love with and love both sexes? Monogamy is a different question altogether and that depends on your own set of values and morals. It's an individual choice.

Even though I'm bisexual, the things I feel for men are completely different to what I feel for women. As a bisexual I have, I hope, a perspective on both sexes. Sure, men and women are different, but both have wonderful attributes emotionally and physically. It's hard to say what one gets from either sex without taking into account the individual person you are involved with. Obviously, that plays the most important role.

I guess I feel oppressed as a bisexual person. Most lesbian and gay organisations don't really cater for bisexuals — I think largely because bisexuals are even less visible than homosexuals. There is also so much distrust of bisexuals in the homosexual community. Sometimes we are seen as sitting on the fence and enjoying the best of both worlds; usually we are seen as being unable to come out of the closet.

I'm not out at work. Even though the people I work with would call themselves progressive, I find them incredibly homophobic. Can you imagine how they'd react to a bisexual in their midst? And I'm also not out to my family. They would not be able to cope. They still mourn my leaving home and not getting married and having children. And, in true conservative Indian style, they still arrange for nice eligible young Muslim men to come and meet me. Of course, the poor suitors take one look at me and smile politely. No-one wants a wife who talks politics and wears men's socks.

Sibongile: 'They fear me because I am sangoma and a lesbian'

I am a lesbian. I am a black woman. I live in the township. Life is not very easy in the township, but I smile through it even though for me, as a black woman and a lesbian, life sometimes doesn't want to make me smile. I come from a Zulu family where the men get first preference for everything, where they get to rule your life if you are a woman.

I love women. I have always loved women. Women are wonderful to me. This thing started very young with me. I wanted very much to marry my best friend, who was a girl. My mother saw this thing and protected me from my family. She encouraged me to have boyfriends just for the family's sake. My uncles, of course, wanted *lobola*, the bride-price, so they were particularly keen on finding me a young man.

I cried and refused this, and this made my one uncle very cross. He rounded up all the boys in the neighborhood and when I came home from school one day I found them all lined them up in our backyard. 'Now', said my uncle, 'you must choose one.' He made great fun of me and asked each one of the boys how many cows he would give for me. I was too afraid to leave, too afraid even to cry. I felt like a toy he could just play with. He didn't understand about my life and my feelings.

So my mother sent me to a boarding school in Natal. There I had my first relationship with a woman, another student. We were sweethearts. But she fell pregnant and had to leave. I guess I wasn't her only lover.

I have never had a boyfriend. After the experience with my sweetheart falling pregnant from this irresponsible boy I vowed to myself that I would not let my family force me into marriage. I did finish school, but it was a lonely experience. My sweetheart was gone.

When I was 20 years old I told my family that I was a lesbian. It was not long after this that I got the calling to be a *sangoma* [traditional healer]. A friend had taken me with her when she consulted a *sangoma*. After the consultation, the *sangoma* pulled me aside and said that I would one day be one too. At the time I was very scared: I didn't want such a thing. I avoided it for a long time, until I knew I was ready for it.

I have a lover now. She is also a *sangoma*. We are both proud and happy to be lesbians. To be a *sangoma* has made me strong. I don't feel afraid of anything. Even when these rough boys come to me in secret, they only want advice and won't harm me. They fear me because I am a *sangoma* and a lesbian.

I don't know what makes me *sangoma* and lesbian. I don't even know if the two have anything to do with each other. All I know is that it feels right that this is the way my life must go. I look after myself.

I do feel for gays and lesbians who are confused, because sometimes they come to me for advice. As I am a *sangoma* I try to help, but I always tell these confused people they must look inside themselves for answers.

Climbing on her shoulders:
An interview with Umtata's 'first lesbian'

Vera Vimbela with Mike Olivier

Vera Vimbela has always been the leader of a pack of boys. In the rural Transkei village near Mount Frere, where she grew up, her home was continually over-run with boys who came to play, despite the urgings of her grandmother that she try to make friends with other girls. She refused to wear dresses, and beat the boys at activities like trapping mice and birds or making clay animals and wire cars.

Now, 20 years later, she is an accounts clerk in the Transkei Health Department, and she still leads a gang of boys. Every Thursday evening, a group of black gay men meet in the living-room of her home in the Umtata suburb of Mboge Park — they include students, teachers, nurses, police officers, and also the odd doctor or lawyer. Vimbela is the only lesbian in the group, and the only one who has publicly come out of the closet. She zooms around Mboge Park on her Suzuki 150cc motorbike, and is unashamedly butch: a short, stocky woman with strong masculine features who always dresses in pants, shirts and a leather jacket and who has never learnt to cook.

Umtata was the capital of the 'independent homeland' of Transkei. In many ways, it is similar to my home, Gaborone, the capital of Botswana. Both are medium-sized regional hubs with sizeable populations of black civil servants and professionals; both have many black gay residents but no organised gay life. In Gaborone we have been trying unsuccessfully, for the past few years, to organise ourselves. I spent some time with Vimbela in Umtata's gay community because I hoped to learn some lessons about how she has managed to take those first steps towards gay community in a place like the Transkei.

Vimbela's living-room has become something of an oasis for Umtata's tentative new gay subculture. Ronnie, one of the men who attends her Thursday evening meetings, puts it like this:

> *Vera has had a tough life, fighting for the right to be herself. I feel ashamed because I could always hide by having a 'girlfriend' and not acting too camp. I've told my parents I'm gay, but I don't want to come out any further, because it's hard to be gay. I don't want to be gay. You are stigmatised and shunned by society, even criminalised or called anti-God. But Vera is leading the way for us. We are now climbing on her shoulders.*

What follows is the edited transcript of an interview I held with Vimbela while in Umtata in June 1993.

* * *

I was an illegitimate child, and so I was taken to live with my grandparents in a small rural village near Mount Frere. My mother married shortly after I was born, but I've never had a happy relationship with her. She doesn't like me as a human being, never mind my being gay. She has her own children and husband, and when I went to visit her she said I should stay away, because I was just there to disorganise her marriage.

My biological father passed away in 1986, and I really do regret that I never spent more time with him. He was a good man, and accepted me even when he knew I was gay — he also liked Busi, my live-in lover. My father and I were good friends. I laugh like him, I look like him, I behave like him.

From an early age I knew I was different. I never had feelings for men, and I always had deep feelings for women. But I never had anyone in the village to talk to about these feelings — in my village gays were unheard of. I tried to suppress these feelings, but eventually they came out. As I grew older I decided I didn't care what society said — I would be myself.

I shocked the whole village in Standard 6, when a rumour spread that I had proposed to another girl. It's true, I was madly in love with this girl, and I would follow her everywhere, from the river to her home.

My grandparents and I were called before the village chief and his council of elders. The whole village turned up to the hearing, to insult me and make nasty comments. They assumed that because I had proposed to the girl I must be *stabane*, a hermaphrodite, with both male and female genitals. I was taken to a hut where a woman forced me to undress and examined me. When they discovered I was 'normal' the chief ordered that I be lashed. I don't remember how many *sjambok* lashings I received; all I remember is crying and screaming with pain as the whole village jeered at me. I was warned never to repeat such behaviour again.

It was only when I was sent off to high school at the nearest town that I felt I could breathe more freely, away from my grandparents, away from the chief and the village gossips. At the boarding school I started proposing to other girls, but some of them went to the boarding master and falsely accused me of touching and fondling them at night. So I was expelled from the hostel and I had to find accommodation with a local family.

Finally, I met a girl who became my friend. We loved each other, but I was terrified to go to bed with her. I felt I needed to have a penis to satisfy her. As far as I knew, sex meant penetration by a penis. On the last day of school, after we had finished our final Standard 10 exams, most of the students got blind drunk during the evening by sniffing benzene. I eventually plucked up the courage to sleep with my girlfriend, and I was so surprised that I was not rejected. She was the first woman who could accept me without a cock.

Shortly after that, I met Busi on a bus. Busi has been my lover for the past ten years. She was sitting at the back of the bus and she was so beautiful that I called her to come and sit next to me. Then I proposed to her and she agreed. So everything went just fine, until, a few months later, I found out she was pregnant and had to leave school. I was very angry, because I had been committed to the relationship. She had the baby, a beautiful boy, but it contracted measles and passed away.

In 1985 Busi came to live with me, because I wanted her to continue her education and her mother could no longer afford to pay for it. Now she's a final-year student at the University of the Transkei. I helped her because I loved her, and I didn't want this pretty young girl to have a wasted life.

But there were problems. I could see all along that she was attracted to men. Unlike me, she wasn't gay, and I was the first woman to have a relationship with her. Whenever she came back late from school, I would get jealous, because I would suspect that she had been with a man.

A few weeks ago, a man came into our house, and he was shouting and very violent, saying that she should leave with him. He just barged in, without knocking. My friends and I were sitting in the lounge, and I could see the bulge of a gun in his pocket. What could we do? The two left together.

Three days later Busi met me in the street in town and said she was sorry, she was now staying with her sister and she wanted to come back. I told her I couldn't have that. I had always been honest and faithful to her — no strange woman had ever come to our house to carry me off! So I'm single now. Of course it will be difficult for me to meet other lesbians. I haven't even heard of any in Umtata, except for a white woman living with her black lover.

After I finished high school, I enrolled to train as a nurse. But the going was tough. I never got on with my instructors because of this 'nursing etiquette'. They wanted me to wear a nurse's cap, a white dress and pantyhose. I rebelled. I would wear a dirty creased technician's coat and I kept the pantyhose stuffed in my pocket. Only when the matron came into the ward would I would dash off to the toilet and put on the pantyhose.

Living in the nurses' hostel was also difficult. The trainee nurses would walk around half-naked, but of course I was too scared to propose to any of them after my experiences at the high school hostel. So I only went to the hostel late at night after everyone was asleep.

Eventually I decided to transfer to an administrative post in the Health Department's accounts section. When I started working there I never hid my sexuality. They made comments about me but eventually I won the respect not only of my co-workers but also of my supervisors. This was because I am the hardest worker there. I am gold. I deal a lot with the public and they always insist on being served by me! Even the Minister phones me directly when he has a query or wants us to do something for him!

But it took me a long time to contact other gay people in Umtata. Seeing Simon Nkoli and others on TV and in magazines really changed my life. When I was in high school, I would see the word 'homosexual' in the dictionary and think, well, maybe there are other people like me on this earth. But then in 1989, when I saw Simon on TV, it was the first time I actually heard someone declare publicly that he was homosexual. In our rural village there were no homosexuals, and if there were, they probably hid themselves because of African culture.

So, after seeing this TV show, I decided to look for other gays in Umtata. I knew about one man, because I had been hearing rumours and gossip about him. The workers in my office would jeer about this dirty man who slept with other men. I think they said this in front of me to provoke me. They didn't realise that they were doing me a favour! I found out his name and phoned him after looking up his number in the telephone directory.

We met and he said he was gay but not out. He said that he had actually seen me two years previously and suspected I was gay. Then, after that, he had heard I slept with women. I asked him why he had not contacted me, and he said that it was hard to talk about homosexuality even to somebody else who was gay.

Through him I met two other gay men, who came to visit me at work. Then they brought along others, and I realised that there was a whole network of gays who are in the closet. Only one man contacted me directly — he phoned me out of the blue and asked me bluntly if there were any gays in the Transkei. I like him a lot. I think he is strong and bold. The first time we met we spent the whole day together talking about ourselves.

Since then we've been meeting every Thursday night at my place, trying to set up a gay support group. They are informal meetings and the size of the group varies from week to week. All in all, there are 29 of us. I think the others are afraid to come out because of their rural backgrounds. Most gays are still afraid to be seen with me on the street because they think they will be suspected. I tell them I don't only walk with gay people. There are lots of straight men who walk with me openly on the street.

We have very little contact with white gays. I met one in 1990 who said that he and three others had tried to start an organisation but failed because they didn't involve black people. This guy said we blacks should first form an organisation and that whites would join later. I didn't like that, as if now it's a black and white thing. I look at it like this: you are engaged in one struggle if you are gay, be you a man or a woman, black, brown or white. I see no colour.

In the Transkei, however, I need strong people who are ready to fight discrimination. The people who are currently in my group are difficult to work with. They are more interested in coming to our meetings to pick up a man for a night and then a different man the following week. They are educated — we have doctors, nurses and lawyers — and they should rather be trying to fight for gay rights.

My plan is first to establish a support group and then to request a meeting with General Bantu Holomisa [the military ruler of the Transkei]. We want to meet him to find out how he feels about gay people. No-one really knows what the status of gay people is in the Transkei. If there is no criminalisation here, well, then there's no need to hide. But if the Transkei is still following South African anti-gay laws than we need to fight it.

And I am prepared to fight. I'm a strong bold person who doesn't accept any nonsense from others. If they try and beat me I do the same to them. That's how I've had to live all my life.

Going underground:
A visit to gay Welkom

Neil Miller[1]

It was Christmas-time 1990, a Saturday night in Welkom, and there was not much happening in terms of entertainment. So, like everyone else in town, we went for a spin in the car. While the straight boys were driving around the horseshoe-shaped downtown business area, we headed out towards the mines.

The night was warm and the car windows were open. We must have been going at close to 120 km an hour. The mines were bathed in a blue and green light. The driver put the score from Andrew Lloyd Webber's *Phantom of the Opera* on the cassette player and turned it up full blast. The music, the illuminated mine shafts, store house, and mine dumps, all created an effect that was eerie, unworldly. It was Welkom, the music video.

I knew that the white population of Welkom was overwhelmingly Afrikaans-speaking, that the city had experienced a year of racial strife in which Afrikaner Weerstandsbeweging (AWB) vigilantes had often seemed to rule the place. I had expected to find conservative racial and sexual attitudes in Welkom. What I hadn't expected to find were the charms of small town life.

But the charms of small town life were precisely what I did find in Welkom (even though with a population of 300 000, including those living in mine hostels, Welkom couldn't exactly be called a small town). On a Sunday afternoon my hosts — two gay men and a lesbian, all in their twenties and involved in a gay and lesbian social group called Gays of the Goldfields (GOGS) — drove their cars on to the front lawn and spent half the day washing and polishing them. There were innocent hours of putt-putt in the town centre and an outing for what was reputedly

1   Neil Miller, an American journalist and author, wrote this piece for the *Weekly Mail* in 1991 when visiting South Africa to research his book, *Out in the World: Gay and Lesbian Life from Buenos Aires to Bangkok* (Penguin, 1993). His account of his time in Welkom appears in longer form in his book.

the largest ice-cream cone in the Free State — vanilla and strawberry combined and hideously artificial-tasting. I could have been in Kansas or North Dakota.

'On Wednesday, we have arranged for you to go underground,' one of my hosts announced. He worked for the mines (although he wasn't actually a miner himself) and had a voice that sounded uncannily like the actor David Niven.

To a large extent I was already underground. Welkom gays and lesbians were very much in the closet, their existence virtually unknown to anyone who didn't share their sexual orientation. The David Niven-voiced mine employee related how, one weekend night, he had been standing at the door of a local hall at an event sponsored by GOGS. When a group of people tried to enter, he explained it was a private party for gays and lesbians. The would-be gatecrashers were mystified. After much discussion they finally understood. 'Homosexuals in Welkom!' they said. 'Homosexuals in the Free State! We thought they were all in Jo'burg.'

In Welkom, gays and lesbians blended in. The women were by and large into traditional butch roles; the men (and women too) were often in heterosexual marriages. When they weren't married to someone of the opposite sex, they talked about marriage to someone to the same sex, 'if only it were legal'. There was a minister in Johannesburg who would perform gay and lesbian weddings, they assured me.

The centre of gay male life in Welkom turned out to be a strip of tar road downtown across from the Pick n' Pay and the First National Bank. Welkom gays referred to it as the *sitkamer* (lounge) and it was both a social meeting place and a pickup spot. In its heyday, I was told, you could see 15 to 20 cars parked there (or driving back and forth) on a Saturday night.

The popularity of the *sitkamer* was due to the fact that there was no gay or lesbian bar in Welkom — no bar, for that matter, where gay people could feel comfortable. So there were private parties, held every second week, and alternating with similar parties in Bloemfontein. In Welkom, it wasn't always easy to find a venue for gay social gatherings, however. A hall where parties used to be held was damaged by a tornado earlier in the year. While the hall was being repaired, parties were held in a variety of places. More often than not, when the owners learned that it was a gay group that wanted to lease the premises, they withdrew their offer immediately.

One of the main reasons why gays and lesbians were so closeted in Welkom was because the mines — the city's biggest employer — were not exactly an environment congenial to gays. My host noted:

> *In the mines, people work very closely. You change together in the changing room. People make gay jokes all the time. Once you say you're gay, though, they won't leave you alone. The management won't fire me because I do my job well. But if I did come out, people I work with would give me such a hard time that by the end of the day I'd resign.*

In Welkom, there were some work environments where being gay was okay, though — a major department store (Dion) for instance. The store had six gay and lesbian employees; at one time there had been 13.

'The store manager thinks gay people make the best workers,' one clerk informed me. He related one store-wide meeting that had taken place before Christmas, in which the manager had concluded, 'I want to wish a happy Christmas to your husbands and wives.' Someone then shouted out, 'What about our affairs?' The manager was unruffled: 'And happy Christmas to your affairs too,' he said.

One evening I had coffee with a burly mine shift boss, his lover of eight years who worked at a local bank, and a young lesbian who worked at a government office. The shift boss collected antiques in his spare time. After a few minutes the young woman excused herself; she had only recently come out, and was nervous talking to a journalist. The shift boss had his own particular view of being gay in the mines:

> *I always used to worry what people would say if they knew I was gay. Now, I've got to the stage where one of the mine captains knows. He and his wife have been to a few of our parties. As for the other guys, some of them know and some of them can't make up their minds but I'll never tell them.*
>
> *They'll take a dig at you now and again and I just laugh at them. They look for people who get upset. So I just give them back what they give me. They tell gay jokes and I can tell more jokes than they can tell me.*

As in most conversations in Welkom, talk eventually turned to politics — and race. The shift boss contended that the gay community tended to be more open on racial matters than the rest of the town:

> *Because, as gays, you are not accepted, you are inclined to accept a lot of other people's differences. I don't think you'll find anyone gay in the AWB for example.*

That might be so, but in fact Welkom's gay community appeared to be totally white. If there were any black gays in Welkom, no-one I met had any contact with them. 'We wouldn't mind if they wanted to come to our parties,' said the shift boss. 'But there are none of us who mix with them.'

Despite protestations to open-mindedness, talking politics with Welkom gays usually consisted of listening to complaints about alleged favouritism towards blacks; blacks refusing to pay water and light bills; blacks receiving loans on easier terms than whites; black miners getting overalls and boots supplied free of charge while white miners had to pay. No one seemed to approve of the AWB. But in the midst of one of these conversations, a young woman handed me a book. 'You should read this,' she said. The title was *God's Miracles Versus Marxist Terrorists*.

Soon enough it was New Year's Eve. The GOGS party took place in an open-air pavilion in a park on the edge of Welkom. Tables and chairs were set up, coloured lights were strung; there was a dancefloor of concrete and place to *braai*.

The moon was full, which almost obscured the fancy disco lights in which GOGS had invested R700.

There were about 40 people present, all of them white, and divided equally between men and women. As in many smaller cities in the United States, there seemed to be more socialising between gay men and lesbians than one tended to find in the large urban centres. In a place like Welkom, gay men and women have no recourse but to stick together.

When I arrived, *Rock Around The Clock* was playing. But the most popular music was the traditional Afrikaans fare — the *tiekiedraai* (folk dancing) and *sakkie-sakkie*. When they came on everyone rushed to the dancefloor.

I chatted with a rather fashionably-dressed woman. She was there with her lover and already seemed a little tipsy. 'I have a complicated story,' she said.

'Let me guess,' I said. 'You used to be married and have three kids.'

'Two kids,' she said. 'They are living with my mother in Welkom. But how did you know that?'

The woman who had fled from my interview with the shift boss the night before took me aside. She was 24 and dressed in jeans and a blue work shirt and was called Marla.

Marla had had a two-year relationship with a 40-year-old woman she met at work. The woman had two grown sons — both of whom lived in Welkom — who had forced their mother to terminate the relationship. Marla was still in love with her eight months after the break-up. 'It's so difficult to find anyone in Welkom,' she said. 'Please, if you find someone for me, let me know.'

At midnight everybody cheered and kissed everyone else. 'Let's hope 1991 is a better year,' one woman said to another.

'Was 1990 so bad?' I asked innocently.

'In Welkom, yes,' they said.

The party went on for several more hours. There was still more dancing and *boerewors* (traditional sausage) simmering on the *braai*. I wondered if this really was very different from any other New Year festivities in white Welkom. By 4.30 am the remaining guests fell asleep on the concrete dance floor, trying to catch a few hours' nap before beginning to party again on New Year's Day. As for me, I went home to sleep and to read *God's Miracles Versus Marxist Terrorists*.

After all, the following day I was going 'underground'.

Wearing the pants:
Butch/femme roleplaying in lesbian relationships

Julia Beffon

'You like her? But she's BUTCH...'

'So...?'

'You're butch.'

'Does that matter? Do you believe in butch/femme roleplaying?'

'Of course not.'

Like most gay women, I have times when I'm butch and times when I'm femme. But when I try to discuss the issue with my sisters, that's about as far as the discussion usually goes. Gay women in South Africa seem to have the same attitude towards butch/femme roleplaying that many heterosexuals have about gays: I've heard it happens, I can spot one from across the street, but in my family, among my friends? No, never...

Even trying to get an adequate definition on what is butch and what is femme can present problems. Much discussion on the subject is grounded in the unspoken belief that gay relationships are, or should be, modelled on heterosexual stereotypes in the Doris Day/Rock Hudson movie mould. This assumes that butch equals macho man and femme equals submissive prom queen and ne'er the twain shall meet. Alas, as with the Rock, it's not that simple.

In attempts to define butch and femme, one aspect is frequently emphasised: dress. Outward appearances play an important role in gay popular culture, and deciphering the visual codes is a skill only learned through submersion in the subculture. The signs can be as blatant as a drag queen's finery or as subtle as a handkerchief. In heterosexual society a woman sends out a variety of messages by wearing a dress with a plunging neckline: in gay society she speaks volumes just by wearing a dress.

Using outward appearance as an indicator, a woman can be classified femme by wearing a dress, makeup and jewellery; or butch by having short hair, wearing trousers and scorning makeup. But while this handy guide might account for Ms Muscles at the pool table and Miss World on the dance floor, it falls flat when you see the Annie Lennox-lookalike in the corner. The cult of androgyny has been much kinder to women than men: Julie Andrews was sexy in a tux, Dustin Hoffman wasn't in a frock. In Western culture today a woman may wear trousers without prejudice, but a man in a skirt is still labelled a cross-dresser or transvestite. This discrimination is magnified in most workplaces — a woman may get a reprimand for wearing trousers to work if that is against the company's dress code, a man in a dress faces dismissal.

If you were to use only the dress criterion to determine whether a woman is butch or femme you would come up with some startling conclusions. A rough estimate at any bar would show that butches outnumber femmes by at least five to one, which either means that the codes fall apart once the clothes come off or that, at the end of the evening, there are four miserable butches to each happy one.

One of the women I spoke to while researching this article — let's call her Debbie — decried my simplification of dress codes. A woman is butch, she said, if she wears *men's* trousers and *men's* shirts. Since shirts and jeans are pretty unisex these days, I asked her what she meant. In answer, Debbie — who's slim and Jo'burg northern suburbs-English speaking — pointed to an overweight, Afrikaans-speaking woman across the room who was wearing a white shirt (I couldn't make out which side the buttons were on at that range) and well-worn blue jeans. 'Now *that's* butch,' she said. Since Debbie was wearing a blue shirt (buttons as per a man's shirt) and designer blue jeans, I asked what the difference was.

'I'm not trying to be a man.'

So the Doris Day/Rock Hudson myth rides again. Butches are trying to be men and femmes are 'real women'. How does Debbie characterise herself? She doesn't play those games.

To get the other side of the story, so to speak, I approached the woman Debbie had pointed out as the epitome of 'butch' and asked her what she thought of butch and femme role playing. 'Yes, it happens,' said Jackie, 'And I'm femme.' And she thinks Debbie is butch and quite cute.

Somewhere in this tragi-comedy was another facet to the butch/femme prism. In a society as riven by prejudice as ours, it is not surprising that the butch/femme debate is often conducted over the same ground as the Boer War. It is also a class issue. In a survey of about 30 white women who go to gay bars in Johannesburg, it came out that more Afrikaans-speaking women than their English-speaking sisters were prepared to admit to butch and femme role playing (and a majority of these said they were femme).

Those who denied playing such roles suggested it was confined to the working classes. True enough, a visit to the swish upmarket Harlequins in Johannesburg's northern suburbs will reveal a preponderance of 'lipstick lesbians' or 'glam-dykes': cascades of hair, layers of makeup and long painted fingernails. If you visit more earthy haunts in Hillbrow, however, you have to fight your way through bikers' jackets and workers' shirts, and you have to watch your step at the pool-table (which is to gay female culture what poppers are to gay male culture).

Hidden in this class snobbery is a grain of practical truth. Education and money are great liberators, especially when it comes to flouting convention. And, where there is less access to other models, the male/female heterosexual paradigm is the 'norm'.

This is not to say that there are no gay women 'trying to be men' as Debbie sees it. A friend, Carol, told me that an ex-lover refused to take off her panties (more correctly, her underpants, since they were Y-fronts) while making love. Carol was also not allowed to touch the other woman in bed. It was a one-way sexual relationship, which had to remain that way if they were to sustain the illusion that Carol's partner was 'a man'.

In this relationship, at least, the 'hidden penis' was an illusion which died the moment one partner said it did not exist. However, Carol said she broke off the relationship because she did not enjoy the completely passive role expected of her, rather than because of the 'penis' issue.

Although this is an extreme example, it does give another way of defining butch/femme role playing. Who does what to whom. Following the traditional male/female role playing pattern, the butch is supposedly the more active partner in bed, while the femme is more passive. The active/passive relationship is not only confined to love making, but extends to the courtship ritual (who asks whom out, who pays for dinner, etc) where the butch assumes most of the 'male' functions.

But once a relationship is established, and particularly where the couple sets up house together, there is quite often a 'role reversal' with the butch assuming many of the tasks which are assumed to be 'woman's work' — such as cooking and cleaning.

Mary and Sharon are a white couple in their late twenties who have been in a relationship (which has had its stormy times) for about four years and have lived together for nearly three years. Although they both frequented the bar/club scene when they first met, their socialising now consists largely of going to the cinema, dinner parties or visiting friends. Mary is adamant that she is butch, and that Sharon is 'her femme'. (Seeing the 'woman' as a 'man's' possession is as prevalent in butch/femme role playing as it is in the heterosexual model it is based on.)

Both come from upper-middle class families, work in white-collar jobs and say they realised they were gay in their teens. In accordance with their role playing, Mary insists that Sharon wear dresses and skirts often, and Sharon insists that Mary goes to investigate any suspicious noises late at night (although Mary is more slight than Sharon).

However, Mary does most of the cooking and cleaning, while Sharon plays football. Also, when their arguments turn violent, it is Sharon who beats up Mary. As in the heterosexual models they imitate, domestic violence is a reality in many butch gay female relationships.

Why do they play roles? Mary says it is because it gives a framework to their relationship. 'I'm butch, she's femme. We know what's what.' She does the cooking 'because Sharon can't cook'. She does the cleaning because Sharon doesn't clean thoroughly enough for her liking.

Through their perception of their relationship as a butch/femme situation, they accept certain unwritten codes of behaviour. It is fine for Sharon to burst into tears, but not so for Mary; it is OK for Mary to swear, but every 'fuck' from Sharon is followed by an apology. (They declined to discuss sex.) Although Mary and Sharon say they have a butch/femme relationship, is it an accurate rendition of the traditional male/female set-up?

No, says Karen, it doesn't matter how you dress, who does the cooking: what counts is who is in control of the relationship. Who wears the pants, in Doris Day-speak. In a patriarchal society like ours, where men hold — and are seen to hold — power in the public and private realms, it follows that the partner who makes the decisions and holds the power in the relationship will be the 'man', or the butch.

By ceding power, the femme frequently attempts to maintain the protective-parent/cosseted-child relationship of her childhood. Many parents, teachers and clergymen still drum into little girls that a woman should not be ambitious or strive for power and that she cannot survive without a man in her life. For the butch, the independence which power brings is a heady drug.

None of these models explains fully why gay women play butch and femme roles — but play them they do, whether in public or in private. Gay women who have a relationship which is a healthy partnership between two equals are as rare as, well, heterosexuals who have a relationship which is a healthy partnership between two equals...

FOUR —

Making noise: Queer cultural forms

The Arista Sisters, September 1984:

A personal account of army drag

Matthew Krouse

> *Be careful of the homosexual who interferes with you sexually.*
> *Avoid him. And if you are one yourself and you become aware*
> *of a specific physical attraction towards another troop, it is my*
> *good advice that you keep your teeth clenched and you keep*
> *well away from that troop.[1]*

This piece of advice comes from the book *Anchors for Servicemen*, which is given to conscripts to the South African Defence Force when they go for counselling. It is originally written in Afrikaans by army chaplains Van Niekerk and Coetzee, and it says much about the official ambivalence we queers encounter in the army.

We are not quite the enemy. Unlike in other national defence forces (the United States being an infamous case in point) we will not be excluded simply because we sleep with other men. We will be included — and then censured. We may fight but we may not fuck. And perhaps we are very important, for, in the eyes of the authorities, our supposed 'womanliness' can be used to reinforce what it means to be a real man.

Being queer will not exempt you from National Service, but, within the SADF, homosexuality is a chargeable offence and anti-gay discrimination is encouraged. Yet at the same time there is an open tradition of drag as part of the troops' entertainment.

Whether performed by gays or straights, drag represents a form of homosexualised culture. This homosexual cultural iconography is exploited by the army when it assimilates the gay sensibility. Through drag, gay people are used as crude mixtures of ally and foe.

I was an SADF drag artist, one of the Arista Sisters. I was conscripted in my early twenties; it was 1984, during PW Botha's second State of Emergency, and I was stationed in Voortrekkerhoogte outside Pretoria, at the Personnel Services School. Camping it up on stage before hundreds of appreciative *troepies*, I came to understand how the SADF uses drag to reinforce certain gender stereotypes — and what the implications of this are for gay men.

From cadets to conscription: Making the South African man

In South Africa, white youths journey through institutions — state-run and family-sanctioned — where supposedly 'normal' standards are set in accordance with so-called traditional values.

In white government schools, Cadets was scheduled once a week and con-sisted of marching, a couple of classes of 'survival skills' such as obstacle races and knot tying, and target shooting.

Once a week we donned khaki safari suits and marched on the rugby field. And then, at the tender age of 15, we were lined up in front of a row of targets of silhouetted people and we shot them.

While shooting, the boys lay on their stomachs in leopard position. And if you were there, if this was the only world you knew, then you too would have lain on your stomach. When that grim master walked up to you and shouted, 'Lie down and shoot!', then you lay down and you shot.

Within schools themselves minor cults of heroism were nurtured. Prizes were given to boys and girls who achieved merit in these fields. The achievers were young people who expounded the values promoted by the school. He who is hand-some shoots well. He who is handsome stands for the fatherland. People viewed the military uniform as an icon of desirable male sexuality. In this way the white school's system has bred the worst kind of patriarchy; and it is here that one finds the origins of white South African male sexuality.

After school one was conscripted into the army for two years — during the reign of President PW Botha that is. Six months of Basic Training and 18 months of labour, or warring. White male graduates in trades or professions were trained and they did the dirty work alongside young school-leavers who had their matric, or school drop-outs of 16 years or older.

The background to white militarism is well documented. Many books pro-duced from both sides of the apartheid divide portray an army of uncompromising force capable of inflicting the worst cruelty upon its enemy. Establishing this force has necessitated the assertion of male dominance. This militarism is built upon already-inculcated values: the values expounded in schools during Youth Prepared-ness and Cadets.

In the barracks, soldiers were told by their superiors that they were fighting the war to protect their wives and children. In practice their wives were the very things they were now deprived of. The things they suddenly could not have. And so they dreamt of their women while they slaved away in the barracks. In fact, they dreamt of taking their wives after battle. Their wives were going to be the things they won. At the end of the day, when they had conquered, they would go back to their communities, kept intact by faithful and committed wives, to demand their prize: submission. This is what the army brochures promised them.

And the wives were encouraged to be faithful and submissive. The booklet *While He is Away*, given by army counsellors to wives when their husbands were posted to fight in the border regions, offered the following advice:

> *To most wives and girl-friends, it seems absurd to discuss the importance of fidelity: of course they'll be faithful to their men while they're away! Of course they will: nobody doubts that, but unfortunately the situation isn't as straightforward as that! For some reason soldiers are particularly sensitive about this matter and they are inclined to jump to staggering conclusions for no reason. Don't be hard on them: playing on his feelings has been one of the most successful techniques of propaganda since men first discovered the importance of psychological warfare.*
>
> *…One very important way of showing your love for you (sic) man is through the post. Post is incredibly important. It is fascinating to see how men will even leave their food when they hear that post is being handed out. And a man who has not received any post is a sad sight. A family who writes, helps the soldier more than they realise. A family who does not write, weakens the whole platoon.*

The overbearing emphasis on heterosexual familial relations has great influence on social attitudes in the barracks. And this is compounded by the official censure of homosexual activity. Homophobia is encouraged in the barracks. I have witnessed a corporal stripped of his rank, after interrogation, for being caught out. People have been incarcerated precisely because they've been gay. Of course this punishment ignores a reality: when men are incarcerated in an all-male environment coupling is inevitable. So the sanatoriums, the asylums and the detention barracks — all of which are used to quarantine and isolate gay men — continue to have systems of gay love manifested within them.

But these are the extremes. This account will concentrate on the everyday experiences of gay boys in the barracks, for not every gay is arrested and tried, or insulted and then assaulted. But there is an ever-present threat that is constructed by the rank. It is an open discouragement of any form of queer behaviour. And since mere discouragement is never enough to do away with normal impulses, a form of hidden terrorism against gays prevails which permeates every echelon of the military environment.

The shower block: Separate bungalows, separate lives

This is the story of two platoons. The first consisted of qualified men over 21 years old. The second was a platoon of school drop-outs, all under 17. Separate bungalows, with separate lives.

It was this separateness that was gross and unmanageable. Inter-platoon competition on an institutionalised level is the means of encouraging aggression in the army. And so one spends months labouring in a war with the men in the platoon across the asphalt. Men one has never seen before. One has to run against them, assemble equipment faster than them, dress neater than them, shave closer, march better. And the punishment for not being triumphant over them is dire.

This is the story of two platoons, one of juvenile cannon fodder and the other of intellectual raw material destined for the army's administration heap.

The youngsters had their own shower block, as did all platoons. Shower blocks were large and hot water from the coal burners would deplete very quickly. And so fellows would wander off to the showers of other platoons in search of hot water. And that is how a bunch of older boys got to shower in the block allocated to the children.

At some stage in the ritual, a kid got paranoid and thought that a queer from the older platoon was watching him while he showered. This is the rumour that abounded through the camp.

The kid got a paranoia and told his corporal. Alarmed, the corporal reported the incident to his superior. Of course, the fact that somebody was showering in the wrong block was cause enough for alarm. It was a dangerous sign that discipline was flagging. The senior platoon was warned that punishment would be severe should they be found showering anywhere other than in their designated shower. And the kids in the under-17 platoon were instructed to shower with their eyes closed, with a corporal posted in their shower to parade up and down the aisle watching that nobody showered with eyes open. This was supposed to have happened. But it could also be that the rumour was circulated as a calculated device to enforce separateness in toilet routines.

There is separatism among gays in the barracks, and very often it is the gays who are blamed for living slightly apart. But I would like to suggest that the isolation is purposefully instituted by the rank through mockery and the circulation of anti-gay rumours, causing a climate of homophobia and fear among youths.

The birthday party

Whether separatism is inflicted through public selection, or whether it is manufactured by gay-identified individuals, it is always there. It is witnessed in pockets. A bunch of queers will colonise the bunks in the corner of the dormitory. A tent of gay boys, a queer platoon. Very often soldiers would jokingly describe how the queers fared (or failed) at sport, physical training or shooting. This separateness, and the view that we are 'outsiders', brings about a type of unity among gays.

One gay boy, who had been appointed the colonel's secretary, arranged a birthday dance with snacks in the soldiers' bar. The dance was to take place after the straight soldiers had gone to sleep. There in the poolhall, around the bar at the dartboard, I saw our nervous nocturnal habits jumping right out the closet. There were the queers, in an alien milieu, running about like sewer rats after lights out trying to facilitate an alternative gay life.

A closer inspection revealed to me how relaxed the birthday party was, how different to the tense and macho stiffness that went on in the soldiers' bar every evening when the moffies constituted a tiny minority, trying desperately not to be noticed. But now the straight soldiers were tucked away, and there was a birthday party at which a majority were queers. In describing the event, one could say that it was our feminine selves at play.

The party was modest: there was free wine sneaked in from somewhere, with lots of sweets and chips from the tuck shop. And there was disco music playing, very different to the regular heavy rock that usually throbbed through the bar.

It wasn't exactly what I had imagined of war. The party, I realised, was just a small bureaucratic oversight, for had the upper ranks taken proper cognizance of it, it might not have been allowed. We felt that by being allowed to party, we were suddenly being treated with a degree of consideration. We perceived this as privilege. And in our campness I feel that we often assimilated privilege with womanliness.

To be treated like a woman meant not having to fight or perform harsh duties. To be let through doors first. To party. To us it wasn't disgusting, it was quite fulfilling. We wanted it that way. It's the queer fantasy, of course. The Lie, The Deception, for our general unwillingness to engage in harsher, stereotypically-straight duties makes us appear soft and inept, fuelling the blatant disgust with which we are viewed by others.

Underlying camp is the perception that womanliness is synonymous with privilege. Underlying homophobia is the perception that 'gay' is synonymous with underachievement and womanliness.

Even if one isn't queer, if circumstances place one in the domain of 'underachievement', one can suffer the queer fate. Witness the testimony of one such unfortunate:

> I was classified G4K3 for medical purposes, allowing me to do duty only of an administrative nature. For the remainder of my two years I was branded by superiors and at times fellow national servicemen as a 'moffie' or 'pansie'. As a group of G4s we were often called 'sissies' or 'girls'. As a result, many of those classified G4K3 attempted to be reclassified. I think it was largely because they felt their manhood was threatened. Anything associated with weakness was considered effeminate.[2]

The ambivalence of drag

Female impersonation has been one of the basic forms of entertainment in barracks, prisons and sometimes even in schools. Female impersonation is a form of satire; it is also an acknowledgement that even within a confined all-male environment, the battle of the sexes is raging. This is the conflict between the feminine as an indication of privilege on the one hand and as an indication of underachievement on the other. Whether performed by straights or gays, drag also comments on gay visibility and separateness.

Armies and institutions allow — and sometimes even encourage — a brief and public display of momentary transgression. It is a sanctioned assertion that there is otherness, an assertion of who the other is. In our case the other is black, communist, as well as any icon of sexuality that isn't white heterosexual male. Blacks and communists have been promoted as the enemy, and the queers are promoted as something midway between woman and man. Competent enough to be present, but part of something weak that shouldn't get out of hand.

Homosexuality is suppressed. Masculinity is elevated. By drawing attention to it, homosexuality suddenly becomes very evident. It fits into a system, and there is a route defined for it. But it has to parade as a charade. And it has to replicate heterosexual values and roles. It has to resemble that which dominates it, heterosexuality. The gays must conform to being a little weaker. They too, in their love of men, must affirm that man is the supreme conqueror. And that can best be done by parading as the weakest and most vulnerable — woman.

Every form of all-male incarceration gives rise to what Klaus Theweleit calls 'transsexuality as regulated play'. He cites various instances of it among straight German soldiers in Munich in 1919, and then goes on to conclude:

> For the soldier males, becoming a 'man' involves performing functions demanded by the military and war. The process whereby they become men is a social one; while their ego becomes 'masculine' through its insertion, as armour, into the whole, their sex remains diffuse. Though they play at 'changing' sex, they do so only in public... The social context makes a more general homosexualisation of the situation impossible. The public serves as a dam against any possible intrusion by sexuality.[3]

Theweleit feels that there is no possible 'intrusion' by sexuality into this charade; that the performed transsexuality is really only a way of reinforcing the proscribed distance that men are expected to keep from one another. I'm of the opinion that, in some way, sexuality does intrude. The 'regulated play' becomes unregulated. And it actually is quite sexy. All who went to school, holiday camp or the army, will remember a concert at which male seniors donned tutus to send-up the famed Signet Dance from *Swan Lake*. Many will remember the sensitive boy who put on the tutu and looked a little too comfortable; or the jocks who used to do it with a loud and awkward conviction. Then afterwards, on the playground they would tease each other, hugging and kissing the boy who looked the best in drag; playful teasing with a slight cutting edge. In contrast to Theweleit I would say that this is where feelings of sexual ambivalence creep in and disrupt the patriarchal male-bonding of the institutions.

This creeping ambivalence is the basis for a wonderful ambiguity in the relationship between the drag performer and his audience. Good drag often leaves the audience feeling both satisfied and betrayed by the illusion: satisfied at the *frisson* of sexual pleasure, but betrayed by the knowledge that it is a man dressed as a woman offering the excitement.

214

But drag can also prove that a system of differentiation is functioning. Sometimes it reinforces the stereotype that queers are indeed midway between man and woman, hermaphroditic. Then there is no ambiguity; only degradation.

The concert: The Arista Sisters

The camp has a compulsory concert. It's a variety performance to celebrate the completion of Basic Training. Notices are posted up informing all soldiers that those with talents should apply for permission to rehearse. In my year, applicants included a clown act, gymnasts, and collections of Greeks and Afrikaners who wanted to do national dancing.

Prior to being drafted I had been working as a professional actor and had once or twice been cast to play female and drag roles. And it was this type of performance that was suggested to me by a fellow gay thespian who, in order to persuade me altogether, suggested that the concert might be a welcome diversion from daily hardship and toils. We grouped, made application, and were granted permission via an appointed lieutenant to begin rehearsing in the afternoons.

Soldiers were referred to by superiors as *kiries*. By my understanding this word is an Afrikaans assimilation of the English word 'kiddie'. The concert, it was decided, would be called the '*Kirie Kabaret*'.

The drag show comprised of three performers, one extra who played a waiter, the Master of Ceremonies, and a unique feature — a body builder from the Permanent Force who had once won a 'Mister Universe' competition.

The costumes were made by a mother of one of the drags. I remember being fetched by the boy's father to be taken from Pretoria to Johannesburg for a fitting. The lad whose mother made the costumes was trading his mother's skills for a journey home. This was one way of going home legally during basics. Interestingly, the parents of the boy had to parade this task as a part of their civilian duty to the war effort: how else could they steal this moment to be together with their child?

The whole system of operation was well within regulations. The wigs were hired, at the army's expense, from the wardrobe of the Performing Arts Council of the Transvaal, whose State Theatre is in Pretoria.

The costumes presented variables of what has become standard drag fare. Corsets, suspenders, stockings and high heels. In her study of female impersonators in America, Esther Newton suggests that this costume/uniform does not originally derive from drag, but rather from pornography. The Mister Universe character then completes the parody of conqueror and conquered. In Newton's words, 'the muscle man and the drag queen are true Gemini: the make-believe man and the make-believe woman'.[4]

In the broader programme, the drag was to take place before the Finale which was to be the highlight of the concert. Two songs by Fats Waller were to be choreographed and staged. The songs were set in an imaginary bordello where three whores lounged about while being waited upon. Waller's 'Lounging at the Waldorf', rendered with its steamy red-hot-mama refrain, was accompanied by a

Permanent Force band. Once the song and dance had built to a climax we sang 'Ain't Misbehavin'' while a large gift-wrapped object was wheeled onstage, out of which erupted a scantily clad Mr Universe. The unwrapped stallion then abducted one of the girls, slung her over his shoulder, while she kicked and beat her fists on his back. The two other drags were left onstage, shaken, without their companion, and thus ended the song. During the performance there was an enormous din of catcalls and mocking masturbatory behaviour.

After the musical numbers, and before the grand finale, all three drags and Mr Universe reassembled onstage for a chat-session with the Master of Ceremonies. Here we gave away our names and credentials to the audience, a couple of thousand soldiers.

After these introductions the men and women of the upper ranks of the attendant camp received joke awards from the drag contingency onstage. The camp matron, the regimental sergeant major and the commanding officer all got invited onto the stage to receive their shields of honour — paper plates spray-painted gold.

As they arrived onstage the drags swept to the floor, curtsying in respect. These awards they received for being womanisers, big drinkers, sadists, or — in the case of the camp matron — saints. Then the 'girl' whose task it was to give out the award would try to kiss the recipient. As you can imagine, the captains and colonels would either go for the kiss, to the delight of the audience, or even better, they would avoid the kiss by craning the neck or jumping out the way. I remember taking off my frilly garter and placing it around the neck of a particularly butch captain. He beamed.

Without the original script it is difficult to explicate the humour. The names we chose for ourselves, however, give some indication of the nature of our parody: all were corruptions of the technical names of pieces of army equipment. The first drag queen was called 'Mossie Dop' which referred to the *Mosdop*, the Afrikaans term for the camouflage hard-hat worn in the trenches. The second was 'Stella Pik', an inversion of the *Pikstel*, the compact knife-and-fork set used by soldiers to eat on field trips. The third was 'Bella Calava' a corruption of *balaclava*, the woolen cap with peepholes worn over the face in cold weather.

Further indication of the humour is found in the program notes, originally printed in an army newsletter that was distributed for free:

SAY HELLO TO BELLA, STELLA AND MOSSIE
THE AMAZING ARISTA SISTERS
The Arista Sisters — Stella, Bella and Mossie, pictured above in something more comfortable, shortly after a tiring evening's rehearsal for their demanding guest appearance in Kirie Kabaret. The girls have recently returned from a grueling tour of the operational area where they have been entertaining (and frightening) the boys (and for that matter the Cubans).

Says Bella, a one-time mercenary, marooned for a while on the Falklands, when a nightly portrayal of Eva Peron was brought

*to an abrupt halt by indignant Argentinian invaders who felt that
'Elaine Page had more class':*

*'Well I wasn't going for class in the first place and when I
told them that was the way Fidel liked it (yes, I have done my
stint across the lines) they all yelled and left immediately. I love
spontaneous people.'*

*Stella agrees with Bella on that subject: 'Yes, do you know
that during a show at Tempe, I casually mentioned my favorite
things (I love presents, doll!) namely crayfish, chocolates and a
taste of sabotage. Well I said that the Taskelder '80 and the Del-
heim '82 were excellent years.'*

*(At this point Bella tactfully points out that Stella probably
means 'pinotage' and not 'sabotage'.)*

*Stella growls, 'what's the diffs anyway, as long as the year's
good.'*

*'Oh, the years have been good, honey,' growls Mossie, her
voice thick with nostalgia (and Gitanes Plain). 'In 1964', she continues, 'after a portrayal of a Valkyrie in a Lebanese concrete
factory commercial, a wonderful Israeli gentleman in my bomb
shelter said it was moments like those that made the Israeli inva-
sion all the more worthwhile.'*

*And future plans, dearie? 'Well, our immediate plans are of
course that glorious number that the lads have arranged for us on
Monday and Thursday. Otherwise we continue daily with our campaign to rid South Africa of unwanted drags. Move over Evita B.
We've done our basics!'*

The concert was performed three or four times. Once for the families of soldiers
and Permanent Force Members, and about three times thereafter as part of the leisure and recreation of soldiers from the various camps servicing Voortrekkerhoogte.

In the dark of the night one witnessed the dramatic sight of hundreds of
boys in formation, being marched by their corporals through the suburbs of Voortrekkerhoogte to the Civic Hall where the concerts take place.

As a further development, some of the Arista Sisters went on to entertain
the troops in other parts of the country. A major performance was done in the large
campus auditorium of Potchefstroom University, attended by some of the highest
ranks in the army, as well as the then-President's wife, Elize Botha. And it was
televised live. This performance featured a Rock-'n-Roll routine by a cast of sing-
ers and dancers, choreographed around a captured Cuban jeep. During rehearsals
for this I heard a military planner reasoning that the brigadiers and generals would
watch the jeep while their wives would watch the queers dancing. And that is exactly what happened.

Conclusion

When I got off the stage my high heels were killing me. As I walked down the
darkened passage behind the stage I saw performers hanging around, silhouetted,

with sporadic rays of light beaming off sequins on their costumes. I heard whispers and giggles, 'Look there, look at her!' My scalp itched with sweat under my wig.

I got to the dressing room, a locker room with one harsh fluorescent light, and looked in the mirror. My make-up was probably dripping down my face; my stockings probably laddered. Then, for me, a strange transformation was to take place as I slowly and laboriously peeled off the wig, the restrictive corset, the false breasts, and wiped off the make-up. I washed, put on my army uniform and waited for the corporals to come and march us back to our dormitories. One of the other 'girls' probably hurried into the dressing room just then, whispering hysterically about the little hitches that had cropped up in the performance. Mister Universe was probably sitting around there too in his scants. I remember that he was simply proud of his overdeveloped body. Showing his body was on a par with what we were doing. You see, we were all parading for the institution, declaring what it was that we cherished as ours. The Greek dancers, the Afrikaans *volkspele* (folkdances) — we were all saying, 'Here I am, this is me, I am Greek,' or 'I am Afrikaans,' or 'I am strong,' or 'I am queer' — for South Africa.

I can only imagine that the upper echelons of the camp must have felt a tremendous sense of strength on those nights. For in their pageantry the concerts must have reaffirmed the state's control over all those types. The entertainment provided admonishment of the power of the state. The state, in this instance, owned one's right to all forms of identification. It had successfully arbitrated a use-value for one of the most powerful of homosexualised cultural icons — drag.

This is a rather bleak note upon which to end. And so I would like to conclude with the idea that in army drag one finds a complex contradiction between collaboration and defiance. Since homosexual love is a criminal offence in the barracks it stands to reason that its propagation is a rejection of the demand that soldiers invest their libidinal energies in the war and that, for the fatherland, they show sexual restraint.[5] In this manner, gay-identifying individuals have always used this sanctioned form of drag to instate their existence, albeit stereotypically.

Notes

1 This and all subsequent quotations from army handbooks are cited in Matthew Krouse, 'The Propaganda of the SADF', *Spark Magazine* 2, 1990.
2 Jacklyn Cock, *Colonels & Cadres: War and Gender in South Africa* (Oxford University Press, 1991).
3 Klaus Theweleit, *Male Fantasies: Vol 2* (Polity Press, 1989).
4 Esther Newton, *Mother Camp: Female Impersonators in America* (University of Chicago Press, 1979).
5 For a more complete description of the same dynamic at play in the single-sex compounds of the South African goldmines, see Patrick Harries, 'Symbols and Sexuality: Culture and Identity on the early Witwatersrand Goldmines', *Gender and History*, 1990.

From Ada to Zelda:
Notes on gays and language in South Africa

Gerrit Olivier

Sociolinguists occasionally talk about 'gay language' or a 'gay sociolect' in South Africa. It is a phenomenon about which very little is known. Lists of 'gay' terms have been compiled, like the one in *Male Homosexuality in South Africa* by Isaacs and McKendrick, who talk about the 'gay vernacular', but we do not have any collection as comprehensive as Bruce Rodgers' *Gay Talk*, Claude Courouve's *Vocabulaire de l'Homosexualité Masculine* or the Dutch *Homo-erotisch Woordenboek*, compiled by Arendo Joustra.[1]

A proper investigation of gay language would involve much more than documenting regularly used words. One would also need to look more closely at the frequency of usage, the social contexts within which the words occur, the social background of the speakers, and the meaning that these speakers attach not only to words themselves, but to the use of the 'gay vernacular' in general.

Many gay people never use the so-called gay vernacular, and some have an active revulsion to it. Apart from this problem of acceptance, the term itself may imply more than one can assume. By talking about a 'gay language' one may fall into the trap of suggesting that gays themselves form a clearly identifiable and homogeneous group in society.

This is the kind of thinking that many gays would want to resist. There was a time when the American army thought that homosexuals could be identified through their language. Knowledge of gay terminology was a bad sign in a recruit.

For the sake of convenience I will talk about a gay language in this article, although there is no such thing in the proper sense of the word. There are words that are commonly used by gay people and mutually understood within certain sections of that community. Many of these words have been appropriated by other groups. For these terms to evolve into anything approaching a language or even a sociolect, a community normally needs to be isolated from the rest of the world for

219

a substantial length of time — or work hard at developing a gay language. In *Parallel Lives*, Peter Burton records the fact that English gays after the war were able to conduct full conversations in gay bars without using a single English word.[2]

The 'gay vernacular' is basically a limited vocabulary or set of what the linguist would call *lexical items*. The use of these words do not have a marked effect on areas of language beyond vocabulary. The following example, quoted by Isaacs and McKendrick, is unlikely to occur in real speech. Nevertheless, it illustrates the point that the 'gay vernacular' essentially consists of individual words:

> Look at that Clora. What a queen. But wada that lunch. It's a picnic basket. I'd love to pomp her up the Ada, but she looks so Dora'd. I suppose she's rent, or maybe even a Priscilla and will only give me a blow-job. My dear, I suppose I'll have to go home and tilly toss-off alone. Moffies are all alike.[3]

In this passage, the use of a spectacular number of lexical items from gay language has no effect on the normal grammatical and syntactic structures of English. The speaker clearly finds himself in a bar or club where he is sexually admiring another person. Gay language does not extend much beyond the description of social and sexual interaction amongst gay people themselves. It would be impossible to open a bank account, ask for a car to be serviced or take part in a panel discussion on *Agenda* using gay language.

Within the vocabulary, common words for gay men include *bit, bunny, faggot, fairy, moffie, pouff* or *poefter, queen, queer* and *trassie*. One could talk about someone being part of the *family* or one of the *sisters*. The term *sisters* could also refer to *dykes, letties, lettuce leaves* or *letty bags*. If the sisters are *BM women* who enjoy the company of moffies, they are called *fag hags*, or occasionally *fruit flies*. And anyone could be called *doll*.

All these words have a range of connotations, even amongst gay users themselves. A number of them did not originate among gays, but in the straight community as pejorative terms for gays. Among gay users, their meaning is not fixed because even though some of them have been appropriated as positive terms of identification, they retain their negative potential. While *moffie*, for instance, certainly has lost much of its pejorative content, the expression *'Hy is 'n regte moffie'* (he's a real moffie), uttered by a moffie about another moffie, may still contain its associations with an effeminate, effete person.[4]

In the category of words referring to sexual organs, practices and preferences we come across a number of items that do not require translation for a wider audience, like *butch* and *femme, active* and *passive*. On the other hand, many of the words in this group would not be known by many people outside the sphere of gay sexual interaction. Words like *belenia, bliss, divine, nommer* or *number, piece* or *stuk* refer to sexually attractive men. With a few exceptions like *rim* and *trade*, terms for sexual intercourse are derived from a wider context, but *chubby chasers* (fat fetishists) and practitioners of the *golden shower* (urine fetishists) may have to explain their needs even to other gays. Regularly used words relating to the activity of cruising are *camp, cottage, glory hole* and *tea room*, while the commonly known *lunch* and *picnic basket* of a *well-hung* person may occasionally be supplemented by terms like *boerie* (for boerewors).

Within the general nomenclature for gays, words referring to male prostitutes and effeminate types form clearly definable groups. In the first group one finds words like *chicken, rent, rent-boy* and *trick.* In the second the ubiquitous *queen* may enter the scene, looking very *camp* while *mincing* with a *clutch-bag* under the arm.

'We are a visual people,' says one of the characters in Andrew Holleran's *The Dancer from the Dance.*[5] Words referring to general appearances and to observable mental states form an important part of gay language and include terms like *bolla* (hairdo, haircut), *coif* (to do/cut hair), *dizzy* (stupid), *finished* (exhausted, drunk), *gil* (to behave excitedly), *gezoosh* (well-dressed), *koekstamp en giggel* (an enjoyable get-together, literally fuck and giggle), *mingle* (to mix socially), *mink* (coat), *wes* (drugged) and *wig* (hairdo, haircut).

Possibly one of the most striking characteristics of gay language is the widespread use of alliterative female names for a range of activities, personal characteristics and objects. The following list of such terms is reasonably representative:

Ada	the buttocks area
Agatha	malicious gossip
Aida	AIDS; someone with AIDS
Annie	anus
Bella	to be beaten up; someone who beats up homosexuals
Betty	buttocks; size of buttocks
Beulah	beautiful man
Celia	offering a cigarette by way of camping
Cilla	cigarette
Cindy	child
Clora	Coloured homosexual
Connie	moment of orgasm/ejaculation; condom
Cora	common person
Debra	depressed; depression
Delia	drama queen
Deloris	delirious; mad
Dora	a drink; to drink; to be drunk
Doris	a drink; dreadful
Ethyl	elderly; elderly person
Fiona	wanting or having sex
Gail	to chat
Golda	Jewish homosexual
Hilda	unpleasant or ugly (person)
Iris	Indian homosexual; irritated
Jessica	jealous
Laura	lover
Lily	the law; the police
Marie	mad or eccentric person

Mary	gay person
Maureen	murdered
Mavis	gay person
Milly	mad
Monica	woman having her period; femme man
Natalie	black homosexual (originally 'Natalie Native')
Nora	stupid; a stupid person
Olga	organised
Olive	beautiful man
Penelope	urinate
Priscilla	police officer(s); the law
Reeva	revolting
Sally	to suck off
Stella	thief
Tilly	masturbate; also 'Tilly Toss-off'
Ursula	sympathetic heterosexual
Vera	to vomit; Valium
Wendy	white homosexual
Zelda	Zulu homosexual

Many readers may want to quarrel with the examples I have given, disputing some words or arguing that many other items are used often enough to be included in the list. I will grant these objections because they illustrate one of my points — that the 'gay vernacular' is not a fixed thing. While some words may gradually become obsolete, new ones appear.

Whereas the nouns, verbs, adjectives and adverbs mentioned earlier overlap with the language of non-gay people, the use of female names would seem to be the one phenomenon that is unique to the gay context. The use of these names is not restricted to the nominal function: one may encounter them as nouns, adjectives or verbs, and some of them, like *dora*, may change their grammatical function depending on the sentence. Whether one has too many *doras*, or *doras* heavily, the end result of becoming or being *dora'd* is the same. Someone who often enough behaves in a *nora* fashion may eventually run the risk of being called *Nora*. The names supply a multi-functional repertoire that allows for a wide range of possibilities. In most cases, the choice of a female name seems to have been inspired by alliteration: *C*illa for *c*igarette, *W*endy for *w*hite. The importance of the sound correspondence is illustrated by such alliterating pairs as *Zelda Zulu* and *Nora No-Brains*.

The use of female names to refer to race, state of mind or sexual activity thus rests on two simple principles of selection that allow for endless new inventions. Whereas the core vocabulary derives from the American example, *Clora* most certainly is a South African invention, and nothing prevents names like *Doreen* or *Brenda* from entering the vocabulary. For all one knows, they may already have done so.

Very little research has been done on the frequency of these terms in different areas of the country or different social contexts. My impression from personal experience is that they occur most frequently in the coloured community of Cape Town, and that the use of it is more widespread in Pretoria than in Johannesburg. Both of these suggest a primarily Afrikaans base, even though the vocabulary itself cuts across the divide between the two official languages, making it equally accessible to Afrikaans and English speakers.

To establish the function of gay language, one will have to enquire more deeply into the attitudes of speakers. Nevertheless, the words listed above have at least three general functions in speech among gay people.

The function of *concealment* is obvious in most of the words derived from female names, as well as in some of the others. This function has a practical advantage in a society where homosexuality is still frowned upon. It allows messages to be transmitted between gay people in the presence of persons who may be completely unaware of the real meaning of the verbal interaction. The question 'Is he part of the family?' would sound like an innocuous enquiry in heterosexual company, but to gay speakers it is an obvious and understood query into the subject's sexual orientation. In the personal advertising columns of *Exit*, these messages are even further codified for obvious reasons. From this an interesting question arises. To what extent is the concealment inherent in this kind of message perpetuated by the use of codified language even when that is no longer required by social pressures?

This question cannot be answered without reference to the fact that gay language also *reveals* and *identifies*. Sociolinguists would probably find that gay language corresponds closely to languages occurring in other sub-cultures. The use of a common language gives to a community of people a sense of solidarity and unity; it allows members of that community to identify with one another and with the group through a mutually understood and exclusive code.

In modern linguistic studies it is commonly acknowledged that every language and every discourse has both an enabling and a limiting aspect. While someone may enter a gay community by identifying with the linguistic codes that prevail within it, the very exclusiveness of the code may isolate speakers from the rest of society, perpetuating the sense of a ghetto existence. This double function probably explains many gays' ambivalence towards gay language.

The double function of gay terms is also illustrated by the history of certain words. The assertive adoption of pejorative terms by the gay community as part of its self-image served to rob some terms of their pejorative meaning. We call ourselves *moffies* without cringing, but we may still object to being called *trassies* or *bunnies*. In the Netherlands and the United States *flikker* and *faggot* have lost their reprehensible meanings because gays have started using them as terms of positive self-identification. But one may not discount the possibility that even the ironic or parodic use of pejorative terms may help to maintain exactly those stereotypical images that society has about gays. Also, terms associated with gay pride may gradually become re-stigmatised. In the *Homo-erotisch Woordenboek* a gay speaker is quoted as saying that the word *flikker* has once again become a cliché.

According to him, it refers to someone who embarks on political action wearing a dress. He would much rather be called a *nicht* (the Dutch equivalent for queen).

Many of the terms listed above, especially the female names, are obviously intended for humorous effect and illustrate a third function, that of *parody* or *self-irony* in gay language. How does one explain the preference for names like *Hilda*, *Cilla* and *Debra*? Cobus Nothnagel, who did research into the gay sociolect at the University of the Witwatersrand, quotes sources who indicate that they perceive these names as belonging to a common, lower class culture. The use of them therefore implies a conscious tongue-in-cheek, self-deprecating attitude.[6]

The use of the female nomenclature is not limited to personal names for males, but occurs across the whole spectrum of gay language. As one could expect from ironic language, the feminisation of experience and social interaction that results from this has several interesting aspects. One could see it as a playful assertion by gay males of their feminine identity. It may also indicate that the social attitudes and role-play of gay males are still conceptualised with reference to heterosexual models, that gays have not succeeded in building a culture that is not a parody of heterosexual relationships. If one adds to this the negative attitude to women that some of the terms imply, the gay terminology is revealed as a double-edged sword. In a mixture of dependence and revulsion, it embodies a constant reaction to the dominant heterosexual culture while emulating that same culture.

A more correct term for the 'gay sociolect' would probably be the 'homo-erotic vocabulary' because that is more or less what is contained in it. The examples discussed in this article amply illustrate that the sociolect which has been documented in South Africa has a relatively limited frame of reference. It allows gays to talk about themselves and to express their sexual identity and preferences. This language can be seen as occupying the opposite pole to the language in which the media talk *about* gays and which contains a vast number of assumptions and prejudices about their way of life, their morality etc.

In South Africa we do not have a public discourse in which gays and non-gays can talk to one another about their sexuality on a basis of equality. While gay language has a number of important functions, one of them being the assimilation of ugly words and the parody of prejudices, its frame of reference is probably too limited for it to become a liberating language.

Notes

1 Gordon Isaacs and Brian McKendrick, *Male Homosexuality in South Africa: Culture, Crisis and Identity Formation* (Oxford University Press, 1992); Arendo Joustra, *Homo-erotisch Woordenboek* (Thomas Rap, 1988); Bruce Rodgers, *Gay Talk: A Sometimes Outrageous Dictionary of Gay Slang* (Putnam, 1979); Claude Courove, *Vocabulaire de l'Homosexualité Masculine* (Payot, 1985).
2 Peter Burton, *Parallel Lives* (Gay Men's Press, 1985).
3 Isaacs and McKendrick, *Male Homosexuality in South Africa,* pp. 78–79.
4 See Shaun de Waal, 'An etymological note on moffies', at the start of this volume.
5 Andrew Holleran, *The Dancer from the Dance* (William Morrow, 1978)
6 Honours essay on 'Gay Afrikaans', Department of Afrikaans and Nederlands, University of the Witwatersrand, 1991.

EXIT:
Gay publishing in South Africa

Gerry Davidson and Ron Nerio

In a time when there is much debate over media policy and planning in a 'new' South Africa, another debate continues on the sidelines — about the gay press. The debate is inextricably linked to the present status and development of the gay movement in this country. As gay rights are tentatively placed on the broader political agenda, and as gays and lesbians begin to be perceived as a potential political force, the need for independent gay publications becomes more and more important.

By looking at *Exit*, South Africa's principal gay and lesbian newspaper, and at its predecessor *Link/Skakel*, this piece will explore the relationship between a gay press and a budding gay rights movement, and will examine the attempts by *Exit*, despite the lack of a united, strong gay rights movement in South Africa, to meet the needs of its readers. To politicise, inform and entertain diverse and isolated gay communities — without alienating its readers or offending its financial base.

Exit is the only publication that has appeared continuously on the South African gay scene since the mid-1980s. There have, however, been several other newsletter-format publications during the past decade, and there have also been several attempts at campus publications by gay and lesbian student organisations.[1]

Recently, coinciding perhaps with the growth of gay consciousness in South Africa, three new publications have emerged: *Inversion*, a Cape Town journal spearheaded by OLGA (the Organisation for Lesbian and Gay Action), which provides explicitly political coverage; *Esteem*, a new commercial men's-only publication; and *The Quarterly*, a news magazine for gay women. By late 1993, *Inversion* had only produced one issue, but *Esteem* and *The Quarterly* promised to appear more regularly.

GASA and Link/Skakel

On 1 April 1982, 24 representatives of three informal gay groups in the Southern Transvaal region met to discuss the formation of a unified organisation to serve a wider cross-section of South Africa's lesbian and gay population and to offer an increased number of services. The social group, Unité, and the political group, Lambda, had been informally negotiating a fusion for several weeks. They were joined by a supper-club, AMO (the Alternative Men's Organisation) to form GASA, the Gay Association of South Africa, South Africa's first formally-constituted gay organisation.

Link/Skakel was launched simultaneously as a monthly newsletter for all dues-paying members. Initially printed in a simple stapled folder format, the newsletter was planned to facilitate communication between GASA's members. But, as GASA grew, it became a marketplace of gay ideas and aesthetics, and was transformed into the tabloid newspaper that is now *Exit*.

A calculation of the demographics of GASA membership in the September 1982 issue attempted to give some indication of who was receiving *Link/Skakel*. Even that early in its history, it was being mailed to all of the provinces and Namibia. But 94.5% of it's readership lived in the Transvaal, with 77.9 % from the greater Johannesburg area. Less than 7% of GASA members were women, and English was the first language of 73.2%.

Even though GASA was officially bilingual, most of *Link/Skakel* was written in English, with only three of four articles in each issue in Afrikaans. One *Link/Skakel* reader wrote to the editor in April 1983 suggesting that GASA's low 'black' membership was due to its language policy. Responding to an editorial lamenting this low number of black GASA members, he maintained that an English-only publication (or in English in conjunction with one or more of the African languages) would convince black gay people that *Link/Skakel* did not associate itself with the apartheid system.

By early 1983, *Link/Skakel* was renting a full-time office with a telephone, and joined the International Gay and Lesbian Press Association. At its height, circulation reached 5 000 (1 200 to GASA members and 3 800 distributed free at gay venues). With the high inflation of paper prices in 1984, the GASA Management Committee decided to open sales to the general public as a means of increasing revenue. *Link/Skakel* was then registered with the Department of Internal Affairs, and all succeeding issues were to be sent to the Registrar of Newspapers, a legal requirement for any publicly distributed publication.

But the first two issues submitted, April and May 1984, were declared undesirable and banned from public display or sale. A letter from the Directorate of Publications in Cape Town, printed in the August 1984 edition, explained that the issues were offensive and harmful to public morals because they were 'calculated to promote homosexuality which, in the view of South African citizens, is an offensive and immoral form of sexual activity.' The Directorate went on to complain that 'homosexuality is presented as normal and right. This publication would exceed the tolerance of the average decent-minded citizen.'

GASA was once again forced to restrict distribution of *Link/Skakel* to members, and continued to subsidise the publication for yet another year, despite high expenses. During this time, the organisation began to experience acute financial troubles. Membership in the national body had fallen drastically due to the growth of a number of more specialised lesbian and gay organisations, and many branches were disenchanted with the Johannesburg leadership. There were also numerous internal disagreements.

Finally, in March 1985, GASA disbanded *Link/Skakel*. Dawid Moolman, an experienced professional journalist, decided to bring out a private gay newspaper, and the first *Exit* was published in July 1985. *Exit* was not meant to replace *Link/Skakel*, but effectively it did so, as it was mailed to much of the newsletter's old readership, distributed in the same gay venues, and staffed by the same people. *Exit* was still aimed at those who had founded and made GASA successful in the previous four years — this meant the subject matter (and thus the readership) remained almost exclusively white and male.

A token look was given to gay liberation, the AIDS situation, gay political interests and the decriminalisation of homosexuality. As with *Link/Skakel*, however, the bulk of the paper was taken up with bar and club round-ups, community news, hunk pictorials, and camp humour, as exemplified in the regular Bitch and Pieces column of Lulu Avender.

Nevertheless, a new column called Outspeak was introduced: written for the most part by Dawid Moolman and founder members of the now defunct GASA, it dealt more explicitly with issues of gay liberation and organisation. And in September 1985, Karen Lotter was retained as a contributor: the first woman among at least ten men on the masthead.

Exit and the white right

Despite the fact that South Africa was in the throes of a national insurrection compounded by the State of Emergency in 1986 and 1987, *Exit* focused almost totally on parochial affairs, with some token coverage of the incarceration of Simon Nkoli, a GASA member who was among the accused in the Delmas Treason Trial.[2] But *Exit* remained primarily the mouthpiece of GASA's founders, and continued to reflect the white gay establishment's attitudes by steering clear of politics — perhaps because of self-censorship, perhaps because of lack of sympathy with the black liberation struggle.

At this time, GASA was in its death throes with many internecine wars being fought around Benefit, a body assembled to raise money for the decriminalisation of homosexuality. Those involved had been accused of fraud and misappropriation of funds. Certainly, the Benefit issue was important and foremost in the minds of white gay activists, but perhaps it should have taken second place to an attempt by the gay community to join with and support the aims of the broader liberation struggle.

In truth, *Exit* defined politics as white. This was made explicit in 1987 when, at a time when there was an open call for a boycott of the 6 May white elections, editor Dawid Moolman decided to use the newspaper to lobby for the support of gay rights by parliamentary candidates. To many, the message was clear: white gay rights were the only ones *Exit* was interested in.

Exit sent letters to all electoral candidates asking whether they supported gay rights and whether they would vote accordingly in parliament. 'Yes' responses were received from 23 candidates of the opposition liberal Progressive Federal Party, from ten candidates of the governing National Party, and from two independents. The majority of candidates did not respond. *Exit* urged its readers to vote for those candidates who had responded positively to its question. For the candidates who had responded negatively, *Exit* wrote in its May/June 1987 edition that:

> *The candidate or his party is totally opposed to any form of gay rights. No gay person would vote for any of these politicians. The party will not support you and the individual can do nothing on his own. Vote for his opponent if he or she said yes, or spoil your paper by writing GAY across it. Do not stay away from the poll. Exercise your right to reduce his votes.*

The issue, for the first time, highlighted gay issues within a broader political arena. A number of PFP and NP candidates wrote encouraging letters to *Exit*, promising to do all they could to rid the politics of anti-gay bias. Conversely, one candidate from the far-right Herstigte Nasionale Party, Mr Gert Swiegers from Algoa, wrote, 'I am pleading with all the homosexuals in my constituency not to vote for me.'

The clamouring of politicians to address the issue was at once empowering and disturbing to the lesbian and gay community. If gay voters were to reject the overtures of the pro-gay candidates, the community might be giving up an opportunity for unprecedented visibility. However, if they were to respond, they would be validating a political system from which most South Africans were excluded, and that a record number of white progressive South Africans were boycotting.

In at least one constituency with many gay voters, Hillbrow, the *Exit* campaign worked: the NP's 'pro-gay' Leon de Beer beat the PFP incumbent, Alf Widman, by a few votes — even though he was later charged and jailed for electoral fraud. Hillbrow had previously been a safe opposition seat, and Widman's defeat was attributed to his lukewarm and equivocating utterances on the issue of gay rights.

Exit's stance — and the role that the newspaper played in helping De Beer win Hillbrow for the government — alienated a large segment of the gay and lesbian community, and a major controversy was sparked off in the pages of the newspaper. In the June/July 1987 issue, for example, the Wits Gay Movement, the gay student group at the University of the Witwatersrand, berated Moolman for his gloating claim '... that the so-called "gay vote" made Hillbrow a Nationalist seat.' And in the July/August 1987 issue, prominent human rights advocate Edwin Cameron slammed the 'active and ostentatious way in which *Exit* had promoted De Beer', calling it 'a debasement of the gay cause and a profaning of its responsibili-

228

ties to the South African gay community as a whole.' In the same issue *Exit* protested that it had never actively promoted the candidature of de Beer, adding that

> *we are keenly aware that only a small minority of gay people are white, which is why we asked our readers to keep in mind the great crowd of gay people who are disenfranchised because of their colour. We want every privilege afforded to whites to be extended to our black brothers and sisters... However, we will use any vehicle to campaign for gay civil liberties, even if it means resorting to the whites only democracy of South Africa.*

Nevertheless, Moolman gave voice to the contradictions of *Exit*'s actions by stating in the June/July 1987 issue that gay voters in Hillbrow had proven that 'they can sway power, even to a candidate like Leon de Beer who represents an unpopular and repressive party, if he comes out strongly enough in favour of gay rights.'

Perhaps in response to the outrage, *Exit*'s October 1988 edition urged readers to vote for 'pro-gay' candidates in the 1988 Johannesburg City Council elections only if they found their political objectives acceptable, and strongly supported the PFP over the NP. Though both major parties had publicly pledged support for gay issues with splashy advertisements in *Exit* promising a gay sportsfield, a community centre, and grants for organisations, it was felt that the PFP generally had a better record on gay rights.

The controversies surrounding the election issue dealt *Exit* a severe blow. The solid right-wing base of the paper was more than visible to both local and international activist gay organisations. When, for example, *The Weekly Mail* called *Exit* the 'politicised gay newspaper', the Cape Town based Gay Action Group responded that this label was 'so far off the mark as to lead past outrage to hilarity. *Exit* is an elitist, sexist paper designed for the large conservative white gay male community.'[3]

This perception was widely shared in activist gay and lesbian circles, and this had a critical significance. Particularly following Simon Nkoli's highly-publicised trial, gay organisations abroad actively funded gay activist organisations and publications. Needless to say, none of this funding came into *Exit*'s coffers.

And so the publication became even more sporadic and uncertain: the number of pages decreased and it displayed an even blander content than before the election debate.

A new Exit in a new South Africa

In 1990, Nelson Mandela's release from prison, the unbanning of the liberation movements and the collapse of apartheid coincided with the coming of age of South African gay politics and the first annual Lesbian and Gay Pride March. Gay activists tied gay liberation strongly to the broader struggle, and *Exit*, with its first new editors/owners in nearly a decade, supported this stance.

After Dawid Moolman's death the previous year, *Exit* had been edited by Karen Lotter and Henk Botha. Lotter's more liberal and feminist perspective meant that more lesbian articles appeared and more coverage was given both to gay politics and to the larger arena of South African politics. But the fact that she had widely divergent political views to those of Botha led to the sale of his share of the paper to Gerry Davidson in January 1990. Davidson subsequently acquired full ownership of *Exit* in September 1990.

Lotter and Davidson, both women, had their own battles to fight within the gay community, openly espousing from the start the causes of activist organisations like the Gay and Lesbian Organisation of the Witwatersrand (GLOW), the Organisation of Lesbian and Gay Activists (OLGA) and Sunday's Women. It was hard (and, some said, inappropriate) for *Exit* to support the workers' struggle in a gay movement dominated by a white male middle class.

However, merely by its existence *Exit* is making a political statement. Would that it could be more definite, more often and more heard. But there is a problem: gay liberation is not yet a widely accepted notion within South Africa's gay communities, and if *Exit* becomes too closely linked to leftist organisations, it will risk losing its financial base — its advertisers in the gay community and many of its subscribers.

Moreover, by 1993, *Exit* was beginning to attract the attention of mainstream advertisers, who began to realise the potential of a gay market. Again, this interest meant that any espousal of a radically liberationist agenda could lose these new advertisers and damage *Exit*'s entry into the mainstream press.

The challenge for the newspaper is to find a balance between activist credibility and acceptability to both readers and advertisers. *Exit* began an approach of gentle persuasion as regards human rights, AIDS education and politicisation. A hunk juxtaposed against an article on AIDS; sexy cartoons used to carry messages; and overseas news, taken off the international press wires, offering explicitly political coverage. The newspaper's cover stories are frankly sensationalist; an invitation to read further and, hopefully, to absorb some of the more serious material.

The formula appears to have worked: the paper has become fatter, more serious, more professional, and carries more advertising and more classified ads. But making this course even more difficult to chart is the fact that, even in the new enlightened era of unbanning, censorship remains a very real threat for gay publications. Recently, censorship has been focussed on the gay community[4] and, as a result, *Exit* has engaged in a fair amount of self-censorship: no ads, photographs or even classified ads which are too sexually explicit. And so, whereas in the past *Exit* might have omitted political material, it now has to consider omitting sexually explicit material — even though this is desperately needed to combat the spread of AIDS. *Exit*, however, continues to tread this dangerous path and test the law in every issue.

In their book, *Male Homosexuality in South Africa: Identity formation, Culture, and Crisis*, Isaacs and McKendrick touch briefly on the subject of the gay press, noting that 'in South Africa (gay) …publications reach only a minority of gay people.'[5] *Exit* is still criticised by the left for not being political enough, and for not having enough coverage of black life and issues.

That the newspaper only reaches a minority of gay people is incontestable. Only 15 000 copies are printed because of financial constraints. However, the great majority of gay men and women are still far too closeted even to consider buying *Exit* or picking it up free at bars and clubs. To compound this, township distributors are unwilling to carry gay publications, either because of their own antipathy or because of their fear of danger in an intensely homophobic environment.

If *Exit* were to become a vehicle for South Africa's black majority of gay men and women, it would immediately lose all support from its current advertisers, who would perceive it to be 'leftist' and 'radical' simply because it dealt with black issues.

Certainly, *Exit* desperately desires and needs to be perceived by advertisers as being in the mainstream. Just as desperately it wishes to reflect and support the 'differentness' and diversity of the gay community.

Until these dilemmas are resolved, *Exit* will continue to sell space to mainstream ad agencies with the intention of strengthening its base so that, in time, it can adopt a more radical editorial policy. In the absence of a windfall of funding from a local or foreign source, and in the absence of a well-organised national South African gay movement that *Exit* could support and that could, in turn, support the publication, there is no other option.

Notes

1 In Durban, for example, a newsletter called *Sunday's Women*, regularly and professionally produced until mid-1992 by a lesbian group of the same name, dealt with feminist consciousness-raising and self-help issues. In Johannesburg, in 1990, a lesbian arts magazine called *Legacy* was founded, and published fiction, art, cartoons and poetry. It folded, however, after a few issues because of lack of finance. A range of other organisations bring out newsletters specifically aimed at keeping their membership updated about their activities. In Cape Town, GASA-6010, a gay service organisation, puts out a newsletter, as does GASA OFS in Bloemfontein, GAIN in Pietermaritzburg, GCC, TOGS and Yachad in Johannesburg and Natal Gay Community in Durban. Among the more activist organisations aligned with the liberation movements, OLGA has put out a handful of newsletters in its five years of existence, and GLOW published *Glow Letter* which, in 1992, was regular and professional, but has now ceased publication. The campus publications have included *Opt Out* at the University of Cape Town and *One in Ten* at the University of Natal/Durban.

2 See Gevisser in this book for a fuller discussion of GASA and the Nkoli trial.

3 Quoted in Cameron's letter to *Exit*, July/August 1987.

4 See Retief in this book for a fuller discussion.

5 Gordon Isaacs and Brian McKendrick, *Male Homosexuality in South Africa: Identity Formation, Culture and Crisis* (Oxford University Press, 1992), p104.

A thousand forms of love:

Representations of homosexuality in South African literature

Shaun de Waal

1

As ek my vreemde liefde bloot moes lê,
Wat sou die vrome skenders van die skoonheid sê?
Sou hul, met heilige verontwaardiging,
Besoedelende vingers God-waarts steek,
En na dié self-regverdigende reiniging
Hul eer aan my kom wreek?
Of sou 'n sprank van hierdie vuur wat in my gloei
Ook hulle aanraak, sodat hul verstaan
Die liefde neem 'n duisend vorme aan?[1]

This poem by ID du Plessis, published in 1937, is a remarkable plea for tolerance of homosexuality. A rough translation:

If I were to reveal my strange love
What would the pious defilers of beauty say?
Would they, with holy indignation,
Stick contaminating fingers in God's direction
And after this self-justifying purification,
Come and revenge their honour on me?
Or would a spark from this fire that glows in me
Touch them too, so that they understand
That love takes a thousand forms?

Although Du Plessis' poetry has been criticised for its vagueness (by DJ Opperman[2] and others), the implications must have been reasonably clear even in the 1930s. As Opperman notes, homoerotic elements had been apparent in Du Plessis' poetry as early as the mid-1920s, and Du Plessis had made Afrikaans translations of Bliss Carman's reconstructions of the poems of Sappho, the lesbian poet of the sixth century BC.

It is perhaps too easy to criticise Du Plessis for evasiveness now, or even 20 years after these poems were written. How simple would it have been for someone who was very much a part of the Afrikaner establishment, a prominent sports journalist, university lecturer and social figure[3], to have been open about his homosexuality? It would certainly have soured his career as a writer of teenage fiction.

The poem 'As Ek My Vreemde Liefde' gives the title to the collection in which it appears, *Vreemde Liefde* (Strange Love). The rest of the volume is made up of a cycle of poems that describe a fleeting, forbidden relationship; loss; humiliation; the pain of memory (later refigured as nostalgia); the poet's unhappiness and loneliness, his unfulfilable yearning; the (unconvincing) acceptance of his lot.

Many of these themes recur in Du Plessis' poetry as a whole. A religious cast is put upon them as the poet considers the nature of sin and temptation — the *bloedrooi luste* (blood-red passions) of the flesh — and engages in a battle (the title of the volume preceding *Vreemde Liefde* is *Stryd*) to overcome such enticements. The remedy, apparently, is selfless service to society, though it is clear that the pain of love denied can never be fully overcome.

The conflict apparent in 'As Ek My Vreemde Liefde' is that of the Law versus Desire. Law represents the mores of society and the church, internalised by the poet; Desire in this case is the forbidden enactment of homosexuality. The site of this struggle is mostly within the speaking consciousness of the poet, treating sin as an internal moral issue (as, for instance, a poet like NP van Wyk Louw might tend to treat issues of guilt and God's grace). In 'As Ek My Vreemde Liefde', however, Du Plessis breaks out of that inner battle and locates the struggle vis-à-vis the sanctioning role of society. Sexual difference becomes sexual dissent.

The poem makes it clear that those who should be the guardians and disseminators of divinely-inspired love are doing the opposite of loving; the admonishing finger pointing *God-waarts* seems to threaten even Him with contamination. This is precisely the type of battle that, say, gay minister Hendrik Pretorius fought with the Dutch Reformed Church in the late 1980s and early 1990s. The kernel is the church's view of (married) heterosexuality as the biblically sanctioned norm and homosexuality as a sin, condemned in Leviticus and elsewhere.

The spectre of social censure is apparent in 'As Ek My Vreemde Liefde' (the poem, in fact, tells us why it cannot be more forthright). The self-justifying heterosexual hegemony is vengeful toward the '*ek*' ('I') of the poem: he who would speak of his 'strange love'. And the speakers strategy for dealing with this threat is remarkably similar to that employed by some campaigners for gay rights today. Gay love is one of the thousand forms of love and is as valid as any other: difference does not equal inferiority.

* * *

In 1993, the Law of church and state as well as the ideological seepage that informs the popular assumption that homosexuality is deserving of mockery, humiliation and sometimes violent assault, is still in place — as it was in 1937.

It is in this context that one must examine those texts in South African literature that represent homosexual desire. One must ask how that representation is structured and to what ideological assumptions it defers. How does the text present the homosexual self, and how does it deal with the transgressive enactment of homosexual desire? What resistances does it offer?

To investigate these ideas, I have chosen to look at the work of five South African male writers, contrasting their varied approaches and textual strategies. First, though, it must be seen that since homosexual desire is illicit in law and stigmatised in daily life, the representation of it in literature is *de facto* a transgression, the breaking of a silence. Yet texts that deal with it must of necessity constantly restage the traversal of the taboo, whether in the process of contesting it, attempting to naturalise it, or destabilising the assumptions on which it rests.

Du Plessis and William Plomer, the first two writers under scrutiny, both from the early part of this century, show an acute awareness of the marginality of homosexual desire. Du Plessis contests this in the poem above; Plomer satirises the conventional mores that stigmatise (the display of) homosexual desire.

The first of the three writers of the latter half of the century, Damon Galgut, uses homosexual desire in an importantly symbolic way in both his novels: as a disruptive force and an act of rebellion. In contrast, Stephen Gray's two novels seek, perhaps, to move beyond the perception of homosexuality as transgressive and marginal, and to reinscribe it as central. This attempted naturalisation is only partly successful. The short stories of Koos Prinsloo, in an altogether different way, deal with homosexual desire as part of a discursive complex in which meanings shift constantly. The transgressive nature of homosexuality is not contested by Prinsloo; he does not seek to recentre it in the way Gray does. Rather, he decentres and fragments many discourses, including those of power, in a way that undermines the construction of the self through language.

2

William Plomer's short story 'Local Colour'[4], first published in *The Child of Queen Victoria* in 1933, deals somewhat satirically with the fracturing of sexual taboos.

Plomer was born in South Africa in 1903. His first novel, *Turbott Wolfe*, caused an uproar (an explosion, said Laurens van der Post) when it was published in 1926 because of the unconventional way it addressed race and sex. The vitriolic attacks on the book and the controversy surrounding *Voorslag*, the literary magazine he published with Roy Campbell and Laurens van der Post, drove Plomer from South Africa, disgusted with what he saw as its parochialism and blindness. He spent some years in Japan, later settling in England.

In 'Local Colour', two young English undergraduates, Grant and Spencer, are holidaying in Greece. They arrange to meet a Madame Strouthokámelos, an impressive lady who takes them to a little place down by the sea '... where we could get a nice Greek lunch and see a bit of the real Greece.' There, they encounter some Greek country boys, whom Madame Strouthokámelos asks to play and dance for the tourists. This they do, but they get carried away, much to Madame's embarrassment:

> *Lilac Shirt rose to his feet, approached the other dancer and clasping one hand round his partner's waist and the other around his loins he called for a tune ... The tune was a tango. With absurdly languorous movements they danced ... Lilac Shirt's trousers were, however, a little too tight for really free movement ... Lilac Shirt's way of holding his partner was perhaps a little too daring, a little too intimate, for the open air, at midday, in public. As the dance continued the goat rose to its feet as if to get a better view. It stared with its pale amber eyes at the dancers, then turned to look at Madame Strouthokámelos ... it was a look that spoke volumes, but banned volumes — and then again fastened its keen, glassy, unblinking stare on the dancers.*

The delicate play of Plomer's irony exposes certain social attitudes, with Madame, the finishing-school woman of the world, as the butt of the satire. The two young men seem to share a secret; they are homosexual themselves, though it is hidden, in contrast to the brazen local youths. The story, in fact, is based on Plomer's own experience: he and a friend travelled to Greece in 1930 in search of the easy homosexual liaisons that were so darkly frowned upon in England.[5] Thus Spencer and Grant would be looking out for precisely the kind of local colour they are presented with in the spectacle of the Greek boys, though Madame Strouthokámelos wouldn't know this, and they would not be able to tell her.

Plomer is perhaps making a wry joke about Greek love, then a codephrase for homosexuality. Madame Strouthokámelos herself is trying to live down the husband who had been a little too Greek in his nature for her taste (though this may refer to laziness more than sexuality). The goat refers to Pan, ancient Greek deity of fertility; it is also a symbol of lust.

In this story we see homophobic attitudes coolly satirised. We are meant to enjoy Madame Strouthokámelos' discomfort, and perhaps to see in the Greek youths' behaviour (they are last seen disappearing behind some rocks together) a healthier exercise of sexual passion than the covert desires of Spencer and Grant. The transgression of the love itself is displaced onto the transgression of being too open about it — which is to make a judgment of the social context rather than the act itself. Plomer, like ID du Plessis, is making a point about the thousand forms of love, though in this tale the spectre of heterosexual disapprobation is not threatening, merely risible.

Homosexual undertones are present in other works by Plomer, for example the short stories 'Bed Number Seventeen' and 'Nausicaa', and the novels *Sado* (1931), *The Case Is Altered* (1932) and *The Invaders* (1934). Plomer found it difficult to write too openly about (his) homosexuality. The gender of the objects of desire mentioned in his poetry and autobiographies is always indeterminate (which, in itself, is a bit of a giveaway).

Like EM Forster, whom he knew well, the fact that Plomer could not fully embody his homosexual self in his work caused him to write less: in fact, he abandoned several novels or parts thereof that were too blatant about it. His reticence was due, in part, to his own unresolved feelings about his sexuality, as Peter Alexander's biography makes explicit. (There was, it seems, a bit of Madame Strouthokámelos in Plomer himself.)

Like ID du Plessis, Plomer was criticised for not making the homosexual element in his writing plain; for not, as one critic put it, grasping the nettle. While homosexuality remains always at the margin of Plomer's work, its unobtrusive presence may indicate a tendency to naturalise homosexuality, to present it as something not necessarily worth comment in itself. In a society that seeks to censor homosexuality into invisibility, or at least to stigmatise it as utterly aberrant and extraordinary behaviour, this can be a radical strategy.

3

Damon Galgut is the author of two novels, a collection of stories and several plays. In his first novel, *A Sinless Season* (1982), published when he was 19, sexual transgression and punishment are problematically entwined.[6]

The primary symbolic opposition, which Galgut deploys in the first few pages of *A Sinless Season*, is mind versus body. Scott, one of three teenagers sent to a surprisingly liberal reformatory for crimes like petty theft, contemplates his reflection in the car window and associates a feeling of repulsion with it: 'Repulsion? No and yes, in an uncomfortable sense: staring at his own flesh and knowing that it was simply a housing for feeling. A generator of emotion. No more, no less.'

The opposition of mind/body is extended as the novel progresses (reason/madness, order/chaos). The reformatory is a model of good society, of rationalism and a trusting social contract. 'We trust you', says the principal, Mr Hall. '... Remember, we have pride here. That is why we do not call this a reformatory ... We have managed to turn our boys into gentlemen. We hope to do the same to you.'

But this neat order will be upset as one boy is murdered, and other sinister events follow. Against the rational mirror of a well-ordered society, Galgut sets a kind of madness, a destructive force that exists in one or more of the boys.

> *There is a crushing normality in their hurried paces through the night ... But, lying deeper than the tread of their feet ... as deep, perhaps as the smooth plunge of cliff* [the scene of murder] *that snarls away to the left, is an awakened insanity ... For here, for now, the madness is begun.*

Centrally symbolic of this growing impetus of 'insanity' is the ritual gang-rape of one of the boys, Raoul, by the others. Like the test of strength in which Raoul burns his own hand, this figure of madness is linked to the role of the body, collocating sexuality and punishment.

It is Scott's attraction to Raoul that has led him astray or awakened his own evil instincts. Later, in the second gang-rape scene, Scott participates, if only in a dreamlike way. The transgression, the sin, is particularised in *A Sinless Season* by murder and so forth, but its primary cause is a generalised madness that, the book seems to say, is potentially present in everyone. The sin may be murder, but sex is causally implicated. It is significant, too, that the sin becomes its own punishment.

One is reminded of the Victorian view of sexual deviance as progressive moral decay, a view not inconsistent with the paternalistic Calvinism that has so deeply influenced dominant white South African mores. (The same logic is applied to drug-taking and, recently, Satanism.) As the Marquess of Queensbury did in his attack on Oscar Wilde, the correlation of sexual perversity and the diseased mind is made.

Thus it may be said that to some degree *A Sinless Season* replicates oppressive ideological formations: homosexual desire is represented as pathological, one mode of a universally present but dormant psychic instability. Once awakened, this madness leads to one transgressive act after another in a downward spiral of moral degeneration.

But there is another reading that may be glimpsed in *A Sinless Season*, though it is no more than an implication. It might be said that the punishment of minor transgressions — sending the boys to a reformatory — precedes the greater transgression, awakens it, in fact. Yet the reformatory is not a place of violent punishment: it is a model of civilisation and human socialisation and rehabilitation. Thus punishment is part of the very fabric of social ordering. There can be no transgression without a Law to break, and small rebellion provokes punishment, which in turn provokes a greater rebellion.

Read this way, the novel hints that society itself, in its attempts to regulate the behaviour of individuals, is the progenitor of the very transgressions it nominally seeks to prevent. The Law exists most vitally in the moment of transgression, as its limits are traversed. (This can make of transgression a repetitive gesture, destined never to go beyond itself as it crosses the same line or a slowly shifting one again and again, but it demonstrates that Desire and the Law exist in a strangely symbiotic relation.)

Galgut's more recent novel, *The Beautiful Screaming of Pigs* (1991)[7], provides a deeper and more accomplished exposition of such concerns. In it, a young man, Patrick Winter, has been traumatised by experiences in the border war-zone. He journeys to Namibia, which is on the eve of independence and its first democratic elections, with his mother. Both are searching for some kind of wholeness, or some assuagement of an alienation they both feel in different ways.

Patrick develops an interest in Andrew Lovell, a Swapo leader recently assassinated by mysterious forces (the character is based on Anton Lubowski). Patrick and his mother go, with her black lover, Godfrey, to Lovell's funeral, which turns into a gigantic Swapo rally. In Lovell, Patrick is seeking an exemplar of someone who resisted the violent patriarchal order (repression and oppression exemplified by apartheid and white supremacy). Significantly, he chooses someone who has already been violently punished for his rebellion.

Patrick's own sense of alienation from the dominant order is figured in part as sexual marginality. His relationship with his macho father and his equally macho brother, Malcolm, and thus with the patriarchal values that structure white South African society, is troubled.

In a 1992 interview with the *Weekly Mail*, Galgut made the link between apartheid as a male-dominated, patriarchal order and the repression of both women and gay people. 'I think the values that made apartheid possible are extremely male values,' he said. 'I see apartheid in its entirety as a male mythology.' He extrapolates from the father-dominated family to society at large, ruled by warlike, traditionally masculine mores: 'For me,' he says, 'the family is the microcosm of everything that happens in the country.' And, later: 'As a gay person, growing up in this country was incredibly oppressive, as it must be for women.'[8]

The patriarch in *The Beautiful Screaming of Pigs*, Patrick's father, is described thus:

> *He was a hunter, my father; and the walls of his study bore witness to this fact. Mounted on wooden plates that looked, to my eyes, like platters, were innumerable heads. He had killed every one, he proudly exclaimed, and he had a collection of guns to prove it. He would take these out and show them, his hands more loving on those brutal butts of wood than they'd ever been on us.*

Patrick identifies more with his mother than with his father. His brother, Malcolm, however, 'is my father's son'. Malcolm torments him with the phrase: 'It's a man's world, Patrick ... It's a man's world ...'

It is this man's world from which Patrick is excluded (though this exclusion is perhaps preceded by a rejection on Patrick's part — a chicken-and-egg conundrum?). In the army, he and a friend, Lappies, are marginalised because they are not good at the violent games of rugby played by the soldiers, an ironic and telling precursor to Patrick's later dissolution in the wake of a bloody battle. (And rugby, of course, has a special place in white South African male society.) Because of their ineptitude, Lappies and Patrick are treated

> *as though we were ill or insane. Conversations broke off when we approached; jokes were made as we left ... We suffered our isolation without much complaint. We had always contained it within us. There was, you see, a brotherhood of men, to which we could never belong. My father, my brother, the boys at my school: they knew things that I didn't know. There was that in*

238

their hands that helped them catch balls; that helped them see objects in flight. Lacking this vision, I felt myself blind … Excluded forever from their strange fraternity, I watched from outside in my shame.

A key episode in the book describes a sexual encounter between Patrick and Lappies, soon after a skirmish in the bush during which Patrick has killed a Swapo guerrilla. The sexual act happens without forethought, and its significance is clear:

It was an act of revenge, undertaken in pain: against men, who had made the world flat. 'Leave me,' I gasped, but it wasn't to him: I was speaking to Malcolm, my father, to Schutte [their commanding officer]. *'Leave me,' I called down the well of my past, to those who'd colluded against me.*

Here desire is an instinctive challenge to the patriarchal law; the transgression is enacted out of a traumatised state as an act of rebellion against the violent heterosexual male order. On a psychological level, it traces the pattern outlined in *A Sinless Season*: the individual has already been somehow stigmatised, marked as a proleptic transgressor and pushed outside the masculine hegemony, denied power. Homosexuality may or may not be the hidden signifier underneath this figuration, but it emerges strongly as a transgression that resists the imposition of that order and the enactment of that power. It is turned back on the law that has first defined it then sought to confine and limit it.

4

Stephen Gray's novels *Time of Our Darkness* (1988) and *Born of Man* (1989)[9] present an altogether different way of writing about sexual transgression. Gray is a poet, novelist, academic and editor whose first volume of poems appeared in 1974; an engagement with homosexuality emerges in his more recent works.

By being quite frank about the gay sexuality with which they deal, these two works of Gray's participate in what has become an international gay literature industry — a genre in its own right. Gray's novels take for granted certain things that writing like Galgut's still questions or defers. But they enact their own range of deferrals and inner contradictions.

In *Time of Our Darkness*, a middle-aged gay man, a teacher, has an affair with one of his pupils, a teenaged black boy. Gray delineates three adjacent sites of transgression: firstly, that of race; secondly, that of age; lastly, homosexual desire. Yet the transgressive nature of homosexual desire is elided to some degree by the novel. It seeks, in fact, to recentre it, to rescue it from its position of marginality (to be affirmative?). As it is written in an essentially realist manner (it is going as a thriller), which enables one to read it simply as a story, the novel is able to displace the transgression of gay love onto the other transgressions it depicts.

The race issue, which overlaps with but does not entirely overlay the sexual, is foremost; the issue of age is significant in the context of a South Africa in which public hysteria greets revelations of paedophilia, which is perceived as an essentially homosexual vice. (It is interesting to note that at the time of the book's appearance South Africa was preoccupied with a number of paedophilia and pornography trials in which such assumptions were apparent.)

The intersection of these categories of transgression serves Gray's purpose in a number of interesting ways. It makes for a fresher look at an area where racial and sexual issues connect, long a concern of South African literature. It also partly naturalises homosexual relationships by foregrounding the racial transgression. Thus there is a double, two-way relation taking place, and the text moves between and handles these terms in a shifting manner.

The declining relationship between Pete, the narrator and protagonist, and his longtime lover, André, is contrasted with Pete's relationship with the black boy, Disley, setting up an opposition of youth and age. This opposition is echoed by both older men's contact with a young rent-boy, Prince. In itself, this does not question the nature of gay relationships but forces one to consider the age issue in and of itself. Gray has said that an element he wished to thematise in the novel was the proposition that 'the entire impetus of the uprising in South Africa in the mid-1980s, during which children assumed the role of adults and adults became, to say the least, vindictively childish, should be acted out literally.'[10]

The nature of homosexual relationships is questioned to some degree by the brief heterosexual liaison between Pete and an English schoolteacher, Jenny. Though this sexually explicit episode is played mostly for laughs, it is enough to throw the binary opposition of homosexual/heterosexual into relief. But this once again serves to transvalue homosexuality in the context: straight sex is an aberration for Pete, a new kind of 'transgression' for him. In an almost satirical way, thus, Gray turns the heterosexual encounter into a symbol of abnormality.

Yet *Time of Our Darkness* operates within a strange double-bind. While it affirms the normality of gay relationships, treating them, in fact, in much the same way a straight novelist would treat straight relationships, the presence in the book of many scenes that explicitly describe sexual acts unsettles this process of naturalisation. Here we enter the area of reader reception. Read within the tradition of 'gay literature', presuming a gay reader, the sex scenes are not shocking in themselves (though some might find elements of them unpleasant). Erotica forms a large part of international 'gay literature': it is a common feature of all kinds of narrative, from the most literary to detective stories. It may be argued that the open representation of gay sex in such texts is a valuable contribution to gay self-recognition and understanding in a world in which images of heterosexual sex are dominant. In this respect, especially in the context of South African literature, Gray is a pioneer.

But read from outside the tradition of 'gay literature' — and *Time of Our Darkness* was sold as a mass-market paperback, successfully so — the mere depiction in such detail of gay sexual encounters is likely to shock and disturb (even as it titillates). Some readers and critics reacted to it in this way, denigrating the book as filth in the most puritan manner. Thus, perhaps, the novel destabilises its own naturalisation of homosexual desire.

Various contradictions are also apparent in Gray's *Born of Man*, a lighter and altogether less complex piece of work. The story of *Born of Man* is essentially fantastical, dealing with the first man in the world to bear a child. Here Gray introduces another transgression: that of biology. As *Time of Our Darkness* displaces sexual transgression onto the racial, so *Born of Man* transfers the sexual onto the biological.

Gray places the book firmly within a genre of avowedly gay writing, framing it as a series of letters by the narrator to friends overseas, describing this extraordinary occurrence of male pregnancy. The language draws on slang and a camp, chatty style that mark it as gay; possibly a kind of 'in-crowd' text. (Read from outside such a gay crowd, this use of special language conveys authenticity.)

Gray's strategies in *Born of Man* are similar to those employed in the aberrant heterosexual scene in *Time of Our Darkness*, though they are taken much further here. He inverts expectations and thereby sends up received social prejudices and norms. The gay self is not interrogated but empirically taken for granted, yet the nature of the body itself — the agent of desire and, significantly in this context, reproduction — is radically undermined. Gray is questioning assumptions of what is natural.

In other ways, however, the novel reinforces certain stereotypes of gay life. The most disturbing of these is that the displacement of sexual onto biological transgression may be reversed. In other words, this collocation may serve to show that homosexuality is a biological aberration that 'goes against nature' in precisely the way that male pregnancy would go against nature.

Also of interest is the fact that *Born of Man* raises the issue of age in gay relationships that is occluded in *Time of Our Darkness*. '*What is it* with older men and younger?' asks the narrator.

> *Perhaps its our way of recapturing our youths ... Then I moved on to thinking it was the way the part of being gay that's kept in the cupboard till last finally comes out: parenthood! Those boys turn into our own sons ... Without **that** moffies are doomed to extinction ... It's my observation that the one thing every male gay I know wants most, and can never have, is a child.* [Gray's emphasis.]

Does this explain the importance of the male pregnancy in *Born of Man*? How far does this go in enabling a re-reading of *Time of Our Darkness* in a different light? Is Gray (or his narrator) really saying that unless older men seduce younger men, collapsing the distinction between lovers and surrogate sons (*making* them gay?), that homosexuality will die out?

The idea that gay men need to seduce younger men to swell the homosexual ranks plays right into the hands of reactionary and repressive forces that are trying to 'stop the spread' of homosexuality, as if it were directly transmissible through sex, like AIDS. Gray perhaps forgets that homosexuals are conceived in a heterosexual act.

5

Koos Prinsloo has published three collections of short fiction: *Jonkmanskas* (1982), *Die Hemel Help Ons* (1987) and *Slagplaas* (1992)[11]. His texts are extraordinarily resistant to interpretation, perhaps because they are already in a state of self-conscious deconstruction. Yet his prose is simple and direct. This is but one of the paradoxes in his work.

A pervasive concern of Prinsloo's has to do with textuality itself. Many of his stories contain the image of someone writing a story, a story which usually remains incomplete, though it gets incorporated into the larger text. Here Prinsloo is drawing attention to the scriptive deed, as well as dramatising (exposing) the incomplete, always deferring, nature of meaning. As Gerrit Olivier notes, Prinsloo's fiction 'rests on a conviction that has more to do with language than with the psyche of the author — the conviction that the subject is constructed by the texts he produces or quotes':

> *... There is no 'I' on which one can get a grip outside of the discourses within which he finds himself; there is no 'I' that can be placed sufficiently in control of his own existence* in language *to make of it an ordered 'story' with a beginning, middle and end; and there is no privileged discourse that can 'rule' over other discourses. The story is just one text among other texts.*[12]

In many of Prinsloo's texts there is a clash of fictional and factual discourse. In the story 'Die Hemel Help Ons' (Heaven Help Us), for instance, a man is trying to write a story about the relationship of two men on a word processor he has recently bought. But his lovers' discourse is invaded by State of Emergency unrest reports, chilling catalogues of death and social upheaval in bland Bureau of Information style. Descriptions of torture in police cells also interrupt the dual story.

The language of oppression infiltrates the personal language of love by mysterious means and seeks to engulf it; it enacts the modalities of repression. Clearly, though, repression can never fully succeed: it must interject, ventriloquise. But the implication is also that the private discourse of desire and relationships will never be left entirely in peace either.

In 'And Our Fathers that Begat Us', in *Die Hemel Help Ons*, the central character (referred to initially as 'the man' but later slipping into a partly concealed 'I') visits his parents' farm. The story is intermitted by quotes from letters written by Prinsloo grandparents and from his father. The lines between the autobiographical and the fictive are blurred; neither constitutes itself strongly enough to dominate. In the light of the works' tendency to question their own authenticity, as outlined above, it is impossible to prefer one text over another, or to place 'truth' above 'fiction'.

On the thematic level, 'And Our Fathers that Begat Us' constructs an opposition between father and son; the father's letter, which interrupts the story the son is trying to write about his father (and ends the text called 'And Our Fathers that

Begat Us'), deals with the father's puzzlement at some revelation of his son's, possibly of a sexual nature. Olivier sees the son as rejecting the heritage of the 'masculine' man, the '... ruler over man and beast, as inherited model'. There may also, however, be a tenuous rapprochement between them.

In 'A Night at the Opera', Prinsloo sets up stylistic oppositions like quotation/invention (juxtaposing fictional narrative and opera programme notes) and English/Afrikaans (switching between the two), though these binaries, like others mentioned above, are never resolved into dominant and subordinate terms. The story depicts a panoply of relationships gone awry: that of Renata and Johann, a couple going to the opera (*Tristan und Isolde*); that of Renata and Oscar, who approaches her at the opera; that of the '*ek*' ('I'), who suddenly appears, revealing that he had broken up with Oscar some time before, and Oscar; that of the 'ek' and the man he picks up in Sea Point in the story he writes for Oscar. The overarching model is Tristan and Isolde, who are supposed to represent, in Wagner's words, the real bliss of love — though it is a tragic love that achieves transcendence only in death.

The story that the first-person narrator writes to Oscar tells of a pick-up at a cruising-spot in Sea Point. He does not post the letter, but sends the story to a literary magazine. It is returned with the comment that it is a bit pointless, so the narrator changes the ending to one which is perhaps equally pointless.

Thus Prinsloo subverts the conventions of closure we expect from fiction; even the story-within-the-story is ambivalent and open-ended or at least double-ended. In his deadpan way, Prinsloo is refusing to erect a hierarchy of meaning that will allow the reader to come to firm conclusions (or the critic to impose too orderly a schema of meaning). It is impossible to tag his work 'gay' or even 'political', although homosexual desire is represented frequently both in a straightforwardly narrative way and symbolically and the texts have a sharp political (in the broadest sense) awareness.

In 'Die Wond' (The Wound), in *Slagplaas*, Prinsloo tells of a man's visit to his sister and brother-in-law. The latter is a policeman who is violent towards his prisoners and employees as well as to his pregnant wife. The sister is wounded by her husband's violence, but she is also wounded by some revelation about her brother. The presence of a censorious mother hovers in the background. Later, with one word, the man is revealed to be gay: he longs to be lying in bed with a '*minnaar*' (meaning lover, but the word is in the masculine form). Is this connected to the damning revelation of which his sister knows? And is this perhaps *his* 'wound'?

If homosexual desire is still transgressive for Prinsloo, he does not seek to recentre or naturalise it like Gray does. It remains marginal, though it can assume symbolic centrality. But then Prinsloo's narrative strategy is dedicated to undermining the very assumptions that would assign marginality or centrality. Prinsloo does not contest the category as such, but subverts the discursive basis on which it is built. Homosexual desire in Prinsloo's work does not have to defend itself or assert itself; it is both natural and transgressive, one text among others.

243

Is it then unsure of its own existence? Perhaps; but it is aware that it takes place in the slippage between the political and the personal. Like the multiplicit 'I' of his stories, it stages itself in the gap between and in the overlap of texts; it is not produced by one final, whole (necessarily repressive) discourse, but in the interstices of language.

* * *

My aim, in presenting a succession of texts that represent homosexual desire, is not to valorise the self-deconstructive text as the culmination of a tradition. The terrain across which the ideological battle is spread is very wide, and strategies adapt themselves to the circumstances.

Yet we see how several writers have chosen to deal with the representation of homosexual desire in literary form, to write out and to write out *of* their own sexual marginality. Notwithstanding the divergences of approach, all of them are positioned in (they read and are read by) a society in which homosexual desire, just in its existence, but also in its enactment and its manifestation, is transgressive.

These texts are situated under the sign of taboo even as they resist it, and they accept and reject that stigmatisation in a variety of ways. For as long as sexual difference is a site of oppression, texts like these may contest, elide or destabilise the transgression with which they deal, but they can never entirely transcend it.

Notes

1 ID du Plessis, *Mens en Ster: Verse 1925-78* (Tafelberg, 1980).
2 DJ Opperman, *Digters van Dertig* (Nasou, 1952).
3 ID du Plessis, *Aantekeninge uit Tuynstraat: Herrinneringe en Beskouings* (Tafelberg, 1975).
4 William Plomer, *Selected Stories* Stephen Gray (ed) (David Philip/Africasouth, 1984).
5 Peter Alexander, *William Plomer: A Biography* (Oxford University Press, 1989).
6 Damon Galgut, *A Sinless Season* (Jonathan Ball, 1982).
7 Damon Galgut, *The Beautiful Screaming of Pigs* (Scribners, 1991).
8 Jane Rosenthal, 'An Extended Cry Against Male Mythology' (interview with Damon Galgut), *The Weekly Mail*, 14-20 August 1992, p34.
9 Stephen Gray, *Time of Our Darkness* (Arrow, 1988); *Born of Man* (Justified, 1989).
10 Stephen Gray, "An Author's Agenda: Revisioning Past and Present for a Future South Africa", in Kirsten Holst Petersen and Anna Rutherford, eds, *On Shifting Sands: New Art and Literature from South Africa* (Dangaroo, 1991), p. 26.
11 Koos Prinsloo, *Jonkmanskas* (Tafelberg, 1982); *Die Hemel Help Ons* (Taurus, 1987); *Slagplaas* (Human & Rousseau, 1992).
12 Gerrit Olivier, 'Die Verval van die Storie', *Vrye Weekblad Boeke*, Spring 1989, p7.

Further reading

Representations of homosexual desire have occurred in South African literature with greater frequency than one might suppose, as Hennie Aucamp's anthology of Afrikaans writing, *Wisselstroom* (1990), demonstrates. In it a variety of responses to homosexuality or homosexual acts is displayed in the works of both gay and straight writers. Aucamp's own work, most importantly his short stories, contains many instances of finely nuanced treatments of homosexuality in guises that range from closet cases to drag queens. (See 'Sop vir die Siekte', 1967; 'Steven en Fay', 1970; 'Georgie', 1970; 'Die Res is Swye', 1972;

'Die Goue Vlies', 1976; 'Tussen Bedrywe', 1978; 'La Divina en die Cowboy', 1981; 'Vir Vier Stemme', 1981.)

Among other work in Afrikaans that treats homosexual desire as theme is ID du Plessis' short story *Die Redder* (1946), Johannes Meintjies' stories *Dis Wonderlik Hier* and *Vervulling* (1947), Marlise Joubert's novel *Klipkus* (1978), Jan van Tonder's *Witvis* (1983), Wim Vorster's *Kruisvaart* (1984) and Marzanne Leroux-Van der Boon's *Klaprose teen die Wind* (1992).

Also worth consideration are Emma Huismans' collection of short stories *Berigte van Weerstand* (1990) and her novel *Requiem op Ys* (1992), Johann de Lange's poetry (*Wordende Naak*, 1990, and *Nagsweet*, 1991, are his two most recent collections), and Joan Hambidge's poetry (*Die Verlore Simbool*, 1991).

Other recent developments in gay literature as it increasingly becomes a category of its own — whether to its detriment or benefit — include an anthology published by the Congress of South African Writers (COSAW), *The Invisible Ghetto* (1993), edited by Matthew Krouse with Kim Berman. It contains fiction, poetry and oral-historical testimony as well as a reconsideration of the (occluded) presence of homosexual themes in the work of Richard Rive. COSAW has been, since its founding in 1987, a major disseminator of the literature of resistance in South Africa. It is significant, thus, that gay writing has come into COSAW's ambit: this represents the growing consciousness of a gay rights movement, and the extension of gay politics into the realm of concerted resistance to oppression.

FIVE —

Making waves: Lesbian and gay activism

Wardrobes: *Coming out as a black gay activist in South Africa*

Simon Nkoli

Editors' note: **Simon Nkoli is perhaps South Africa's most well-known gay activist. From a background of radical student politics, he moved into gay activism in the early 1980s. His work, however, was interrupted in September 1984 when he was jailed for his involvement in a rent boycott demonstration in his home township, Sebokeng. He spent four years in prison and was charged with murder and treason, alongside 21 others, in the Delmas trial of 1986.[1] After his acquittal, he founded the Gay And Lesbian Organisation of the Witwatersrand (GLOW). Here, in a series of interviews with Mark Gevisser, he recounts his two most difficult 'comings out'.**

* * *

One of my strongest childhood memories is of locking my parents in the wardrobe. They were illegal squatters in the Vaal township of Sebokeng, and, when we heard the policemen's knock, they bundled themselves into the big wardrobe in the bedroom and told me to lock them in and hide the keys before opening the door. I told the police my parents were not at home, and they left. I was nine years old at the time.

Ten years later I came out of my own closet when I met a man, fell in love with him, and told my parents. Ever since then, I seem to have been coming out of closets all the time. In the Congress of South African Students (COSAS), where my homosexuality nearly lost me my position as Transvaal Regional Secretary. At the Delmas Treason Trial, where my co-accused at first did not want to be tried with me. And now, every time I speak publicly about the need for lesbian and gay rights or AIDS education in South Africa.

In so many ways, the closet I have come out of is similar to the wardrobe my relieved parents stepped out of when I unlocked them after the police left. If you are black in South Africa, the inhuman laws of apartheid closet you. If you are gay in South Africa, the homophobic customs and laws of this society closet you. If you are black and gay in South Africa, well, then it really is all the same closet, the same wardrobe. Inside is darkness and oppression. Outside is freedom. It is as simple as that.

Sangomas and psychologists

I was brought up by my mother and stepfather. My stepfather only went up to Standard 6, and then went to cooking school. When I was growing up he was a chef at a hotel in Vanderbijlpark. My mother only went up to Standard 4; first she was a domestic worker and then, through a Portuguese woman, she got a better job at the fruit market. She went to nightschool and passed Standards 6 and 7, and eventually got a job as a saleswoman at Edgars.

When my parents organised a 20th birthday party for me, my mother said, 'Simon you've never brought a girl home. Your brother's got a girlfriend and you always come alone. What's happening?'

At this point I was involved with André, a white man, my first love. He had written to *Hit* magazine requesting black penfriends. I had responded, and an affair had developed — first by mail, then on a trip to Durban. He had brought me back to Sebokeng from Durban in his father's Mercedes, and when I entered the house, covered in the gifts he had showered upon me, my mother was upset: 'You've got your own family,' she said, 'Why are taking things from a white man?'

Now, a few months later, in response to her question about girlfriends, it was time to tell her who André really was. She hit the roof:

> *I can't believe it's happening to me. What have I done to deserve this? What is my sin? My God is punishing me. First you were involved in politics and you got harassed and I got a bad name, the neighbours saw police and you lived like a criminal. Now things are clearing up and you bring this thing! What will I tell the neighbours? What will I tell your grandpapa? How will I explain to your uncle?*

My stepfather tried to support me, telling my mother that at his hotel there were many men like me — businessmen, doctors, everyone. But my mother's response was to turn on him too: 'This means you're also one of them! Tell me! Every time Simon went to sleep in your hotel, you did things!'

My stepfather and I were very close. He'd be the person to take me to movies and he helped me a lot with my English when I stayed over with him at the hotel. But now I was forbidden to even run an errand to him in town. Because he had never laid a hand on me, that became further proof for my mother there was something between us and that he was not a real man. They nearly divorced over this thing. When bedtime came my mother would say, 'I don't want to go to sleep with another woman.'

Once my mother cooled off, she decided that I needed to be cured. And so began my year-long tour of the *sangomas* [traditional healers] of Sebokeng. My mother is a Christian, but, like many African families, we took out the double insurance of using *sangomas* along with our Christianity. Every time the children wrote external examinations, for example, they would need to get blessed to pass: the *sangoma* would arrive with a steaming basin of foul-smelling things for us to inhale. I hated it and only did it once.

Now, my mother took me to a woman. She put her bones down and said, 'Hmmm. Dangerous.' I laughed. I remember how I laughed. She said, 'Your child is bewitched.'

I said 'No, I don't think so'.

The *sangoma* asked my mother to keep me quiet 'because he is disturbing my bones.' She said, 'The woman who bewitched him …'

'Woman!' my mother screamed.

'Mammie, no!' I tried to interrupt. 'Now you're going to suspect all the women in the location!'

When my mother said she wanted more details, the *sangoma* demanded more money to name names. An extra R10 bought my mother the name of her neighbour — who also happened to be a *sangoma*, a rival *sangoma*. I said, 'Don't you say that, because maybe you want my mother to put the blame on another *sangoma*.'

The *sangoma* became very angry. 'See how he speaks,' she said. 'It's the *tokolosh* [evil spirit]. It's not him. He's bewitched.'

When we arrived home, both my mother and I were shocked to discover that the neighbour already knew exactly where we had been. She said she had heard about our visit to her rival in her dreams and told us, 'That woman and I are fighting. I didn't bewitch your child. Your child is a gay person. He is. And there's nothing you can do about it.' She was a very good *sangoma*. 'Even psychologists and doctors can't change it,' she said. 'I've dealt with these cases. A person is not sick.'

The neighbour suggested to my mother that she take me to another *sangoma* for a second opinion. So off we went, to a man this time. He jumped around and did frightening things. I thought he was going to kick me. He threw his bones. 'I don't see any problem,' he said. 'You've got a very intelligent son. He's not sick. Nothing. I can't take any money from you. Try another one.'

And so off to a third one, who repeated, like the first one, that I was bewitched. But this time it was my aunt who had done it. I said, 'Now you believe that your own sister who is not even a *sangoma*, who is a church member, would do this! Now will you start hating your own sister because of this *sangoma*?'

My mother was clearly in crisis. I said, 'Go to another one, someone else will have bewitched me! All that these people want is money, so they're telling you what they think you want to hear!'

We did go to another one, a fourth one, who said, 'The child has got a big problem. The person who bewitched him is dead.' She counselled my mother to slaughter a sheep and four chickens, and to feed me the blood of the chickens.'

I said, 'That'll be the day! I'll be gay whether I drink that blood or not, so I'm not going to do it.' So my mother asked the *sangoma* for an alternative.

They told me to go out, and my mother came out very angry. 'She told me to boil eggs with aloe vera and bluegum and your sister's urine and give it you!' she said. 'I give up on this!'

So that was it with the *sangomas*, but there was still the church to deal with. The minister just cut me out completely. At first he tried to counsel me. He showed me Leviticus 18:22. He told me about abomination. He blamed André, white and older than me, for leading me into temptation. I believed him even less than the *sangomas*.

Then, in the middle of this crisis, André's mother began phoning my mother. After much screaming between the women, in which each one blamed the other's son for corrupting her own, André's mother said she had met a very good psychologist who would help, and offered to pay for both André and me to see him. My mother was impressed with her concern. At this point, I think she was willing to try anything.

And so off André and I went, every Wednesday. The psychologist did these tests, made me look at things, did concentration exercises, showed me pictures. I was depressed — not because of being gay but because I was being taken up and down and made to see all these people. The psychologist was very good. He had a good smile. He would show me a picture of a pair of trousers and one of a dress and ask me which I liked. I said, 'I am a man. I like the trouser.'

After all these tests he said, 'Simon you're a 100% gay man and you must learn to accept it.'

I was skeptical: 'Are you telling me you can't do anything?'

'As a psychologist', he replied, 'I am here to help you discover yourself, to accept yourself. I'm not going to take your parents' money and say I can cure you.'

We saw him for four months, until November, when he said 'I'm finished with you. I can see the two of you dearly love each other — why don't you move in together?' It was still 1980, so it would be difficult, but he suggested that we get our own flats, and that I enter André's building by pretending to be his servant.

Then he opened a bottle of champagne, to celebrate our relationship. And he told us that he too was gay! I told my mother, 'Mammie, do you know that the psychologist is gay too!' My mother said, 'Then I've failed. If that educated man is gay it seems like everyone's gay!' My stepfather was really laughing. He said, 'I told you so!'

This was already a year after I first came out, and my mother was much better. She got support. She had told my uncles and aunts, and while some rejected her, most supported her and told her there was nothing she could do. Some people said if she didn't support me I'd kill myself, and that they had met other mothers whose children had committed suicide because they were gay. And she didn't want to lose me.

My relationship with my mother was very good when I was a child. She was very proud of me, the first born and a good scholar. She's still proud of me now. We have a very close relationship. My mother's reaction showed concern. She didn't want to reject me. She wanted to rectify things. She blamed herself. She thought maybe she had spoiled me. She blamed my stepfather. She blamed my biological father. But in the end, I was lucky she was concerned. I've counselled lots of people whose parents weren't as concerned as she, whose parents just threw their clothes into the street or turfed them out of the house. My mother, at least, tried to help me, in the ways that she knew how.

Coming out to comrades:
COSAS and the Delmas Treason Trial

In 1984, I was no longer living in Sebokeng, but because I was the sole breadwinner of my family's household, I went down there often, and I became involved with the Vaal Civic Association.

I spoke often at meetings, and of course when the stayaway of the 3rd of September was announced, I went along. Many people died in the clash between the police and the community, and, at the funeral on 23 September I was arrested. I was kept in detention for 16 months until, in January 1986, I was brought to trial along with 21 others in the famous Delmas Treason Trial.

This was my second detention: in the 1976 uprising, aged 15, I had been a student leader and was detained for three months after the high school I attended was burned and looted. Since then, I had been very active in COSAS, and by 1981 I was the organisation's regional secretary for the Transvaal.

My homosexuality became an issue within COSAS. Because of the continual pressure to bring girlfriends to parties, I had come out in 1981, and the regional executive felt so strongly about it that they called a general meeting. The entire region met to discuss my sexuality and whether the fact that I was gay meant I should stand down as their secretary. The arguments against me were that homosexuality was not African; that we cannot accept to be led by a gay person; and that I had been dishonest by hiding this vital information. Luckily, however, the arguments for me won out, and I managed to get the 80% I needed to remain as secretary.

Coming out had affected my work in COSAS. Sometimes I would be reluctant to put forward suggestions because I felt I wouldn't be taken seriously. Some people mocked me. That year, for example, there was a white man who raped two boys in Hillbrow. People used to tease me about this and say, 'Look what you people are doing'.

In many ways I was lucky. I had support, from my friends within COSAS and also, by now, from my mother. But my experiences had left me worried and I knew, now that I was one of 22 accused of high treason, along with such high-profile figures as Terror Lekota and Popo Molefe,[2] that I would have to face the issue again — if not from my co-accused, then at the very least from the state, which was bound to bring it up in the courtroom.

I had good reason to fear this. During my initial interrogation, the homosexuality issue was frequently raised. The police kept on saying, 'You say you're fighting for the people. But you're a moffie. Do you really think the ANC and SACP would be mad enough to take a moffie on?' They'd bring in things like a baton and tell me to go fuck myself with it. They also said they'd put me in prison with others and get me raped.

Then, during further torture and interrogation at John Vorster Square, one policeman, who had seen snaps of white men in my photo album, became particularly angry. 'Why do you like fucking white men?' he asked. 'What have they done to you? Why don't you have sex with your own people?'

I knew I had to raise the issue with my co-accused before the trial, and I and my closest friends had been strategising a way to handle it. And then, in Pretoria Central Prison while we were awaiting trial, something happened, entirely beyond my control, that brought the whole thing to a head. One of the accused was found to be having a relationship with a convicted prisoner.

Suspicions began when this guy started asking for cigarettes and tobacco even though he did not smoke. And then the prison warder in charge of us, a black man, found a love-letter written in this guy's handwriting to the convict. A white prison warder also seemed to be involved with the two of them. And so the leaders of the accused, Terror Lekota and Moss Chikane, were called in and given the letter. 'Look at your people,' they were told.

We were all called into Cell 47, the biggest one, for an urgent meeting, told only that something terrible had just happened. Since I like meetings I was the first one there — I wanted the best seat. I could see Terror was furious. I couldn't hear him very well; all I heard was, '... that's why I don't want to be arrested with homosexuals.' I started looking around and thinking, 'God what have I done?'

Everyone was in. Only those who knew me looked at me, but I was puzzled. Terror said, 'Comrades, I've got this loveletter. It's disgusting,' and he named the guy who wrote it. People started hammering the writer, who replied that it was a mistake and would never happen again. He said he had been harassed by the convict, and that all he needed was forgiveness.

I was taken over by rage, and the next thing I knew I heard my own voice, interrupting, 'What about me?' Terror was dumbstruck: he had only ever had political discussions with me. The older men didn't understand. Popo Molefe was aware there was going to be tension, and so he tried to prevent me from bringing in another issue.

But then others started interjecting. One guy said, 'We should have our own trial. I'm not going to stand accused with a homosexual man. All of us here have girlfriends, wives, supporters from overseas. What will they think when we have a homosexual man with us?'

I stood up and said, 'I think I should leave this meeting now. This is including me as well. Here you're not talking about the person who committed this act. You're actually talking about homosexual men and I am one.'

Everybody's jaw dropped. The old priest, Father Moselane, was particularly shocked. 'I cannot believe it,' he said. 'You and I addressed the meeting together. And when you spoke you spoke like a man, even though you've got a small voice. You look like a man. Don't tell me you do these things.'

I said: 'I'm telling you who you don't want to go to the trial with and that's me. It'll be fine. My trial will be much shorter if I'm alone. That person has apologised, so accept him and forgive him and forget it. What I do I will continue to do.' I was very angry. Everyone was quiet.

My friend Gcina Malindi intervened: 'Simon is angry and emotional. We have to take his case as well.'

Terror was at a loss. I don't know if he knew I was gay, but he said, 'There it goes.'

I said, 'So far we have one confessed homosexual and one heterosexual person, who had an affair.' Then I was accused of dishonesty: if this incident had not happened, would I have come out at all, they wanted to know?

For weeks, this homosexuality thing dominated. Daily meetings were held on the issue. First they did not want to be tried with homosexuals. Then they did not want me on the witness stand. All because of the possible problems public disclosure of my homosexuality might cause. I felt I had to testify because of my indictment. The primary charge against me was murder: I was alleged to have thrown a big rock. I was adamant that I had to take the witness stand to defend myself, as I was innocent.

Even the lawyers were consulted on the issue and the two senior queer lawyers of the progressive legal fraternity were brought in to talk to us! All the lawyers supported me, and said that they would pull out if there were two trials. Their attitude was that people were not being charged because of their sexuality. Most supportive, in fact, was George Bizos, the advocate who was to lead my defence. When I was depressed and everyone was confused about my being homosexual, George would call me outside and tell me to be brave. He said that if the state brought the issue up he would object. I was closer to him than any other advocate.

Perhaps what helped me most was that I received so many letters. Everyone was writing to me, from anti-apartheid organisations and gay organisations the world over. I got much support from the anti-apartheid movements in Britain and Holland — I think that in Europe, I was the focus of attention in the trial, especially because of my homosexuality. In December 1986, for example, I got more than 150 Christmas cards from gay individuals, organisations and friends. And so I would say to the others, 'Look people won't be against us. Look how much support I'm getting.'

Over time attitudes did change. Some people didn't come to my cell anymore. Others came to ask questions. Some were really concerned. The old priest finally came to speak to me about whether he could help me. The person who seemed most affected was my friend Jake. We had been together since the beginning of our detention and we were very close. I'd eat with him, read with him, go to medicals together with him. I had just assumed that he knew about me — my cell, after all, was full of men's posters and clippings from gay papers, and I had even once told him about my relationship with my lover. I don't know if he was hearing selectively or what, but he was really shocked.

But after the revelation, he would came to visit me even more often, and became very supportive, saying that I was being treated very unfairly. When we were out on bail, I continued seeing him, and I'd often stay over at his flat. People thought we were sleeping with each other, and the rumours upset me. But Jake only said, 'So what?' That was the only time there was any insinuation about my friends.

Popo Molefe was always supportive. And, as time went by, Moss Chikane too became very supportive. Once, I remember, there was a press clipping about Elton John having been arrested with little boys. A prison warder came in and said, 'I like Elton John.' And Father Moselane said, 'Why do you like him?'

Warder: 'He's got good music.'

Moselane: 'But he sleeps with boys. That's an abomination. God made man and woman, not man and man!'

I screamed from my bed, 'Father, you're saying these things because you know I'm here. I don't sleep with young boys. I sleep with a person like you if I want!' He was so insulted.

At this point Moss Chikane intervened: 'Father you started this. Since last year Simon has told us he is gay. Why are you preaching about God now?' Tom Manthatha also silenced him. Tom liked me so much, he used to say I was like a son to him.

And at the end of the whole thing, when we were all about to go to the witness box, there was no one against me. When I was in witness box, everyone, including Terror, made a point of telling me how well I was doing! Terror had been the most shocked in the beginning, but by now things are much better. We're good friends, and his attitude has changed.

The irony was that the prosecutor didn't even bring the issue up. I did. I needed to prove that I wasn't at a meeting, and so I told the truth, which was that at that time I had been at a GASA (Gay Association of South Africa) event. Only then did the prosecutor start up on my homosexuality, but the judge angrily intervened, saying that he was not interested about who was gay and who was not, and that the prosecutor's line of questioning did not prove whether I had conspired. I was finally acquitted, in no small part, I think, due to my gay alibi!

I'm sure that my continued involvement with the African National Congress after my acquittal has helped to gain credibility for gay rights within the liberation movement, and it has also helped many other gay and lesbian people within the liberation movement in their coming out. It's difficult for me to tell exactly what the relationship is between my anti-apartheid activism and my gay activism, but there are two things I know for sure. The first is that my baptism in the struggles of the township helped me understand the need for a militant gay rights movement. The second is that this country will never protect the rights of its gay and lesbian citizens unless we stand up and fight — even when it makes us unpopular with our own comrades.

Notes

1 The Delmas Treason Trial, in which prominent members of the United Democratic Front were charged with high treason, was the showpiece of PW Botha's State of Emergency repression, and one of the most significant political mobilising points for the mass democratic movement in the 1980s.

2 Lekota and Molefe were two of the ranking officials of the United Democratic Front: Molefe was Secretary-General and Lekota was National Publicity Secretary. Both now hold senior positions in the ANC. Other treason trialists referred to in this piece are: Moss Chikane, a senior UDF official from the South African Catholic Bishops' Conference; Father Geoff Moselane, an Anglican minister from Sharpeville; Tom Manthatha from the South African Council of Churches, and Gcina Malindi, a youth activist from the Vaal region who grew up with Nkoli.

Ivan Toms is a fairy?:

The South African Defence Force, the End Conscription Campaign, and me

Ivan Toms

The first volleys in the disinformation campaign against me and the End Conscription Campaign (ECC) were amateur enough. Yellow posters saying 'Ivan Toms is a fairy?', part of a batch of homophobic posters with declarations like 'ECC does it from behind' and 'The ECC believes in fairy tales'.

Then the graffiti. 'Ivan Toms fucks young boys' in the University of Cape Town subway; 'Toms is a moffie pig' spray-painted on my house and car. Other slogans sprayed on walls in Mowbray and Observatory included 'Toms does it rectally', 'ECC Homo perverts' and, rather bluntly, 'Hang Toms'. And later, the more sophisticated artwork on street poles throughout Cape Town: 'Toms AIDS test positive' and 'Ivan Toms dumped by lover Graham Perlman'. Along with these were the usual death threats, the advertising of my car for sale at a ridiculously low price, the delivery of a load of pig manure, and black condoms sent with obscene messages that linked anti-gay and anti-black prejudice.

The hate-campaign started in 1983, and continued until 1988, when I was finally tried and sentenced to 18-months imprisonment for refusing to complete my military service. My stand was a high-profile one, as I was the first person to challenge publicly the harsh new amendments to the Defence Act. To the South African Defence Force (SADF), it seemed obvious to use the fact that I was gay to discredit me. Surely I would lose popular support if, while claiming to be a Christian, I was also openly gay? And aren't all moffies cowards anyway? And so, for five years, the 'dirty tricks' department of the SADF, stationed in the Castle at Cape Town, tried to smear me.

I had already done some time in the army: after completing my medical degree in 1976 I had been conscripted for two years, six months of which I had spent as a lieutenant in the Medical Corps on the 'border' in Namibia. But I had not done the obligatory camps that all national servicemen are required to complete: instead of responding to my near-annual call-ups, I had worked for seven years as a doctor in the Crossroads squatter camp on the Cape Flats.

Working in the squatter camp, I witnessed first-hand the brutal inhumanity of apartheid. Oppression can often be ignored, but I felt that in some small way I could understand what discrimination was all about, perhaps because as a gay man I had experienced it myself.

Not continuously, though: like many gay men I could 'play straight' and tow the heterosexual line when it was too difficult to stand up and be counted as gay. And my experience of discrimination was not nearly as brutal as that of my patients in Crossroads. What I had felt was the fear of being gay-bashed for walking hand in hand with my lover along a Pringle Bay road. The absolute amazement, the staring, the anger and rejection. Patriarchal society excluding and condemning me, not because of the colour of my skin, but for the love I felt for someone of the same sex. The sense of being rejected simply for being the very person God had created.

So, within me, as my work in the squatter camps and my growing gay consciousness deepened my understanding of oppression, a new fight developed. The reality of apartheid meant that I could never again put on that SADF lieutenant's uniform hanging in the back of my cupboard. By 1984 the 'border' was no longer thousands of kilometres away, but right on my doorstep: Langa, Guguletu, Crossroads; the townships of Cape Town in which the army was now deployed. I decided I would go to jail rather than serve.

Between 1984 and 1988, the SADF would call me up and then back off days before the camp was to begin: I was, after all, the only doctor in Crossroads. But it would not stand down on my July 1987 callup: I was charged in contravention of Section 126A(1)(a) of Defence Act 33 of 1957, and the prosecution was calling, according to its interpretation of the law, for a mandatory sentence of one and a half times my outstanding time, which would mean 21 months in jail.

My decision to object and stand trial was most certainly informed by my growing gay consciousness. Ultimately, objection to military service is a deeply personal issue: one person standing up for the principles he or she believes in. And as being gay had truly been part of the formative growth on the road to refusing to serve in the SADF, I wanted to stand as a positive role model for gays and lesbians — to show that gays were just as brave and principled as the many straights who had refused to serve.

But, interestingly enough, it was not only the SADF that was troubled by my open homosexuality. In the End Conscription Campaign, which was funding and organising my defence, the issue provoked heated debate. I had initially wanted to refer, in my statement of reasons for refusing to serve in the SADF, to my experiences of oppression as a gay person. The ECC felt, however, that any espousal of gay rights would detract from its primary function — to oppose conscription — and my coming out might in fact work against the broad-based coalition that had been formed around the single issue of challenging white conscription and thus challenging the apartheid war.

The ECC was indeed a particularly effective and powerful organisation in the fight against apartheid, perhaps because every white family was affected by the conscription of sons, husbands, lovers or friends. The ECC was a one-issue campaign that was able to mobilise large sections of the white community who were against conscription, no matter what else they believed.

To this end, the ECC used innovative and creative ways to draw in ordinary people. Peace festivals, fasts for a just peace, sand-castle building, fairs, 'Rock Against The Raatel' concerts, all helped build an effective organisation offering a wide range of people the space to challenge what they believed to be wrong. This rather trendy way of involving ordinary people meant that ECC was able to appeal to many groups that traditionally steered clear of anti-apartheid politics. And gay men too found in the ECC a place where they could work creatively to challenge an unjust system.

On the surface these gay men were fully accepted, and at least three high profile activists in the Cape Town branch were openly gay. But this acceptance and openness hid the much more subtle fears and ambivalent homophobia that is often to be seen on the left. In the heated debates on the subject between the ECC and the Organisation of Lesbian and Gay Activists (OLGA), of which I was an active member, the issue was always clothed in terms of what would most powerfully push the anti-conscription message. Interestingly, the most vociferous opposition to the inclusion of my gayness in my reasons for objecting came from other gay men within the ECC.

Retrospectively, I can explain this reticence as self-oppression. But, to be truthful, I myself was ambivalent at the time about pushing both messages. I found myself in the unusual position of being externally out of the closet, yet still struggling internally with the long battle to see myself positively as a gay person. I had let my closet be kicked open, yet part of me was still desperately trying to stay inside.

And all along the way I did secretly feel I was not being true to myself. I had to cope with the continual pressure of 'What if someone brings up the gay issue?' during my frequent public platform appearances throughout the country. I had raised it in small groups and with the different organisations that made up the ECC — but never stated it publicly during the campaign. If they had known that I was gay would they have supported me in the same way? This question plagued me after each public appearance. As I saw it, the public was creating and strengthening a myth — a straight Ivan Toms.

I never at any stage tried to claim that I was straight. What ECC wanted — and got — was that I did not actively raise the fact that I was gay; I did not talk about how being gay had developed my understanding of oppression and political issues in South Africa.

I was able to raise this issue in interviews for French television and in an interview for a video that was distributed by the Committee of South African War

Resisters. And I was able to deal with being gay on occasion in discussions with university students and women's groups. But, due to my agreement with the ECC, I was unable to raise the issue proactively with the general South African public.

Retrospectively, I can only but speculate about how the campaign might have differed had I been open and public about my homosexuality. What I do know, however, is that our attempt to hide my sexuality made no difference in the end. The prosecution was intent on using it in an attempt to undermine my moral and ethical standing, and chose to highlight the fact that I had *not* brought it up myself.

Citing a newspaper report on a discussion I had had about lesbian and gay rights with two leaders of the exiled African National Congress in Harare, the Prosecutor took me to task for avoiding mention of my gay activism in the trial. Why, he wanted to know, had I not mentioned my involvement with OLGA in my evidence, when I had been so forthcoming about all the other organisations I had participated in?

I answered simply by stating that 'OLGA was working towards a non-racial, non-sexist, democratic, non-heterosexist democratic South Africa' and that its mission was 'to support lesbian and gay activists who were working in the struggle in South Africa and to raise the issue of lesbian and gay rights within the broader democratic movement.'

But the prosecutor would not let it drop, and attempted to offset my gay activism — which he had now triumphantly proved — with my avowed Christianity: 'Did you also enjoy the full support of your church?' When I answered that I 'received the support of my parish priest and of the majority of the staff,' he pressed on: 'How would you anticipate the synod of the Church of the Province of Southern African [Anglican] would have reacted?' I replied: 'I know of many bishops who would be supportive of my involvement and many priests, but I would not like to know what the vote at a synod [would be].' It was difficult terrain for me: despite the support my own parish and a few senior clergymen had given me, the church, on the whole, remains a bulwark of homophobia in this society.

Nevertheless, by raising the issue of the church's attitude towards my homosexuality, the prosecution gave my own counsel, Edwin Cameron, the opportunity to flesh out the church's position on gay issues and to develop clear support for my stand on lesbian and gay rights.

Cameron asked Anglican Bishop David Russell, for example, what the church's attitude would be to my stance on gay rights. Bishop Russell responded by indicating that the Church was grappling with these issues and said: 'In my opinion the fact is there would be general sympathy concerning the right of gays and lesbians to seek re-thinking and re-understanding on these matters.' Similarly, Rev John Freeth, my parish priest, said:

> *I personally would hope very deeply that members of the Christian church following the example of Christ would be committed to seeking to bring about change in whatever area was appropriate and possible for them in our society, provided that*

change is moving towards truth, moving towards greater justice, greater fairness for all ... towards wholeness. I encourage and support him in those lesbian and gay organisations.

In his closing arguments, Cameron told the court that he believed my involvement in gay organisations to have 'no relevance to the issues of this trial', and that he had advised me that 'it was not relevant to this Court to discuss those issues.' And interestingly, not even the Afrikaans newspapers covering the trial raised the gay issue in their reports. It was irrelevant to the key issue of my moral and ethical reasons for refusing to serve in the SADF. Even the magistrate ignored the gay red herring and went on to say:

You are not a criminal. Our jails are there for people who are a menace to society — you are not a menace to society. In fact you are just the opposite, you have always been an asset to society in the services you have rendered.

He nevertheless sentenced me to 18-months imprisonment, because he read the law as saying he had no other option.

A small example of how the whole trial was received was the response of the policeman who sat in court throughout the proceedings and then took me to Pollsmoor Prison. He would not lock me up in the cells in the court, and went out of his way to get a car to take me to prison. There, he shook my hand and said he had been very impressed by all that he had heard — and regretted having to leave me in prison.

* * *

The long walk down to C Section of Pollsmoor Prison seemed to go on forever. Cold grey corridors ending with the grating sound of keys in the steel door of my cell. This was the start of my nine months in Pollsmoor Prison, and the first experience of that one sound that continues to haunt me — the ever-present locking and unlocking of grills, doors and gates.

Although most of my time in Pollsmoor was solitary and uneventful, one incident remains vivid in my memory. I had the frightening experience of being assaulted by a psychopath in the bathrooms of C Section. He was the most aggressive prisoner in the section — smashing up his cell and even the punishment cell, 'the bomb', where he was then sent. On a number of occasions warders had bashed him into submission and placed him in a straight jacket.

He had an insatiable sexual appetite that turned to men while in prison. After being beaten up by a gang of younger prisoners who he tried to molest, he turned on me, making repeated passes which I angrily ignored. And then, one day in the bathrooms, we were locked in together with two other prisoners and no warder in sight. He grabbed my arse while I was cleaning out the bath, saying something sexual. I pushed him away telling him to 'fuck off and leave me alone!' But again he came at me. Then all the tension that had been building up through the whole traumatic process of trial and imprisonment overcame me. I cracked — and punched him full in the face, knocking out two front teeth.

262

All hell broke loose! His eyes glazed over and he wrestled me to the ground, hitting me in the face and all over my body. He was like a wild animal; all I could do was cry for help and try to protect my face. The other two prisoners tried to drag him off me while screaming for the warder to open up the locked gate of the bathroom.

With blood all over my face from a bleeding cut below the eye, I was marched off to the head warder. I could hardly believe the aggression that had welled up in me: it was the first time in my life I had ever hit someone: an explosion of pent-up aggression at the homophobia and lack of freedom that had obviously been eating away at me throughout the four months I had been locked up.

Sitting for 22 hours a day alone in my cell I developed my thoughts on gay rights. I realised the shortcomings of the left: the fact that our supposedly sophisticated political insights did not necessarily extend to insights into sexual oppression. And I realised that in the left (be it ECC or the African National Congress), 'political correctness' and deep insight into the oppression of blacks did not necessarily mean an equal insight or commitment to rights for lesbians and gays.

I realised the extent to which homophobia existed, particularly amongst gays who have only partly come to terms with their sexual orientation. But I also realised, more fully than ever before, the difficulties of coming out. For lesbians or gays, coming out of the closet is not a once-and-for-all experience — a fling of the door and out we come in all our splendour! And public exposure does not necessarily speed things up — it remains a drawn out, exciting (and exacting) process of self-acceptance as well.

The more open we are, the less we have to hide and fear further exposure. It sounds so simple, and yet my experiences during the trial proved how complex it really is. Life, and particularly public life, involves an intricate balancing trick of being open about one's sexuality and being sensitive to the best use of opportunities. I'm not sure that I found the right balance — but maybe, finally, a balance was found in spite of me!

I was released on bail after nine months, pending my appeal. The appeal was successful: the Supreme Court found that the magistrate did not have to give a mandatory sentence, and that I thus did not need to serve any more time. So I was free. But the sounds that dominated those nine months of imprisonment still resonate — the growing din of steel cell doors being slammed shut and locked, of gates being mastered. Even now, four years following my release, I find myself unlocking doors within doors. Coming out is a long walk out of a cold, grey corridor.

Identity crossfire:
On being a black gay student activist

Hein Kleinbooi

My name is Kleinbooi, Hein Arthur Kleinbooi. Kleinbooi tells you that I am one of those people designated 'coloured'; that my ancestor was probably Khoisan, with a name unpronounceable to white tongues, enslaved and called 'little boy', Kleinbooi. Such has been the construction of slavery and apartheid. But digging up the seeds of my family's surname, planted in the days of Cape Colony slavery, says very little about the person, Hein, born at a time of great stirring three centuries later, born six years before the Soweto uprising of 1976.

I was later to become part of what was and still is called the struggle. I am a black South African and a gay male. My own personal struggle has been an endless fight to be just what I am, without painful self-loathing, and without racist gay white men or homophobic black comrades telling me that there is something wrong with me.

I enrolled in the University of Cape Town in 1989, choosing it because of its reputation as a 'liberal' campus with strong radical student tendencies; because of its tradition of fighting apartheid. But on campus my white gay comrades told me that the oppression they experienced as homosexuals was equivalent to the oppression I experienced as a black South African growing up on the poverty-stricken Cape Flats. And my black liberationist comrades told me, whenever I brought up the issue of gay rights, that I was 'hijacking the struggle'. Caught somewhere between these two misguided attitudes was my own identity, struggling to find its place.

I have painful memories of those days. University life was so different. I felt that there was nobody who understood me. Nor was anybody at home willing to listen to what I had to say about the place being 'strange'. For my family, the mere fact that I had made it to university meant that I could cope with anything. I spent most of my first semester at university trying to find out what was going on around me. UCT's culture, predominantly white and racist, was profoundly alienating, and university life was so much more impersonal, so much more anonymous and 'free'; in that sense radically different to the background I came from. The overcrowded conditions at home also meant that I had very little space or time for myself. It was only once I moved out of home that I could talk and think of myself as a UCT student; and that I could truly begin to unpack my various identities and look at the way they interacted with each other.

One of the first organisations I joined was the then BSS (Black Students' Society, which later became SANSCO). My reasons for joining were really just to be part of something that I could identify with in a new and alien environment. The country was still in the throes of the PW Botha dictatorship and the student movement formed a significant part of the struggle against the apartheid government. My own experiences in SANSCO were limited to participating in meetings and rallies; just being a member took care of a very significant part of my identity.

But by the end of my first year, I was coming to terms with another part of my identity, that of being gay. I remember my stunned disbelief when I read the words 'Gay And Lesbian Association' in the UCT student diary under the heading, 'Student clubs and societies'. I could not believe that such things were allowed at UCT; I also knew that the words triggered off something deep and mysterious inside me. I was curious and wanted to investigate, but did not do so for almost two years.

It was only towards the end of my second year on campus that I took the first tentative steps. By this time the Gay and Lesbian Association (GALA) had brought out several posters and a magazine called *Opt Out*. I remember sitting in the Students' Union one day, and seeing people distributing copies of *Opt Out*. The thought entered my mind: 'What if I go and ask them what the magazine is all about?' I got up and my knees just could not carry me. I stood there shaking and decided to sit down again. Then I saw the man and woman were walking in my direction — how was it possible that they knew about me? As it turned out, they were simply looking for a place to eat. I decided to remain as quiet as possible and try to listen to what they had to say to each other — I always wanted to know what 'queer' people talked about. After about five minutes I managed to scrape together all my courage. I turned to them and asked: 'When is the next GALA meeting?'

I made sure that I attended that meeting. I joined GALA and paid a few visits to the Gay Association of South Africa (GASA) community centre in Cape Town. There were so many different things happening: the lunch-time meetings, the first ever gay party I went to, the GALA activist forum. The lunch-time meetings somehow never really did anything for me. I went to them in search of the comfort and support of others who were, like myself, facing great difficulties in being open about themselves in a repressive society. But I did not get the support I was looking for and felt alienated most of the time.

What made my sense of alienation even more acute was that the meetings seemed to be great fun for everyone else. The videos shown were pirated copies of the British 'Out on Four' series, but I very seldom identified with the humour, the 'culture' presented in them and the general tone of the meetings. The white 'yuppie culture' that was presented in GALA's programmes seemed so foreign from my own experience.

In SANSCO, where everybody was black, I felt more at home. It was an explicitly political organisation and there was very little space and time for the 'personal' feelings and processes. In GALA, on the other hand, I was one of a handful of black students in an organisation that was not political and that defined itself primarily as a support group for lesbian and gay students. Perhaps because GALA defined itself as a support group, I had great expectations of finding a 'safe haven' in the organisation. But black students' lack of participation in GALA said something about the nature of the organisation. What I found most difficult was that this informal boycott by black students did not seem to bother the majority of GALA's white members.

One of the first GALA activities I involved myself in was the initiation of its activist forum. Our mission was to challenge the oppression of gays and lesbians in the political struggle, but from the start, we struggled to survive: most of GALA's members had little, if any, interest in political activism.

One of our major tasks was to compile and distribute an educational package on 'non-heterosexism' as a political principle. This was in response to the fact the a motion on non-heterosexism had been rejected at a previous congress of the South African Students Press Union (SASPU). The package consisted of essays on socialism and gay liberation, on structural foundations of the gay world, and on the nature of gay oppression. It also included the personal story of a white gay man at a liberal university. So everything in the package was either hyper-intellectual or the personal story of a white person.

I was asked to read the package and comment on it. I could barely contain my fury upon reading the white gay man's personal account of homophobia. He asks: 'Don't these black men who scream "queer" at me know what it feels like to have people yelling "kaffirs" at them?' I was shocked. It seemed to me that black homophobes were being treated with racist contempt, and those white macho types we all know so well on racially-mixed campuses were being neatly let of the hook. Black men were being made to carry the can for a whole society's homophobia.

I later realised that this was an alarmingly common way for white lesbians and gay men to deal with black people's homophobia. The strategy to introduce the principle of non-heterosexism — as one that deserves the same political credibility as any other progressive political principle — was always done by means of an analogy drawn between racism and heterosexism: 'Heterosexism', the 1990 National Union of South African Students congress was told by a prominent white gay activist, 'dehumanises lesbians and gays as effectively and brutally as racism does blacks.'

To black lesbian and gay students this political strategy raises expectations of an organisation that is completely non-racial. But many personal experiences show that there is not always certainty about race and class issues amongst white lesbians and gays. The analogy is also a very shallow one: to say that heterosexism is the same as racism is actually trivialising racial oppression. A lesbian or gay person born into a white middle class family somewhere in sunny South Africa inherits so many social privileges, and is in no way exposed to the brutalities of forced removals or police attacks in his or her own dwelling just for being gay.

Before I became involved in the GALA activist forum, I did not see being gay as a political issue and hence never regarded being 'out' as important. The issue of gay rights was also not on the struggle agenda, and so I remained secretive about my sexual orientation within SANSCO.

I think my crisis was partially resolved by joining the off-campus Organisation of Lesbian and Gay Activists, a group affiliated with the United Democratic Front that was as anti-apartheid as it was pro-gay rights. It felt like I could breathe again: I suddenly did not have to compromise my politics or be secretive about my sexual orientation. And so I gradually came out to friends in SANSCO.

It was not until the now-infamous Winnie Mandela trial — and the accusations about her homophobic defence — that the politics of sexual orientation was openly discussed in SANSCO. This was a particularly difficult time for me, as I was the only openly gay person in SANSCO and often felt that people were insensitive to the issues that I tried to raise.

The fact that I was out as gay within SANSCO was, to my surprise, not seen as any problem by the people who knew about my sexual orientation. But it was also not regarded as politically relevant, and this was the cause of great anger and frustration for me. Certainly, SANSCO leadership distanced itself from all forms of discrimination, including heterosexism. But this did not translate into the organisation instantly becoming a haven for gay and lesbian students. Nobody really paid much attention to lesbian and gay students (outside the organisation, in the broader student community) or called for the issue to be recognised as one that should be on the agenda of all progressive organisations.

And, although I never experienced it personally, some SANSCO comrades would be openly homophobic, using their position as leaders of the black community on campus in an attempt to control the perceived 'embarrassing' behaviour of black gay students. An openly gay black student in one of the university residences, for example, told me that some of my SANSCO comrades accused him of trying to 'recruit' heterosexual people into his circle of gay friends. He was also told to stop 'converting' heterosexual first year students. Through this person I met a few other black gay students on campus. We all had similar experiences of alienation from both the traditionally black political organisation, SANSCO, and the white GALA. Unfortunately my other black gay friends were not interested in gay politics. One told me he had an aversion to anything political — precisely because of the homophobia of some of the people in political organisations like SANSCO.

I was once asked to lead a workshop on non-heterosexism at a regional SASPU media festival in the Western Cape. When the floor was opened for questions, a comrade from UCT asked me (with a facial expression that could only suggest that he was deeply concerned) if I was aware of the fact that I was trying to 'hijack the struggle'. I cannot remember how I responded, but I left feeling really angry at people's inability to understand what I was trying to say. I took a hard look at student gay politics and came to the conclusion that, while there was no doubt of my accuser's homophobia, the 'hijacking' accusation, often levelled at lesbian and gay activists, was not always as far-fetched as these indignant lesbian and gay activists (myself included) believed.

Certainly, when it come to issues of gender and sexuality, the nationalist liberation movements do not have proud track records. But the same holds true for gay and feminist liberation movements with regard to anti-apartheid struggles. This has brought about a situation where accusations of being 'oppressive', 'uncivilised', 'Euro-centric', 'African macho' are endlessly thrown around. The gay activists are forever fighting the homophobia of those in 'progressive' organisations, who often argue that the gays are not 'oppressed' at all. All this leaves those of us who are black and gay in the middle of an extremely unpleasant crossfire. What do we do? Who do we side with? Is there any way out?

I have to believe that the issue of gay and lesbian rights can be introduced into political movements that are 'progressive' in the broad sense. This will enrich the struggle against all forms of oppression, including heterosexism. But until both gay and black activists realise that they are both victims of oppression, and that any denial of rights is a struggle worth fighting for, these questions will remain unanswered, and black gay people like myself will continue to be faced with the crisis of being forced to choose one inextricable dimension of our identities over another.

As I near the end of my university years, the solution becomes clearer: black activists in political organisations like SANSCO must stop using 'black culture' or 'the struggle' to excuse unacceptable prejudice and bigotry. And gay activists must realise the extent to which their hardship is part of a far larger and more virulent oppression, and must fight to eradicate all forms of oppression. That way, we gay activists will find space for our voices within every single sphere of the struggle.

The lavender lobby:
Working for lesbian and gay rights within the liberation movement

Derrick Fine and Julia Nicol

At its Policy Conference in May 1992, the African National Congress formally recognised lesbian and gay rights as part of its policy, by acknowledging, in its Bill of Rights, 'the right not to be discriminated against or subjected to harassment because of sexual orientation'.[1] In addition, the ANC included 'sexual orientation' in its policy on Human Resources Development:

> *The ANC's goal for Human Resources Development is full em-*
> *ployment with a rising standard of living and quality of social*
> *and working life for all South Africans, regardless of race, sex,*
> *class, religion, creed, sexual orientation and physical or mental*
> *disability.*[2]

By including these clauses, the ANC became the first mass-based movement in Africa to acknowledge formally the rights of lesbians and gay men. The ANC Policy Conference was thus an important milestone on the path to recognising and securing our rights as lesbians and gay men in South Africa, and was the result of intense organisation, education and lobbying by lesbian and gay groups within the broad anti-apartheid struggle. These rights have since been included in the draft South African constitution formulated during 1993 at the Multi-party Negotiating Forum.

The first-ever initiative in raising the issue of lesbian and gay rights in the broad South African democratic struggle came in June 1986, when a small number of Cape Town activists organised themselves as Lesbians and Gays Against Oppression (LAGO). In late 1987, LAGO changed into the Organisation of Lesbian and Gay Activists (OLGA), a grouping with identical objectives: the establishment of a non-racial South Africa free of all forms of oppression, focusing in particular on the oppression of lesbians and gay men.

These activists were motivated by two central factors: the failure, as of mid-1986, of any of the country's existing lesbian/gay organisations to adopt a meaningful anti-apartheid stance; and a perceived need to present an organised challenge to the homophobic ethos which Capetonian lesbians and gay men experienced as prevailing within anti-apartheid organisations in which they were active.

OLGA worked at establishing itself as a lesbian/gay sector within the Western Cape, and was an affiliate of the loose alliance of anti-apartheid organisations known as the United Democratic Front until the dissolution of that body in 1991.

Lobbying the African National Congress

In late 1989 OLGA became involved in the debate around the constitutional dispensation in a post-apartheid South Africa. The organisation took a decision to formulate a response to the draft Constitutional Guidelines issued by the still-exiled ANC in the previous year. There was no mention of lesbian and gay rights in this document. OLGA felt that it was vital that the matter be formally raised in response to the ANC's published request for grassroots feedback to its Guidelines. The organisation felt important strategic gains could be made even if its representations were rejected.

What sort of response could OLGA expect from the ANC at this point? In late 1986, a delegation of university students, visiting the ANC's Lusaka headquarters, was told that the movement had no policy on lesbian and gay rights, since this had to date not arisen as an issue for the organisation.

Then, in September 1987, an article appeared in the London newspaper *Capital Gay*, headlined 'ANC dashes hopes for gay rights in SA'. The article carried an interview with ANC National Executive Committee member Ruth Mompati, in which she stated that lesbians and gay men were 'not normal'. She also said: 'I cannot even begin to understand why people want lesbian and gay rights.' Mompati justified the ANC's lack of policy on lesbian and gay rights by stating: 'We don't have a policy on flower-sellers either.'[3]

Negative reaction from a variety of British anti-apartheid and lesbian/gay groupings was swift. Amongst the most vocal were the British Anti-Apartheid Movement, the London-based Committee on South African War Resistance (COSAWR), and the Notting Hill Gay Youth Organisation. As news of the interview spread, protests were also issued by a number of Dutch and Scandinavian anti-apartheid and civil rights organisations. Some of these groupings threatened to withdraw their support for the ANC if it did not retract Mompati's statements.

By late November, the ANC had responded by offering *Capital Gay* an exclusive interview with spokesperson Frene Ginwala, in which the following more sympathetic views were expressed:

> *ANC policy towards gays and lesbians and towards other groups in South Africa which are discriminated against has to be the same, because it is an issue of principle enshrined in our*

Freedom Charter. The raison d'être of the ANC's existence is to fight discrimination, and deprivation of gays and lesbians cannot be excluded from that process.[4]

And, in the same issue, Thabo Mbeki, then Director of Information of the ANC, offered an official policy statement:

The ANC is indeed very firmly committed to removing all forms of discrimination and oppression in a liberated South Africa ... That commitment must surely extend to the protection of gay rights.[5]

These were the ANC's formal statements on lesbian and gay rights at the time when OLGA began planning its response to the Constitutional Guidelines.

In early 1990, OLGA called a discussion forum of lesbians and gay men, and set up a working group to research and formulate a response to these guidelines. This process was stimulated by meetings OLGA held with various members of the ANC, including Ginwala (who has since been appointed head of the movement's Women's Emancipation Commission), and Albie Sachs and Kader Asmal, two members of the ANC's Constitutional Committee. All three unreservedly welcomed the OLGA initiative and saw the need to raise the issue of lesbian and gay rights both as part of the recognition of gender rights and as a broad human rights issue.

Albie Sachs in particular publicly encouraged and legitimated OLGA's work, by situating the oppression of lesbians and gay men in the context of overcoming the effects of apartheid:

What has happened to lesbian and gay people is the essence of apartheid — it tried to tell people who they were, how they should behave, what their rights were. The essence of democracy is that people should be free to be what they are. We want people to be and feel free.[6]

After consulting with the lesbian and gay constituency in the Western Cape and writing to a range of lesbian and gay organisations throughout the country asking for their views and support, OLGA made an extensive submission to the ANC's Constitutional Committee in September 1990.[7] The Committee was charged with formulating the ANC's draft Bill of Rights. OLGA's submission called on the ANC to include the principle of non-discrimination against lesbians and gay men through the inclusion of 'sexual orientation' as one of the grounds for non-discrimination against individuals, along with race, colour, gender, disability, etc. OLGA's motivation was as follows:

♦ that lesbian and gay rights were fundamental human rights;
♦ that, because of public discrimination against gays and lesbians, sexual orientation was a public and not merely a private issue;
♦ that sexual orientation, while a personal issue, was also a political issue that needed to be dealt with as part of a whole package of gender issues in the development of social and economic rights for all individuals.

271

In its draft Bill of Rights published in November 1990, the ANC included non-discrimination on the basis of sexual orientation in a Gender Rights clause: 'Discrimination on the grounds of gender, single parenthood, legitimacy of birth or sexual orientation shall be unlawful.'[8]

The ANC draft Bill of Rights acknowledged OLGA's contribution by stating, in its Introductory Note, that it had benefited from 'receiving proposals from a wide range of organisations associated with the United Democratic Front... including those concerned with... lesbian and gay rights...'[9]

The acceptance of the principle of non-discrimination against lesbians and gay men in the draft Bill of Rights was seen as a major victory for the lesbian and gay movement in South Africa. It was the result of years of groundwork not only by the progressive lesbian and gay movement, but also, very importantly, by anti-apartheid and other human rights groupings in Europe (particularly in the United Kingdom). These groupings helped to build a human rights culture and to establish firmly the principle that any genuinely democratic ethos needs to incorporate an acknowledgement that lesbian and gay rights are human rights.

At the same time, there was the sobering realisation that the Bill of Rights was still only a draft that needed to be approved by the ANC's broader membership, and that an enormous amount of ongoing lobbying and education work lay ahead to ensure that gender and sexual orientation issues were debated and understood by rank-and-file ANC members, and indeed by the public as a whole.

Thus, OLGA continued to engage the ANC by participating in ANC workshops on gender and health issues.[10] Individual OLGA members also made a point of raising sexual orientation issues as ANC members within their branch and regional structures.

The Winnie Mandela assault and kidnapping trial in 1991 was a major test of the ANC's real support for the lesbian and gay rights clauses included in its draft Bill of Rights. Along with GLOW (Gay and Lesbian Organisation of the Witwatersrand), OLGA members in the ANC were particularly active in debates the trial sparked off within various ANC branches in the Cape and Transvaal. A number of these ANC branches formally expressed concern about the homophobia displayed at the trial: ANC supporters outside the court bore placards such as 'Homosex is not in black culture', and Mandela's defence lawyers used the perceived need to protect young men from homosexuality as a defence to charges of brutal assault. The contradiction between the ANC's deafening silence in dealing with this homophobia and its draft Bill of Rights was effectively highlighted in an open letter to the ANC National Executive Committee from GLOW, which OLGA publicly endorsed.[11]

This particular phase of lobbying work within the ANC reached its most crucial point at the ANC's National Policy Conference in May 1992. This conference was charged with formalising ANC principles and policies for future national elections, and it was here that the ANC's draft Bill of Rights, including its provisions on sexual orientation, would be accepted or rejected. By formally recognising lesbian and gay rights, elected delegates ratified the proposals of the Constitutional Committee, and put the issue squarely on the ANC's policy agenda.[12]

Lobbying other political parties and organisations

While OLGA had previously singled out the ANC as a priority target-group for its lobbying work, the organisation now felt that it was equally important to begin lobbying other political parties and organisations across the political spectrum. This coincided with a debate about OLGA's own political affiliation to the UDF and the compromising effect that this might have on OLGA's lobbying efforts, in that OLGA could be seen as partisan. OLGA accordingly took a decision to remain independent of any formal political affiliation following the dissolution of the UDF in August 1991.

In June 1991, OLGA wrote to 10 political parties and organisations explaining its position on non-discrimination on the basis of sexual orientation as a human rights issue. Each party or organisation was asked to state whether it supported the general principle of non-discrimination against individuals in a Bill of Rights, and specifically whether it supported the inclusion of sexual orientation as one of the grounds for non-discrimination. The responses to the OLGA lobby were as follows:

♦ The Democratic Party responded positively, referring to a clause in its draft Constitutional Proposals:

> *The Bill of Civil Rights will guarantee all persons irrespective of race, ethnicity, colour, religion, gender, sexual preference or other arbitrary criteria, the following fundamental rights:*
> *(a) Equal protection of the law...*[13]

♦ The National Party[14] and Labour Party[15] supported the general principle of non-discrimination against individuals, but were non-committal on the inclusion of 'sexual orientation'.

♦ The Conservative Party responded by stating that it did not believe 'that it would be of any value to enshrine anything in a Bill of Rights' and that 'the Ten Commandments serve as the best Bill of Rights and all rights are sufficiently enshrined therein.'[16]

♦ In spite of several reminders, the other six parties and organisations failed to respond to the OLGA request. These were the Azanian Peoples' Organisation (AZAPO), the Inkatha Freedom Party (IFP), the New Unity Movement, the Pan Africanist Congress (PAC), the South African Communist Party (SACP) and the Workers' Organisation for Socialist Action (WOSA).

The reasons for parties and organisations not responding were not clear, but could conceivably be that the issue was not felt to warrant a response,[17] or that no policy had to date been developed on the question of lesbian and gay rights.[18]

The results of the lobby emphasised the amount of work that still needed to be done, and, in 1991 and 1992, OLGA participated in forums where there was potential for lobbying and alliance-building around common issues. An example was participation in the Women's Alliance structure in the Western Cape, which brought together various women's organisations around gender issues.[19]

The changing political climate also presented new opportunities for OLGA to engage in the previously uncharted territory of apartheid or state-controlled structures. The participation of OLGA and GLOW in the December 1991 SABC TV *Agenda* programme on lesbian and gay rights in a future South Africa was a breakthrough. Another example of this new approach was OLGA's decision to reply formally to the Law Commission's draft Bill of Rights, which was adopted as official government policy in March 1992. OLGA called for the specific inclusion of 'sexual orientation', rather than the Commission's vague reference to non-discrimination on the basis of 'other natural characteristics'.[20]

Also in March 1992, OLGA made a formal submission to CODESA (the Convention for a Democratic South Africa) in response to calls for interest groups to make submissions to the various CODESA working groups. The submission to CODESA's Working Group 2 on General Constitutional Principles called for the inclusion of the principle of non-discrimination against individuals in a Bill of Rights, with 'sexual orientation' as one of the grounds for non-discrimination.

The CODESA submission also focused on the need for additional essential measures to make principles such as non-discrimination effective, namely:

- decriminalising homosexuality, ie repealing or no longer applying laws which criminalise or discriminate against lesbians and gay men;
- introducing positive anti-discrimination laws, eg, making it unlawful to discriminate against lesbians and gay men in the areas of employment, health care and housing;
- implementing effective mechanisms to enforce new protective laws, eg, a suitably staffed and trained Human Rights Commission;
- embarking on accessible countrywide public education programmes, eg, including positive material on sexual orientation in school and community programmes.

Developing a Lesbian and Gay Charter

Early in 1990, when OLGA held discussion forums in the Western Cape to formulate a response to the ANC's Constitutional Guidelines, there was a strong feeling that a proactive campaigning strategy was needed. It was therefore decided to compile a Charter of Lesbian and Gay Rights.

Such a charter would express concrete demands, dealing with specific areas of discrimination such as those related to employment, housing and social welfare benefits and the lack of recognition of lesbian and gay relationships. And, as with the lobbying, the content of the charter would be a useful focal point for educating the general public on lesbian and gay issues.

The creation of this charter is a larger-scale and longer-term project than lobbying the ANC and other political organisations in that it will seek to draw on the widest possible range of views among lesbian, gay and bisexual individuals and organisations, and to foster unity among lesbian and gay organisations nationwide.[21] Ultimately, it is envisaged that the charter will serve as a judicially-recognised guideline for the interpretation of future non-discrimination provisions protecting the rights of lesbians and gay men.

By May 1990, OLGA had drawn up a draft Lesbian and Gay Charter, which was subsequently circulated to other lesbian and gay organisations nationally for their consideration. And in October 1991 the charter was discussed nationally at the second momentous national lesbian and gay pride march organised in Johannesburg by GLOW. The lesbian and gay organisations present undertook to revive the charter idea by consulting as widely as possible in their respective regions to get fresh ideas on the content of a charter.

In the first half of 1992, OLGA pursued this process in the Western Cape by conducting a survey in English, Xhosa and Afrikaans to ascertain the concerns and demands of as wide a cross-section as possible of lesbians, gay men and bisexuals. Networking on the Lesbian and Gay Charter has also taken place through the Cape Town Forum, an *ad hoc* alliance of lesbian and gay organisations in the Western Cape, who come together to organise events such as the first-ever Cape Town lesbian and gay fair in May 1992.[22]

In October 1992, based on feedback from its charter survey, OLGA drew up a revised and extended draft charter, circulating it to all lesbian and gay organisations nationally, inviting comments on the new draft and proposing a 1993 National Conference of all lesbian and gay organisations to work out a united approach to lobbying and campaigning for our rights.

Conclusion

The changing political climate since February 1990 made OLGA critically reassess itself and realise that the battle for liberation from lesbian and gay oppression is a long and ongoing one, requiring consistent and concerted work from all lesbian and gay people and organisations and our allies, regardless of present political affiliations.

This represents both a short-term dilemma and a long-term challenge to the lesbian and gay rights movement in South Africa: a dilemma, because current affiliations and limited resources restrict our ability to work together; a challenge, because tradition, culture and religion make our oppression a deep-seated one that will take years of joint effort to change.

Yet the strength of our cause in fighting for lesbian and gay rights is that we are calling for the upholding of basic human rights. This makes our call one of principle to be respected and implemented by any party or coalition of parties holding the future reins of political power and claiming to uphold basic human rights. There is great potential for the lesbian and gay movement to play an ongoing and non-sectarian watchdog role in monitoring abuses of our rights or the non-implementation of new laws. The signs are hopeful that we will be able to forge and play such a role under a more democratic government, one bound by a justiciable Bill of Rights and committed to the protection of personal freedom.

We fervently look forward to the day when the law and social climate have changed to the extent that we are all able to live full and proud lives as lesbians and gay men, free of discrimination, harrassment and abuse.

Notes

1 Clause B5.1.7, ANC Policy Guidelines for a Democratic South Africa, as adopted at National Policy Conference, 28-31 May 1992.

2 Clause K1.1, ANC Policy Guidelines for a Democratic South Africa, as adopted at National Policy Conference, 28-31 May 1992.

3 *Capital Gay*, (London) 18 September 1987.

4 *Capital Gay*, 4 December 1987.

5 *Capital Gay*, 4 December 1987.

6 *South*, 17 May 1990, at an OLGA press conference following a meeting between Albie Sachs and OLGA.

7 The OLGA submission was supported by 11 other lesbian and gay organisations nationally: COGS (Cape Organisation of Gay Sport), Gay Advice Bureau (Johannesburg), Gay Switchboard (Johannesburg), Gay Library (Johannesburg), GAIN (Gay Association of Inland Natal), GALA (Gay and Lesbian Association, University of Cape Town), GLAD (Gay and Lesbian Association of Durban), GLOS (Gay and Lesbian Organisation of Students, University of Natal), GLOW (Gay and Lesbian Organisation of the Witwatersrand), TOGS (Transvaal Organisation of Gay Sport), and Yachad (Jewish Lesbian and Gay Group, Johannesburg).

8 Clause 7(2) of ANC Gender Rights clause, the rest whereof reads:
1. Men and women shall enjoy equal rights in all spheres of public and private life, including employment, education and within the family...
3. Positive action shall be undertaken to overcome the disabilities and disadvantages suffered on account of past gender discrimination.
4. The law shall provide remedies for sexual harassment, abuse and violence.
5. Educational institutions, the media, advertising and other social institutions shall be under a duty to discourage sexual and other types of stereotyping.

9 ANC draft Bill of Rights, November 1990.

10 For example, in November 1991 OLGA made a submission towards the formulation of an ANC draft Mental Health Charter. The submission recommended legal reform and public education as bases for redressing the psychological stress caused by societal proscriptions against homosexuality.

11 See Holmes in this volume for the full text of the letter and a more detailed analysis of the implications of the Winnie Mandela trial.

12 For a critique of the ANC provisions with respect to sexual orientation, see Cameron in this volume.

13 Democratic Party Draft Constitutional Proposals, August 1991.

14 National Party letter to OLGA, 30 July 1991.

15 Labour Party letter to OLGA, 24 July 1991.

16 Conservative Party letter to OLGA, 12 September 1991.

17 See AZAPO's response in a subsequent interview by *Exit* newspaper: 'At the present time AZAPO does not consider homosexuality a priority. It seems to us that this phenomenon is largely affecting the more affluent sections of the community.' (Strini Moodley, National Publicity Secretary, *Exit* 53, December 1991)

18 In November 1991 the PAC decided not to take part in an SABC TV *Agenda* programme on lesbian and gay rights because the organisation did not have a policy on the issue.

19 OLGA is now one of the participating organisations in the Western Cape region of the Women's National Coalition, which was established in October 1992.

20 The Law Commission's 'other natural characteristics' proposal has now been adopted by the National Party in its Charter of Fundamental Rights, published in February 1993 — see Cameron for a fuller discussion of these proposals.

21 Women's and workers' organisations are following similar processes in developing Women's and Workers' Rights Charters, and in so doing uniting people regardless of their political affiliations.

22 This kind of co-operation has been part of a concerted effort by OLGA to reach out to and work with a wider range of lesbian and gay organisations. This important shift in emphasis in OLGA was embodied in its decision in March 1992 to change its name from 'Organisation of Lesbian and Gay Activists' to 'Organisation for Lesbian and Gay Action' (still 'OLGA' for short). This, together with other changes to OLGA's internal constitution, such as removing limitations restricting OLGA to working with progressive groups, was an attempt to open up OLGA's membership to lesbians, gay men and bisexuals who were committed to working for objectives such as lesbian and gay rights and visibility, but who did not define themselves as 'activists' in the narrow, more exclusive sense of the word.

Pride or protest?:
Drag queens, comrades, and the Lesbian and Gay Pride March

Mark Gevisser and Graeme Reid

Look at the images of the annual October lesbian and gay pride march in Johannes-burg, and you'll see some astonishing juxtapositions. In amongst the township kids, avuncular men, proud mothers and affectionate couples, you'll note angry comrades (fists in the air and slogans on the T-shirts) marching alongside outlandish drag queens with shocking-pink hair and falsies.

The march is unique in South Africa, in that it is simultaneously angry and carnivalesque; both deeply earnest in its call for lesbian and gay rights and wildly subversive in its challenge to heterosexual stereotyping. It has a strangely dual character, illustrated, perhaps, by the incongruity of comrades and drag queens.

On the one hand, the march fits into and invokes the tradition of human rights protest marches in South Africa, from the Women's March on Pretoria in 1956 through to the marches of the defiance campaigns of the 1980s that signified the collapse of apartheid. On the other hand, it draws its style and indeed its name from the carnivalesque tradition of the pride march, initiated in North America after the Stonewall uprising of 1969 (when gay patrons of a Greenwhich Village bar rioted after a police raid in June 1969).

Since the first Annual Johannesburg Gay and Lesbian Pride March on the 10th October 1990, Africa's only such event has taken place in Johannesburg on the second Saturday of October each year. Organised by GLOW, the Gay and Lesbian Organisation of the Witwatersrand, it begins at the University of the Witwatersrand and winds its way through Braamfontein and Hillbrow under a rainbow of balloons and banners.

Perhaps the march in October 1992 came closest to drawing the traditions of pride and protest together. More explicitly political than in previous years, the

278

theme — 'Marching For Our Rights' — was linked directly to the inclusion of a specific clause within the African National Congress's Bill of Rights to protect the rights of gay men and lesbians. But it was also a march that attracted a wider range of gay men and lesbians than ever before: people who, regardless of their political views, joined up for the fun of it, for the colourful procession and the partying at the carnival in Pieter Roos Park that followed the procession through the streets.

Publicity campaigns in bars, however, revealed that the majority of white gay men who participate in Johannesburg's commercial gay sub-culture stay away from the march: they find it too political and too closely linked with the aspirations of the anti-apartheid liberation movements. Nevertheless, mainstream white gay social organisations are becoming more and more involved: in 1992, for example, TOGS (Transvaal Organisation for Gay Sport) provided marshalling services.

Apolitical white gay men are not the only ones to stay away — so too do black gay men and lesbians from the townships. The march remains a white affair, despite the fact that more than 60% of GLOW's members are black — nevertheless the number of black participants has risen steadily from 5% in 1990 to more than 25% in 1992, and one reason why the ratio was so much higher in 1992 was that a new, largely-black organisation from Cape Town, ABIGALE (The Association of Bisexuals, Gays and Lesbians), brought up a busload of more than 50 people. Interestingly, the ratio of female participants has always been higher than the ratio in lesbian and gay organisations themselves; while GLOW, for example, has no more than a 20% female membership, the number of lesbian marchers in 1992 exceeded 40%.

GLOW, like all progressive lesbian and gay political organisations in South Africa, is presented with a fundamental dilemma: how to reconcile the need for militant gay and lesbian activism with the needs of its members, which tend more often, in these early days of gay liberation, towards the provision of support and social space.

GLOW remains an expressly political organisation, but it has tried to organise its black membership more efficiently in various ways: an active Lesbian Forum provides a consciousness-raising space for its largely-black membership, and GLOW tries to focus its activities in the townships by holding meetings there, and by linking organisational meetings with social events. The GLOW Annual General Meeting, for example, takes place in Soweto and is always followed by the immensely popular Miss GLOW drag competition.

But this strategy is only partly successful: what tends to happen is that a few activist stalwarts — mainly black and white people living in town — make the trip out for the meeting, and the number then swells to the hundreds for the show, with busloads of spectators coming in from townships all over the reef. GLOW township chapters, while populous, remain weak and inert except in places like kwaThema on the East Rand — where a community has been built around an older woman who has opened her home to the township's gay community — and some areas in Soweto, where the chapter rides on one or two strong personalities.

And so the march, while presenting a public spectacle, does little to build organisation in the townships. It is a costly affair that swallows most of GLOW's budget and takes up the most of the time of the activists who organise it. Perhaps, if more time and money went into organising the townships, township chapters of GLOW would march under their own banners, proudly proclaiming their presence in a show of pride and defiance. The march would then present to South Africa a more representative public spectacle of gay life. The real work of organising gay men and lesbians in the townships remains undone, and there is a strong argument to be made that the money could probably be better spent on small-scale projects that enhance gay and lesbian visibility in a slow and incremental manner.

Despite this problem, however, there is demonstrable worth in 1000 or more South African gay men and lesbians taking to the streets on an annual basis. If nothing else, the march, and the increased media attention that inevitably follows in its wake, provides an annual moment of public visibility. It is not coincidental that homosexuality has entered South Africa's public consciousness in the very years that the march has taken place.

Not surprisingly, the most media hype came after the first march in 1990. As the first lesbian and gay march in Africa, it settled for a fairly neutral theme, calling for 'Unity In The Community'. Even so, the sense of apprehension was strong. In an attempt to assuage fears, the organisers offered paper-bag masks to those still in the closet. South Africans were thus presented with the bizarre spectacle of people marching incognito for openness and pride. If nothing else, this presented a tangible image of how difficult it is to be open and proud in this society.

But despite the neutrality of the theme and the controversial (and misguided) paper bag option, several of the more conservative gay organisations chose not to participate: many, for example, were put off by the in-your-face militancy of the planned kiss-in which was scheduled to take place at the end of the march, but which ultimately did not happen.

Nevertheless, 800 lesbians and gay men participated in that first march through pouring rain — accompanied, significantly, by many non-gay supporters from other progressive organisations who have not been nearly as visible in subsequent years. And at the park, the feeling of triumph at having braved the streets was exhilarating.

The second march, in 1991, had a more politically explicit theme: 'Marching for Equality'. About 1000 people participated and, coincidentally, thousands of Christians marched on the same afternoon, crossing the pride carnival at Pieter Roos Park. The Christian marchers hurled biblical injunctions: the gay marchers threw abuse back. Every year, in fact, a group of Bible-punching Christians doggedly follows the march, and they have become as much part of the spectacle as the drag queens.

Well, perhaps even more of a spectacle. In 1992, the bible-punchers, holding banners like 'Turn or Burn' and yelling 'Don't you queers wanna be saved?' were more numerous and more bellicose than ever before. Certainly, there was something menacing about them: one particularly straight-laced prophet brandished a firearm when a marcher attempted to kiss him. But, ironically, their presence is critical: in 1992, for example, their arrival turned a rather quiet stroll into vigorous outrage.

Conversely, in 1992, the drag queens were scarcer than ever before. Perhaps this is because they do not feel welcome at a march that tends more and more towards political protest. But, more likely, it is because the media's inevitable focus on the garish and outlandish elements of the march has caused a degree of self-censorship among gay people themselves. The drag queen issue has raged after each march: do we present a public face that is clean and acceptable, even if it means ostracising those members of our own community in the very way we have been ostracised by a homophobic world? Or do we embrace and celebrate our diversity, even if it means playing in to stereotypes and allowing the media to sensationalise the march and ignore its very real, substantive issues?

At the end of the 1992 March, a group of particularly edgy black transvestite hustlers, who had joined the procession at the Skyline bar in Hillbrow, leapt onto the stage in the park and did a wild and ecstatic dance, a performance of true abandon, to blaring disco music. They were cut short by a modulated voice that interrupted the music with words of caution: 'Please be careful,' the voice said. 'We must remember that the whole country is watching us, so we must be very careful how we present ourselves.'

It was a sad and telling moment: the conflict of gay abandon with gay respectability. And, if nothing else, it demonstrated the prickliness and sensitivity of lesbian and gay people to the way they are represented by the media. For any gay and lesbian pride march has one central function: to facilitate public visibility. This is particularly important in South Africa where, for example, there is the common misconception — as the placard of an ANC supporter at the Winnie Mandela trial put it — that 'Homosex is not in Black Culture'.

Without doubt, the marches are the most visible public event organised by gay men and lesbians, and they do help create awareness of gay and lesbian issues. They have ensured that our demand for equality becomes an issue of social concern. This is the political face of the march — the march as a protest against inequality; a march as a demand for equal rights; a march that says that in South Africa all oppression must be challenged. For a community that is hidden and mostly silent, this is of great importance.

The marches attract public attention and force straight society to recognise the existence of gay men and lesbians — 'We're here, we're queer, you'd better get used to us'. This constitutes the second aspect of the march: a public acting out that celebrates the lives of lesbians and gay men, affirming a sense of identity often at odds with the straight world. The sense of solidarity and unity created for gay men and lesbians themselves is at least as important as the march's more explicitly political face. It is a sense of community that allows many people to take to the streets, often coming out publicly for the first time. To march through the streets in comparatively small numbers in a homophobic and intolerant society is a brave and courageous act. And in spite of the pressures to remain in the closet, every year more people come together in a noisy, colourful public event proclaiming their pride in being gay; the numbers have risen, slowly but consistently, from 800 in 1990 to nearly 2000 in 1992.

Most significantly, the march focuses media attention on lesbians and gay men: not only the event, but the issues it presents, are thus transmitted to a wide range of South Africans. Ever since 1990, the media — newspapers, popular magazines, radio talk-shows, television programmes — has shown unprecedented interest in gay and lesbian issues. And while only some of the coverage is serious, and much of it is sensational or homophobic, there is a belief that any discussion is preferable to the silencing of the gay and lesbian experience. Within media coverage, however sensational, we find a space to talk, publicly, about our own sexuality.

When, for example, after the first march in 1990, the black popular magazine *Bona* published an appallingly homophobic article, the response was nevertheless overwhelming. Two years later, GLOW was still receiving enquiries from people who first heard about the organisation and the existence of other gay men and lesbians through that article. What is revealing is how coverage changed over the three years, particularly on national television. Following the first march, SABC viewers were treated to nothing more than a couple of sound-bites from particularly outrageous drag queens. Following the 1992 march, however, both *Agenda* on TV1 and *Newsline* on CCV broadcast in-depth documentaries on homosexuality in South Africa, treating the subject with a seriousness and a respect that would have been unheard-of a couple of years ago.

The call for an apolitical annual carnival remains strong, and there is no doubt that such a pride march would bring the crowds out of Champions and Connections in their thousands. Many older gay men, for example, remember with much nostalgia the Gay Day parties, organised by GASA (The Gay Association of South Africa) at Kyalami in 1982 and in Broederstroom in 1983.

Although the Broederstroom party took place on the anniversary of the Stonewall Rebellion, the 'Gay Days' were, like the association that organised it, expressly apolitical and overwhelmingly white and male. Rather than dangerously flaunting their dissidence on the streets of Johannesburg, hundreds of gay men held a celebration, shut off from prying and judgemental eyes at a country club in Kyalami on a secluded stretch of the Crocodile River.

There is no doubt that events like the Gay Days of 1982 and 1983 — or the Shaft 8 parties that took place in the late 1980s as fundraisers for legal reform — are worthwhile: the creation of gay community depends as much on these moments of social interaction and celebration as it does on explicitly political public activism. If GLOW were to dispense with its drag show, for example, it would probably lose most of its members and it would do away with a space that brings black gay men together like no other. If GLOW really wants to strengthen its base in the townships, it will have to consider even more of these purely celebratory events.

Pride or protest?

But the political edge to the pride marches has had two important positive effects. Firstly, it has provided gays and lesbians with a sense of self worth — by giving us the opportunity to put our bodies on the line for something we believe we deserve as our natural birthright. Secondly, it has given South Africans, and particularly those who have fought for the eradication of apartheid, a graphic indicator that any consideration of human rights in a democratic society must include the entrenchment of rights of sexual minorities. The sight of two elderly African women on Pretoria Street in Hillbrow, standing bemusedly on the pavement with their shopping bags at their feet as the moffie carnival passes by, and then thrusting their fists in the air and shouting 'Viva!' as they realise this is a protest march too, brings this point home.

The challenge, in future marches, will be to be as inclusive as possible of all gays and lesbians while at the same time addressing the political demands of gay men and lesbians without separating these demands from the broader struggle for democracy and human rights in South Africa. Ultimately, a pride march divorced from the realities of South African society would divorce our own future from the future of other oppressed groups in the country. This would be morally indefensible, as well as strategically shortsighted.

'White rapists made coloureds (and homosexuals)':
The Winnie Mandela trial and the politics of race and sexuality

Rachel Holmes

On 22 April 1991, the South African press reported that Winnie Mandela had attended the launch of an African National Congress Women's League branch in Toekomsrus. There she made the following statement: 'You are called coloureds because not long after they [Europeans] landed here in 1652 these despicable people raped our grandmothers.'[1]

We can infer that Mandela's reading of inter-racial contact is as follows: colonial whites disrupt black culture by defiling it, and multi-racial identities are therefore just another form of violated colonisation. Clearly, Mandela makes a crucial point about the deeply embedded relationship between South African colonial history and European despicability. But the remark is an indication of Mandela's tendency to read any multi-racial contact as colonial contamination effected through rape and abuse.

This comment dismisses the histories and identities of a large and important socio-political constituency — the majority population of the Western Cape — by consigning its subjects to the fixed and unshifting status of rape victims.

Winnie Mandela made this statement during the progress of a Supreme Court criminal trial, where she was being tried for kidnap, assault and intention to do grievous bodily harm, along with three co-accused. Mandela's defence case, conducted by George Bizos, codified homosexuality as sexual abuse, and characterised homosexual practice as a white, colonising depredation of heterosexual black culture. 'Homosex is not in black culture', read a placard held by one of

'White rapists made coloureds (and homosexuals)'

Mandela's supporters outside the court, invoking homosexuality as a white exploitation of black culture and in itself, just another form of colonisation.

There is a logical congruence between the portrayal of homosexuality in the 1991 Winnie Mandela trial, and Mandela's historical account of mixed-race identity offered at Toekomsrus. Under this rubric, both homosexuality and inter-racial sex (be it homo or hetero) are not just equivalent to, but are in themselves actual rape and abuse. Thus, any alternative political, sexual and racial identities, such as exists in both homosexual and mixed-race practises, are discounted as simply irretrievable white masculinist colonising contamination.

The Mandela trial therefore highlights a range of issues around sex, race, gender and political activism which are of vital importance to South African politics and human rights in the following ways. Firstly, Mandela's defence strategy relied totally upon a deliberate exploitation of public susceptibility to homophobia. Secondly, through media representation and public statements, the defence made implicit statements about the power relationship between race and sex in South African communities. Thirdly, the trial demonstrated the obstructive degree to which heterosexuality and 'the family' dictate social and political organisation — even within constituent parts of a radicalised liberation movement, in this case the African National Congress.

In May 1991, Winnie Mandela was found guilty on four charges of kidnapping and four of being an accessory after the fact of assault. She was sentenced to six years' imprisonment. In July 1991, she was granted leave to appeal against her conviction and sentence, and, in June 1993, the appeal court set aside the charges of assault, but upheld those of kidnapping, reducing her sentence, however, to a fine of R15 000.

Mandela responded that she had been 'vindicated' in her claim that she would 'never lift a hand onto a child',[2] and, despite much criticism of the judgement within South Africa's legal community, the judicial system has ruled, finally, on the extent of Mandela's guilt.

Nevertheless, even after its formal conclusion, the Mandela trial continues to act as a barometer of deeply contested ideological ground, and it is neither possible nor appropriate to offer any conclusive readings of what is an ongoing political process. Rather, this article seeks to explore what it is that this trial tells us, as lesbians, gay men and sexual radicals, about the public discourse of homosexuality in South Africa today.

Winnie Mandela trial, or error?

In January 1989, *The Weekly Mail* and *The Guardian* published a scoop story[3] revealing that on 29 December 1988 four youths had been abducted from a Methodist Church Manse in Orlando West, Soweto and taken to the Diepkloof Extension home of Winnie Mandela.[4] Here they were allegedly questioned, subjected to a variety of accusations, seriously physically assaulted and then held captive. The victims of this abuse were: Kenny Kgase (29), Thabiso Mono (18), Pelo Gabriel Mekgwe (19) and Stompie Moeketsi Seipei (14).

These revelations produced an uproar over the (mis)conduct of the Mandela United Football Club (the MUFC, Winnie's personal team) and over the disappearance and alleged murder of Stompie. There was also much speculation about the extent of Winnie Mandela's complicity and personal involvement in the events — the 'youths' claimed that she personally had assaulted them. This story, and subsequent trial, led to Jerry Richardson, former 'coach' of the MUFC, being found guilty of the kidnap and assault of Mono, Mekgwe and Kgase, and of the murder of Stompie.[5] At Richardson's trial, Mandela argued that the 'boys' had been removed from the Manse to protect them from sexual abuse by the Methodist priest in charge, Reverend Paul Verryn.

The Richardson trial cleared Verryn of the allegation of sexual abuse. Verryn had already been cleared by both a local community enquiry and a formal Methodist Church investigation. These events marked the beginning of a series of doubts and questionings regarding Winnie Mandela's status in the liberation community.

Mandela herself was brought to trial on 4 February 1991. In the presence of a gallery packed with high-profile ANC-alliance leaders,[6] Winnie Mandela and three co-accused, John Morgan (63), Mrs Xoliswa Falati (36), and her daughter, Nompumelelo Falati (18)[7] were charged with kidnapping and assault with intention to do grievous bodily harm, and a basis of common purpose was alleged. All pleaded not guilty to the charges. Key witnesses for the state prosecution were Kgase, Mono and Mekgwe, the remaining survivors of the assault.[8]

When testifying, Mandela denied that she had assaulted anyone or that any assault had been committed in her presence. She claimed that in December 1988 Falati had approached her and alleged that (homo)sexual abuse was occurring in the Manse. According to the *Sowetan* reportage, Mandela asserted that Falati

> *informed me that some of the youths were following Verryn's example in indulging in homosexual practices and that a youth Katiza Cebekhulu had, as a result of indecent assault on him by Verryn, become mentally disturbed.*[9]

Note how this invokes the theme of homosexual practice as producing or being equivalent to mental and emotional instability, reproducing the prejudicial view of homosexuality as mental disorder and/or clinical condition that can be cured. Mandela claimed she had responded by suggesting to Falati that Cebekhulu be brought to her, and that on 29 December they visited the surgery of Dr Abu-Bakar Asvat where Cebekhulu was examined. Following this, she stated that she left Soweto. Only on her return on 31 December did she hear that Falati had arranged with Jerry Richardson for four 'youths' to be brought from the Manse. This, she claims Falati told her, was to deter the absent Paul Verryn from frustrating investigations into the alleged sexual abuse, and to prevent the spread of such practices amongst the 'youths' staying at the Manse.

Dr Abu-Bakar Asvat was shot dead in his surgery on 27 January 1989: whether he found that Cebekhulu had been raped or not is therefore only conjectural. However, his surgery notes and Winnie Mandela's testimony state that he recommended that Verryn and Cebekhulu seek psychiatric treatment. Mandela therefore justified the removal of the 'youths' from the Manse on the grounds that they were being sexually assaulted.

Xoliswa Falati was apparently the origin of this allegation. The main co-accused in the trial, Falati worked in the Methodist Manse and was involved in the care of its inhabitants at the time of these events. From the way it appeared in media coverage, Falati's testimony seems to have been a combination of contradiction and self-righteousness. For example, at different times she stated that Cebekhulu had been raped by Verryn, or that Verryn had attempted to rape him. Her testimony included extensive reference to the 'insertions' of genitalia into 'private parts', 'touching all over', buttocks, 'thigh rubbing', and 'rape'. Interestingly, the only consistent aspect of her testimony was that, however much she confused who exactly was doing what to whom at what particular time, all the 'youths' were involved in having sex with each other. This seems to be something of a give-away: if she was genuinely attesting to abuse, then presumably she would easily have distinguished between victim and perpetrator. But what actually emerged was a language of sexual policing whereby *all* those concerned required salvation or discipline.

A statement accorded to her by the *Daily Dispatch* echoes unmistakably with Winnie Mandela's own characterisation of homosexuality as colonial abuse, and notably uses the possessive language of the family to authorise the self-appointed right to protect social subjects: 'What should I have done about Reverend Paul Verryn raping our children?'[10]

The defendants' insistence on the relevance of Paul Verryn's imputed sexual behaviour was further indicated in John Morgan's testimony. Morgan, a former driver for the MUFC, and driver of the vehicle that 'collected' the 'youths' from the Manse on the night in question, claimed that Jerry Richardson had questioned Stompie specifically about his relationship with Verryn, charged him with being an *impimpi* (informer), and slapped him.

From March 1991 onwards, the emphasis of the case, as characterised by the media, shifted from concentration on the alleged kidnapping and assault by Winnie Mandela and her co-accused to the imputed sexual abuse by Paul Verryn.[11] Defence advocate George Bizos' line was very clear: if it could be proven that Winnie Mandela believed Verryn had been sexually abusing the Manse inmates, then the removal of these inmates could be seen as justified, as presumably could verbal abuse, *sjambokking* (whipping), slapping, beating, dropping to the ground from a height and holding people against their will.

Bizos appeared to be arguing that the 'young boys' were not abducted, but rather removed to protect them from a damaging environment. He did this by linking homosexuality with child abuse in a way that calculatedly did not distinguish between the two. On 11 March, the *Sowetan* cited Bizos as follows: 'The primary concern of Verryn was that he did not want allegations of sexual misconduct to be made public.' This wording reflects Bizos' approach. The language is ambiguous: *sexual misconduct* could be read as *abuse* or, feeding off homophobic moralism, could be interpreted as simply a reference to homosexuality; that is, 'misconduct' as a reference to 'inappropriate' sexual behaviour. The blurred distinction between the two made them appear to be the same thing.

This habit of speaking as if homosexuality and abuse were synonymous was augmented by large sections of the media, who either uncritically followed the defence's blurring of terminology or used their own deliberately ambiguous formulations.[12] It could be argued that this ambiguity cut both ways. At several stages during their testimonies, the complainants denied both knowledge or experience of homosexual 'misconduct'. Clearly, to deny sexual abuse and misconduct is not to deny homosexual experiences, except from a homophobic perspective.

The defence case attempted to connect homosexual practice with abuse in terms of it being an exploitation of the vulnerability of disadvantaged people. This was apparently the reasoning behind Bizos' relentless pursuit of details about the alleged sexual relationships Verryn had with the victims of apartheid in his care. The approach was a powerful one which fed off social bigotry, not only as demonstrated in the 'homosex is not in black culture' placard slogan, but in press language which can be summed up by the following example from *City Press*:

> *Is Methodist Minister Rev Paul Verryn a sex abuser who corrupts black youths or is he a dedicated Christian martyr who has made many sacrifices in the struggle? And was the Orlando West Methodist Manse a refuge for the unfortunate, or a den of iniquity?*[13]

These rhetorical questions, placed in the context of the charges against Verryn, immediately suggest that male homosexuality, by now hopelessly conflated with sexual abuse, is incompatible with political dedication to the struggle. This division between, at a basic level, 'appropriate politics' and 'appropriate sex' placed those located in Verryn's Manse as politically suspect homosexuals and/or abusers, and those in Mandela's home as dedicated members of the struggle endeavouring to maintain its (heterosexual) 'moral' values.

At no time was the issue of consent raised in relation to what was, or was not, going on in the Manse, despite the fact the so-called youths — also sometimes referred to as 'boys' or 'children' — were far from being children: their ages ranged, as indicated above, between 14 and 29 at the time of the alleged 'misconduct'.

The testimonies of Kgase and Mono seemed to suggest that the real location of 'abuse' and 'assault' was in fact Mandela's home rather than the Manse. Both claimed that they were questioned in a back room of Mandela's home, that Mandela herself attended, and that Richardson instructed them to refer to her as 'Mummy'. They maintained that Mandela stated Cebekhulu to be hysterical because he had been raped by Verryn, and that she beat them. Stompie, as indicated above, was accused of being an *impimpi*, and Mekgwe and Mono were accused of sleeping with Verryn. Kgase alleged that Winnie Mandela stated that 'We were not fit to be alive,' and that he was gripped by the hair and shoulders and asked why he had to protect a white person he had made friends with: 'She kept punching me, saying that I was an intellectual ignoring my call to free Africa.'[14]

Therefore, to the accusation of homosexuality as politically irresponsible was added a combination of both whiteness and intellectualism as betraying the fight against oppression. Under the loaded condemnation of *impimpi*, betrayal and untrustworthiness were aligned to homosexual behaviour.

Two questions arise from the way the theme of sexual abuse was embedded in the defence case. Firstly, what was the basis for this claim? Secondly, what specifically was taken to constitute sexual abuse? The existing testimony is ambiguous and unsatisfactory. Under cross examination, Kgase confirmed that he had been tickled by Verryn in bed. He said that he did not particularly like this, and had told Verryn to desist, which Verryn did. This is as close as one gets in testimony by one of the abducted and assaulted witnesses detailing a specific form of physical encounter at the Manse. By pursuing this issue with Kgase, it seems as if the defence was asking the court to accept that tickling, even though desisted from when not welcomed, constituted sexual abuse.

Bizos also drew the witnesses out regarding a pattern whereby new arrivals at the Manse would spend their first night in Verryn's bed, accompanied by one or two other residents. Mono and Kgase are reported to have confirmed this as having been their experience, and it is in respect of this that the testimony of Peter Storey, Methodist Bishop of Johannesburg, becomes relevant. Storey claimed that in mid-October 1988 it was reported to him that rumours regarding homosexual practices in the Manse were being circulated in the local community. Verryn himself reported these rumours to the Bishop. Initially Storey did not act, but later set up a pastoral commission to investigate the charges. As no-one provided the commission with evidence to support these rumours, Verryn was cleared of the imputations against him.[15] Knowing that, due to shortage of space at the Manse, Verryn shared a double bed with its residents from time to time, Storey advised him to make his bedroom out of bounds. Verryn was agreeable, but pointed out that it would take time to arrange this. Mono confirmed in his testimony that there were insufficient beds, but that he was not aware of any resulting 'improper activity'.

Material shortages of resources and space result in the overcrowding, bed-sharing and shift arrangements familiar to many subjects of apartheid residential conditions, such as in industrial compounds and hostels. To pursue a line of questioning which seemed to imply that 'unnaturally' close proximity due to material necessity inevitably produces 'unnatural' practices can be seen as another version of the homosexuality-as-colonial-defilement model. That the oppression of white apartheid capital produces inadequate and unacceptable living conditions which are an offence to human rights is incontestable. However, to infer that apartheid is the *cause* of homosexual practices that take place in these environments, is to recapitulate Winnie Mandela's version of 'homosex' as a white contamination of black culture. This is a directly oppressive dismissal of the rights of black lesbians, gay men and bisexuals.

Clearly the defence case's emphasis led to a detraction from the accused's charges of abduction, violence and assault. Tickling and bedsharing seemed to be the best evidence the defence could offer to confirm sexual abuse. Despite this lack of hard evidence, however, the issue seemed to be to determine whether the defendants' violence was *justified*, not whether or not it took place.

Whose liberation politics?
GLOW soundings and ANC silences

In response to the homophobia generated by the trial, GLOW (The Gay and Lesbian Organisation of the Witwatersrand) took the lead, with a prompt and formally-organised campaign. On 13 March 1991, GLOW sent an open letter to the National Executive Committee of the ANC and bought advertising space to publish it in the national press.

The letter situated its opposition to Mandela's defence strategy in the context of Article 7(2) of the ANC's draft Bill of Rights; this states that 'Discrimination on the grounds of gender, single parenthood, legitimacy of birth or sexual orientation shall be unlawful.' The letter referred to the anti-homosexual slogans displayed by ANC supporters outside the court, the damaging effects of failing to distinguish between homosexuality and sexual abuse, and the defence's use of allegations of homosexuality to detract from the real issues of the trial:

> ...we feel that the defence is attempting to capitalise on conventional and reactionary prejudices against homosexuals. This is particularly disturbing as this defence is being raised by the head of the ANC's Department of Social Welfare [Winnie Mandela]. The line of defence is irreconcilable with basic principles of human rights outlined in the ANC's proposed Bill of Rights... The ANC's failure to respond to the above raises doubts regarding its stated commitment to the recognition of lesbian and gay rights. We therefore demand that the NEC states clearly and unequivocally its position on the rights of lesbians and gay men.[16]

GLOW also announced a campaign to request local and international progressive organisations to re-affirm their commitment to the protection of lesbian and gay rights in a future democratic South Africa. GLOW called for public support for the letter. Although other lesbian and gay organisations endorsed GLOW's position and forwarded their support, none initiated any active protest or campaign of their own.

By 1993, the ANC National Executive Committee had yet to respond, or, indeed, to make any statement about the homophobia generated by this trial. Despite the fact that a large number of local ANC branches formally expressed concern about the homophobia displayed by Winnie Mandela and her supporters at the trial, and that the issue was raised at the 1991 National Policy Conference, ANC leadership structures have never discussed the issue. The liberation movement's leadership has thus failed to match its general articulations about equality and non-discrimination to the very real needs of a sector of its constituency. These failures seem to be the result of an executive-level inability to deal with real public differences within the ranks of the liberation movement.

Since the trial, the ANC has made two significant acknowledgments of lesbian and gay rights. Firstly, the warm message of support sent by Secretary-General Cyril Ramaphosa to the 1991 Lesbian and Gay Pride March in Johannesburg. Secondly, the ANC's *Policy Guidelines For A Democratic South Africa*, adopted at the National Policy Conference in May 1992, which formally recognises lesbian and gay rights in Clause B5.1.7, and also acknowledges rights to non-discrimination under other subject sections of the document.[17]

But the fact that there has not been any official response to the homophobia in Winnie Mandela's defence strategy indicates that the ANC's commitment to upholding any policy on gay and lesbian rights may be questionable.

At the time of writing, lesbian, gay and bisexual groups in South Africa are drafting a Lesbian and Gay Charter. And the Multi-party Negotiating Forum has approved a draft constitution for South Africa that guarantees equality on the basis of sexual orientation. While this is a worthy and invaluable gain, the Winnie Mandela trial should be the clearest warning yet that documentary commitments do not guarantee correlative action, protection and support from either an umbrella liberation organisation or a future government. As GLOW's letter reminds us, Section 7(2) was in place in the draft Bill of Rights at the time of the trial — and made absolutely no difference.

Queerbashing with family values

On 17 April 1991, breaking her press silence, Winnie Mandela said that she had wanted to hold an indoor enquiry into the allegations of sexual abuse she had heard about Reverend Paul Verryn. The Methodist minister, she stated:

> *was doing the same kind of work that I was doing, providing food, shelter and educational facilities. For that I held him in high esteem. I intended to contain this problem among ourselves and I had hoped that Paul Verryn would allow himself to be assisted by a psychiatrist. I could not understand how a man who was doing such valuable work could at the same time abuse children who had no choice but to depend on him.*[18]

The identification Winnie Mandela makes here between her own role and Verryn's role is absolutely crucial. The characterisation of those in receipt of food, shelter and educational facilities as 'dependent children' suggests that Mandela perceived herself and Verryn as fulfilling parental, nurturing roles. In Mandela's construction, both Verryn's Methodist Manse and her own Diepkloof Extension home were versions, or models, of the family; one of which, the Methodist Manse, was presided over by a man.

As a reform church, Methodism does not require its priests to be celibate. The priest is thus a familial representative in a sexualised way (he cannot be assumed to be celibate). He is a 'father' given to the reproduction of his Christian 'family' in conjunction with the 'mother' of the 'family', Mary. Methodism imagines the church as the 'home' of the Christian family, and is a form of religion that can conceivably replicate the heterosexual family structure in the church community.

In the Winnie Mandela trial, however, the gender relations of the family were altered by the perception of Verryn as performing the dual role of mother and father. Sex is the great family taboo, and in heterosexual environments is rendered invisible, because it is deemed to be 'natural'. But in Verryn's case, the accusations of homosexuality served to sexualise a supposed family environment.

In contrast, Mandela's characterisation of the events in the Methodist Manse coded her own home as a heterosexual family structure, with Mandela self-styled 'mother' in relation to her attendants (the MUFC) and the community. That this might validly be argued to be a political, rather than biological, version of the family, does not alter the fact that it is the ideological framework of the family that provided a way of describing, and an attempt at excusing, the abduction and assault of the four Manse inmates.

'Mother' is not a static, essential category. Neither is it intrinsically 'good' or 'bad' until harnessed to a conceptual framework that seeks to fix it in a particular, unchangeable place. In the case of Winnie Mandela's actions leading to her trial, the function that the category of mother performed was, quite specifically, the 'saving of children'. As can be seen, in this instance the 'saving of children' narrative *infantilised* homosexual practice and the political agency of dependent people. This infantilisation is also reflected in the model of the Mandelas as a couple 'parenting' the nation, a symbolism most frequently reiterated in various forms by the national and international press and by hagiographical biographers.

It is important to note that this very same family/husband/wife imagery has been used to negate a black woman's political activism through an approach that fetishises Winnie Mandela's sexuality and demonises her as 'disreputable', 'wicked', 'wayward' and 'betraying'. She is, we read in the media, 'a shrieking shrew of a wife'; a murderess and an overreacher who reduced her husband to a 'guilty', 'doting', 'lovesick fool'[19] and as such a threat to national political security.[20] As one respectable foreign correspondent put it: '*Private Eye*... was not entirely exaggerating when it drew a line of descent for Mrs Mandela through Lucrezia Borgia, Myra Hindley and Lady Macbeth.'[21] These kinds of representations of Winnie Mandela are both racist and sexist. The effect of such rigid stereotyping is to decontextualise Winnie Mandela's actions, statements and strategies from structural political relations. To explain the events as aberrations of individual personalities misses this crucial point.

It has to be remembered that Mandela's own defence insisted on casting what was in effect a *political difficulty* as a *moral difficulty*, thus deliberately obscuring political issues with the language of 'moralistic' defense. In order to engage with the issues raised by the trial in a way that does not accept the homophobic terms of this defence, it is necessary to focus on these events as a struggle over local power politics framed by the ideology of 'the family' — in this case a political rather than a biological notion of the family. The defence's use of this ideological model of 'the family' attempted to justify the sexual policing and violence carried out in Winnie Mandela's household *in the name of the family.* By insisting on a fixed heterosexuality, this particular ideology of the family repudiates and excludes the possibilities of and the rights to plural sexualities by attempting to contain and police their practice. It is this operation of power and control that constitutes the heterosexism of the family.

In this way, the heterosexist family itself becomes a central site of oppression for those who do not conform to its model of 'appropriate' sexual behaviour, and who thus become familiar with the sexual policing, mental, verbal and physical abuse carried out and justified in the name of the family. It could thus be said that Winnie Mandela's Diepkloof Extension arrangement produced violence *not in spite of, but because of* being structured like a heterosexist family.

Conclusion

In April 1992, Nelson and Winnie Mandela officially announced their separation. And in August 1992, while her case was still on appeal, Winnie Mandela finally resigned from all leadership positions within the ANC.

It is interesting to note that this resignation was immediately precipitated by the leaking of a letter to *The Sunday Times* allegedly from Mandela to her 28-year-old lover, Dali Mpofu, thereby further demonising her as sexually voracious and politically irresponsible.[22] The letter was the final step in the demotion of Mandela from the fixed and essentialised identity of 'good mother' into 'bad mother'.

Other possible reasons for her resignation include allegations of her misuse of power in the ANC Women's League and her misappropriation of Social Welfare funding, both of which were still under investigation by the ANC at the time of writing. While the homophobia of her defence certainly served to further alienate her (and her counsel) from some sectors of the white liberal establishment, and while it played a significant role within the ANC of drawing attention to the need for gay rights, it did not have anything explicitly to do with her resignation.

With the appeal court's final ruling in June 1993, the Winnie Mandela trial is now officially over. But the specific issues the trial raised are unresolved, and there is thus a continuing need for the fledgeling South African lesbian and gay rights movement to mobilise around these issues. Most urgently, the liberation movement needs to account to those militant sexual activists — either within their own ranks or affiliated supporters — who regard their campaigns as an inherent part of the fight for non-racial democracy.

The issues raised by the trial cut to the heart of questions about what constitutes democratic politics, and why the radicalness of the bid for democracy necessarily includes the question of sex. The homophobia of the Winnie Mandela trial should serve as a reminder of the need to challenge constantly the apartheid logic of fixed identities locked into unchangeable power relations.

Characterising homosexual practices as a default of apartheid, renders colonialism directly 'responsible' for homosexuality, and thus dismisses homosexuals as unworthy of rights in a just, post-apartheid society. The discourse of public homo-sexuality constructed by the defence in the Winnie Mandela trial tries to tell us that 'homosex is not in black culture'; that homosexuality among black people is the result of members of black culture becoming tainted by homosexuality in white culture.

This argument can only be sustained by continuing to promote the damag-ing misconception that it is meaningful to talk of fixed, static, singular and separate cultural and sexual practices divided along rigidly demarcated racial lines, a logic of racial segregation which is the legacy of apartheid ideology. The idea of colour-coding sexuality is as ludicrous as the notion of separate development itself. It is not homosexuality, but the insistence on fixed and unhistorical categories of 'essen-tial' racial and sexual identity which causes violence, sexual policing and the subsequent alienation of sexual radicals from the democratic process.

Notes

1 *The Argus* and *Sowetan*, 22 April 1991.
2 *Business Day*, 4 June 1993.
3 *Weekly Mail* and *Guardian*, 26 January 1989.
4 A fifth inmate of the Manse, Katiza Cebekhulu, went willingly.
5 This verdict was accorded a death sentence.
6 Nelson Mandela, Alfred Nzo, Joe Slovo, Chris Hani, Popo Molefe and Jay Naidoo.
7 Four other accused, all former MUFC members, had jumped bail and disappeared at the end of 1988, including Katiza Cebekhulu.
8 On the 10th February, the day before he was due to testify, Pelo Mekgwe disappeared, an event which caused extensive speculation as to whether he had been kidnapped or not, and if so, who by; and that also made Kgase and Mono temporarily afraid to testify.
9 *Sowetan*, 12 February 1991.
10 *Daily Dispatch*, 13 April 1991.
11 For examples, see: *The Sunday Times*, 10 March 1991, *City Press*, 17 March 1991, *Sowetan*, 11 & 15 March 1991, *Weekly Mail*, 15 March 1991.
12 *Weekly Mail* was the only national South African newspaper to draw attention specifically to and protest about this conceptual collapse. See Shaun De Waal: 'Mandela trial: Legitimate defence or homophobia?', 15 March 1991, and Mark Gevisser: 'Sex, Lies...and political debates', 19 December 1991.
13 *City Press*, 17 March 1991.
14 According to *Sowetan*, 8 March 1991.
15 That a commission was held by the church seems to suggest that Verryn was tried by the church before he was tried in the Mandela trial.
16 *Weekly Mail*, 25 March 1991.
17 See Cameron and Fine/Nicol in this book for a fuller discussion of the ANC's official policy regarding lesbian and gay rights.
18 *Sowetan*, 18 April 1991.
19 All of these references can be found in: *Daily Dispatch*, 16 May 1991, *The Independent on Sunday*, 19 April 1992, *Weekend Guardian*, 25 April 1992.
20 See the ultimate in reactionary anti-revolutionary sentiment shored up by the morality of marriage in 'This tragic marriage that could wreck a nation', *Daily Mail* (London), 15 May 1991.
21 John Carlin, *The Independent on Sunday*, 19 April 1992.
22 *Sunday Times*, 6 September 1992.

'Lesbians in love and compromising situations':
Lesbian feminist organising in the Western Cape

Mary Armour and Sheila Lapinsky

In South Africa, as elsewhere, there can be no neat definition of lesbian feminism, since among those who claim that description for themselves are found many different viewpoints; and in any event, each of us is involved on an ongoing journey.

However, we can go so far as to state here that lesbian feminism implies movement away from the domination of the worldwide edifice of heterosexual patriarchy: that is, the worship of maleness, social relationships that support male power, and the destruction of female energy and power. Lesbian feminism embodies a desire to love and value ourselves and other lesbians — *as* lesbians. It involves an opposition not only to sexism, racism and economic exploitation, but also to hierarchies of all kinds involving a higher authority than oneself — a giving up of personal power and deferring or submitting to another. This is not to say that there will not be influences of these oppressive belief systems in our own interactions, but we try to be aware of them and counter them when they occur.

As lesbian feminists living in South Africa, we are fully aware that many of the values we adhere to were first formulated by women in North America and Europe: they are 'imports'. This circumstance makes our position at once easier and more difficult: easier, in that much of the hard work of struggling through to clear theoretical positions has been done for us; harder, in that we sometimes feel as if we are living in a lesbian feminist desert — an environment in which it is exceptionally difficult for these values to survive, let alone have been born. As is the case in the First World countries, we are a minority within a minority, yet we feel it even more keenly than they: we don't have the strength of numbers. As lesbian women

295

living in the large urban centre of Cape Town, we have found it relatively easy to find other lesbians; but lesbians who are *for* lesbians are thin on the ground indeed. It seems that the misogynist and homophobic values of the heterosexual patriarchy are very firmly entrenched in our own communities.

Where do we locate the international roots of lesbian feminism? It is generally considered that the resurgence of feminism in the later part of this century occurred simultaneously with and was influenced by the civil rights movement in the United States. Betty Friedan's 'problem without a name'[1] and Germaine Greer's writings on the invisibility of women came to be analysed as oppression.[2]

Indebted as many women were to the black civil rights movement at the outset, disillusionment at the sexism of black consciousness groups and the male-dominated Left gradually set in. A particularly notorious example of sexism was Stokely Carmichael's utterance, 'The only place for women in the black consciousness movement is horizontal.' Women began to agitate and organise on their own and with the mushrooming of consciousness-raising groups, an awareness of the extent of women's oppression and violence against women spread.

Inspired both by feminist activism and the gay liberation movement that gathered momentum after the Stonewall riots of 1969, lesbian women began to come out of the closet and demand rights. The public coming out of feminist activists such as Kate Millett caused consternation in women's groups and split the powerful National Organisation of Women.

Ti-Grace Atkinson declared: 'Feminism is the theory, lesbianism the practice';[3] and right from the beginning it was clear that lesbians who aligned themselves with the feminist movement were often radical and uncompromising. They were also the first to support the critique of feminism from the perspective of black and Third-world women, which came to be widely acknowledged only in the later 1970s and the 1980s. African-American lesbian feminist Barbara Smith provided a clear analysis:

> The reason racism is a feminist issue is easily explained by the inherent definition of feminism. Feminism is the political theory and practice to free all women: women of color, working-class women, poor women, physically challenged women, lesbians, old women, as well as white, economically privileged heterosexual women. Anything less than this is not feminism but merely female self-aggrandisement.[4]

Those women who, in calling themselves lesbian-feminist, took on a dual political identity, were also obliged to struggle with the notion of interrelated oppressions, experienced simultaneously and inextricably — they were compelled to consider what it meant to be oppressed as a woman as well as by the pervasive heterosexism of society, together with knowledge of the damage done by racism, classism, ageism, ableism. Lesbian feminists found, together with other multi-oppressed women, that it was impossible to rank these oppressions with regard to relative importance. As Cherrié Moraga writes of the United States:

'Lesbians in Love and Compromising Situations'

In this country lesbianism is poverty — as is being brown, as is being a woman, as is being just plain poor. The danger lies in ranking the oppressions. The danger lies in failing to acknowledge the specificity of the oppression.[5]

Lesbianism has always existed, but never within the bold self-proclaimed historical identity we claim for ourselves now. Just as feminists have made one of their priorities the reclaiming of a lost and erased past, so too have lesbian feminists searched for a specifically lesbian history. But this project has been complicated by the difficulties of definition — where does female friendship end and lesbianism begin? Adrienne Rich attempted to open up this debate with her notion of a 'lesbian continuum':

I mean the term lesbian continuum to include a range — through each woman's life and through history — of woman-identified experience, not simply the fact that a woman has had or consciously desires genital sexual experience with another woman.[6]

Together with Lillian Faderman,[7] who reclaimed romantic friendships as unconsciously lesbian experiences for 19th-century women, Rich has been accused of 'desexualising' lesbian experience. In counterpoint, one can look at the work done by Joan Nestle[8] in restoring erotic credibility to butch relationships of the 1950s, although Sheila Jeffries has warned against 'glamourising' such history by ignoring its oppressive aspects.[9]

* * *

In the historical overview of local lesbian feminism that follows we shall be confining ourselves to the situation in the Western Cape. This survey is not intended to be comprehensive or the last word on the subject, but rather to serve as a stimulus to debate and to the recording of invisible lesbian history in our own society.

From the early 1970s onward, consciousness-raising groups were formed by various feminist organisations, notably the Women's Movement at the University of Cape Town. For many women, these were the first place they felt free to articulate their feelings of attraction to other women and to consider what the political implications of this might signify. In the early 1980s, *Stir*, a local journal for feminists with a strong emphasis on creative writing, lent itself to some lesbian-feminist debate.

In 1983, encouraged partially by the emergence of the Gay and Lesbian Association (GALA) on UCT campus, South Africa's first lesbian-only organisation was formed. This was LILACS, the acronym standing for 'Lesbians in Love and Compromising Situations'. LILACS meetings were a combination of socialising and discussion groups on issues affecting members' lives as lesbians. But after about a year, initial enthusiasm for the organisation tapered off and tensions arose between those members who favoured serious debate (including feminist and political content) and those wanting only to 'jol' (play). Attendance at meetings dwindled, and by the end of 1985, LILACS had ceased to exist.

297

In 1984-85 the Cape Town branch of the Gay Association of South Africa (originally established in 1982 under the name 'The 6010 Group') received a degree of input of lesbian-feminist ideas from the presence of Sheila Lapinsky as chairperson. GASA had very few women members, however, and for Sheila the experience was in many ways exhausting and isolating. Since the collapse of GASA, 6010 continues to be a predominantly male-oriented organisation.

In 1985, a discussion group calling itself Gender was set up by a small group of lesbians and gay men, most of them members or former members of GASA-6010, who felt a need to analyse what it meant to be lesbian or gay specifically within the South African context. The debates in Gender were strongly informed by feminist concepts. By common consent this group disbanded after a period of a year.

June 1986 saw the establishment in Cape Town of the first lesbian/gay organisation with a political activist agenda: Lesbians and Gays Against Oppression (LAGO). The central aim of LAGO was, according to one of its pamphlets, 'to situate the lesbian and gay struggle within the context of the total liberation struggle'. LAGO's method of operating was explicitly based on non-hierarchical feminist principles. As far as the organisation's actual programme was concerned, however, the small membership and the embattled political climate of the time meant that the organisation's limited resources were all focused on generalised issues of gay/lesbian liberation, and not on specifically women's issues.

In late 1987, LAGO metamorphosed into the Organisation of Lesbian and Gay Activists (known since late 1991 as the Organisation for Lesbian and Gay Action). OLGA, which was an affiliate of the anti-apartheid United Democratic Front until the demise of that organisation in 1991, continued with the work of bringing the issue of lesbian and gay rights into the agenda of the broad liberation struggle.

By the end of 1989, the number of OLGA's supporters in the Western Cape had expanded to the extent where it became possible to cater for specialised interests; and the first in a series of meetings of a 'Lesbian Sexuality Group' was held at the end of 1989. These meetings, in which a feminist standpoint was a base assumption, continued through the following year, attracting an average of five to 15 women each time.

Late in 1990, women in OLGA decided that the altered political scenario had opened up important areas in the Western Cape where lesbian voices needed to be heard. As a result the Lesbian Sexuality Group changed its name to the Lesbian Caucus, and broadened its programme to incorporate the promotion of lesbian visibility in Western Cape political structures. The Lesbian Caucus has maintained a consistent presence of OLGA representatives at meetings of the Women's Alliance, the umbrella grouping established in the Western Cape in 1991.

Lesbian feminists are a small but vocal minority amongst the lesbians of Cape Town. At present, only among the women members of OLGA could one expect to find a sizeable number of self-identified lesbian feminists, although it should be noted that Rape Crisis (Cape Town) has provided a comprehensive analysis of feminism over the past 25 years and has opened up a space for lesbian-feminist voices to be heard. However, most self-identified lesbians in the Western Cape do not call themselves 'lesbian feminist' (or even 'lesbian' for that matter — the preferred term is 'gay'); and they choose to participate in bar culture, private parties, or lesbian and gay clubs rather than discussion groups or other events held by OLGA. (An exception should be noted here, namely the liturgical services and socialising carried out by the Gay Christian Community and the Free Christian Fellowship.)

Reasons for the preference of a bar culture range from a disinterest in politics, to disagreement with the progressive politics of such groups, to feeling intimidated by the format and content of OLGA meetings. Both the terms 'lesbian' and 'feminist' are perceived by many 'gay' women as distasteful or threatening. Women involved in butch role-playing are afraid of being criticised for this by lesbian feminists. And working-class lesbians (black and white) find the emphasis on articulate debate alienating. A further difficulty is that many women have simply never been exposed to lesbian-feminist ideas: lesbian feminism remains largely the preserve of university-educated women.

It is important to note here that lesbian feminism, in South Africa at any rate, is in no way synonymous with lesbian separatism. Because there were no lesbian-only organisations, with the exception of the two-year period of existence of LILACS, those lesbians who held separatist views stayed away from lesbian and gay groups except for the occasional women-only activity and, more recently, the Lesbian Caucus of OLGA.

In Gender, in LAGO, and in OLGA, the lesbian members have consistently been outnumbered by the male gay members. The perennial scarcity of women in mixed-gender lesbian and gay organisations is in part to be explained by the existence of several women-centred and women-only organisations like the Black Sash and the United Women's Congress, where many lesbian-feminist women have preferred to place their energies. These organisations provided an ideological home for them so long as they downplayed their lesbianism.

Another reason for the scarcity of specifically lesbian organisations in South Africa may have to do with the reluctance of lesbian women to work on issues that have to do with lesbians alone: to 'deal with our own stuff'. In a country where institutionalised racism and capitalist greed have been the predominant social evils, both black and white women have felt pressured to ignore other forms of oppression, especially those connected to the politics of identity. It can be argued that many lesbian women have opted for a politics of 'caretaking', in which we work on taking care of any oppressed persons except ourselves.

In Cape Town in mid-1990, the first Women's Centre in South Africa was opened, funded partially by a private sponsor and partially by membership fees. This provided a safe space for homoerotically-inclined (though not necessarily feminist) women to meet and socialise with one another. The Centre presented challenging controversies of principle for those involved in it, such as whether the presence of lesbian women alienated heterosexual women. Many conflicts amongst

Cape Town lesbians came to be focused on the Centre. It is interesting to note that the tensions between those women wanting a purely social club and those wanting a space for discussions, art exhibitions, lesbian discussion groups and the like, almost exactly parallel the stresses experienced within LILACS a decade ago.

Further dissatisfaction centred on the prevalence of what might be termed 'therapism' in the programmes on offer at the Women's Centre; that is to say, a predominance of focus on topics such as depression, dream work, and relationships. Some women viewed this as an inappropriately individualistic approach to problems confronting women: an approach which failed to take cognisance of the essentially societal, structural causes of these problems. Although the centre has subsequently closed, it is hoped that future projects will build on its accomplishments and those of LILACS.

In closing, we would like to stress what we see as a need for greater unity in South African lesbian-feminist circles. In beginning to contradict the internalised oppressions that prevent us as women from 'dealing with our own stuff' and from empowering ourselves, we need to put the politics back into lesbianism. We need more than therapy and lesbian support groups; we need alliances within lesbian circles that are effective and durable. Only then will we be able to present a strong and resilient front from which to challenge the misogynist and homophobic society in which we live.

Notes

1 Betty Friedan, quoted in Mary Allen, *The Necessary Blankness: Women in Major American Fiction of the Sixties* (University of Illinois Press, 1976), p381.
2 Germaine Greer, *The Female Eunuch* (McGraw Hill, 1971), p30.
3 Ti-Grace Atkinson, quoted in editorial, *Signs* 4 (Summer 1979).
4 Barbara Smith, 'Racism in the Women's Movement', in Cherríe Moraga and Gloria Anzaldúa (eds) *This Bridge Called My Back: Writings by Radical Women of Color* (Persephone Press, 1981), p61.
5 Moraga and Anzaldúa, *This Bridge*, p29.
6 Adrienne Rich, 'Compulsory Heterosexuality and Lesbian Existence', in *Blood, Bread and Poetry* (Virago, 1990), p213.
7 Lillian Faderman, *Surpassing the Love of Men: Romantic Friendship and Love Between Women from the Renaissance to the Present* (William Morrow, 1981).
8 Joan Nestle, *In a Restricted Country* (Naiad Press, 1991).
9 Sheila Jeffries, quoted in Lillian Faderman, *Odd Girls and Twilight Lovers* (Harper Collins, 1992), p402.

Living with loss in the best way we know how:
AJDS and gay men in Cape Town

John V Pegge

It is almost a misnomer to talk about 'gay' people in South Africa, as 'gay' implies communal political identity, and, in this country, men who have sex with men and women who have sex with women have not yet achieved this. Most do not yet have enough trust in a movement that will allow them to shed the fear of exposure and give them the collective courage to stand together and be counted. They meet in the bars and the clubs they have claimed as their own, they meet in each other's homes away from their families and employers who could hurt them. Homophile groups are emerging and growing, but depend on the few with vision enough to trust the rewards of a movement.

By 1992, these groups were beginning to discover the issues they held in common and those that divided them. But the formation of gay identity in South Africa is complicated even further by the fact that, at the very time we are beginning to see the emergence of a homosexual people, we are also having to live with HIV infection. The impact of HIV on gay men in South Africa has already been catastrophic, but unlike in Western Europe and North America, homosexuals in the AIDS scenario of southern Africa are a minority amongst those who are infected, a minority that can be safely ignored by the majority and those who hold power.

In North America and in Western Europe, homosexual people had already coalesced into gay communities with powerful political lobbies by the time the epidemic struck in the mid-1980s. Thus, not only was there already an appropriate gay political movement in place to lead the fight against AIDS, but this fight could actually be used as a mobilizing tool, to further buttress and strengthen the gay movement itself. In South Africa however, HIV hit homosexual men at a time when gay community was still in its earliest stages. Unlike gay people in San Francisco or London, we did not have a strong enough movement upon which to build. Worse yet, rather than strengthening our emerging gay movement, AIDS threatened to destroy it entirely.

Certainly, the seeds of gay consciousness have been sown in South Africa, but although awareness increases, little account has been taken of AIDS and how this virus could make or destroy the emerging gay community; on the one hand, of how the fear of illness and stigma could make coming out so much more difficult and, on the other, of how the need for action could facilitate community growth.

AIDS may well be a virus and a devastating syndrome of frightening illnesses, but it is also the trauma and the terror of lovers being separated prematurely by death in the prime of their lives and of children dying before their parents. With AIDS, as never before, I have seen the bravery, the humour, the stamina and the loneliness of a people discarded as the flotsam of this world by the majority and those who hold power.

The years of the epidemic: 1983-1992

It was 1983, he was young, sensuous and serious and had recently qualified as a specialist anaesthetist. He had a high-profile position in a large provincial hospital, and was very much in the closet. At the time I was the volunteer director of the newly-established GASA-6010 Counselling Service, which was struggling to make an impact on appropriate human service provision for gay men and lesbians. He made a formal appointment to see me, and very seriously told me that in the United States, in cities like New York, Los Angeles and San Francisco, there was a new disease I should take note of, and that as a Counselling Service we should do something to prevent its spread amongst gay men in Cape Town. He told me that he was not an epidemiologist or a specialist in infectious diseases, but his reading of the literature suggested that this was a viral disease and that the infective agent was probably transmitted in semen.

I looked at him in sheer amazement: we hardly had the resources to keep together a 24-Hour Telephone Counselling Service and he was asking me to bother about a strange new disease reported amongst a handful of gay men in the United States. I did not take him seriously — after all, we did not have saunas and bath houses, dark rooms and black holes in Cape Town and anyway medical science was such that there was bound to be a cure around the corner. I remembered his visit and I remembered his warning. I pushed it to the back of my mind, because there was so much else to do. I really believed it could not happen here.

* * *

It was 1984, he was 23, with jet black hair and piercing blue eyes. He was a foreign national, employed by South African Airways as a cabin attendant. He lived in a Cape Town suburb with his lover of four years who was also employed by South African Airways. He came to see me. After ensuring confidentiality, he broke down and started crying. When the emotion cleared, he told me that he had just been discharged from hospital where he had been treated for a rare kind of pneumonia; doctors had told him he had AIDS. I froze and recalled my conversation with the young doctor the previous year. It was here, it was in our midst and I did not know how to deal with it. This beautiful young man recounted the litany of horrors regarding the way that he and his lover had been treated in a provincial hospital; he had been made to feel like an unwanted criminal, a leper. He and his lover had told their friends and now they had none. He ended by saying that he was a Catholic and wanted to make his confession and receive communion; they had called their priest, but he had not bothered to come.

My first encounter with a person with AIDS was not with an emaciated, living skeleton, but with a beautiful young man, who did not look very ill. He and his lover were my first teachers, how it was to live with this virus and see friends flee, doctors take to space suits, and, when the very last thing on your mind is sex, have healthcare professionals interrogate you about what you did in bed. Only weeks after our meeting this beautiful young man developed his second bout of pneumocystis carinii pneumonia and died. The day he died, we learned the cruel extent of the horror awaiting us. We could not find an undertaker to remove his body or a Catholic Church in which to hold his requiem mass.

* * *

It was still 1984, he was a young man doing his Masters in Educational Psychology at the University of Cape Town. He subscribed to the American gay magazine *The Advocate* and was the best informed person to undertake a safer-sex campaign amongst men who have sex with men attending gay bars and clubs in downtown Cape Town. We didn't have a budget, and so he conducted his one-man campaign on a person to person level. He went to the bars two or three times a week and started engaging people in discussions about AIDS and how to prevent it. He was ridiculed and rejected. 'Don't come in here and spoil our fun.'

* * *

It was 1985, he was 30, and he couldn't breathe. His general practitioner had some excuse as to why he could not do a house call, and suggested that an ambulance be called to take him to hospital. His housemate called the ambulance, it arrived 20 minutes later, and she told the crew he had AIDS and that he could not breathe. They told her that they could not take him because persons with AIDS had to be conveyed in a specially-equipped vehicle. They said they would summon it by radio, the wait would not be long. He could not breathe and waited two hours for the ambulance to arrive.

* * *

It was still 1985 and he was young, in hospital and he too could not breathe. He had been there quite a while, but his family and friends had not visited him. He asked the sister in charge to telephone me, and asked me to visit him urgently. I did so and held his hand and heard what he wanted. He wanted to make a will and bequeath R10 000 to GASA-6010 for the care of gay people living with AIDS. He

303

wanted to leave his signet ring to his nephew. I left and briefed a trust company on his instructions, they drew up his will and sent it to the hospital. He signed it five days before he died and the bequest he had made left his family very angry.

* * *

It was 1986, the townships were burning and young gay men were dying. Both drew the headlines. Despite the emerging debate and the increasing consensus that people with AIDS had a right to confidentiality and privacy, the *Cape Times* took perverse delight in reporting the names, identifying particulars and sensational smut about the young gay men who died of AIDS. Without political power, with other gay men saying they did not want to know about AIDS, there was little that could be done to ease the fear and the pain of the friends and the families of the young gay men dying of AIDS.

In a country where freedom of the press and freedom of speech was something of a fantasy, the press could suddenly not understand the rights of the individual to privacy and confidentiality. Names, we were told, should be revealed in the public interest, because then the men who had slept with these men would know that they were at risk. In the bars and the clubs the safer sex campaign went on, and still the men who had sex with men said, 'Do not spoil our fun; this is a rare and largely foreign disease; it can't happen to us.'

* * *

It was 1987 and he was 30 and gaunt. The call came from the police at DF Malan Airport. The constable said, 'We believe you work with people with AIDS. We have a man here who has flown in from New York; he is sick and has nobody to fetch him and nowhere to stay.' Long before the African National Congress was unbanned, long before formal agreements on the return of exiles, our first exile had returned. I picked him up at the airport and brought him home, his parents lived nearby, but did not want him in their home.

He had left Cape Town years before and settled in New York in search of freedom from oppression, freedom from rejection by his family, and the pursuit of a successful career as a ballet dancer. He danced in New York for as long as he could, he had lived in an apartment on the East Side and for the past year, he had been in and out of St Vincent's Hospital and watched his friends die. He had had pneumonia on two occasions, he showed signs of AIDS dementia complex, and when he ran out of money the Americans put him on a plane and sent him home, destitute and dying.

I got to know him well during the few months he had left. He showed me with pride the photographs he had brought back, images of a young and healthy man, dancing and successful. The reality of his present situation, destitute and dying, emaciated and yearning for reconciliation with his family, made me cry. He talked his family into letting him come home, and they let him sleep on the lounge settee. In the couple of months he had left, he managed to persuade his parents to accept him for who he was and love him in the best way that they could.

304

Living with Loss in the Best Way we Know How

* * *

It was June 1988, and I attended my first International AIDS Congress in Stockholm, Sweden. There were 8 000 delegates and I was overwhelmed. I met gay men from all parts of the world, all of whom were either living with HIV or caring for their fellows. One night during the congress we marched in our thousands, ten abreast with our candles burning. On my right was a doctor from Johannesburg, on my left a leatherman from Leningrad. There were thousands who shared my values and my commitment to life and to living. We reached the Tor, the tower in the centre of the city, and left our candles burning on the steps. As semi-darkness enfolded Stockholm at midnight, our candles lit the Tor and said we cared.

I returned to Cape Town feeling envigorated and strong; a friend met me at the airport and brought me home. Ten minutes later there was a knock at the door. Two men in jeans with guns tucked into the back of their pants produced identity documents stating they were police officers and said they had reason to believe there were drugs in my house. I froze, took fright, and let them in. They didn't begin to look for drugs, but asked me if I had video tapes and pornography. I said I did not, but they proceeded to search my home, room by room. They took all my video tapes and returned them three days later without an apology. I had told them the truth, there was no pornography. I clenched my teeth and knew I was back in the land of oppression. To ease my pain, I thought of us marching through Stockholm, with the police escorting us on horseback, the clickity-clop of hooves the only noise breaking the silence of our solidarity in remembering those we had lost, and rekindling our determination to fight this epidemic with love.

It was 1989 and the men who have sex with men, who meet in the bars and the clubs, no longer said 'Don't spoil our fun, it can't happen to us.' They took the condoms we offered and asked for more.

* * *

It was 1989 and the numbers had grown. There were several who were homeless, one of whom slept on Greenmarket Square, and so we rented a house in which they could have shelter and care for one another. We had no money to appoint a member of staff. They lived there well, but four of them died and the pain was too much for those who survived. This was not the way to care for those who lived with this virus. There was no reason for their alienation and separation from those who did not live with this virus. We would only win the battle when all of us, gay and straight, believed that this was our disease and we would have to fight it together.

It was during this time that a powerful purple-clad cleric phoned me and said he didn't want to intrude, but would it be alright if he visited those who lived in the house? He said he was busy and would not have much time, but he would call on his way to a meeting in town. He is known for his humour and deep compassion, most whites regard him as a troublesome priest, most blacks pin their hopes on his power. His name is Desmond Tutu, Anglican Archbishop of Cape Town and undoubtedly the most powerful priest in the land. He came with a priest whom he left in the car and said, 'I will only be a short while, we have a meeting

307

to attend.' He entered the house and found a young white gay man washing the body of a terminally ill young black woman. He stayed for over an hour and was very late for his meeting. I do not know what he said to those who lived at the house, but they were deeply honoured by his visit: those who were white no longer saw him as a troublesome priest, those who were black were affirmed in what they knew all along, that he really cared. He left the house and entered the car, turned to the priest and said, 'I know that I am late, but that was important, I did not minister to them, they ministered to me.' One who held power knew the truth and was no longer afraid.

* * *

It was the same year, 1989, and at the next International AIDS Congress in Montreal, Canada, I delivered a paper entitled 'Networking, The Survival Strategy of the Gay Minority in South Africa'. Those who lived with this virus and those who cared knew that oppression and prejudice were the issues we must fight, and said so. But back home, the men who lived with this virus and those who cared were still too frightened to fight. The scientists had made much progress and there were now drugs which could really contain the ravages of this virus for a significant time. But back home the state healthcare system said we could not have these drugs, they were too expensive. Back home the medical insurance industry said it could not bear the costs and set limits on claims for HIV-related disease. How strange. The state healthcare system does heart and kidney transplants and the medical aids schemes are happy to pay. But when it comes to this virus, another standard applies: suddenly we are Third World and there is not enough money to go around.

* * *

It was 1990 and Mandela was free. The laws that separated us according to the colour of our skin were scrapped, but the laws that tried to prevent men from loving men and women from loving women remained on the statute book. The police raided our bars and our clubs and took away our condoms. We went to see the Divisional Commissioner of Police who said it couldn't happen. We went to see the Regional Director of Health, who wrote a letter to ensure it would not happen again.

The men who have sex with men, who meet in the bars and clubs were frightened and did not hit back: they knew there would be more condoms and they would continue to love men, in the best way they knew how. The men who love men and who live with this virus knew they were no longer alone. It was no longer rare or strange to hear of others who live with this virus; who were sick or dying. Those who lived with it and those who did not were coming together, to help in the best way they could.

* * *

Living with Loss in the Best Way we Know How

It was still 1990 and he was 27 and had just qualified as a chartered accountant. He and his lover were buying their first home. The building society said he must insure his life before he could have the bond, so they sent a broker to him and he took out a policy. A week later the broker phoned and said he must see a doctor for a medical, to be paid for by the insurance company. He saw the doctor who completed the form and took a tube of blood from his arm. He was not asked to return and went on his way, happy to have completed the formality which would secure him his home.

A few days later the doctor phoned: 'You're fine, but I am sorry to have to tell you, that your HIV test came back positive.' The doctor said he was welcome to come and see him, but the test had been done, the insurance company would no longer pay. He went cold, 'How could this be? It can't be me.' His dreams and aspirations were suddenly gone, 'How do I tell my lover? No I can't. How do I tell my family? No I can't. How do I live my life? No I can't.' Twelve hours later the police found his car on Table Mountain Drive, in it his body was cold. The note to his lover told the truth. Everybody cried, except the building society, the insurance company, the doctor and the police.

* * *

It was 1991 and I had seen more than a thousand young men who have sex with men live with this virus: 139 of them no longer lived in this place of misunderstanding, prejudice and bigotry. There was now an industry of those who wanted to prevent the spread of this virus and provide care. But there was much competition and little sharing of expertise; those who lived with this virus looked on with suspicion and asked, 'Where are the drugs and when will you listen?'

It was the month of May, it was cold and grey and time to go to the Cathedral to light the candle which says, 'I remember those I have lost and care about those I have not.' I thought of the young smiling faces of those whom we had lost. I thought of my brothers and sisters across the globe that day, who from Tokyo to Anchorage, all around this planet, were gathering like me to light candles that say, 'We remember and we care.' They made me feel strong as I entered the Cathedral and saw it was full. I thought back to the 30 men and three women, who had started this ritual in the hope that we would win. In the Cathedral now, four years later, were those who lived with this virus, who sought the strength to go on. In this Cathedral were the lovers and friends, the mothers and fathers, aunts and uncles of those we had already lost. In this Cathedral were those who cared and wanted it to end. No longer were we alienated and isolated, for in this Cathedral gay and straight together lit flames of power, warmth, compassion and love. In this Cathedral were some who held power: an ambassador, a mayor and the most powerful priest in the land. Now there were three who held power, who knew the truth and showed that they cared.

* * *

It is 1992 and every week I see new men who have sex with men learning that they too live with this virus. Most come quickly to terms with their mortality, know that their lives might be limited, and surge into life and living. In July the government said that the route of transmission of 53% of those newly-diagnosed with AIDS had been heterosexual intercourse. Nobody said that 47% were still men who had sex with men. They still meet in the clubs and the bars, and they cruise at the Wall on the seafront. All of them know it can happen to us; they take 16 000 condoms a month and ask for more. I watch them dance in the clubs and cruise at the Wall, part of the celebration of life for men who have sex with men. Many will die, but some will survive.

It is 1992. He is 25 and a pretty boy; they sent him to prison for shoplifting. The prison tested his blood and found he was positive. They put him in a single cell and then sent him to hospital. The hospital told him his immune system was seriously impacted. The hospital told him there was a drug which could help, but they could not give it to him; he would have to pay. He went back to prison and wrote me a letter asking for help. The prison told me nobody visited him, and so I arranged for a volunteer to do so. The volunteer phoned his family, but still they did not visit him. He wanted the drug and nobody would pay. Last night he covered his head with a blanket and set it on fire. Now he is critical and in intensive care. He is unconscious and breathing his last; his family has finally visited him. They phoned a short while ago and asked for a priest, who would sign him with a cross and send him on his way.

I go to the bar and order a beer. I look at the men who love men and catch one who smiles. I order two beers, one for him and one for me. We talk and I know that he needs to love me and I need to love him. He is a beautiful young man and I invite him home. In bed we talk and I stroke, caress and hold his firm body. He tells me he lives with this virus, I hold him closer and say, 'Who doesn't?' I need to love this young man and he me. We put rubbers on our cocks and love each other the best way we know how, the way we always have and always will.

Of gay rights and the pitfalls of the 'PC': *A polemic*

Digby Ricci

That unjustly maligned Victorian Jeremiah, Matthew Arnold, once lamented that he lived in an age in which the old was not yet dead, the new not yet born. At a time in which grotesque government corruption, 'covert' atrocities, and police conniv-ance at massacres indicate that there is, alas, life in the rabid Nat dog yet, South Africans cannot claim with any conviction that the bad old days have come to an end. At the same time, there are disturbing indications, admittedly by no means comparable in magnitude to the excesses of the existing tyranny, that the new South Africa may well enter the world of the Politically Correct, unless considerable vigi-lance is exercised. It would be sad indeed if South Africa went from reactionary 'old' oppression to trendy 'new' oppression without any stage of true democracy in between. The flickers of 'PC' intolerance form a lurid will o'the wisp rather than a raging conflagration, but they should not be dismissed because of their comparative triviality. Already there are signs that dissenting voices will be little beloved in the post-apartheid South Africa.

In August 1989 we were confronted with the unsavoury spectacle of black students, aptly dubbed *Wits wolwe* by the cartoonist, Andy, disrupting a debate be-tween Van Zyl Slabbert and Zach de Beer (the former and current leaders of the white liberal opposition), whom they ludicrously denounced as a capitalist Klaus Barbie; we have recoiled from the sight of demonstrators at the Winnie Mandela trial waving banners declaring 'Homosex [sic] is not in Black Culture'; we have had to endure the egregious spectacle of Martin Orkin applying the label 'racist' to anybody who does not take the 'cultural materialist' (read Marxist) line on Shake-speare. Freedom of speech, sexual freedom, freedom of thought — all these prerequisites of real democracy are under attack by South African advocates of the 'PC'. One must never forget that the narrow exclusivity of the 'PC' has nothing to do with any genuine struggle for freedom. Real liberators are inclusive in their

311

views. You do not find the Sylvia Pankhursts and Germaine Greers, the Martin Luther Kings and Albert Luthulis, the Oscar Wildes and Gore Vidals of the world attempting, on the grounds of sexism, racism, homophobia, or Eurocentricism, to curb the intellectual curiosity and knowledge of politically concerned human beings.

The campaign for gay rights has come comparatively late to South Africa, and it may seem foolishly over-cautious to warn its adherents to guard against the 'PC' idiocies and excesses of far more established and powerful protest groups. Yet, are not early days exactly the time for self-criticism, which should never — as it so often is by militants — be confused with self-hatred? What follows is a polemical attempt by an unashamed liberal humanist to argue South Africa's new gay activists into avoiding the pitfalls of the 'PC', and to exhort them to establish a movement both powerful and tolerant, both effective and open-minded.

Terminology

In the beginning is trouble about the word; even in these early days, an element of shrillness has crept into views of what terms should and should not be used. 'What do you prefer? "Faggots?"', a gay activist snapped at me when I expressed my aversion to the use of the word, 'gay', itself. The entire question whether militant minorities should impose usage on language users in general is, I should think, a vexed one. After all, no general consultation of all English speakers has taken place about the adoption of 'gay' to mean homosexual. Any unfortunate teacher who has had to endure sniggers over Yeats's great 'Lapis Lazuli' ('Hamlet and Lear are gay') or Pope's line, 'Belinda smiled and all the world was gay', has felt the anger that should accompany the distortion of the meaning of a perfectly acceptable word by a special-interest imposition. How many homosexuals — let alone heterosexuals — really want the new meaning of 'gay' to be generally imposed?

John Simon's argument that 'gay' in its latest sense is restrictive and insulting, suggesting both fatuous jollity and promiscuity, seems to me definitive:

> As Eric Partridge's *A Dictionary of Slang and Unconventional English* makes clear, the word comes from early nineteenth-century British slang, where the adjective *gay* referred to women leading... a harlot's life... [T]here is every reason to object to a supposedly official word that carries clear implications of whoring. Apparently some homosexuals who advocated it must have been of the screaming queen type, which ostentatiously acts out a parody of homosexual behaviour.... Other homosexuals may have felt that the prevalent patterns of promiscuity in homosexual behaviour (probably socially conditioned rather than inherent) justify the use of such a whorish word. That, however, is self-hate and should not be legitimized. And some self-deceivers and hypocrites may have actually believed that homosexual lives are merrier than heterosexual ones and so

*merit the appellation **gay**. Yet such manifest untruth cannot be endorsed.*[1]

To complain at this stage about a term that I myself have reluctantly adopted may seem needlessly carping, but perhaps the sheer silliness of taking up 'gay' can serve as a useful warning. Protests should be made not only against what CS Lewis called 'verbicide' (the destruction of a useful meaning), but also against horrible coinages. 'Heterosexism', for instance, has all the noxiousness of a truly 'PC' coinage, suggesting that *we* are virtuous and *they* are wicked. Anyone who believes in the necessity for a word that suggests that sex-based bigotry is a specifically heterosexual vice has not listened to the misogynistic outbursts of all too many male homosexuals.

The insistence on a uniform style of speech and writing for a specific protest group is, in any case, disturbingly tyrannical, and suggests a belief in monolithic conformity, rather than in a diversity of opinions among those who share a common cause. About a year ago, I attended a Johannesburg panel discussion during the course of which an ill-informed, professed feminist kept asserting: 'We say "personhole" ', conveniently failing to define the 'we', and forgetting that such eminent feminist thinkers as Germaine Greer and Brigid Brophy have questioned the whole process of tampering with existing language. Obviously, all terms of abuse and patronage ('chick', 'bint', 'authoress', etc) must be angrily rejected, but some liberated women prefer 'chairman', for example, to the awkward 'chairperson', putting forward the perfectly scholarly argument that one should reclaim the original Anglo Saxon 'mann', which had a meaning that was not gender-restrictive.

Gay activists should take heed of Greer's characteristically illuminating and tolerant warning that a movement should not become a religion, 'complete with things you [can't] say ... observances you [have] to carry out. There's crypto-fascism in that position.'[2] Greer, of course, is not rejecting outrage at manifestations of real bigotry, but simply pointing to the necessity for careful definition and the acceptance of differing perceptions of what constitutes abuse. As always, we can learn much from the women's movement.

The real enemy?

There is a distressing tendency in gay circles to apotheosize and to demonize. Overpraise because of shared sexual orientation is always foolish and harmful. It casts doubt on one's ability to assess real excellence, and gives one's opponents scope to question *all* one's judgments. Edmund White's skilfully controlled mandarin prose and David Leavitt's affecting blend of wit and pathos deserve high praise, but one should not make the error of speaking of them in terms worthy of a Jane Austen, a George Eliot, a Flaubert, a Faulkner.[3] The greatness of Marlowe, Verlaine, Wilde, Tennessee Williams is denigrated if we raise to their ranks those who are not altogether deserving of the elevation. As Gore Vidal once commented airily, 'it's not enough to be homosexual; one must be talented too.' South African gays who insist on giving serious attention to the pornographic trash of Stephen Gray and foolishly regard the toothless camp bitchery of Pieter-Dirk Uys as fanged satire should mull over this comment very carefully.

The celebrity-list defence of homosexuality should also be avoided. Not only is such a defence irrelevant and, frequently, inaccurate, but it can also prove to be a double-edged sword. Those of dangerously little learning who claim Milton for the homosexual ranks simply because his delicate good looks caused him, as a student, to be nicknamed the 'lady of Christ's', and who insist that Shakespeare 'had to be one of us'[4] must consider the fact that such flamboyant name-dropping requires them to drop the names of the infamous as well as of the celebrated. Do we mention Titus Oates of the 'Popish Plot', McCarthy's henchman, Roy Cohn, Leopold and Loeb, and Anthony Blunt in the same breath as Alexander the Great, Plato, and Tchaikovsky? Honesty should compel us to do so, and the ranks of notorious homosexuals will, naturally, balance the ranks of the justly renowned. So it is with all human beings; it's a fallen world. Human rights are for all of us fallible people; one should not fight for them beneath the banner of the famous.

Demonizing putative foes is equally harmful to a cause that wishes to command respect, rather than to alienate potential sympathisers. After all, one can reject taints of baseness in the views of the great — TS Eliot's anti-semitism, for instance — without belittling their considerable achievements.

George Orwell's attacks on the 'pansy left' should not lessen our admiration for *Animal Farm* or *Homage to Catalonia*, and I have never found that Rebecca West's undoubted recoil from homosexuality has decreased my admiration for her glittering, labyrinthine prose or her profound political insights. It is always necessary to decide when regret is the appropriate response rather than militant opprobrium.

In any case, there is always the question of priorities. Breaking butterflies (or even the most noxious bugs!) upon a wheel is really time-wasting when there are inexplicably applauded monsters to slay. Once again, we should take a leaf from the feminists' book. Germaine Greer trounced Norman Mailer and William F Buckley in debate; she did not waste her time on that farcical chauvinist hog, the faded actor, Oliver Reed. There is so much major injustice for homosexuals to combat. Let us demolish the illogical vituperation of Paul Johnson, who, blithely disregarding African statistics, insists that AIDS is a purely homosexual phenomenon; let us campaign against Clause 28[5], against the continued criminalisation of consensual sodomy in 25 American states, against South Africa's discriminatory age of consent for homosexuals. Let us not emulate those idiots who, by using homosexuality as a bludgeon, attempt to injure often neutral, or even sympathetic public figures. What did the protesters who screamed 'dyke' at the understandably bewildered Jodie Foster hope to achieve? All they did was imitate heterosexual homophobes by using the term as a 'shocking' insult.

The practice of 'outing' does not seem to have entered South Africa yet, and I, for one, fervently hope that it never will. I do not claim that it isn't occasionally a tempting weapon. Whenever a corpulent queen writes a homophobic column for a reactionary newspaper, one may long to create thousands of incriminating posters, but this dangerous temptation has to be resisted. 'Outing' exploits the tragic fact that the revelation of homosexuality can still destroy reputations and lives. This wicked injustice should be eliminated, certainly not used as a strategy by those who advocate an end to sex-based oppression. In any case, one could argue that the self-deceiving misery of the completely closeted life is punishment enough, even for those who belong to what Christopher Hitchens dubbed 'that special group of closet homosexuals who delight in joining the gay-bashing pack'.[6] The fate of Robert Bauman, extreme rightwing Maryland Republican, who actually opposed a housing bill because it *didn't* discriminate against homosexuals, reads like a Mediaeval exemplum of the dangers of hypocrisy. Bauman's eventual arrest for soliciting, the disgrace, the desertion by professed friends — all seem horribly inevitable. 'Outing' could hardly have caused more suffering, and, anyway, I do not believe that it should ever be the desire of campaigners for freedom to inflict misery upon others.

Strategies

Strategy is often regarded as a dirty word by those who crusade for a just cause: it seems to smack of deviousness and window-dressing. Yet good sense dictates — or should dictate — that the use of certain tactics will assist a cause, while others will do it considerable damage. When, in 1911, a chiffon-clad Mrs Pankhurst informed an American audience that she was 'what you would call a hooligan', she knew that the elegance of her appearance would further her cause by ironically underlining the difference between the human reality of a feminist leader and the virago caricature of Asquith's propaganda. Such an intelligent refusal to conform to the definitions of the prejudiced should be part of gay thinking too.

Alas, there is little evidence of such awareness in South African gay circles. The impact of the first two gay pride marches in Johannesburg was considerably undermined by the fact that the media concentrated solely on the drag queens in the processions. To those who were upset and surprised by this emphasis, one was tempted to say, 'Wake up and taste the coffee!' What on earth did they expect, and why weren't we prepared *temporarily* to curb a minority's rights for the sake of assisting gays to present a serious, not risible, front? A refusal to allow homosexuals to march in drag would hardly have been a Stalinist act, and it could have done much good in promoting the gay cause to the mass public as a significant movement, not a sequined joke.

The South African gay movement should also examine searchingly and critically its attitudes towards the heterosexual community. All too many activists who believe that homosexual slang, with its plethora of reductive terms for women ('fish' is probably the most offensive) is amusing, and assert that drag shows are not distasteful attacks on women, are outraged by terms like 'queer' and 'fag', and reject with disgust heterosexuals' mincing caricaturing of homosexual behaviour. It appears that 'our' prejudices are acceptable; 'theirs' are not. Such a horribly slanted perception is obviously absurd and self-destructive. I find the misogynistic statements of many male homosexuals particularly disgusting, and the 'all gays should be mutually supportive' view that permits them equally reprehensible.

One should never defend the indefensible. Instead of promoting Stephen Gray's venomously misogynistic *Time of our Darkness* and *Born of Man*, the local gay newspaper, *Exit*, should have denounced them in no uncertain terms. After all, heterosexual feminists have frequently and courageously put themselves on the line for our cause — think of Gloria Steinem arranging a 'Kate is Great' rally for the vituperatively abused bisexual, Kate Millett — and the least we can do is to return the support. Indeed, support for women and awareness of their continued oppression (if you think times have changed that much, then a reading of Susan Faludi's depressing, scathing *Backlash: The Undeclared War Against Women* should put you right) are, I think, essential for the true fighter for gay rights. The words of Olive Schreiner's Lyndall should still be a glorious exhortation: 'There was never a man who said one word for woman but he said two for man, and three for the whole human race.'[7] An inclusive movement with good sense, vision, realism, and tolerance as its most apparent qualities: that is the kind of gay rights movement *I* want, and that, I believe, is the only kind of movement that will manage to achieve equality.

Notes

1 John Simon, *Paradigms Lost: Reflections on Literacy and Its Decline* (Penguin Books, 1984), pp25- 26.
2 Quoted in Marcia Cohen, *The Sisterhood: The Inside Story of The Women's Movement and the Leaders Who Made It Happen* (Fawcett Columbine, 1988), p353.
3 I am fully aware of the fact that, in this age of demented deconstructionist theories, a Stephen King can be subjected to the same solemn analysis as a Margaret Atwood, but, fortunately, there is still a thinking reading public outside the poisoned groves of academe which continues to draw distinctions between great, good, and trashy writing.
4 Eric Partridge is scholarly and illuminating on this vexed issue. 'Had Shakespeare, so frank and courageous, been a homosexual, he would have subtly yet irrefutably conveyed the fact. Had he ever been much interested in the subject, he would have mentioned it far more often.' Eric Partridge, *Shakespeare's Bawdy* (Routledge & Kegan Paul, 1968), p16.
5 '[T]he infamous clause sought to prohibit [British] local authorities from "promoting" homosexuality.' Simon Shepherd and Mick Wallace, *Coming on Strong: Gay Politics and Culture* (Unwin Hyman, 1989), pp16-17.
6 See Christopher Hitchens, 'It Dare Not Speak Its Name: Fear and Self-loathing on the Gay Right', *Harper's*, Volume 275, No. 1647 (August, 1987).
7 Olive Schreiner, *The Story of an African Farm* (Penguin Books, 1979), p192.

SIX —
Testaments

Promise you'll tell no-one:
A memoir

Koos Prinsloo
translated by Johannes Bruwer

*Ik kan di lesers van hierdie eenvoudige jagtersverhale ferseker
dat hierdie gebeurtenisse wat ik beskrijf nie uitgedink is of uit
geleesde boeke kom nie. Alles het werklik gebeur en is nie
fersindsels nie, maar ware manlike ondervindings.*[1]
— Jacobus Petrus (Koos) Prinsloo (1885–1950), the author's
grandfather, in an unpublished text *Mij Ervarings op Safari in
Kenia*

The first time I touched somebody else's cock was one summer afternoon in a
farmyard near Ingogo, a tiny place with a post office, a police station and a railway
station at the foot of the Majuba mountain, a few miles from Newcastle in Natal.
Except for Amcor, the coal mines and the power station in the vicinity, Newcastle
was just another farm *dorp* with one traffic light.

It happened in 1963, the year we heard on the morning news that John F
Kennedy had been shot dead in his open car and the year in which I squealed on
my sister: while the grownups were playing canasta around the powdered wooden
table in the kitchen of the neighbouring farm, Tant Sarie's son Eddy kissed my
sister on the sofa in the sitting room. I told my mom and dad that night. She was in
Standard 7 or 8 and mad about Cliff Richard and the Beatles. My dad was furious.
It was also the year in which Beauboy, the eldest son of friends of ours from
Kenya, died of leukemia. (Tant Sarie, who had been born with a caul, had a premo-

---

1 I can assure the readers of these simple hunting tales that these events that I describe have
not been invented or taken from books that have been read. Everything really happened and
has not been made up, but these are true manly experiences.

nition that day.) My mother hugged me to her in the bathroom, the same bathroom in which my dad and I bathed together on some evenings.

On that afternoon in 1963 I was playing in the backyard with the older boys who were helping with the sheep-shearing, when two of them pinned a third down on the ground. He laughed and struggled, but they held him down and undid his fly buttons. Later they also egged me on to push my hand into the front of his khaki shorts and to feel. I was six years old, but I was the son of the *baas*. He must have been a teenager because his cock lay thick in my hand. He laughingly broke free and the three of them went chortling along the footpath through the thicket of poplars on their way to the huts.

On our farm on the Uasin Gishu plateau near Eldoret in Kenya my minder, Cheblengingh, would join me on safari in my green American jeep pedalcar with the white five-pointed star down the terrace in front of our stone house. It was during the time of the Mau-Mau and the servants, Kebie and Bundotich, had to be out of the house by sundown. Then we would shift the beds in the bedrooms so that someone outside couldn't just take a pot-shot (as my mom always says) through the window at night.

Cheblengingh also had to push me in the swing next to the lane of pine trees, and one day I pinched him until he stole the dry tips of my dad's game biltong from the wire for me. I also remember the time when our foreman Arap Rongiag's little boy and I pulled down our pants for each other down at the chicken coops. Enchanted, I watched as he squeezed out a turd with his buttocks in the air and then did the same.

All I knew of sex was that Felicity, the daughter of our British neighbours on the White Highlands, had a little hole and later, on the Ingogo farm, when I wanted to know why my middle sister had to get a bra, the grown-ups just laughed. It was there that I crept out on hands and knees over the wooden floor one Sunday afternoon to see what was contained in the doctors' books forbidden to me. And it was there that my dad hit my middle sister with a *takkie* (sports shoe) after we had played sky-rocket and I had broken my arm. I sat on her feet and she launched me into the air and therefore it was her fault, my dad probably reasoned. That Christmas I kissed Niens, a little girl my age, at the reservoir and gave her a plastic ring from a Christmas cracker as a gift. And then the neighbour shot my dog, Spot (a bullterrier/foxterrier cross), because he allegedly caught sheep and the hail wiped out the harvest. My dad sold the farm and got shift work at the Ingagane power station, 15 minutes' drive away on the other side of Newcastle.

The white neighbourhood had about 200 neat face-brick homes, a public swimming pool, a tennis court, a *jukskei* (frontier game) court, a shooting range and a library. The recreation hall was still being built so we went to watch *Tammy and the Bachelor* with Debbie Reynolds one Saturday night down at the prefab area where the construction people lived, just this side of the black single quarters. That's also where Sunday school was held, and Escom's Christmas party.

Now my mother would no longer teach me and I was to join the other kids on the bus to school, the Kilbarchan State School for the Grade 1 to Standard 2 kids of the area.

George, the fat, blond little boy from the Ballengeich carbide factory with whom I made friends on the first day at school, later told me more about sex; he and Lodewyk, who lived only two houses away from us. One day in Grade 2 or Standard 1 Lodewyk pulled down his pants in the boys' toilets and showed us the black bruises on his buttocks. His dad had hit him and his elder brother like that because they sneaked away to a movie one night. They were Apostolics and movies were a sin. It was in the same toilets that we once took turns to scrutinize a gigantic turd in the bowl and then decided jointly that it could only be the black gardener's.

George came to stay over with Lodewyk one weekend and they laughed at me because I asked, 'What is that?' when George in the swimming pool spoke about 'fucking'. George explained that babies grow from 'pus'. Lodewyk's dad keeps his 'pus' in a little bottle, George said, and Lodewyk and his brother fuck their little sister. Lodewyk said that George was lying and that it was really the son of our neighbours at the back, Dicky in Standard 3, who fucked his sister, Amanda. Later I wanted to fuck Amanda with the twins, René and André, but she said no because her mother had caught her and Dicky in the maid's room that time and had beat her terribly. Later she did pull down her pants for me in the coal bin and I pulled down mine for her. My 'chingeling' (as my mom called it) was stiff. But before we could do anything — not that I would have known exactly what — her brother found us. We said we were playing hide and seek. Lodewyk also said that white men were tortured in the old days by being tied naked to masts and that black women (he said *meide*) would then rub their cunts against them. If the men got a cock-stand, their cocks were chopped off, he said. It was soon after this that an emergency flash interrupted the Springbok Radio stories one afternoon and I had to run down the corridor to tell my mom behind the Pfaff sewing machine that Dr Verwoerd had been stabbed with a knife.

One afternoon when I got off the bus, I heard my new dog, Bonzo (a black corgi/skipper cross), yelping. He was trapped in the corner of Lodewyk's yard and Lodewyk's dad was hitting him with a sjambok. I ran home and I think my mom went to save the dog from old Eksteen. But I was still uncertain about where babies come from and of wanking I knew little. It was the same year in which my eldest sister would fall and hurt her back. She had to go to hospital and gave up varsity. My father would resign his job at the power station early the next year and we would all move to Rhodesia, my eldest sister included. But during the December holidays before we went to live on the farm near Gatooma I heard more about fucking and pulling wire.

My older cousin Robert asked me during that Christmas vacation at Gwelo (the same vacation in which he gave me a blue eye and Ouma Ben made him sit in the corner) whether I knew why there was a fly in my father's pants. Not only for pissing, he said, but also to fuck my mom through. Where did I think I came from, then? He tried to teach me to smoke *stompies* behind the bamboos and in the bathroom, with uncles and aunts around the table in the next room assembling a jigsaw puzzle, he tried to teach me how to wank. He also tried to fuck me one afternoon under one of the single beds on the stoep (all we could see was Ouma Ben's feet), but his cock wouldn't go in. A week later with my other cousins at Umtali, Robert and the others egged on the youngest, Pietebaas, to taunt me, 'You're a sissy, you're a sissy', and the eldest, Jannie, tried to strangle me with a tie one evening. (Years later they found Pietebaas' body next to his motorbike and shotgun in a mealie field on his uncle's farm near Hartley. He had just come out of the army.)

Back at Ingagane, while my mom and the others were packing for the move, one afternoon in the bathroom I managed to wank. Immediately afterwards I locked myself in my room and started doing it again, but my mom came hammering at the door, furiously demanding to know why I had locked it.

When we moved we gave Bonzo to the neighbours.

In Standard 3 in the hostel in Messina I wanked once or twice with the Standard 4 boy in my room and he taught me an English rhyme:

Down in the valley where the grass grows long,
There sits a lady with nothing on,
Here comes a cowboy clippity clop,
Down falls his pants and out comes his whop,
Three months later all went well,
Six months later she did swell,
Nine months later Bing, bang, pop,
Out came a baby with a six foot whop.

But whether babies came out in front or behind, he couldn't tell me. During the Easter holidays (Oupa Ben had been dead a month already) at my mother's cousin on a farm on the other side of Beit Bridge, I tried to fuck the bitch dog, but her cunt was too small. Ouma Ben died two months later and my dad said he had seen what had happened in the Belgian Congo and Kenya, Rhodesia is going the same way. By September we were back at Ingagane (Bonzo came to live with us again) and I with my Messina Laerskool blazer was in Standard 3 in the Junior School at Newcastle. But my eldest sister had stayed behind in Salisbury. She would come home at Christmas and say she was engaged. Father said even though they had never met the man they trusted her judgment for she was an adult.

The Saturday afternoon before we saw her to the train I had to help my father wash the car. We started arguing because I hadn't dried the hub caps. First he hit me with the wet towel twisted into a sheep's tail, but then in the bedroom he fetched a belt from the wardrobe. Afterwards my mom drew a bath for me and disinfected the broken skin with mercurochrome. 'And we always laughed at old Eksteentjie,' was her only comment. In the passage my dad told my eldest sister if she had only been spanked more she wouldn't have been such a slut today. (Years later he said he had seen I was getting out of hand and had only done it for my own good.) That evening at home after we had gone to see my sister off, my parents made me promise that I wouldn't tell anybody what had happened and for the rest of the summer holidays I wore my long pants and didn't go swimming. I was ten and my dad never hit me again, only one time in Standard 8 three weeks before my music exams he locked the piano after we had been at odds.

It must have been in Standard 4 or 5 that I started to hug Bonzo tightly, sometimes so tightly that he yelped. I also taught him to lick my arse while I pulled my wire and tossed him off sometimes. (Years later, when I was already at university, the dog started whining from rheumatism and my dad had him put down.)

Only in Standard 6 (Iscor was already being built and the *dorp* (small town) was expanding rapidly) did I again touch somebody's cock. One summer afternoon Dirk (he was two standards ahead of me), two girls and I stood in a row with our legs apart on the shallow side in the swimming pool. Like a string of dolphins we would dive in the water one after the other and swim underneath each other's legs. In the men's changing room Dirk and I later wanked. Again a week later, in the stretch of veld beyond the swimming pool on the way to the ash dams (there were beggar-ticks on my towel), and then one Saturday evening during intermission at a movie show in the recreation hall we slipped out to the shooting range. It even happened in the back of the school bus on the way home one afternoon. (Later Dirk spread the story that Jannie, who had been in the Drakensberg Boys' Choir when he was small and who took music with me, and I fucked each other. Poor Jannie.)

In the same year stories also started circulating in the school about Venter, a Durban boy from a broken home who had been dumped in the hostel at Newcastle. First he fucked Stoop, a boy in my class. The hostel father caught them. (The same Master made me stay behind during one break and took me into the little bookroom. Do I have problems at home, he asked me while he wildly kneaded the front of his pants. Later he was transferred to another school. There were rumours about him and a little guy in Standard 6.) Stoop came into a cold-drink tin, it was said. At break Rudie, a boy in Standard 9, shouted at him on the playing ground: 'Is your arse sore?' Stoop only laughed sheepishly and I knew it was true. There were also stories that Venter had poked one of the hostel girls on the rugby field. Then the big story broke. Led by Venter, three other boys (among them Dirk's brother who was in the same standard as I) fucked a girl in the hall's cellar under the stage. She (was her name Aletta?) apparently said yes at first, but became frightened when she started bleeding and went to squeal. Venter was expelled and two of the other boys were sent to a school in a neighbouring town by their parents. The twin brother of one of them, Leslie, and three other soldiers were mistaken for Swapo by their buddies on the Border in 1976 and shot dead. (What could have become of Venter?)

By Standard 7 I still did not have a name for this thing. At night I tried to console myself that I was only halfway like that. And I prayed that it would go away and that I would like only girls. Then *The New Illustrated Medical and Health Encyclopedia* came to my salvation, four books my dad got as a bonus with a set of the *Colliers Encyclopedia*. The saleslady had a French accent and halfway through her presentation she said: 'I want to make peepee'. My dad bought the

323

books. I started reading at *reproductive system* and then worked my way through from *cervix* to *vulva. Homosexuality* was among the entries.

It was also that year that a man pushed open the door of the public toilet in the town one Saturday afternoon when I was standing there reading the graffiti on the wall. He was wearing a gold ring which chafed the skin off the head of my cock. When I saw him from the school bus two years later he was pushing a pram with a baby in it, a rundown woman at his side.

At the beginning of Standard 8 I fell in love with a new Dutch girl in the school with red hair and blue eyes. I watched her every break at the tuck shop, but when at last I scraped up the courage to talk to her she called me a *klootzak* (scrotum). By October that year I was writing poems for a new English boy in Standard 9. I only watched him during breaks where he stood to one side. Once I sneaked into his classroom to take an exercise book from his bookcase and read his name: Grant Thayer.

It was on a Sunday afternoon the following year that I took Bonzo for a walk in the stretch of veld behind the swimming pool. (My dad had forbidden us to swim on Sundays.) A distance in front of me a man in a khaki shirt and pants was walking. I didn't take notice of him until I came across him at a drift where he was lying behind a heap of earth. His pants were unbuttoned and when he saw me he immediately stopped masturbating. I walked closer. My breath was racing. '*Sawubona*' (Good day), I said when he jumped up. 'He wants to bathe,' he said and pointed to the ash dams. We stood watching each other for a time. His muscled diaphragm was moving up and down rapidly. Then I said: 'I want your thing.' I pointed to his pants. 'No, he hasn't got money, *baas*,' he replied, flustered. I jumped away and headed into the veld. (Had I but known that afternoon that my dad would tell me years later, when I told him I fuck men, that my sister had not been in hospital for her back in 1967 but in a Dutch Reformed Church home for unmarried mothers.) Only when I ran into a wire fence did I calm down. I whistled for Bonzo. He came running through the long grass and we started walking back to the residential area. When I eventually looked in the direction of the ash dams again, I spotted him immediately. He was standing on the heap of earth. Above his head his khaki shirt flapped wildly in his hands. Without looking back again, I just kept on walking home along the fence.

My childhood as an adult molester:
A Salt River moffie

Zackie Achmat

*Family history, of course, has its own dietary laws. One is sup-
posed to swallow and digest only the permitted parts of it, the
halal portions of the past, drained of their redness, their blood.
Unfortunately this makes the stories less juicy; so I am about to
become the first and only member of my family to flout the laws
of halal. Letting no blood escape from the body of the tale, I
arrive at the unspeakable part; and, undaunted, press on.*
— Salman Rushdie, *Midnight's Children*

There is no place called Salt River. There are no people called moffies. Children
don't have sex. Muslim men don't beat or oppress their wives. This testimony is
fantasy because everything is fantasy. In real life, no-one has sex. Names and
places in this fantastical testimony have been changed to protect the guilty. Everyone is guilty. Guilty of enjoying sex...

I am South African, black, male, 28, unfree and gay. For many years of my
life, in fact, I have been militantly gay. During a religious instruction period in
Standard 7 or 8, the teacher, Mr F (a Christian) asked me: 'Which religion do you
follow?' Reply: 'I'm an atheist.' Gasps in the class. Sharon: 'Ah, he's just a show
off.' Mr F: 'Why are you an atheist?' Reply: 'Sir, my parents were born and remain
devout Muslims. For many years I was a good Islamic scholar. I chucked it in
Standard 5. Then I converted to Catholicism for two weeks. Now I am an atheist.'
A low murmur spreads across the class. 'Why? Well, its written in the Quraan and
the Bible that homosexuals will burn in hell. I've done nothing wrong and I don't
want to end up in hell for it.'

Pandemonium in the class! Sharon the dolly-bird rises from the back where she is holed up with the *manne*[1], struts like the Madonna to my desk with tears in her eyes for the blasphemy, and hastily leaves her sticky paw print across my face. From then on even my best friends in class refuse to acknowledge my existence. They still won't.

I have learnt that gay people combine honesty sometimes bordering on brutality with lies, lies and more lies, in order to survive.

* * *

My first sexual memory at three. I can barely walk. I'm in Johannesburg, in Fietas (Vrededorp — before Group Areas evictions), in a room with my biological parents. A rare occasion in itself — that's why I remember it so vividly. I'm lying on my tummy. Ma has just bathed me. I'm ready to go to sleep. My dad hobbles across the room and starts serenading my mom in the most romantic deep voice. My mom is moved by Nat King Cole's *Mona Lisa*. Her name is Mona. She rises from the bed where she is tending me. She looks like an angel towering above my dad. She stoops down to let him embrace her in a grotesque waltz. Sex? From that moment I disliked my father and thought my mother unclean.

My birth certificate says: Cape Malay born in the Transvaal. I was born in Johannesburg; Baragwanath Hospital to be exact. But I grew up in Salt River. As children, my sister, Fika, and I were given to my grandparents when they moved to Cape Town. Fika and I were always used as pawns in the battle between my parents and grandparents. South African Railways seemed central to this struggle, shunted as we were up and down the country from Johannesburg to Cape Town to Johannesburg and back to Cape Town.

My parents lived in Fietas. My dad grew up in Sophiatown and my mom in Fietas. My parents had a room in a yard with several other families. Some were relatives, others just friends. We shared toilets, trials (*fahfee*[2] losses) and tribulations (domestic violence). Our house was next to a field, and a mosque adjoined it on 23rd Street. The street was the border between Mayfair and Fietas. Mayfair was a white working class area then, not the mixed-race suburb it is now.

We had regular wars with the poor white kids. They were children's wars, fought with fists, sticks and stones. We were all poor, so it was not class war. Boys and girls fought on both sides in rare displays of gender solidarity. So it was not a battle of the sexes. It was plain children's war in which the dividing line was race.

My best friend was Nomvula, the daughter of Beauty, the *shebeen*[3] queen. Every Saturday afternoon Nomvula and I had great fun. We would get lollipops, we would take her doll and Fika's (Fika would take my gun) and nurse our children on the steps of the stoep. Kippie Moeketsi, Spokes Mashiane, Dollar Brand would play loudly from the yard and we would watch the migrant workers gather on the field next to the mosque, dancing, arguing, conversing and relaxing.

---

1 guys/men
2 illegal Chinese gambling game
3 illegal tavern

We would watch Beauty serve the *mqombothi*, home-brewed beer, stored during the week in the entrance to our yard. Then would come the best part. Almost every Saturday without fail, Nomvula and I would scream with fear and delight as the *gumba-gumba*[4] arrived to chase the men. It was grown men chasing grown men. Grown men hitting other grown men. It was the children's war played by adults. Except some adults were armed and others not; many were taken away. It was only ten years later that I realised what the pass laws were. It was only then that I realised that almost 20 million men, women and children were thrown into prisons because of these laws. But those Saturdays, Nomvula and I enjoyed ourselves. Later we learnt fear.

My first schooldays were at Krause Street Primary. I was there for only three months until the railways claimed Fika and me. One evening before school started, my dad was supposed to buy my school uniform, but didn't. He never discussed finance with my mom. Sometimes he gave her money for food, sometimes not. That night she waited for him. We were all meant to have supper at Grannie's (his mother, who had had seven husbands). He arrived late, without the school uniform. They fought.

My mother, pregnant every second year, was preparing one of the babies' bottles. The milk she used to feed the babies was S26, mostly supplied by sisters or friends. He hit her several times.

She retaliated. He was covered in S26. My mom ran; he couldn't follow her because he is disabled. Fika and I cried in tune to the hit song on the radio — *Blue, Blue, My World Is Blue*. Since then the song has had a definite associations with my mom and dad.

The next day Beauty the shebeen queen from Transkei bought me a school uniform. I went to school a day late but with a shiny uniform. My dad was not all that bad. The yard's children had a collective nanny — Aunty Emma. Grannie was very racist. Aunty Emma always sat at the table and had her supper with us. Grannie was invited to supper one day. She saw Aunty Emma at the table and refused to cross the threshold: she would not sit down with 'a kaffir'. My father insisted that Grannie would not be welcome unless she treated Aunty Emma with respect. Grannie stayed away for two years, but Aunty Emma never left the table.

One afternoon, when I arrived back from school, my mom was being interrogated by two white policemen. They were very rough with her. They searched the house. My mom's only pride in her marriage was her trousseau, especially the white linen. It was dirtied and damaged, soiled like her marriage, as they searched the rooms. My mom was in tears but adamant: she would not tell them who was illegally brewing beer. They wanted to arrest her because the beer had been found in our part of the yard. Beauty arrived and told them that 'the shebeen queen only comes on Saturdays' and that my mom knew nothing. They left.

Many more fights between my mom and dad. Many more songs; *Blue, Blue, My World Is Blue*. Fika and I had to pack our baggage; the railways sent two tickets. My mom was too heart-broken to come to the station to say goodbye, but

---

4   police truck

as the train pulled out of Park Station, moving west, it passed Mayfair-Fietas. And there, running along the fence was my mom shouting 'Zayne! Fika! My children!' I swear I could see the tears. Nomvula and Beauty just stood there waving. I wanted to jump off the train. I didn't. Until then I had loved my mother; since then I have only pitied her — all love disappeared. She did not fight to keep us. She did not fight to keep the children she loved and who loved her in turn. Since that time I have mistrusted love.

* * *

Another sexual memory. I'm living with my grandparents in Salt River. Like Table Mountain, tranquility reigns through the presence of Mammie, my grandma — when it is not shattered by the demanding growls of my wonderful grandfather. My mom's eldest brother, Ebrahim, visits every Saturday at lunchtime. My uncle retires to the couch in the dining room, where he removes his size nine shoes. I'm hiding under a chair between the couch and the imbuia sideboard of the dining room suite. He snores! I emerge from the hideout. His face turned towards heaven, his feet in the direction of Mecca, my lips touch his. I get an erection. He wakes up and soothingly says: 'Never do that again.' He never told anyone. I have discovered I'm gay.

At the same time I have discovered the stigma, the taunting, the disgust, the degrees of toleration in the person of Sis Gamat. At my youngest aunt's wedding in 1968, Sis Gamat is called in to do the cooking. Sis Gamat is a moffie. Sis Gamat sends all the women into hysterics; the men twitter nervously around him and ignore him. I hear the whispers: 'Sis Gamat likes men.' They tease my aunt: '*Sis Gamat smaak jou man.*'[5] I wonder — am I like Sis Gamat? For the next three years, I take the keenest interest in cooking and kitchens.

Mogamat or Muhammad is the name of the last prophet of Allah in the Muslim religion, Islam. It is a name most often given to Muslim boys. Gamat is diminutive for Mogamat. *Gamat* is also the derogatory slang used to refer to Muslims. I have a poster of the gay film *Looking For Langston*; I stole it from a cinema during a film festival. The poster is ornately defaced with the word *SIS*. *Sis* means dirty in local slang. *Sis* or *sisi* can also mean sister. Sissy we know means faggot. More than 20 years after my aunt was married, if a man or boy is referred to as 'Sis Gamat' in our family, it means he's gay or considered effeminate.

* * *

1970 was a great year for family crisis. The railway was to carry my mother and her newborn twins and the two older sisters to Cape Town for the last time. My father had sold all her furniture and the goodwill on the house and just put her on the train. For the next five years they would live together for a few months at a time; for the next two years my mother would struggle against the patriarchs of the Muslim Judicial Council to get a divorce from my father.

---

5 Sis Gamat wants your man!

My Childhood as an Adult Molester

My eldest aunt, Nana, who took responsibility for my mom and all her children, had meantime married. She did not want to, but Mammie said: '*My kind, voor ek my oë toe maak, moet ek voel jy is besorg.*'[6] Nana looked after the whole family but Ouma felt she needed to be looked after by a husband. Dutifully, she found my youngest aunt's brother-in-law, the village idiot, and married him because: '*Ek soek nie 'n man wat op my kop kak nie. Kyk maar net vir Mona.*'[7]

Just before Mammie died in 1970, a 'squatter' family moved into the back of the garage in the yard: the mother Sis Kulsum and the father Boeta Dienie. They lived in a room with six children. Upstairs, in our single bedroom flat with Mammie and Daddy (my grandfather), were my mom's six children — the railways brought all of them to Cape Town; the youngest, the twins a year old, always dozing in that ugly turquoise twin pram. Nana and her husband also lived with us, as did Fatima, my youngest aunt's daughter.

Twelve people in a single bedroomed flat in Salt River. There was no electricity. The only personal privacy was to be found in the outside toilet. All the adults (and later even I) developed the habit of sitting in the toilet for at least half an hour. Every night we had to fetch Bertha before we could go to sleep. Bertha was big. She spent the days on the balcony and the nights in the kitchen. Bertha was a king size mattress which slept six children in front of the black coal stove in the kitchen. We were never cold.

My grandfather, Daddy, never once beat my grandmother, but he terrorised her daily. When he was around, my father beat my mother weekly. All of us eight children were beaten every second day: by my mom, my aunt, my father and, god help us, the monthly beating from Daddy.

Boeta Dienie beat his family too. He must have been nearly seven feet tall; the blackest man I have ever seen. Always blacker with grease, often drunk, regularly beating everyone in his family — twice, three times a day. Thereafter he would escape to one of the three toilets in the yard for some privacy.

After one such beating... It's about 5pm when he enters the toilet. I'm deeply, sexually aroused by this man. I dream, I fantasise, I think only of him all the time. I sit at the bottom of the 19-step concrete staircase, right opposite the toilet. I hear him cough with smoke-damaged lungs. I hear him gnash his teeth. He must be aware of my presence. It's 6pm. It's 6.30pm. It's 6.35pm. My mother goes mad: 'You must get ready to go to mosque!' Boeta Dienie coughs. He uses newspaper to clean-up (*Subaganallah*[8]). He pulls the chain. He comes out of the toilet. He pretends not to see me, but his pants are unzipped and in them is the biggest erection I have ever seen. He goes to beat his wife.

Our family felt superior to Boeta Dienie's family. The adults thought we were better because we were poor, clean and godly. They were poorer, dirty and they drank. But Mammie liked Boeta Dienie and his wife. She died while Fika and I said her last prayers with her. Jerry, her cat, disappeared that same day.

---

6 My child, before I close my eyes I must make sure you're taken care of.
7 I'm not looking for a man who's going to shit all over me. Just look at Mona.
8 Allah help us!

Smarting from Boeta Dienie's ambiguous rejection, I tried to repress my sexual desires. I turned to religion, joining the Tableegh — a religious sect, fundamentalist in the extreme. Here I learnt to do 'political house-visits'. Of course we refused to speak to the women if their husbands were not at home. Maybe it was the fact that the Tableegh wore flowing robes that attracted me — it always made the male body look so supple.

But religion — its dogma, its intolerance — did not captivate me. I turned to books. I read voraciously; anything and everything printed. *True Confessions* (especially the stories about naughty priests), Shakespeare's *Collected Plays, See, Kyk, Keur, Sister Louise, Ruiter in Swart, Grensregter, Anne of Green Gables*, James Hadley Chase, *The Diary of Anne Frank*. In the magazines and photostories I always looked at the men. My parents' quarrels seemed so remote from the real love in these magazines. But nothing, not one word about Sis Gamat, moffies or gays.

* * *

By now I was nine years old and knew I was a moffie. At school the boys called me that. There was one boy called Rashied. He wanted me to kiss him; I refused. He went to my grandfather and told him I had kissed a girl in the toilet. On one of the rare occasions that Nana and my mother spoke to each other I heard them say: *'En dis die wit mans wat so van moffies hou. Jy kry nie 'n bruin man of 'n Native wat met moffies rondgaan nie.'*[9] But what about me, then? I was not white, I was black. Could they not see? Moffies are not coloured or black; moffies, Fika would say years later, are a different nation.

Peter Moffie was the other moffie I knew. He was a different nation. He wore a wig. He wore the best dresses. His high heels were the envy of all the women in our family. Not once did anyone see him with his stockings ripped. Everyone hated Peter Moffie. He lived in Fenton Road. White men in fancy cars brought him home. But very often they did not. Then he used the bus.

He would get off at the bus stop near us. We knew what time he would arrive from work and we would lie waiting for him. I would lead five or ten children, all throwing stones at Peter Moffie. Shouting: 'Moffie! Moffie!' I can still see his bulging eyes filled with tears; I can see him holding his head high, dignified, while I tried to exorcise the *Shaytaan*. It did not work.

The *Shaytaan*, of course, is Satan. And stonethrowing has a particularly important place in Islam. It is not only used to punish adulterers, fornicators, homosexuals and thieves, it has a far more cathartic function. The *Shaytaan* is not only in the world, but is also within the individual. When Muslims go to Mecca and reach Mount Arafat, one of the holiest places in Islamic mythology, the place where Abraham had to sacrifice his son, they have to cast the *Shaytaan* out of their persons, with stones.

---

9 And it's the white man who likes moffies! You never see a brown man or a Native going round with moffies.

My Childhood as an Adult Molester

A few weeks ago Fika said to me: 'Hey! Did you know Peter Moffie was dead?' Now Peter is dead, and what can I say. There is no-one to ask for forgiveness. In Islam, you have to be forgiven personally by the one you have wronged. I won't be forgiven.

There was a boy in my class. He was so beautiful, everyone noticed him. Shy, reticent, he never played with anyone and refused to make friends even with me. Today he is out of the closet and lives in Observatory; a fashion designer. His sister, Tanya, was the school's cheerleader. She was boyish and strong. I fell in love with both of them, but her in particular. I still blush when I see her, and often wonder whether falling in love with Tanya was a way of exorcising the *Shaytaan* or whether there was a genuine bisexual side to my desire. I would like to develop it.

* * *

In 1972 I turned ten. I discovered active sex and never turned back. Nana was still working in a clothing factory. She has worked in the industry for more than 40 years. At the time she was supporting all my mother's children, her father, her husband and, at times, her younger brother. Nana was the most self-sacrificing person I have ever met. Once I fractured my ankle, jumping over six milk crates on a Sunday afternoon, and the next morning she took off work. We did not have money for bus fare so she carried me on her back from lower Rochester Road to Woodstock Hospital, a distance of five kilometers.

The division of labour in our family was as follows. Nana worked in the factory and cooked on Sundays. Ma looked after the children, did the washing and cooking during the week. And I, being the oldest, had responsibility for the household budget and shopping, as well as scrubbing and polishing the floors after school and before *Madressah*[10]. One afternoon while polishing the floors (God, it had to shine!) I had the most wonderful fantasy. A tall, strong, powerful man holds me down on the floor, kisses me, and fucks me. Today most people won't believe I had this fantasy. They just don't have imaginations.

A few weeks later. Sunday. Nana is cooking. I am sent to the shop to buy tomatoes. Being myself, I daydream all the way there and on my way back a car's hooter stirs me from it. It is a kombi, maybe a Hi-Ace. A white man beckons me. He opens the passenger door in the middle of the Main Road and shows me his cock. It is hard as a rock. He begs me to get into the vehicle. I drop the tomatoes and run.

In the kitchen Nana, who cooks on Sundays, bellows: 'Where's the damn tomatoes?' I run back; the tomatoes are squashed. Forgetting the tomatoes for a minute, I run up and down looking for the kombi, wishing I had got into it. At home I earn a hiding because I cannot account for the tomatoes. I'm not allowed to tell the truth because children are not allowed to discuss their sexual desires.

I continued reading. I read two books a day. At night, I did not go to sleep; I'd read at the kitchen table instead. During the day, I'd sleep at my desk at school. The Salt River Public Library was and still is a mobile unit. It was clean and neat,

---

10 Muslim school

but despite being open only two afternoons a week, I read most of its books in three months.

The coloured librarian, Mrs Kies, was very prim and neat. She was one of those people who believed that 'coloured people should better themselves through education', and the fact that I read so much made me an ideal guinea pig to prove that 'whites and coloured are equal when educated'. Embarrassed that she had no more books in the mobile, she hit on a wonderful plan: 'I am going to write to the Chief Librarian at Observatory Library (the white library) and tell them that you have read all the books here. They have a huge library which is open daily. I will beg them to let you use it.' I was thrilled at the prospect of a big library, though sceptical even then about the notion of equality through education.

Observatory Library had shelves and shelves filled with books. It had spaces to sit and read. It was quiet, there were no intrusions of street life. You could read and study and escape life at Salt River. I used to bunk *Madressah* to go to the library. At this stage my daily schedule looked something like this. Wake up at six in the morning, light the coal stove, make breakfast for the kids. Go back to sleep till 8.15 am. Then Fika would wake me rudely, because she had to knot my tie and do my shoelaces before going to school. I would stand there in my underpants with a tie and shoes and socks. I'd dress leisurely, eat something, get to school just after prayers, and sleep through class.

When school closed I would run home. Get to my grandfather's radio, where we would sit down and listen to those wonderfully romantic Afrikaans serials. I can still hear Miets, Gerhard and Ma Matilda of *Ompad*. I could never forget Tant Ralie. I hated weekends and public holidays, because I missed *Die Geheim van Nantes, Ongewenste Vreemdeling* and *Die Dans van die Vlaminke*. After the serials I would clean the house, do shopping and pretend to make off for *Madressah*. Instead, I would go to the library.

Observatory Library was then only open to whites. But, armed with my letter from Mrs Kies, I became one of the few coloureds to use it. The Cape Town City Council has always been liberal. But at that stage the liberalism did not extend to toilets. I could use their library, read and borrow their books, but I was not allowed into their toilets. One afternoon, I desperately needed to go; despite my insistence that it was an emergency, I was directed to the nearest public toilets.

Any toilet in Muslim mythology — whether whites only, blacks only, mixed, public or private — is evil. The *Shaytaan* dwells in the toilets. You enter them with your left foot reciting a special toilet prayer. After using a toilet, all Muslims must wash themselves three times, reciting another prayer. This process is known as *Istinjaa*. It is *haraam* (forbidden) to leave the toilet without washing. On leaving, you set out on the right foot, completing the cycle of toilet prayers.

Observatory Station is two minutes walk away from the library. I had to rush there. I walked into the Whites Only toilets; there were no guards. As I entered, three or four men hastily moved in all directions. I was driven by natural forces into one of the two cubicles. The toilet doors were painted a railway orange-brown colour. The black of koki pens transformed them into works of art. It was not the drawing, it was not the misspelt words or even the rhyme and rhythm of prison gang poetry, that transformed these symbols into art. It was what they said. They spoke of unspoken, unwritten and unsung love. They celebrated sex between men. They advertised sex between men. They told wonderfully erotic stories of sex between men. I loved it. Toilet doors became galleries for the art of love between men.

The men who were there waited for me to finish, but I would not leave. I stayed in that toilet till 7pm. Then I went home where I got a hiding for missing early evening prayers. I rushed to mosque for *Eshaai*[11] but I did not pray. I went to the mosque toilets, hoping to find the songs of love between men on the walls. I forgot toilet prayers; maybe that is why I did not find any drawings, messages, stories, desires on the doors and walls. I waited till all the men had left the mosque.

The next day I returned to Observatory toilets via the library. There was a man. A white man, about 20 years old. He had brown hair. He tried to pretend that I was not there. He looked at me and looked away. I stood at the tap. I looked at him. Eventually, I walked up to him and put my arms around him. He whispered nervously: 'You are only a child. Go home.' He spoke softly and he was strong, but I wouldn't go. I always suspected that learning poetry and Quranic verses by rote would have some use. Now it did. I could recite the poetry of the toilet walls to him. I had memorised it. He saw that I was not going to relent. I had an erection and so did he.

He kissed me. He held me. But he could not hold out against me. He would not enter me, but he entered me. He was gentle. He fucked me slowly, carefully, but with tremendous power and passion. I felt him everywhere. I could taste him in my mouth. We came together. I had an orgasm which came from inside my arse, exploding out of my cock. We kissed and I insisted that he meet me the next day. I went to meet him completely in love. He wanted to give me a present. I refused because I would not have known how to explain it at home. He had to return to Jo'burg. He left. I cried. But I soon got over it. I had the toilets.

I had sex at the toilets every day, sometimes twice or three times a day. I would go to the library to get books, which I would read in the toilet, so that when something happened I would be there. Almost all the men were scared to touch me because of my age. But once they discovered that I was into it, they enjoyed themselves. I had sex with anyone who wanted to: old, young, black or white, fat or thin, it did not matter. The sex and tenderness mattered, and there was lots of both.

Apartheid worked in mysterious ways. From denying me the use of one set of toilets, it opened the world of another set to me. But apartheid was not just about toilets. At ten I knew some things about apartheid. It was about sitting upstairs in the bus. It was about using separate entrances at the post offices. Apartheid meant that Salt River was a coloured area and Observatory, like Mayfair was a white working class area.

Apartheid also meant that my dad's mother, Grannie, not only refused to eat with Aunty Emma, but blatantly favoured her fairer-skinned grandchildren. She

---

11 last of the five daily prayers

gave the darker ones less food, smaller presents — if she did not forget their birth-days entirely. This has caused intolerable strains in our family. This is what I knew about apartheid. Apartheid forced me to use Observatory Station toilets, but apart-heid was destroyed in those toilets. By men who had sex with men, regardless of race or class.

* * *

1973. 'Man is dead but his spirit lives.' This was the slogan of the African workers in Durban. Apartheid had killed thousands through pass laws, land laws, starvation and plain brutality. I only learnt the significance of the Durban Strikes years later. But that year I discovered love in the compounds.

In Salt River there was a coloured building contractor. He employed about 30 African men and one white worker to oversee them. He had four Bedford trucks. The men were all migrants from the Transkei. They were housed in a dilapidated room. The room was covered in soot from cooking on a primus stove or over an open fire. It was not larger than the flat my parents lived in. In the bitter cold Salt River nights, these grown up men did not even have a mattress.

The white supervisor was named — rather appropriately — Whitey. He lived with the men. He was an ex-con. He had never been to school. He had one front tooth missing. He had red hair and a scraggly red beard. He very seldom laughed, but when he did, his green eyes shone. Whitey was extremely thin. I became friends with Whitey and Khaya. They asked me to read to them. I read them stories. I wrote letters for the families of the workers in the Transkei. They were workers, but the machines and tools their boss owned were much better looked after than they were. They didn't have any bathrooms. They had no place to wash. Khaya's skin was cracking. His eyes were bloodshot. He always coughed long and hard. Khaya and Whitey both only had one set of clothing each. They would ask me if they could wash it at the tap in our yard.

One day I went to the shop and was mugged by some of the gangsters. Khaya and Whitey rounded up all the workers and, within minutes, they had forced the gangsters to apologise to every adult member of my family individually and to return the grocery money.

Whitey tried to teach me to play rugby. In the cold winter nights, he and Khaya sat in one of the Bedford trucks drinking. I tried to drink but they wouldn't let me. The toilets had emboldened me: sitting in the truck with them I waited till they were drunk, and then I started playing with them. They tried to stop me but I would not hear any of it. I started having sex with Khaya and Whitey. Sometimes together, mostly with one or the other. I let them fuck me. At first they did not want to, like all the other men. Then they insisted they'd only fuck me between the legs, but eventually passion ruled and I would be happy. Less than five hundred meters from my parents home.

Coloured communities have a higher proportion of gangsters than any other community. Salt River had gangs. Ice used to stand on the corner, with the Wonder Kids. He was their leader. At night he would sing. And the songs he sang I could hear in Bertha the bed. I fantasised about him. I was in love with him. Whenever I went to the shop I would find an excuse to speak to him. Eventually, one night I asked him to sing. He sang. He was alone on the corner. I returned from the shop and he called me over. We went into the lane and he kissed me. Nothing more.

The Wonder Kids sold liquor to the workers of the construction company. One of the Wonder Kids was a boy called Qader. His mother was a very religious Auntie, a Salt River paragon of virtue. One night we were all asleep when we heard a cry from the quarters of the workers. I ran out onto the balcony and saw Qader and some boys running away. The ambulance arrived and I ran downstairs. Qader had stabbed Khaya in the heart. Khaya had tried to stop him selling liquor to the men. Qader was 18. His mother went to see the dead body in the room. She fainted and they had to carry her home. Qader was arrested. Khaya was now dead. A dead African migrant worker, killed by a coloured gangster whose mother managed to raise the bribe for the white policeman investigating the murder. Qader was released without charges.

* * *

For weeks I could not sleep or eat. My aunt and mom did not know what was wrong. I could not tell them either. At school some boys continued calling me a moffie, some maliciously, some out of sexual interest. 'Unisex' was a word that fired Imam Omar of Tennyson Street Mosque up to apoplectic heights when he preached on Fridays. Fashions were unisex, so were hairdressers. According to the Imam, men and women who were fashionably unisex would burn in *Jahannum*.[12] The word 'unisex' taught me more about moffies. Salt River's famous moffies were Doulah Moffie and Hakkie Moffie. They owned unisex hairdressers. But their hairdressing salons were unisex long before the word or the fashions were coined.

Doulah Moffie's hairdressing salon is still in Lower Main Road. Back then (and now) it was a meeting place for moffies. Moffies were men who dressed like women, or who dressed in high style. Moffies were men who were really women in spirit. They spoke like women, flirted openly with men and kept men. The moffies in these salons had wonderful parties. But the moffie hairdressers were also places where 'straight' men could go for a 'regular blow job' as a blow-dry was then known. My youngest aunt's husband visited moffie hairdressers regularly. In the community, all fashionable women had their hair done at the hairdressers. At *Eid* after the Fast, virtually every Muslim household had members in the moffie hairdressers getting blow-dry's.

The community in Salt River and elsewhere has always had ambiguous attitudes towards the hairdressers, ranging from feigned disgust to sexual curiosity and its satisfaction. But the verbal and sometimes physical abuse horrified me. *Eid* was the only time I really visited the hairdressers. My mom and aunt always had to force me to get a haircut — I was sent home from school three or four times a year because I always refused.

---

12 Hell

I hated having my hair cut. I also hated the way the moffies were treated; I feared being treated the same way. When I was about six I loved dressing up in my mom's clothing. But when I got a little older I started hating high heels. I wanted to be like the other boys at school; except, I also wanted to have sex with them.

At school, the Adams boys were friends with my sister Fika and me. Yaseen, the older brother, and I were in the same class; his younger brother Hasim and Fika were in the same class. Hasim and I were friends because we loved reading; Yaseen and Fika loved playing 'cowboys and crooks' and 'Russians and Americans'. Yaseen was very macho; he did judo and karate at school. He was a soccer player and he smoked. Some cousin of ours got married and my mom and aunt went to their place for the weekend to help with the cooking. So Yaseen came to stay over with us. He brought with him a black-and-white photograph of a man fucking a man, and showed it to me. We slept on my mom's bed and fucked so hard that the mirror on the dressing table broke. It's broken to this day. I got a terrible hiding for that broken mirror, but it did not hurt nearly as much as Yaseen teasing me and smooching with Fatima at school.

Ten years later, in 1983, Nana phoned me at the flat where I lived with my lover. I was worried as Daniel handed me the telephone, because she never phones. Her only words were: '*Ek moet met jou praat.*'[13] I jumped into the car and drove to Salt River. Had someone died? My mother? My father? No, the catastrophe was worse. Yaseen Adams, who had gone to an Islamic college in Greytown, Natal (and had always been held up as the example of a good Muslim youth) had returned to Salt River. Was he an Imam? No! *Subaganallah!* He has moved into a hairdressers with Abassie Moffie!

Yaseen lived with Abassie Moffie for eight years. Every week, in a fit of jealous rage, he would beat Abassie in the hairdressers. The customers would watch, many of the women shaking their heads in solidarity with Abassie. Once I went to have my hair cut and Yaseen washed my hair. We chatted about our families. When Abassie came to cut my hair, he said: 'Yaseen told me that he has not enjoyed sex with anyone as with you.' I felt flattered but I could not help thinking that Abassie, one of Salt River's sexiest moffies, could find a better lover than Yaseen; one who would not beat or rob the poor boy. I remembered what a bully Yaseen had become at school after we had sex. Once he beat me so bad, I had to tell my mom I fell of a bicycle in the road.

* * *

One morning, instead of going to school, I told my mom and aunt I needed to speak to them. I started speaking slowly and deliberately: '*Ma and Nana weet ek is nie soos ander laaities nie. Ek hou nie van hulle games en onoselheid nie. Ek hou ook nie van meisies nie. Die anner kinders sê ek is 'n moffie.*'[14] Almost simultaneously they said: '*Moenie sulke dinge sê nie. Jy weet daar's niks verkeerd met jou*

---

13 I must talk to you.

14 Ma and Nana, you know I'm not like the other boys. I don't like their games and nonsense. I also don't like girls. The other kids say I'm a moffie.

nie. As jy weer iets hiervan se dan trek ons jou gatvel af.' [15] So much for trying to come out.

At night, for the next few weeks, I just cried. I did not visit the toilets or cruise. In the end I decided to kill myself because no-one wanted to discuss my desire for men with me. One morning, after giving the youngsters breakfast, I emptied out the medicine box. There were Panados, vitamins, Phensics, Amasecs. In all I must have swallowed about sixty pills.

At home we did not have a bathroom. There was only one sink in the kitchen from which we got water for everything. We were not allowed to wash dishes or food in that sink because we also had to wash ourselves there. The next thing I remember is standing at that white sink in the kitchen, my head spinning. I puked a rainbow of pills. I felt a hand on my shoulder and looked up. It was my aunt rubbing my back. She had tears in her eyes and said: *'Moet dit nooit weer doen nie, dis 'n coward se way en jy is nie 'n coward nie.'* [16] I cried, she dried my tears and walked me to school. That afternoon I visited my grandmother's grave and tried to speak to her about Khaya's death. I could not forget him.

* * *

In 1974, I left the Muslim primary school and went to a Christian school. At this new school the boys were particularly snooty: English and cruel. They teased me mercilessly because I came from an Afrikaans school. To their disgust I took the English and Afrikaans class prizes. Only one thing helped me survive — sex.

My best friend at this time was Danny. He went to Dryden Street Primary. We were the same age and in the same standard. But Danny decided to leave school in Standard 5. They had a huge family; the three brothers and two sisters had all been in jail or reformatory. Danny was a very quiet and reserved kid; even my aunt thought he was sweet.

Danny was one of Salt River's best athletes. He would have been better than the Lakay family, but no-one encouraged him. I hated school sports, but I have always enjoyed long-distance running on my own. Danny and I started running long-distance together. One evening, about an hour before sunset, he asked me to run to Rhodes Memorial with him. We ran up Rochester Road, past Groote Schuur Hospital, crossed over the highway and went through the University. Then we reached the lions at Rhodes Memorial. I'll never forget the beautiful lilies. Danny was taller than I. His black hair was short and his shorts were tight. I noticed his erection but did not do anything. As the sun set we sat among the lilies and Danny kissed me. We made love. We ran to Rhodes Memorial every Monday evening. Why Mondays? I don't know.

Ida was my best friend. She was a year ahead of me at school. We did everything together: we bunked, laughed, cried, lied, wore each other's clothing, organised dates. We hardly ever needed to communicate our desires to each other

---

15 Don't say such things! You know there's nothing wrong with you. If we hear any more of this we're going to whip your hide off.

16 Don't ever do that again. That's a coward's way and you're not a coward.

— we translated each other's feelings instinctively. When she was at Salt River High in Standard 7, I was still in Standard 6 at Wesley. I used to bunk school and attend her English classes. I remember them doing *Romeo and Juliet* as a setwork.

All Ida's classmates knew why I attended her English classes: I was in love with the English teacher, Mr Jordan. He used to let me read all the parts — Romeo, Mercutio, Benvolio, the Nurse, even Juliet. I would read for 15 minutes without stopping and the class loved it: they could escape Shakespeare while I courted their teacher. While reading I would slowly unbutton my shirt allowing my chest and silver St Christopher chain to show. He would stare all the time, blushing.

The entire school was fascinated. I was from another school and a lower standard and the teacher was in love. But I could not stand the tension of making love through the pages of Shakespeare; I was pining for Mr Jordan like Romeo for Juliet. Ida decided to act. One Sunday morning, while my aunt was busy making *koeksisters*, Ida fetched me for swimming lessons. She dragged me to the teacher's house in Observatory, which she had tracked down by following him home one Friday afternoon. I was shy — it's one thing seducing your teacher through Shakespeare, and quite another making out with him when he is not really your teacher. Ida would have none of this coyness — she rang the doorbell. Mr Jordan came to the door in a pair of shorts and Ida just pushed me in the door and waved goodbye. I stayed, and went back daily for three months.

Then disaster struck. My grandfather Daddy died the same week that *The Towering Inferno* opened at The Palace in Salt River. I have still not seen the film. My grandfather was a great man. He had come to South Africa from India without any education. He could speak Hindi, Urdu, Gujerati, and here, in South Africa, he learnt English, Zulu, Tswana and Afrikaans. He also learnt to read and write. Every morning and afternoon he would send me to buy the *Cape Times* and *The Argus*. He would read them to me and discuss the news of the day. The only time I saw him really cry was when he read about the Indo-Pakistani wars in 1972. He would get up much earlier than *Subuh* (dawn prayers) or at midnight for *Tahajud* (special supplications) to pray for an end to the wars. 'They are brothers,' he would say, 'how can they kill each other?'

I owe much to him. His death also meant that the simmering civil war between my mom and aunt, my mom and my dad, my dad and my aunt came to a head. All of us were devastated by his death.

I remember the *Ghatam* after Daddy died. All the men were busy praying and all the women were in the kitchen talking, cooking. All my mom's sisters, cousins, neighbours and friends were there. Ida's mom, Safie, was also there. The subject turned to children, and my mom was congratulated on what wonderfully obedient kids she had. Safie sensed that it was time for eulogies: I was, she said, the most wonderful friend Ida had ever had. She went even further, proclaiming loudly: *'Zayne is mos 'n moffie en ek voel Ida is altyd in safe hande met hom. Hy sal mos niks met haar maak nie.'* [17] My poor mom and aunt learnt the meaning of

---

17 Zayne's a moffie and I feel Ida's in safe hands with him. He won't get up to any mischief with her.

the saying: If you try to force reality out through the door, it just comes in through the window.

* * *

By now, January 1976, Ida and I were regularly bunking school. Saunders Rock was one of our favourite haunts, and there we pestered white men for suntan oil, Coke, food and lifts. I had to supply sexual favours in return for the more earthly material goods.

Observatory Station had introduced me to the world of toilet sex. I never got great grades for maths but logic was never a problem. I quickly deduced that if men had sex at Observatory Station they would have sex at other stations. It was around this time that I discovered the most important stations of all, Newlands and Rondebosch.

Last year I was browsing at Exclusive Books in Hillbrow. I noticed a man in his forties starting to cruise me. I walked up to him and said: 'Hallo, your name is Don'. He turned red: 'How do you know my name?' I smiled. He said: 'Can I buy you a drink?' I told him to drop the formalities and asked where he lived. As we walked to his flat, I informed him that, in 1976, he lived in Kalk Bay and worked in the South African Navy. By now Don was sure that I was working for Military Intelligence. I assured him I was not. As he put his arm around me I told him that he had a lover called Hein. Shocked, he asked me to describe his house, which I did in detail. I even remembered the name of the dog: Abigail!

Don had forgotten that, way back in 1976, he had picked me up at Rondebosch Station. He was stunningly beautiful then: a navy boy, blond curls and blue eyes...

We enter the train (they still ran late in those days), get carried away, start fucking. Both of us with our pants down, the train whizzing past Steenberg, Retreat, Muizenberg, we are suddenly aware of the presence of three ticket examiners. They stare, then, silently, intimidated, they turn around and go back to where they came from. As we pull into Kalk Bay Station they return and ask politely for our tickets.

Don and I reach his home in Kalk Bay. We are thrashing around in his bed when our luck runs out. Hein returns. He was supposed to have spent the night with some friends in town, but he didn't. At two in the morning, he and Don storm up and down, in and out. Don shows me to the guest room. In order to demonstrate to his boyfriend that it did not really mean anything, Don offers me money the next morning when I wake up. I refuse...

As we finished our coffee in Don's Hillbrow flat, I pointed out to him that I would expect him to pay for sex this time round, and that I did not think he could afford it. I departed as I did 15 years before, in 1976.

* * *

The youth revolt of 1976 sealed the fate of apartheid, and has become part of the legend of struggles against racism throughout the world. On 17 June, my Afrikaans

339

teacher told me to come to her house, to watch the news on television. We heard that youth in Soweto were revolting against Afrikaans, and that their revolt was communist-inspired. We also heard that scores of students were shot and killed.

The next few months were very tense at school. First University of Western Cape students boycotted, and they were followed by students in Langa, Nyanga and Guguletu. At Salt River High we had two campuses, one on Kent Street and the other at Rochester Road. I was at Kent Street and Ida at Rochester Road. On 1 September, a Wednesday, the African students marched into town. The next day we locked the principal in his office after stoning him with eggs. He had a terrible complex about his height, and was a reactionary Muslim from Bo Kaap. Then we held a mass meeting. We decided to form a Students' Representative Council and to boycott classes. *Jock of the Bushveld,* and all our history textbooks, were to be burnt. While our meeting was in progress, hundreds of students from the Rochester Road campus streamed into the school; we were also marching to town!

Why did we participate in the strikes and struggles of 1976? The deaths of so many children shocked the whole country. The police brutality unified the coloured and African youth. We found rebellion exciting. In the end, we rebelled not only against the state, but also against teachers, principals, parents and stuck-up students called prefects. All of us had witnessed racism and all of us were scarred by it. Apartheid was part of our bodies; it was not simply a system.

We marched through Victoria Road, into Darling Street, up Plein Street. Ida and I were marching together. The seniors taught us songs: *We Shall Overcome*; *This land is your land*; *Senzenina* reverberated as Salt River High students became the first coloured students to march into town. As we marched along Parliament Street, and down into Adderley Street, the riot police charged. We overran the flower sellers and ran into shops. Ida and I were beaten. We fled into the post office and sat down. The pursuing riot policeman ran straight past us. We then regrouped with other students near the Parade and started marching again.

It was a Thursday. Every Thursday morning my mom would go to town to the magistrates court with Mogamat, Nana's son, to collect the R28 a week my dad had to pay for the maintenance of the six kids. Sometimes she would return crying, and then we would know that he had not paid a cent. Apparently when my dad appeared in court he had told the magistrate: *'Edelagbare, ek kan nie elke week hof toe kom nie om geld te betaal nie want ek is kreupel.'* [18] The magistrate replied: 'Meneer, jy was nie kreupel toe jy ses babas gemaak het nie.'[19]

Just as we turned into Darling Street, I saw my mom and Mogamat. I saw a riot policeman knock my little cousin down as he ran in our direction. It was then that my mom saw us.

At two o' clock in the afternoon on Thursday, 2 September 1976, we got a lift from a truckdriver back to Salt River. Tired, Ida and I went to find other students and we all decided to march back into town the next day. As I reached home, my mom and aunt were waiting with belts. They gave me a hiding worse than the

---

18 Your honour, I can't come to court every week because I'm a cripple.
19 Sir, you weren't a cripple when you made six babies.

one I had got from the police. My aunt said: '*Jy kan nie teen die Boere baklei met jou kaalhande nie. Beter mense soos Dr Dadoo, Ahmed Timol en Solly Sachs kon nie die boere klaarmaak nie. En julle is net kinders.*' [20] My mom and aunt believed that we would get shot. And they were not wrong: scores of students in Manenberg, Bonteheuwel, Langa and Guguletu were shot and even killed. But that night I hated my mom and aunt. I sought solace elsewhere.

The Caltex Garage in Lower Main Road had a night-watchman. He was from Queenstown. He called me over as I escaped from home. My body was aching all over from the beatings. I felt miserable. The watchman made me some tea over his open fire. I told him what happened and he started caressing my body. He stripped my clothes off and stared, transfixed by my legs. I thought it was the blue marks of the belt but it wasn't! '*Imfene!*' (Baboon) he cried as he started pulling the hairs on my legs. He had never touched anyone with hairy legs. He laughed as he fucked me and insisted that I was related to the baboons.

1976 changed my life forever. In the next few years, I became a political activist and was detained several times. Family-life became intolerable. I left home and lived on the streets and with friends. Later I met Daniel, who became my lover for almost ten years. In those years I discovered that sex is political and that, as moffies and letties, we had to be part of a revolution to change everything. It was the beginning of a life of sex and politics.

---

20 You can't battle the Boers with your bare hands. Better people than you, like Dr Dadoo, Ahmed Timol and Solly Sachs couldn't finish the Boers off. And you're just children!

'Pretended families':
On being a gay parent

Neville John

I have been out of the closet, from long before my child was born, in most areas of my life — to my parents, at work, and in my social life. I have always been open with my child about my sexuality.

My father once claimed that he had no problem with the fact of my homosexuality, but that as a father I had no right to practise it. Being an openly gay man, he said, would have extremely prejudicial consequences for James, my son. He said that James would be beaten up in the playground, that he wouldn't have any friends, and that I would be an embarrassment to him.

In the end, what helped resolve the question for me was an open letter written by a gay father to his children in *GLPCI Network*, the newsletter of the Gay and Lesbian Parents Coalition International. He was dealing with this same issue: why he, a parent, chose to be so openly gay. He wrote:

> *Well kids, I have a choice. I can be visible as a gay father and in so doing expose you to the gay bashing that your classmates may subject you to. OR I can be secretive and subliminally give you the message that it's not 'okay' to be gay. That is the choice I have to make ... It's not an easy choice.*
>
> *Before making this choice, I thought long and hard and talked to a lot of people. I talked to a panel of children at a gay and lesbian parent's conference. 'Read the button you're wearing', they said, 'PROUD PARENTS MAKE PROUD KIDS. It's the proud voices in the world that give us strength. Without someone speaking out, particularly our parents, we are all alone.'*[1]

In writing this piece, I have followed the above advice only partially. As I mulled the dilemma over with James' mother, Anne, we worried about the consequences of 'outing' a five-year-old boy in print. Anne is a lesbian, and neither of us has problems with being completely open. But, we felt, it should be left to James, when he is a little older, to decide upon how public he wants his unusual but loving family to be. And so 'Neville', 'Anne' and 'James' are pseudonyms.

A lesbian parent once said to me of her nine year old son, 'Oh, it's not an issue. He understands and it's not a problem.' I think she's very wrong; that she's wishing away problems she and her son are going to have to face. I think that her kid and James and all the children of gay and lesbian parents will have to deal with a whole lot of homophobia and gay-bashing. And I think that what we have to do — probably all we can do — to help our children cope with society's prejudice is to try to educate other people about gay parenting.

Gay parenting — and indeed homosexuality generally — has remained hidden in South Africa for longer than in the United States, where the above letter was written. In the United States, the GLPCI has been going for 13 years and holds well-attended annual conferences. In South Africa, I know a few lesbians who are parents, and even fewer gay men. On the whole, it seems that gay parents in South Africa are mostly people who lived heterosexual lives before coming out. For them, coming out often meant losing custody of their children — for some, even access to them — and much anguish. But, increasingly, gay men and lesbians here have decided to find ways of fulfilling their dreams of having children of their own and making their own kinds of families.

Anne and I fall into this latter category, and so I don't want to pretend to write about the experiences of the many gay men and lesbians who have come out to themselves and their children later on in life: theirs is an entirely different set of problems. But in the end, I think that the general concerns and fears expressed here for my child apply to every gay or lesbian parent, whatever the circumstances of the birth of that child.

When I told my mother that we were going to have a child, one of her first responses was to say that she had given away all the clothes I had worn as an infant because she thought that, as I was gay, I wouldn't ever have a child. Most gay men and lesbians who come out to their parents are confronted, at one point or another, with the accusation, 'Now we won't have grandchildren.' The myth that gay men and lesbians don't want children is so pervasive that I have even encountered it in 'progressive' straight circles. More than once, people with whom I work and for whom homosexuality is not an issue have asked, after noticing a picture of James on my office notice-board, 'Do *you* have a child?' And I must explain that, yes, I, a homosexual, have a child, and yes, as a homosexual I decided to have a child.

Faced with these attitudes, it is quite easy to accept that as a homosexual one will be childless. I had started to believe this myself, even though Anne and I had spoken of having children for many years. But Anne was more determined, not the slightest bit concerned by, or interested in, the view that gay people don't have children. And so, one day, while Anne and I were sitting in the kitchen of a friend who was packing up to move to Cape Town and talking about the future and the world, she said to me that the time had come. I agreed, rapidly and eagerly. In that moment we made real what I had often imagined and wanted but thought could not really happen.

James was born in January 1988. He had a natural childbirth at which I was present. We didn't know whether it was going to be a boy or a girl, although I had jokingly demanded a boy. And then, two weeks late and after a night of labour, there he was. He looked so serious. I remember that he was frowning when he was born, a look I still occasionally glimpse when he 'reads' a book or when I shout at him. When he came home, a tiny little child that I could hold in one arm, I was overcome with emotion and, holding him as he slept, I wept.

He was a relatively easy child. He slept well, and apart from an allergy to milk, he has thrived. Today he is healthy and, I think and hope, happy. He seems to have a relatively serious nature, but he likes to joke and to 'trick' us. He is an intelligent, articulate child, whose school and psychological assessments indicate that he is well-adjusted and progressing well.

He lives mainly with his mother on one side of a pair of semi-detached houses. My lover, Matthew, and I live on the other side. James has a room on both sides, and moves freely from one side to the other. Once during the week and on the weekend he spends the night with Matthew and me. Matthew and I are openly affectionate with each other and James knows that we love each other. James thinks of himself as part of a family that comprises himself, his mother, his father and his father's lover. This notion of who his family is has been sufficiently important to him that my mother, initially openly hostile to Matthew and echoing my father's views on gay parents, has now come to refer to all of us — Anne, Matthew and me — as 'James's family'.

But of course, nothing goes all smoothly. Anne and I have had our problems and so have Matthew and I. In addition, Matthew was faced with a 'package deal' — a situation which he had no say in the making and in which he had to establish and define relationships with both James and Anne.

Parenting raises many problems. A gay parent must deal with all of them — discipline, diet, schooling, violence on TV — and a whole lot more. The problems begin with the decision to have a child. While gay adoption is not explicitly prohibited by law, gay men and lesbians find that adoption agencies refuse to let them adopt children, regardless of the fact that they would provide excellent homes for the great number of children waiting to be adopted. Artificial insemination is unavailable to lesbians and self-insemination is illegal. Sexual orientation should not be an issue in determining whether or not a person can adopt, whether or not custody should be awarded to parents who divorce, whether or not women can get artificial insemination, but it is. And so, having decided to have a child, it's extremely difficult to go ahead and do that.

Making sure that your child will be financially secure in the event of your early death is another difficult issue. I know of an insurer that doubled the premium on a life insurance policy when it discovered that the insured was a gay man — although he had tested HIV negative, although there was an AIDS exclusion clause in the policy, and although the insured had been involved in a monogamous relationship for some period of time. The man in question had a child, and part of the reason for seeking the additional life cover was to ensure that his son would be properly provided for in the event of his early death. By making sexual preference a factor in determining the cost of life insurance, insurance companies not only discriminate against gay people but also their children.

On the positive side, it is possible that we will see a future where these forms of discrimination will be unlawful. The Bill of Rights proposed for a future South Africa by the African National Congress will outlaw discrimination against, or harassment of, people because of their sexual orientation. In addition, the ANC's Bill of Rights provides for all persons the right to establish families.[2] Assuming that the ANC comes to power, and that these proposals are not negotiated away, gay people will be able to challenge the laws which deny them access to artificial insemination, the agencies which turn down their applications to adopt on the basis of their sexuality, and the insurance companies which charge them more for life cover.

Unfortunately, the societal prejudices and bigotry that gay people have to deal with on a day-to-day basis will probably be around for a lot longer. Even more worrying and painful is the knowledge that it is highly unlikely that your child will be able to avoid having to face and deal with society's homophobia himself. Already, at the age of five, James has been told at school that boys don't hug or kiss. I find it strange that parents and schools still reinforce these gender stereotypes at an age when spontaneity and emotional growth should be encouraged. Right now it's fine for James to say: 'That's not true. My dad hugs and kisses Matthew all the time.' But what will it be like when he's older and the kids are telling moffie jokes? I go cold thinking of it, especially as it was James, and not his teacher, who countered his friend's comment.

And so the choice of school, if one has a choice, becomes more complicated that it already is for straight parents. Not only must you find an institution that provides good education, but also one that will actively ensure that your child has, as far as possible, a safe environment in which to grow and develop — a school which will actively fight homophobia and promote an awareness that a good and happy family and home life has nothing to do with the number of mums and dads, straight or gay.

We anticipated being seen as oddities in heterosexual circles. What we hadn't anticipated was that gay people could be equally hostile. Indeed, some of our fiercest critics were gay people. Sometimes the criticism was overt, sometimes more subtle. Some of them just stopped seeing us. Some of them, whom we expected to be around to help just weren't. Some, of course, were wonderful. And sometimes the speculation becomes intrusive when almost-strangers ask of Matthew, 'Was Neville gay when you met him?' or of me 'How's it all working out?' But the real issue is that throughout his life, James will have to deal with the hostility, the criticism, and the speculation.

All the above problems manifest themselves in various ways. There is the urge to be the most perfect parent — to prove them all wrong. There is the urge to produce the most perfect child — to prove them all wrong. There is the urge to have the most perfect relationships — to prove them all wrong. And there is the urge to assume that everything that goes wrong with James, even a common cold or tonsillitis, must in some way be related to his parents' sexual orientation — to prove them all right. As parenting becomes more and more part of our lives, though, all these urges are more easily overcome.

It's difficult for all parents to explain certain things to their kids. For us, though, these difficulties do seem amplified. How do you explain the nature of a homosexual relationship to a child, when all that he sees, all the books that he has read to him, define relationships in heterosexual terms?

James has always accepted the explanation that men can love men, women can love women, and men and women can love each other. But he still was insistent to know who Matthew was in his family. Just as an aunt or an uncle has a title in the family — 'my aunt', 'my uncle' — so too Matthew needed a title. At first James tried calling Matthew his 'other Dad'. When it was explained that he only had one father, he asked, 'Is he my step-mother?' — a title that Matthew didn't appreciate.

Finally we settled on 'Matthew is your Dad's lover'. James uses the title with much pride. Once, when trying to be discreet in front of her 80-year-old aunt, Anne announced that I was coming to visit with a friend. James assertively contradicted her: 'Matthew's not my Dad's friend, he's my Dad's lover.' So long was the silence that ensued, that James asked, 'I'm not wrong, am I, Mum?'

Often, in trying to deal with these issues, I feel that we are groping in the dark. One can read a great deal on parenting, but there seems to be little literature available, in South Africa at any rate, on the problems of gay parenting. And there are no sex education books explaining to children and teenagers what gay sexuality is all about. I'm sure that we'd find life a good deal easier, and be far more effective in helping our children cope, if there were an organisation for gay and lesbian parents in South Africa. But gay and lesbian parents remain largely invisible in all aspects of South African life, even within the gay community: the question of child-care, for example, never arises at gay events.

Even in other countries, where there are significant gay communities and strong organisations of gay and lesbian parents, the dominant ideologies make parenting very difficult indeed. In Britain, for example, Clause 28 prohibits local governments from disseminating or publishing material that 'promotes' homosexuality, or 'the teaching in any maintained school of the acceptability of homosexuality as a pretended family relationship'.

Clause 28 is a direct attack on gay men and lesbians as parents, and much of the language used at the time in Parliamentary debates in support of the clause illustrates this. For example, Tory Baroness Strange said in the House of Lords:

> *A human being is created by the love of a father and mother of a different sex. The basic principle is the family, on which all life and civilisation depend. We owe it to our forebears, to ourselves, to our children, and to God who created us, to keep it so.*[3]

'Pretended families'

For the promoters of Clause 28, relationships involving gay men or lesbians and children are not 'families'. They are at best 'pretended family relationships' — which by law may not be promoted. As a result, support is denied to not only the gay or lesbian parents, but also to their children.

What happened in Britain with Clause 28 might seem irrelevant to our lives in South Africa — particularly given that we have neither local authorities that support community activities nor education authorities that teach any form of sex education. But the attitudes and prejudices that prompted Clause 28 are exactly the same as the ones that face us here in our every day lives.

So how do we prepare James to deal with this? We have taught him that all people should be treated equally. But because he is still young, he has not yet encountered things like homophobia or racial prejudice. When he does, we hope that the basic belief in the equality of all people will be sufficient to enable him to counter them.

Anne, Matthew and I have no illusions about the 'differentness' of the family we have made. But while our family might defy many of the surface text-book rules of parenting, we believe it obeys the more profound ones. As any parent does, we try to provide our child with a secure environment. Part of this means trying to make sure that he knows he is loved and wanted at home. It also means trying to make him know that he's a valued member of a broader community.

Notes

1 *GLPCI Network*, Summer 1992, p9.
2 See Mbali Mncadi, 'The right to choose: gay and lesbian rights', *Mayibuye*, July, 1992.
3 Quoted in Sarah Roelofs, 'Labour and the Natural Order: Intentionally Promoting Heterosexuality', in Tara Kaufman and Paul Lincoln (eds), *High Risk Lives: Lesbian and Gay Politics after the Clause* (Prism Press, 1991), p195.

In memory of Rocky:
An obituary

Anne Mayne

The telegram came from John: ROCKY DIED PEACEFULLY 0850 SUNDAY MORNING LOVE JOHN.

I can see him now, so thin he is like a brown shadow on the white hospital sheets. He probably died curled up in the foetal position like his friend Joseph did. He probably looked like that ancient Egyptian corpse in the British Museum, found dessicated and preserved under the desert sand. Dried out, skin and bone, face sunken in like an old man's, although he was only 32. John says he kept his sense of humour until the end. That was probably only possible because he was supported by his own kind of people, gay men, who cared and understood. I wish I had been there to say goodbye to him. I wish he had out-lived me, as he should have.

I met him first when he was seven. Thinking about it makes me cry. He was a sweet, soft little boy, one of a band of scavengers, seven of them, ranging in age from three to 12. I didn't take all that much notice of him because he was not one of the assertive ones; he was quiet and retiring. But I did notice that he always looked after the little ones. If it was raining, he would carry a little one under his coat. He always watched over them, held their hands crossing the road, saw that they got their share of food — although, in fact, the little band were meticulous about sharing. The older children contemptuously called him 'the moffie'. In our society, those gentle, caring qualities in a male are seen to denote inferiority. How crazy!

My sister Jenny and I lived in a flat near some run-down, rat-infested tenements off the Buitensingel. Friday was pay-day, so the parents of these children got drunk and, on Saturday mornings, the children had to forage for food until the adults sobered up. Jenny and I developed a routine. Because we were home from work on Saturday mornings, we bought in extra milk and bread and cheese and fruit and nuts and raisins. We had a sort of Breakfast Club every Saturday morning!

Sometimes, when we had the time, we would take them to the beach or to the zoo or somewhere fun.

I remember their names. Pauline, Basil and Kuku were from one family; Pauline and Basil, tough, strong, like those weeds that push through the pavement; Kuku, a pretty, fair-haired, blue-eyed child of three, with that lovely blush, brown gold skin. Cilla, who looked Malaysian, shy and graceful, with huge clever dark eyes. I have a faint memory of a younger brother called Yusef, or Yusiboy. Rocky, with large slanting eyes and soft, curly hair and a shy smile. Patrick, the oldest, light brown hair, green eyes and freckles, tough and athletic. Now and then they would bring a dark, glowering little girl of about four, whose name I forget, but she was the best fed and cared for of them all.

After about a year's association with these children, they began to disappear. We discovered from Rocky that they were being moved to new housing estates on the Cape Flats, and that the tenements were being demolished. This meant that the families would all be split up, and the little survival band would be scattered over the sand dunes, housed in draughty, monotonous council estates. They would never be able to keep in touch, because it was too expensive to travel to visit each other.

Rocky remained behind, because he had no parents. Well, he did have them, but they didn't want him. His mother had given him to her mother-in-law, after she had unsuccessfully attempted to abort him when she discovered, in the midst of her pregnancy, that his father was marrying someone else. Once, when Rocky met and spoke to his mother, she had told him this. When he in turn told me, the sense of shock was still with him.

He was very aptly called Rockland. He was like the seed of a graceful plant fallen on very stony, rocky land. There was nothing much to nurture him. It was the haphazard kindness of people round him that helped him to survive.

His father was an alcoholic and had tuberculosis, and spent most of the latter part of his life on a disability grant. His mother was a fast-food cook who died of a stroke while on the job. Rocky arrived too late for her funeral because he only heard about it indirectly. His grandmother, on his father's side, was a washerwoman who collected laundry from door to door, washed it at the public wash-house, ironed it, and delivered it back, from door to door. She was a small, sweet-faced woman. I saw her alive only a few times. On the last day of her life, I was told, she did her ironing, folded it neatly, then lay down and died. I saw her laid out in her coffin. She looked beautiful surrounded by the satin lining. Probably the only time that she had satin near her skin was when she was dead in her coffin.

These three people were alive when Rocky was a child, but they were incapable of looking after him, so he looked after himself. He worked for his living, probably from the age of five or six. Wherever he stayed, he minded the children, swept, cleaned, ironed, cooked, and more than earned his keep. He was sweet-natured and always attached himself to women. He knew how to be entertaining and amusing, but he was badly treated at some of the places where he stayed, so he would move on. There always seemed to be people who would have him.

After his friends were moved to the Cape Flats, Rocky attached himself to me. If we had lived in a humane society, I might have fostered him. But I was insecure, confused, and a sort of waif myself, cut off from my family (I was at loggerheads with my father) and with few friends, not much money and no sense of direction. I wasn't capable of taking responsibility for a child in a society that would hound and reject me for doing it. I did what I could for him, as one privileged waif could for a waif without one single guaranteed right in the land of his birth.

Where did he come from, Rockland Abrahms? His mother's surname was Cupido, Spanish/Portuguese; his father's name was Abrahms, probably from the Muslim/Malaysian people, or possibly from a Dutch Abrahms. He preferred his father's surname and took it when he was about 14. He surely also had Xhosa and Khoi-san ancestry. Once I showed him a map of the world. I wanted to show him where his genes came from, to show him that his ancestors came from interesting, wonderful cultures and parts of the world, to show how they got to Cape Town. But he looked very distressed and tearful and said that he didn't want to know. I was puzzled then, but, when I think of it now, perhaps from his perspective I was highlighting his tragic condition, abandoned by all his progenitors in a society that denied him his basic human rights. Unless I could offer him some security, he didn't want to think about it.

At least he lived to meet the 6010 AIDS Support Group and see that it was possible for gay people to form political and social organisations. At least he lived to see the huge step forward taken for human rights when Mandela was released and established himself as a leader to be reckoned with; at least he lived to see the ANC unbanned.

I tried to make sure that he had decent clothes. I would buy him winter clothes and summer clothes, every year. I once bought him a bike, but the people he was living with smashed it up out of jealousy.

I never thought of seeing a social worker about him, because I saw myself as an outsider, a rebel. The social workers represented the state and, in my developing political awareness, the state was the enemy. I knew I was different and I couldn't trust these people, the establishment. I felt the need to protect both of us and allowed myself to be guided by what he wanted, and he didn't want to be placed in care. But I was unaware until much later that both he and I were gay. Which is probably where this sense of mutual protectiveness came from.

My life took many nasty turns. I lived for eight years with a man who battered and terrorised me. The sexual abuse I had experienced as a child left me unable to protect myself from further abuse, and I was locked into a pattern of allowing myself to be abused and exploited, unable to take control of my life.

Rocky helped me through many bad times. He would come and visit, listen to my long distressed stories, cook me *gesmoorde eiers* [scrambled eggs], and just be kind and companionable. He was also a very interesting and amusing gossip,

350

and would take my mind off my problems with his stories. He had distress stories too, of exploitation and abuse. He never talked about his love affairs or his gay life as a young man; he kind of hid his wild, camp side from me.

Bo Kaap, where he lived, was in many ways a wonderful community to grow up in, as District Six once was. If you grew up there, there were networks of friends and contacts who would help you survive, teach you about life, and teach you skills. You could exchange work for food and shelter, and there was a rich cultural life. I met some wonderful people through Rocky. I don't want to romanticise poverty, violence and oppression, but it was through Rocky that I first learnt that the people I was taught to think of as inferior were far from that. They were often materially poor, but they were rich in intelligence, kindness, wisdom and humour.

Rocky grew up to be a homosexual, a housekeeper, a childminder, a messenger, a transvestite, a hairdresser. And he knew Cape Town so well: Bo Kaap, District Six, Woodstock, Salt River, Kensington, and the people and things that went on there. He knew hundreds of people and was liked by many. He was bright and shrewd and talented, and he didn't achieve half of his potential, though not through lack of his own efforts. He was physically well-proportioned, but he did not grow to his full height and strength because of malnutrition. He became a sought-after hairdresser, with almost no education, totally self-taught.

He never had a long-term sexual partner because, as he told me once, 'It's dangerous for me to be in love, because then I get *bevok* (crazy). I am so possessive that if I think my friend is being unfaithful, I could either murder him or kill myself! So I avoid falling in love.' He was aware of a bottomless pit of emotional need, but, knowing it would annihilate him if he went too near it, he skirted around it and survived. He wasn't a shallow person, he was a thinker. He sometimes got very depressed and angry and then he would escape into booze or dagga, but he wasn't an alcoholic or an addict, except to nicotine.

One day I had a long conversation with him about being gay and proud. I only realised I was a lesbian at the age of 36, and when I came out, it was in the most supportive atmosphere, at a conference on violence against women, in Brussels! When I returned to Cape Town, I discussed the situation with Rocky. He said he didn't like moffies, only real men. He only got turned on to real men! I explained that most of the real men who went with him were probably moffies too, and that the role-playing was because society oppressed us so much, and we tried to copy the dominant culture to minimise our differences. I told him that some of the finest men and women in history were gay men or lesbian women, and that it was only the Judeo/Christian/Islamic doctrines that decreed this kind of loving to be a crime in our society; that not all societies had this view. He understood everything I said, and his attitude changed.

When he became ill I introduced him to the gay men of the 6010 AIDS Support Group. He was fascinated by them and their positive attitude towards their homosexuality, and he asked me many questions. He tried to help his gay friends who had AIDS or were alcoholics. He sat up night after night with his friend

Joseph when he became ill as a result of AIDS, and counselled him and comforted him.

Long before he showed symptoms of AIDS, he told me that he was afraid because he thought he had it. I didn't believe the disease was in South Africa, and tried to reassure him. When he became ill and was not responding to treatment, I took him to hospital to see a specialist, and when they diagnosed AIDS, I nearly died of fright! He was, in fact, the first coloured in South Africa to be diagnosed as having the virus. I felt dreadful because he had had to deal with the news alone: we were away for the weekend when the results of the tests came back. We found him in an isolation ward, frightened, looking like a trapped animal, staring out of the window at the sea, and saying that he wanted to get out of the hospital.

I fluctuated between fear and anger. The fear was for both my own and my partner Leah's life. We thought we had been exposed to the virus because we had many times shared meals with him and he had, on occasion, coughed on us. The anger was because he had AIDS and not tuberculosis, which is what I had initially thought.

In order to be of proper support to him and to deal with our own terror, Leah and I had to learn as much as we could about this disease. It was a deeply traumatic experience. The way the 6010 Support Group helped us was wonderful; we developed such an enormous respect for the people working there.

I can't stop thinking of Rocky as the beautiful plant seed that fell on stony, rocky ground and battled and struggled to flourish and bloom and bear fruit. Amazingly, he did succeed! He will be remembered with love and gratitude by many people. He looked after many children who loved him, and who will remember him with love. He made hundreds of women look beautiful with his hair styling. He told many wry tales about people and their foibles, not maliciously, but full of humour. Whenever he had any money he would share it with his friends. He borrowed and lent freely. When people who had treated him badly fell on hard times themselves, he felt sorry for them and not glad, and tried to help them. I can think of numerous occasions when he amazed me with his big-heartedness.

He could be unreliable, but he survived by avoiding things he couldn't cope with and doing things when the mood was right. When I came into financial good fortune, I did try to share some with him, but money and possessions slipped through his fingers like water, so I gave him what I could and stopped being angry or disappointed when he lost it or gave it away.

When I decided to try to live in England, it was with great anguish and soul-searching that I left him behind. But it was too late for him to come too; he was too ill. He had many good friends in Cape Town and reliable support from the 6010 AIDS Support Group, so I left money in trust for him and this group.

I didn't have the courage to talk to him honestly about my leaving, and my not being there to support him through his last weeks. Once, when he was drunk after our friend Joseph died, he cried and said that I must not abandon him. I tried not to — I wrote to him, left him money, but still I feel guilty because he needed much more. I am so grateful that friends were at his bedside when he died. I am so glad that there were 50 people at his funeral, and I am so glad that my sisters went to pay their last respects to him.

On Friday 1 June 1990, my sister Jenny phoned to tell me about the funeral. Later that evening I went with friends from South Africa to the opening event of the North London Lesbian Strength Gay Pride Festival, a cross-cultural cabaret and dance organised by the Black Lesbian and Gay Group, and Shakti, the South Asian lesbian and gay organisation. I sat in the dark and watched some black men dancing together, and I cried. Rocky should have been there.

I wish I could believe there was a life hereafter where his soul could go. I wish I could believe that his soul would rise out of that shrivelled body, smitten down by disease in his prime, and float into another dimension where he could go on growing and developing, and achieving his potential and enjoying himself. But I think that if one believes that, one doesn't work hard to make it happen here on earth. For me his spirit lives on in the image of the outrageous *Kaapse* moffie, mincing down the street in his mules, his wildly flamboyant clothing flapping in the Southeaster, his quick repartee tossed over his shoulder with total disdain for heterosexual norms, his racist, classist, sexist insults. Long may his brave, funny, generous, irrepressible spirit live.

Contributors

ZACKIE ACHMAT is manager of the AIDS Law Project at the University of Witwatersrand's Centre for Applied Legal Studies. He has been a youth and community activist in Cape Town since 1976, and is a founder-member of ABIGALE. His documentary film work includes "Gay Life is Best" and "Die Duiwel Maak My Hart So Seer", broadcast on SABC in June 1993. He is working on his master's thesis on homosexuality in South Africa from 1848 to 1948.

MARY ARMOUR is a member of OLGA, and works as a researcher. She has done previous work in the field of feminist theology.

JULIA BEFFON, formerly Sports Editor at *The Weekly Mail & Guardian,* is currently a sub-editor at *Business Day* in Johannesburg.

EDWIN CAMERON is a practising human rights lawyer and academic at the Centre for Applied Legal Studies at the University of Witwatersrand. He helped found the AIDS Consortium and co-drafted the Charter of Rights on AIDS and HIV. His books and articles include work on labour and employment law, conscription, trust law, gay rights, and the judiciary.

TANYA CHAN SAM is a qualified teacher. She has been a member of the GLOW Executive since 1990, and is currently the organisation's Secretary-General. Her poetry has appeared in COSAW's *The Invisible Ghetto: Lesbian and Gay Writing from South Africa* (1993).

DHIANARAJ CHETTY is an historian and educationist. He has recently work as a researcher at the Education Policy Unit at the University of Witwatersrand and as a trainee at UNESCO's International Institute for Educational Policy in Paris. He is working on a doctoral dissertation for Columbia University, New York, on South African history.

GERRY DAVIDSON, who has been in the publishing and design business for thirty years, is editor and publisher of *Exit* and *The Quarterly.* She is presently engaged in research for an honours degree in sociology. Her poetry has appeared in COSAW's *The Invisible Ghetto: Lesbian and Gay Writing from South Africa* (1993).

SHAUN DE WAAL is the Literary Editor of the Johannesburg *Weekly Mail & Guardian,* and was co-editor of the alternative arts magazine *Blits* in 1989. His short story, 'Stalwart', won second prize in the 1992 Sanlam Literary Award and is published in COSAW's *The Invisible Ghetto: Lesbian and Gay Writing from South Africa* (1993).

DERRICK FINE has been an active member of the Cape Town-based organisations LAGO and OLGA. He is involved in community education and para-legal training.

PETER GALLI is a financial journalist at *Business Day* and has an honours degree in English from the University of Witwatersrand.

MARK GEVISSER is a Johannesburg-based freelance journalist who writes mainly for the Johannesburg *Weekly Mail & Guardian* and is the South African correspondent for the *Nation* in New York. He has done radio work for the BBC World Service and the SABC, and his writing has appeared in numerous publications, including the *New York Times* and the *Village Voice* in the US, and the *Guardian* and the *Observer* in Britain.

RACHEL HOLMES, who was brought up in South Africa, is a lecturer in Lesbian Studies at Sussex University, and was formerly English Lecturer at London University's Queen Mary College. She is working on a Ph.D dissertation on sex, space and South Africa and is a member of ABIGALE.

NEVILLE JOHN lives in Johannesburg, where he is a lawyer working in the field of urban development and housing.

HEIN KLEINBOOI is an activist in OLGA and in the South African Students' Congress at the University of Cape Town, where he is an engineering student.

MATTHEW KROUSE is the editor of COSAW's *The Invisible Ghetto: Lesbian and Gay Writing from South Africa* (1993), and his poetry has appeared in COSAW's anthology, *Essential Things*. His has worked in theatre in Johannesburg, most recently as Madame in Genet's *The Maids* at the Market Theatre. He has co-written two plays, *Famous Dead Man* and *Score Me The Ages* and has made two short films, both of which are banned.

SHEILA LAPINSKY has been a member of GASA-6010, LILACS, Gender, LAGO and OLGA and works in a factory.

JACK LEWIS is the co-director of the Out-in-Africa Film Festival, South Africa's first gay and lesbian film festival. He has a Ph.D in Economic History from the University of Cape Town, and lectured the subject for eight years at the University of the Western Cape. He has been active in adult education, community health and AIDS awareness work, and is now involved in film-making.

FRANCOIS LOOTS was born in Prieska in the Northern Cape and now lives in Cape Town, where he teaches English as a second language at a skills-training centre. He is a member of ABIGALE and has been active in AIDS awareness work. He has a master's degree in German from the University of Cape Town.

ANNE MAYNE worked with Rape Crisis in Cape Town before emigrating to the United Kingdom in the late 1980s. She lives in London.

HUGH MCLEAN, an active member of GLOW, is a musician by training. He has worked in rural development, and is currently projects officer at the Liberty Life Foundation.

NEIL MILLER is a Boston-based author and journalist. His books include *In Search of Gay America* (Atlantic Monthly Press) and *Out in the World: Gay and Lesbian Life from Buenos Aires to Bangkok* (1993). He is currently working on a survey of lesbian and gay history from the late nineteenth century to the present day, to be published in 1994.

LINDA NGCOBO, a founder-member of GLOW, was trained as a teacher and lived in Soweto. His work for GLOW included organising the annual Miss GLOW drag shows. At the time of his death, in February 1993, he was putting together an education and training programme for GLOW's members.

RON NERIO spent some six months in South Africa in 1990 doing research for a Master's degree on the gay movement in this country. He is presently completing his studies at the University of Michigan-Flint in the USA. He is an American.

JULIA NICOL has been an active member of the Cape Town-based organisations GALA, GASA-6010, LILACS, Gender, LAGO and OLGA. She works as a librarian.

SIMON NKOLI was born in Soweto and brought up in Sebokeng. A youth activist, he spent two years in prison as one of the defendants in the 1986 Delmas Treason Trial. He was the founder of The Saturday Group, South Africa's first black gay organisation, and later of GLOW in 1988. He has travelled extensively as South Africa's "gay ambassador" and was one of the speakers at the Stonewall 25 rally in New York City this year. He now works as an AIDS counsellor and educator for the Township AIDS Project.

GERRIT OLIVIER is a critic and essayist who heads the Department of Afrikaans and Nederlands at the University of Witwatersrand. His publications include *Ongerymdhede* (Haum-literêr, 1987).

MIKE OLIVIER lives in his native Botswana where he works in radio.

JOHN V PEGGE, who is the father of two children, is the service director of ASET (the AIDS Service Education and Training Foundation), South Africa's oldest AIDS service organisation. He was a founder member of 6010 and heads the organisation's counselling services. He has been a social work practitioner for 24 years.

KOOS PRINSLOO died of AIDS-related illness in February 1994. He was born of Afrikaans parents in Kenya and came to South Africa as a child in 1962. He has published three highly-acclaimed collections of short stories: *Jonkmanskas* (1982), *Die hemel help ons* (1988) and *Slagplaas* (1993).

LUIS RAFAEL has worked in psychiatric rehabilitation and holds an honours degree in literary theory.

GRAEME REID was one of the organisers of the 1992 Johannesburg Lesbian and Gay Pride March. He was the African Literature Coordinator at Khanya College and is currently administrator of the Handspring Trust for Puppetry and Education.

GLEN RETIEF is a queer activist who graduated from the University of Cape Town and did research into policing at the Institute of Criminology there.

DIGBY RICCI was former English lecturer at Rand Afrikaans University and is now head of English at King David High School, Johannesburg. His film and theatre criticism has appeared in the *Johannesburg Weekly Mail & Guardian,* and he is the editor of *Reef of Time* (1986), a collection of writings about Johannesburg.

IVAN TOMS lives in Cape Town, where he is Director of SHAWCO. A medical doctor, he worked in the Crossroads squatter camp for 11 years. He was a founder-member of LAGO and the End Conscription Campaign, and is an active member of the Anglican Church.

VERA VIMBELA is the founder of a lesbian and gay support group in Umtata, and works in the Transkei Department of Health.

SUBJECT INDEX

INDEX OF PERSONS